COLOMBO'S BOOK OF CANADA

COLOMBO'S BOOK OF CANADA

Edited by
John Robert Colombo

Hurtig Publishers
Edmonton

Hurtig Publishers
10560 105 Street
Edmonton, Alberta

Canadian Cataloguing in Publication Data

Colombo, John Robert, 1936-
Colombo's book of Canada

Includes index.

ISBN 0-88830-155-3 cloth
ISBN 0-88830-161-8 paper

1. Canada.   I. Title.
FC60.C64   971   C78-002071-5
F1008.3.C64

Printed and bound in Canada.

To
F.R. Scott
The Compleat
Canadian

I know what I have experienced,
and I know what it has meant to me.

VILHJALMUR STEFANSSON

Inscribed in Icelandic, English, and French
on the renowned Arctic explorer's monument
at his birthplace, Arnes, near Gimli, Manitoba

Contents

VII   National Songs

VIII   Some Facts, Some Figures

IX   A Chronology

Preface

I realized that there was a need for an anthology like *Colombo's Book of Canada* about four years ago when the following incident occurred.

I was waiting in line for a teller in the branch of the Bank of Nova Scotia in Lawrence Plaza, around the corner from my home in northern Toronto, when a woman entered the bank and took her place behind me in line. She was well dressed, well groomed, middle-aged, accompanied by a huge husky dog which was straining on its leash. Dogs are not generally found in banks, especially magnificent huskies.

I am a friendly person by nature, so I complimented the woman on her dog. She accepted the compliment with a wan smile but said nothing. "What's the dog's name?" I asked.

She paused before answering. "Kring."

"Kring? That's an unusual name. It sounds like an Eskimo word. Is it?"

"It is—or at least we think it is," she replied. "My husband and I bought the dog from a breeder who had a longer name for him. But all we can remember is Kring."

"I wonder what it means."

"We haven't the slightest idea," she said.

"I'll remember that name. I have an Eskimo-English, English-Eskimo dictionary at home, and when I return home I'll check the meaning of Kring."

"An Eskimo-English dictionary! What an odd thing to have," she said, almost without thinking about it.

I did not reply to the woman, but I thought about her remark on the way home. The more I thought about it, the more I realized that while it might be odd to have an Eskimo-English dictionary in Bangladesh or Bulgaria or Brazil or Belgium, it was *not* an odd thing to have such a dictionary in Canada. Yet how few Canadians have Eskimo-English (or Eskimo-French) dictionaries in their homes, or have ever seen one? Canada, after all, is one of the few countries that has Eskimos.

When I returned home, the first thing I did was take down my dictionary and check the dog's name. I found that the word Kring is, indeed, an Eskimo word and that it is part of a longer word, Kringmerk, which in the eastern Arctic means. . .dog.

The husky in the bank was called Dog. The couple who owned the lovely beast did not know the meaning of his name. Then I posed the following question to myself: "Would they be interested in knowing his name?" I realized that they would, that there was a certain appropriateness to the name, and that this knowledge would enrich their lives in a small but nevertheless significant way.

It was then that I decided to compile this collection of material about Canada. To enlighten that couple, to let them know the name and nature of their beast, and to delight and instruct Canadians everywhere.

Colombo's Book of Canada is two books in one, for it is both a primer of basic Canadiana and a reader of unusual Canadian writing. As a primer, it offers the reader such basic reference material as the complete words, in French and English, of "O Canada"; population figures for the provinces and principal cities; a chronology of important events in our history; photographs of the prime ministers; and reproductions of federal and provincial crests and flags. As a reader, it does not try to duplicate the work of existing anthologies of prose and poetry, for it has as its aim to delight the general reader and surprise the specialist with a wide array of general-interest writing that seldom finds its way into popular anthologies. The verses, songs, poems, plays, stories, quotations, letters, speeches, and other documents that make up the bulk of this book were selected for their human interest as well as for the light they shed on the history and spirit of Canada.

Like all collections, this one reflects the tastes and thoughts of its editor. I am partial to material a little off the beaten track, so I have taken the reader down a few country lanes, instead of along the national highway, in order to widen the area covered, so that this collection includes a wealth of writing, not just a little literature. I have selected dramatic material, often eye-witness accounts written by the participants themselves, over more polished writing by commentators far from the action in point of time. If the collection has a somewhat populist feel, it is because I have tried to build on what the reader may already know and to focus on those events that have affected the lives of not hundreds of people but hundreds of thousands of people.

There are dimensions of our national life that are not represented here or that are represented only peripherally. I have concentrated on history and writing, and in the visual sections on the pictorial and symbolic nature of the country, so I have had to exclude music and dance, art and architecture, politics and education, religion and medicine, etc., not because these are foreign to my conception of the country, but because these are subjects dealt with in other books; there is not room for everything, especially for cursory treatments of subjects of importance. The countryside, with its fauna and flora, goes uncelebrated not because the landscape has lacked its singers but because there is not a people in the world that has failed to extol the beauty of its own terrain. No attempt has been made to give equal representation to the regions of the country nor to the groups, ethnic and otherwise, that make up the mosaic of our modern life. The representation given to French Canada is a measure of the degree to which it impinges upon the lives of English Canadians. The historian will search in vain for more than passing references to the evolution of responsible government, and the folklorist will lament the absence of regional lore. Truth to tell, no single book could hope to encompass the whole of the Canadian experience. So room remains for many sequels. . . .

As I envisage it, the book you are holding in your hands is, like the country itself, a collage or a mosaic, a jigsaw or a patchwork. It is one view of the variety and contrariety of the history and spirit of Canada. It may be a personal view, but it is one tamed by wide reading and tempered by some reflection on the people and places, the movements and events, the texts and documents that have both recorded and sparked the national spirit in the process of asserting itself. The book, then, is a variegated vision of a country so vast, so on-going, that the wealth of detail is meant to do no more than suggest the greatness of some future whole.

Acknowledgements

Although very much the product of one person's work, *Colombo's Book of Canada* owes much to earlier collections devoted to the national spirit. Among these are Margaret Fairley's *Spirit of Canadian Democracy* (1945), John D. Robins's *A Pocketful of Canada* (1946), Malcolm Ross's *Our Sense of Identity* (1945), William Toye's *A Book of Canada* (1962), A.J.M. Smith and F.R. Scott's *The Blasted Pine* (1957, 1967), William Kilbourn's *Canada: A Guide to the Peaceable Kingdom* (1970), Raymond Reid's *The Canadian Style* (1973), N. Brian Davis's *The Poetry of the Canadian People* (1976), and Edith Fowke's *The Penguin Book of Canadian Folk Songs* (1973). I found exceptionally useful *Explore Canada* (1973) published by Reader's Digest and the Canadian Automobile Association. Books I regularly consulted include *The Oxford Companion to Canadian History and Literature* (1967) by Norah Story and *Supplement to the Oxford Companion to Canadian History and Literature* (1973), edited by William Toye. I also made good use of *Colombo's Canadian Quotations* (1974) and *Colombo's Canadian References* (1976).

Many friends and fellow writers took an active interest in the evolution of this work. Special assistance was rendered by four researchers, Alexandre L. Amprimoz, Don Curtin, B.G. Fingerote, and Philip Singer, to whom I am grateful. Others who assisted in specific ways include: Jack Batten, J. Michael Bliss, Bill Brooks, Ernest DeWald, Doug Fetherling, Howard Fink, Mark Frank, Jacques Godbout, J.L. Granatstein, Cyril Greenland, Jack D. Griffin, Tony Hawke, S.W. Horrall, Gordon Johnston, Gerald McDuff, Lorraine Monk, Michael Richardson, Morris C. Shumiatcher, Guy Sylvestre, William Toye, and Robert Weaver.

I am indebted to Mel Hurtig, the publisher and nationalist, for commissioning the book. Carlotta Lemieux edited it, and David Shaw designed it, with customary concern and style. Bill Brooks assisted in the photo selection. Ruth Colombo contributed many valuable suggestions. The newly opened Metropolitan Toronto Library, so imaginatively and handsomely designed by Raymond Moriyama, provided fine quarters in which to work; the MTL staff was helpful without fail. I also used facilities provided by three other libraries: the John P. Robarts Research Library of the University of Toronto; the North York Public Library system; and the Ottawa Public Library. Asher Joram of Acadia Books and Beth Appledorn and Susan Sandler of Longhouse Bookshop, both based in Toronto, answered some last-minute queries. The final editing was undertaken while I was writer-in-residence at Mohawk College of Applied Arts and Technology; for this pleasant experience let me record my gratitude to Don Brennagh, William FitzGerald, Jim Foley, Ron Slavik, and Dr. Sam Mitminger. While at the college I benefited from discussions on multiculturalism with Kamala Bhatia.

No grants or subsidies were requested for the compilation or publication of *Colombo's Book of Canada*. However, I am grateful to the Canada Council and the Ontario Arts Council for past assistance. I have taken the liberty of dedicating this book, largely the work of others, known and unknown, to F.R. Scott, the distinguished Montreal poet and lawyer, writer and teacher, activist and thinker, whose contributions to our national life seem so admirable and so considerable.

I
Our History in Poetry

Canada has never had a Homer to tell the story of its people in epic form. Two Bostonians have come close to being Homers, however. In a series of stirring narratives, the historian Francis Parkman has recounted the epic struggle waged by the French and the English in the forests of America; and Henry Wadsworth Longfellow has retold in verse form two episodes in the Canadian saga, the history of Hiawatha and the story of Evangeline. The only Canadian so far to set himself the task of preserving our past in artistic form in a major mode is E.J. Pratt, who, as "the national poet," made two events uniquely his own: the story of the Huron missions and the construction of the Canadian Pacific Railway. To complement the work of Parkman, Longfellow, and Pratt are the contributions of a multitude of individual writers, both known and unknown, whose poems, verses, and songs celebrate our heroes and villains, and remind us of the stirring and stark events that compose the gradually unfolding story of Canada. Out of all of these I have constructed this section, which I like to consider a *cento*, a literary composition which makes use of the words of others to form a new literary whole. I have chosen thirty-three episodes of interest and importance from our past, briefly described each of them, and then found works of some literary interest with which to dramatize them. Some events have inspired chroniclers in their own day; others have moved later chroniclers. Many of the poetic annalists sing patriotic tunes, but not all, for there are some who hum intensely chauvinistic ones or sound unpatriotic notes. I have included them all, for I think, as literary compositions, the works here grant us an unexpected and immediate insight into our past. They bear reading and rereading. Together they constitute our homeric history.

The Dawning of Consciousness

No one knows the age of the Eskimo or Inuit creation myth that follows. All that we know is that it was told by Apagkaq, an Eskimo teller of traditional tales who lived with his people in the Mackenzie Delta area of the North-west Territories. Apagkaq told it to Knud Rasmussen (1879-1933), the half-Danish, half-Eskimo explorer who headed the famous Fifth Thule Expedition of 1921-24 into the Canadian Arctic. Apagkaq's account of the dawning of consciousness is quite long, so only the opening section has been reproduced here. The full creation myth may be found in *The Mackenzie Eskimos: After Knud Rasmussen's Posthumous Notes: Report of the Fifth Thule Expedition* (1942), edited by H. Ostermann.

The First Man/*Apagkaq*

He was squatting in the darkness.

He was quite alone on earth, when suddenly he became conscious and discovered himself. He had no idea where he was. Nor did he know how he had come there. But he breathed and there was life in him. He lived!

But who was he? A being—something living. More than that he could not comprehend. All about him was dark, and he could see nothing.

Then he groped about with his hands. His fingers brushed over clay wherever he felt. The earth was clay; everything about him was lifeless clay.

He let his fingers glide over himself. He knew nothing of how he looked, but he found his face and felt that he had a nose, eyes and mouth, arms and legs and limbs. He was a human being—a man!

Norsemen Discover the New World, 1001

If a poetic account of the Norse expeditions from Greenland to the eastern coast of the North American continent was ever composed, it has not survived. Nor has any later poet succeeded in capturing the thrill of those early voyages. But *The Greenlander's Saga*, composed in Icelandic prose by an unknown author sometime after the events themselves, is a work of genuine poetic power, especially in the sombre translation made in 1976 by George Johnston (b. 1913). The *Saga* tells of Leif Ericsson—Leif the Lucky—and his three important landfalls at Helluland, Markland, and Vineland. According to the Norwegian explorer Helge Ingstad, these landfalls can be located: Helluland (or Flatstone Land) may be identified as Cape Dyer, Baffin Island; Markland (or Forest Land) as Cape Porcupine, Labrador; and Vineland (or Wineland, Land of Vines) as L'Anse aux Meadows. It is at the latter site, on the northeastern tip of Newfoundland, that Ingstad claims Leif wintered. In the 1960s, Ingstad uncovered there remains of the first indisputable Norse settlement so far found in North America.

The Greenlander's Saga

Now they readied their ship and put to sea when they were ready, and came upon the land first that Bjarni and his crew had seen last. They sailed up to the land and cast anchor and launched their boat and rowed ashore and saw no grass there. Great glaciers were all the higher part, and it was like one flat rock all the way to the glaciers from the sea, and to them this land looked barren.

Then Leif spoke: "It has not turned out for us at this land as for Bjarni, that we did not go ashore. I shall give a name to this land and call it Flatstone Land."

Then back they went to the ship.

After this they stand out to sea and come upon a second land; once again they sail up to the land and cast anchor, launch the boat and go ashore. This land was flat and wooded, and white sand in many places, and sloping gently to the sea.

Then Leif spoke: "By its worth shall this land be named, and called Forest Land." Then they went right back out to their ship.

*

But they had such a curiosity to go ashore that they would not wait until the tide came up under their ship, and they ran ashore at a place where a river flowed out of a lake. And when the tide came up under their ship they took their boat and rowed to the ship and towed it up into the river, and then into the lake, and anchored there and took their bed-sacks ashore and put up shelters there; made up their minds then to stay there over the winter, and built a big house.

There was no dearth of salmon, either in the river or in the lake, and bigger salmon than they had ever seen before.

Living was so good there, as it seemed to them, that they would need no fodder for cattle in winter; there was no frost in winter and the grass hardly withered. Days and nights were more of a length than in Greenland or Iceland; the sun had mid-morning and mid-afternoon there on the shortest day. . . .

And when spring comes, then they got ready and sailed away, and Leif named the land for what it grew and called it Wineland. Now they stand out to sea, and there was a good wind for them all the way till they came in sight of Greenland and its mountains under the ice.

Hiawatha Invents Picture-Writing

There is no entry for Hiawatha in the volume of the *Dictionary of Canadian Biography* (1966), which covers the years from 1000 to 1700. Yet there is some reason to believe that Hiawatha, the Iroquois culture hero, did exist, so that the stories about him may be considered to be legends rather than myths. An important legend concerns Hiawatha's role in the establishing of the Great Confederacy in the Great Lakes area about 1390 (see the section "Records of Our Past" for a description of the planting of the Tree of the Great Peace); another important legend concerns the invention of "picture-writing," attributed to Hiawatha, the enlightener of his people. Since 1855, Hiawatha has been the world's best-known Indian, for that was the year Henry Wadsworth Longfellow (1807-82), the New England poet, published *The Song of Hiawatha,* using — and apparently misusing — the aboriginal research of Henry Schoolcraft, an Indian agent residing in the Sault Ste. Marie area. It seems that in 1851 Schoolcraft published a description of some Indian pictographs he had never seen, basing his account on the word of a native who claimed he knew of a cliff face decorated with ochre figures of a horned panther, a mounted man, a crested serpent, etc. Schoolcraft's account of Inscription Rock inspired Longfellow's account of Hiawatha as the enlightener of his people. Does Inscription Rock actually exist? One hundred and seven years later, in the summer of 1958, taking Schoolcraft's directions seriously, Selwyn Dewdney, an art instructor in London, Ontario, succeeded in locating the site of Inscription Rock. The cliff face at Agawa Bay, Lake Superior, Ontario, is a tourist attraction today. The text of "Picture-Writing" comes from *The Song of Hiawatha* in *The Poetical Works of Longfellow* (1908).

Hiawatha's Picture-Writing/
Henry Wadsworth Longfellow

In those days said Hiawatha,
"Lo! how all things fade and perish!
From the memory of the old men
Pass away the great traditions,
The achievements of the warriors,
The adventures of the hunters,
All the wisdom of the Medas,
All the craft of the Wabenos,
All the marvellous dreams and visions
Of the Jossakeeds, the Prophets!

    "Great men die and are forgotten,
Wise men speak; their words of wisdom
Perish in the ears that hear them,
Do not reach the generations
That, as yet unborn, are waiting
In the great, mysterious darkness
Of the speechless days that shall be!

"On the grave-posts of our fathers
Are no signs, no figures painted;
Who are in those graves we know not,
Only know they are our fathers.
Of what kith they are and kindred,
From what old, ancestral Totem,
Be it Eagle, Bear, or Beaver,
They descended, this we know not,
Only know they are our fathers.

"Face to face we speak together,
But we cannot speak when absent,
Cannot send our voices from us
To the friends that dwell afar off;
Cannot send a secret message,
But the bearer learns our secret,
May pervert it, may betray it,
May reveal it unto others."

Thus said Hiawatha, walking
In the solitary forest,
Pondering, musing in the forest,
On the welfare of his people.

From his pouch he took his colours,
Took his paints of different colours,
On the smooth bark of a birch-tree,
Painted many shapes and figures,
Wonderful and mystic figures,
And each figure had a meaning,
Each some word or thought suggested.

Gitche Manito the Mighty,
He, the Master of Life, was painted
As an egg, with points projecting
To the four winds of the heavens.
Everywhere is the Great Spirit,
Was the meaning of this symbol.

Mitche Manito the Mighty,
He the dreadful Spirit of Evil,
As a serpent was depicted,
As Kenabeek, the great serpent.
Very crafty, very cunning,
Is the creeping Spirit of Evil,
Was the meaning of this symbol.

Life and Death he drew as circles,
Life was white, but Death was darkened;
Sun and moon and stars he painted,
Man and beast, and fish and reptile,
Forests, mountains, lakes, and rivers.

For the earth he drew a straight line,
For the sky a bow above it;
White the space between for daytime,
Filled with little stars for night-time;
On the left a point for sunrise,
On the top a point for noontide,
And for rain and cloudy weather
Waving lines descending from it.

Footprints pointing towards a wigwam
Were a sign of invitation,

Were a sign of guests assembling;
Bloody hands with palms uplifted
Were a symbol of destruction,
Were a hostile sign and symbol.

All these things did Hiawatha
Show unto his wondering people,
And interpreted their meaning,
And he said: "Behold, your grave-posts
Have no mark, no sign, nor symbol.
Go and paint them all with figures;
Each one with its household symbol,
With its own ancestral Totem;
So that those who follow after
May distinguish them and know them."

The Discovery of Canada, 1534

Jacques Cartier (1491-1557), the French explorer from Saint-Malo, commissioned by François I "to discover certain islands and lands where it is said that a great quantity of gold, and other precious things are to be found," was put in command of two ships and sixty-one men, and crossed the Atlantic in twenty days. On 24 July 1534 he erected a thirty-foot cross at Penouille Point, Baie de Gaspé, and claimed the land for France, despite protests from the Iroquois chief Donnacona. "What is most to his credit," wrote historian Marcel Trudel, is that "in 1535 he discovered the St. Lawrence River, which was to become the axis of the French empire in America, the vital route which would carry eager explorers towards Hudson Bay, towards the mysterious horizon of the western sea, and towards the Mississippi. Cartier discovered one of the greatest rivers in the world, and he marks the starting-point of France's occupation of three-quarters of a continent." The song lyric, "Jacques Cartier," which follows, was written by the Montreal-born Quebec rock star, Robert Charlebois (b. 1944), and translated by Philip Stratford. It first appeared in English in *Voices from Quebec* (1977), and it expresses sentiments that French and English alike have experienced in Montreal and elsewhere — especially during our long winter months.

Jacques Cartier/*Robert Charlebois*

Cartier, Cartier
O Jacques Cartier
If you'd only steered clear
Of our wintery ways
Cartier, Cartier
O Jacques Cartier
If you'd just sailed that ship
On a summerside trip
Think what we'd have today!
A Sherbrooke Street lined in coconut palms
With flocks of parrots perched in their fronds

Mount Royal covered in banana trees
With cute little monkeys at play in their leaves
And St. Lawrence swimming would be really grand
Or just lying on the sand for a nice winter tan!

Cartier, Cartier
O Jacques Cartier
If you'd only steered clear
Of our wintery ways
Cartier, Cartier
O Jacques Cartier
If you'd just sailed that ship
On a summerside trip
Think what we'd have today!

On Victoria Bridge, built of creepers and vines
Shopping bags on our heads and laughing in time
We'd make our barefoot way, O Jacques Cartier
To the sound of tom-toms or the ukulele
And orange orchids along Peel Street
Mint, jasmine and lotus would smell so sweet!

Cartier, Cartier
O Jacques Cartier
If you'd only steered clear
Of our wintery ways
Cartier, Cartier
O Jacques Cartier
If you'd just sailed that ship
On a summerside trip
Think what we'd have today!

Giraffes would stare on Pine Avenue
At the squirrels there like things from a zoo
White elephants stroll down De Lorimier like pets
And Place Ville Marie with its slim minarets
And blizzards of sand, hot, golden and clean
Would make January drifts a great place to dream!

Cartier, Cartier
O Jacques Cartier
If you'd only steered clear
Of our wintery ways
Cartier, Cartier
O Jacques Cartier
If you'd just sailed that ship
On a summerside trip
Think what we'd have today!

Montreal in Dakar, Tangiers or Conakry
Montreal in Tokyo, Kyoto or Kobe
Montreal in Aden, Fremantle or Bombay
Montreal in Java, Borneo or Papeete
Montreal in Phnom-Penh, in Bangkok or Hue
Montreal in Hong Kong, Canberra or Sydney

Cartier, Cartier
O Jacques Cartier
Think what we'd have today!

The Death of Champlain, 1635

"The Father of New France" is the title posterity has granted Samuel de Champlain (1567-1635), for this native of Brouage, France, established the first French colonies at Acadia and Quebec, thus laying the groundwork for the French presence in North America today. To Marc Lescarbot (1570-1642), a lawyer and poetaster from France who wintered at Champlain's colony in Acadia in 1606-7, Champlain was as much an explorer as he was a colonizer. Lescarbot's sonnet "done at Campseau Islands in New France" was doubtlessly known to Champlain himself, for it originally appeared in Lescarbot's *Histoire de la Nouvelle-France,* published in 1609, twenty-six years before Champlain died on Christmas Day at Quebec. This translation from the Old French was made by the present editor.

To Samuel Champlain/*Marc Lescarbot*

A *Numidian* King moved by fine desire
Did seek out once the source of that river
That to *Egypt* and *Libya* gives water,
Taking in his pursuit a unique pleasure.
  CHAMPLAIN, for long I saw how your leisure
Was spent so stubbornly and without respite
In seeking out the waves that from *Newfound-Land*
Do over many a leap these banks command.
  Should you attain your noble enterprise,
No one could guess the glory that one day
Would to your name accrue for grasping it.
  You seek a boundless river's origin
So in the future making there your visit
You will attain for us the route to *la Chine.*

The Life and Death of Brébeuf

"I am an ox, and I am fit only to carry loads," confessed Jean de Brébeuf (1593-1649), the Jesuit missionary, punning on the presence in his last name, Brébeuf, of *boeuf,* the French word for "ox." He arrived in New France in 1625 and the following year journeyed to Huronia, where he commenced his life's work: proselytizing among the Huron Indians. He helped build Saint-Marie-among-the-Hurons, a palisaded settlement with numerous log buildings, destroyed by the Jesuits themselves in 1649 and painstakingly reconstructed in the 1960s. Caught by the Iroquois, Brébeuf and his Jesuit companions were (in the words of the historian René Latourelle) "taken prisoner and carried off to Saint-Ignace, where they suffered one of the most atrocious martyrdoms in the annals of Christianity." Martyred on 16 March 1649, Brébeuf and his fellow companions were canonized in 1930 and proclaimed patron saints of Canada in 1940. About eight years before his death, Brébeuf wrote in the Huron language the celebrated "Huron Christmas Carol," two versions of which follow. The first, a literal translation by John Steckley, is published for the first time in its entirety. Following "Iesous Ahatonnia" is "Jesous Ahatonhia," a free adaptation by the versifier J.E. Middleton (1872-1960), first published in 1926. To present a slightly different view of things, the two carols are followed by "Brébeuf and His Brethren," a satiric verse by F.R. Scott (b. 1899), from *The Eye of the Needle* (1957).

Iesous Ahatonnia (Jesus, He is Born)/*Jean de Brébeuf*

Have courage, you who are people, Jesus, He is born,
The oki spirit who enslaved us has fled,
Do not listen to him, for he corrupts the spirits
   of our thoughts;
   Jesus, He is born.

The oki spirits who dwell in the sky are coming
   with a message;
They are coming to say: rejoice!
Mary has given birth, rejoice!
   Jesus, He is born.

Three men of great authority have left for the place
   of His birth;
Tichion, a star appearing over the horizon, leads
   them there;
That star will walk first on the path to guide them;
   Jesus, He is born.

As they arrived where Jesus was born,
The star stopped not far beyond it;
Having found the place, he said: Come hither,
   Jesus, He is born.

When they arrived and saw Jesus,
They praised His name, saying He is good and kind;
They greeted Him with great respect,
   Jesus, He is born.

They say let us place His name in a position of honour;
Let us act reverently towards Him for He comes to
   show us mercy;
It is the will of the spirits that you love us, Jesus, and wish
that we may be adopted into your family;
   Jesus, He is born.

Jesous Ahatonhia/*Jean de Brébeuf*

'Twas in the moon of winter time when all the birds
   had fled,
That Mighty Gitchi Manitou sent angel choirs instead.
Before their light the stars grew dim,
And wandering hunters heard the hymn;
   "Jesus, your King, is born;
   Jesus is born; in excelsis gloria!"

Within a lodge of broken bark the tender Babe was
   found.

A ragged robe of rabbit skin enwrapped His beauty
   'round.
And as the hunter braves drew nigh,
The angel song rang loud and high;
   "Jesus, your King, is born;
   Jesus is born; in excelsis gloria!"

The earliest moon of winter time is not so round and fair
As was the ring of glory on the helpless Infant there.
While Chiefs from far before Him knelt,
With gifts of fox and beaver pelt.
   "Jesus, your King, is born;
   Jesus is born; in excelsis gloria!"

O children of the forest free, O sons of Manitou.
The Holy Child of earth and heav'n is born today for you.
Come kneel before the radiant Boy,
Who brings you beauty, peace and joy.
   "Jesus, your King, is born;
   Jesus is born; in excelsis gloria!"

Brébeuf and His Brethren/*F.R. Scott*

When de Brébeuf and Lalemant, brave souls,
Were dying by the slow and dreadful coals
Their brother Jesuits in France and Spain
Were burning heretics with equal pain.
For both the human torture made a feast:
Then is priest savage, or Red Indian priest?

The Defence of Long Sault, 1660

For three centuries the heroism of Adam Dollard des Ormeaux (1635-60) has merited special attention in Quebec. Dollard (who is sometimes called Daulac) was the commander of the garrison at Ville-Marie (later called Montreal). He became the hero of New France when he led seventeen soldiers against the Iroquois. He laid an ambush against the Iroquois who threatened Ville-Marie in an abandoned fort at the Long Sault on the Ottawa River, near present-day Cornwall, Ontario. After ten days of fighting, the Frenchmen and their Indian allies were either killed or captured, 1 May 1660. The brave resistance has been credited with saving the life of the infant colony of New France. André Vachon, the contemporary historian, has noted that one must "take care not to exaggerate the importance of this episode in the Iroquois wars." Yet Dollard's last stand inspired Canon Lionel Groulx, as late as 1919, to deliver an inspirational address, "If Dollard Were Alive Today," which concludes with some inspired rhetoric: "Together we shall work for the reconstruction of our family's house. And should you command it, O Dollard, O powerful leader, we are ready to follow you to the supreme holocaust for the defence of our French tongue and our Catholic faith." The selfless exploit led an English Canadian, the lyric poet Archibald

Lampman (1861-99), to tackle a narrative subject. "At the Long Sault: May, 1660" occupied him until a few months before his death. It was published for the first time in *At the Long Sault and Other New Poems* (1943), edited by E.K. Brown.

At the Long Sault: May, 1660/*Archibald Lampman*

Under the day-long sun there is life and mirth
   In the working earth,
And the wonderful moon shines bright
   Through the soft spring night,
The innocent flowers in the limitless woods are springing
   Far and away
   With the sound and the perfume of May,
And ever up from the south the happy birds are winging,
   The waters glitter and leap and play
   While the grey hawk soars.

But far in an open glade of the forest set
   Where the rapid plunges and roars,
Is a ruined fort with a name that men forget, —
   A shelterless pen
   With its broken palisade,
   Behind it, musket in hand,
   Beyond message or aid
   In this savage heart of the wild,
   Mere youngsters, grown in a moment to men,
   Grim and alert and arrayed,
   The comrades of Daulac stand.
   Ever before them, night and day,
   The rush and skulk and cry
   Of foes, not men but devils, panting for prey;
   Behind them the sleepless dream
Of the little frail-walled town, far away by the plunging
   stream,
   Of maiden and matron and child,
With ruin and murder impending, and none but they
To beat back the gathering horror
Deal death while they may,
   and then die.
Day and night they have watched while the little plain
Grew dark with the rush of the foe, but their host
Broke ever and melted away, with no boast
But to number their slain;
And now as the days renew
Hunger and thirst and care
Were they never so stout, so true,
Press at their hearts; but none
Falters or shrinks or utters a coward word,
Though each setting sun
Brings from the pitiless wild new hands to the Iroquois
   horde,
And only to them despair.

Silent, white-faced, again and again
Charged and hemmed round by furious hands,

Each for a moment faces them all and stands
In his little desperate ring; like a tired bull moose
Whom scores of sleepless wolves, a ravening pack,
Have chased all night, all day
Through the snow-laden woods, like famine let loose;
And he turns at last in his track
Against a wall of rock and stands at bay;
Round him with terrible sinews and teeth of steel
They charge and recharge; but with many a furious
   plunge and wheel,
Hither and thither over the trampled snow,
He tosses them bleeding and torn;
Till, driven, and ever to and fro
Harried, wounded and weary grown,
His mighty strength gives way
And all together they fasten upon him and drag him down.

So Daulac turned him anew
With a ringing cry to his men
In the little raging forest glen,
And his terrible sword in the twilight whistled and slew.
And all his comrades stood
With their backs to the pales, and fought
Till their strength was done;
The thews that were only mortal flagged and broke
Each struck his last wild stroke,
And they fell one by one,
And the world that had seemed so good
Passed like a dream and was naught.

And then the great night came
With the triumph-songs of the foe and the flame
Of the camp-fires.
Out of the dark the soft wind woke,
The song of the rapid rose alway
And came to the spot where the comrades lay,
Beyond help or care,
With none but the red men round them
To gnash their teeth and stare.

All night by the foot of the mountain
   The little town lieth at rest,
The sentries are peacefully pacing;
   And neither from East nor from West

Is there rumour of death or of danger;
   None dreameth tonight in his bed
That ruin was near and the heroes
   That met it and stemmed it are dead.

But afar in the ring of the forest,
   Where the air is so tender with May
And the waters are wild in the moonlight,
   They lie in their silence of clay.

The numberless stars out of heaven
   Look down with a pitiful glance;
And the lilies asleep in the forest
   Are closed like the lilies of France.

The Expulsion of the Acadians, 1755

One of the darkest days in the history of early Canada fell on Friday, 5 September 1755, when the British governor, Charles Lawrence, arranged for the reading of his proclamation banishing the Acadian population from the province of Nova Scotia and dispersing them among the other British colonies in North America. This document was read at the Church of St. Charles at Grand Pré, Nova Scotia, now part of Grand Pré Historic Park. During the next month, between twelve and fifteen thousand French colonists, mainly farmers and their families, were uprooted and expelled. In the confusion, families were broken up and lovers separated. An instance of the latter is the tragedy of Emmeline Labische, who was separated from her lover. She finally located him in Louisiana only to find he was engaged to marry another woman. This incident was told by an Acadian lawyer to a Boston minister who related it to Nathaniel Hawthorne. When the novelist declined to make use of it, Henry Wadsworth Longfellow (1807-82), the Boston poet, rose to the occasion and spent three years working the material into his famous long poem *Evangeline: A Tale of Acadie* (1847). The section from Part V, describing the actual departure and the separating of the two lovers, Evangeline Bellefontaine and Gabriel Lajeunesse, is taken from *The Poetical Works of Longfellow* (1908). Grand Pré is tranquil enough today. In front of the chapel stands a statue of Evangeline by Philippe and Henri Hébert. As the observer moves around the bronze figure, the young Evangeline seems to grow gradually older and sadder.

Evangeline/*Henry Wadsworth Longfellow*

There disorder prevailed, and the tumult and stir of
    embarking.
Busily plied the freighted boats; and in the confusion
Wives were torn from their husbands, and mothers, too
    late, saw their children
Left on the land, extending their arms, with wildest
    entreaties.
So unto separate ships were Basil and Gabriel carried,
While in despair on the shore Evangeline stood with her
    father.
Half the task was not done when the sun went down, and
    the twilight
Deepened and darkened around; and in haste the reflu-
    ent ocean
Fled away from the shore, and left the line of the sand-
    beach
Covered with waifs of the tide, with kelp and the slippery
    sea-weed.
Farther back in the midst of the household goods and the
    wagons,
Like to a gipsy camp, or a leaguer after a battle,
All escape cut off by the sea, and the sentinels near them,

Lay encamped for the night the houseless Acadian
    farmers.
Back to its nethermost caves retreated the bellowing
    ocean,
Dragging adown the beach the rattling pebbles, and leav-
    ing
Inland and far up the shore the stranded boats of the
    sailors.
Then, as the night descended, the herds returned from
    their pastures;
Sweet was the moist still air with the odour of milk from
    their udders;
Lowing they waited, and long, at the well-known bars of
    the farmyard, —
Waited and looked in vain for the voice and the hand of
    the milkmaid.
Silence reigned in the streets; from the church no Angelus
    sounded,
Rose no smoke from the roofs, and gleamed no lights
    from the windows.

The Conquest of Quebec, 1759

"The Plains of Abraham! Yes, my mind was full of Montcalm and Wolfe fighting it out up there towards the roof of the world. The French and Indian War, I believe we call it. Seven long years of fighting. It was probably this battle on the Plains of Abraham, which my weak memory places somewhere in the vicinity of Quebec, that decided the fate of the French in North America. I must have studied this bloody war in detail in school. In fact, I'm sure I did. And what remains? *The Plains of Abraham.*" So mused Henry Miller, the well-known American novelist, on the site of one of history's most celebrated battles, which took place the morning of 13 September 1759. Five thousand Red Coats under Major-General James Wolfe (1727-59) landed at Wolfe's Cove, two miles above Quebec, and taking an old trail, scaled the cliff and gained the plain which stretches west of Quebec's walls. There they assembled in battle formation and faced the hastily assembled, numerically superior French forces under the command of the Marquis de Montcalm (1712-59). Twenty minutes later the battle was over, the French forces having been decisively defeated by the British. Wolfe lay dead on the Plains of Abraham, and Montcalm fell there too, mortally wounded, to linger on until the following day. (Francis Parkman describes the deaths of these two valiant officers in the section "Records of Our Past.") Quebec, on the promontory of Cape Diamond, the stronghold of New France, the centre of the sixty thousand French in Canada, the oldest city in Canada, capitulated. This scene remains the single central tableau in the minds of English (if not French) Canadians. Today the Plains of Abraham, part of 235-acre Battlefields Park, attract hundreds of thousands of visitors every year.

The traditional song that follows is of unknown authorship and appears in *Canada's Story in Song* (1965), edited
by Edith Fowke and Alan Mills. Fowke notes that as no
horses were taken up the cliffs, Wolfe was horseless, not
mounted.

Brave Wolfe/ *Traditional*

Come, all you old men all,
    Let this delight you,
Come, all you young men all,
    Let nought affright you.
Nor let your courage fail
    When comes the trial,
Nor do not be dismayed
    At first denial.

I went to see my love,
    Thinking to woo her;
I sat down by her side,
    Not to undo her;
But when I looked on her
    My tongue did quiver;
I could not speak my mind
    While I was with her.

"Love, here's a diamond ring,
    Long time I've kept it
All for your sake alone,
    If you'll accept it.
When you this token view,
    Think on the giver;
Madame, remember me,
    Or I'm undone forever."

Then forth went this brave youth
    And crossed the ocean,
To free America
    Was his intention.
He landed at Quebec
    With all his party,
The city to attack,
    Both brave and hearty.

Brave Wolfe drew up his men
    In a line so pretty,
On the Plains of Abraham
    Before the city.
The French came marching down
    Arrayed to meet them,
In double numbers 'roynd
    Resolved to beat them.

Montcalm and this brave youth
    Together walkéd;
Between two armies they
    Like brothers talkéd,
Till each one took his post

And did retire.
'Twas then these numerous hosts
    Commenced their fire.

The drums did loudly beat,
    With colours flying,
The purple gore did stream,
    And men lay dying.
Then shot from off his horse
    Fell that brave hero.
We'll long lament his loss
    That day in sorrow.

He raiséd up his head
    Where the guns did rattle,
And to his aide he said,
    "How goes the battle?"
"Quebec is all our own,
    They can't prevent it."
He said without a groan,
    "I die contented."

The Death of Brock, 1812

"Most of the people have lost all confidence," boasted
Major-General Sir Isaac Brock (1769-1812) a few months
before his death. "I however speak loud and look big."
The commander of the British forces in Upper Canada
and the hero of the War of 1812, Sir Isaac died before
learning of his knighthood, bestowed for the bloodless
capture of Detroit earlier that year. He fell before a
sniper's bullet on 13 October 1812 while leading an
attack on Queenston Heights, the American-occupied
promontory that overlooks the Niagara River. He fell a
short while after issuing the celebrated command to the
Toronto militia: "Push on, brave York Volunteers!" The
Battle of Queenston Heights was concluded later that day
when General Roger Sheaffe drove the American invaders, under General Stephen Van Rensselaer, from the
heights. Brock lies buried beneath the 184-foot monument which bears his name and towers over the countryside and the Niagara River below. The monument, raised
in 1824 but damaged during the Rebellion of 1837, was
re-erected in 1854. This is the monument, designed by
William Thomas with a tall fluted Corinthian column in
the tradition of Nelson's Monument in Trafalgar Square,
that stands today. Its dedication was celebrated by
Charles Sangster (1822-93), in one of the few such public
poems written in this country. What it may lack in inspiration it more than makes up in intention. "Brock" is
reprinted from *Hesperus and Other Poems and Lyrics*
(1860).

Brock/*Charles Sangster*

October 13th, 1859

One voice, one people, one in heart
  And soul, and feeling, and desire!
  Re-light the smouldering martial fire,
  Sound the mute trumpet, strike the lyre,
  The hero deed can not expire,
    The dead still play their part.

Raise high the monumental stone!
  A nation's fealty is theirs,
  And we are the rejoicing heirs,
  The honoured sons of sires whose cares
  We take upon us unawares,
    As freely as our own.

We boast not of the victory,
  But render homage, deep and just,
  To his—to their—immortal dust,
  Who proved so worthy of their trust
  No lofty pile nor sculptured bust
    Can herald their degree.

No tongue need blazon forth their fame—
  The cheers that stir the sacred hill
  Are but mere promptings of the will
  That conquered then, that conquers still;
  And generations yet shall thrill
    At Brock's remembered name.

Some souls are the Hesperides
  Heaven sends to guard the golden age,
  Illuming the historic page ·
  With records of their pilgrimage;
  True Martyr, Hero, Poet, Sage:
    And he was one of these.

Each in his lofty sphere sublime
  Sits crowned above the common throng,
  Wrestling with some Pythonic wrong,
  In prayer, in thunder, thought, or song;
  Briaereus-limbed, they sweep along,
    The Typhons of the time.

The Rebellion of 1837

There is a temptation to see the Rebellion of 1837 in comic-opera terms, for neither side—neither Patriot nor Loyalist—wished to institute a civil war in Lower and Upper Canada. Bloody uprisings in present-day Quebec, led by Louis-Joseph Papineau (1786-1871), took place at Saint-Charles, Saint-Denis, and Saint-Eustache in November and December 1837. The principal battle in present-day Ontario, led by William Lyon Mackenzie (1795-1861), took place at Montgomery's Tavern, now in north Toronto, in December 1837. All were quickly aborted and resulted in the loss of life and property

damage. Yet the grievances felt by "the rebels" against the Château Clique in Quebec and the Family Compact in Ontario were at least partially recognized and redressed by Lord Durham, sent by the British government to look into the causes of the uprisings, in his famous *Report,* published in 1839, which recommended a modified form of responsible government for the colonies. Both Papineau and Mackenzie were amnestied and returned home. I have represented the Rebellion of 1837 with three songs. The first two take the form of additional verses to be sung to the tune of "God Save the King." The Patriot side is represented by "Lord! Free Us All!" from *Mackenzie's Gazette,* 3 November 1838. The Loyalist side is presented in "National Anthem" from the *Montreal Transcript,* 13 February 1838, where it is ascribed to "J.P.H. Cobourg." The texts of both are taken from John S. Moir's *Rhymes of Rebellion: Being a Selection of Contemporary Verses about the "Recent Unpleasantness" in Upper Canada, 1837* (1965). These two martial airs are followed by an English version of "Un Canadien Errant" by Antoine Gérin-Lajoie, a moving lament for the French Canadians exiled to Australia following the rebellion, written by the author while still a student. The translation "From His Canadian Home" is by John Murray Gibbon (1875-1952) from his book *Canadian Folk Songs: Old and New* (1927, 1949).

Lord! Free Us All!

Tune—"God save the King"

Lord! o'er our own loved land
Spread thy protecting hand!
    Help! ere we fall!
Free us from Monarchy—
Free us from Hierarchy,
Sabres and *Squirearchy*—
    Lord free us all!

O, men of England! rise!
Arm for the precious prize,
    Your birthright, all!
With firm heart, with iron-hand
As *One* let *Millions* stand,
A true and steadfast band—
    Triumph, or fall!

Lord! o'er our own loved land,
Spread thy protecting hand!
    Help! ere we fall!
Free us from tyrant-knaves—
Let us no more as slaves
Find out inglorious graves,—
    Lord; free us all!

National Anthem

Additional Stanzas

Lord, on our side be seen,
Prosper our rightful Queen,
      Bless our young Queen!
Her loyal people bless,
And give their swords success,
Shield us from all distress;
      God save the Queen!

Put down th' invading band
Threat'ning our happy land,
      Mocking our Queen.
Set every fear at rest,
Animate each breast;
On thee our cause we rest:
      God save the Queen!

From His Canadian Home/*Antoine Gérin-Lajoie*

From his Canadian home
   Banished a wand'rer came,
And full of tears would roam,
   Countries that strangers claim.

Thoughtful and sad one day,
   Down by a river bed,
As the stream slipped away,
   These were the words he said:

"If you my land should see,
   My so unhappy land,
Say to my friends from me
   They in my memory stand.

"O so delightful days,
   Vanished you are—adieu!
And my own land, alas!
   Never again I'll view.

"Plunged in unhappiness,
   From my dear parents torn,
Now through the tears I pass
   In luckless moments born.

"For ever set apart
   From friends that were so sweet,
Alas! no more my heart,
   My heart for grief can beat.

"No, yet in dying still,
   O my dear Canada!
My drooping eyes I will
   Turn toward thee afar."

Confederation, 1867

"I am obliged to go to Ottawa tomorrow for a few days for some business," wrote Lord Monck from his official residence at Quebec City. What the future governor general of Canada did not explain in the letter he addressed to his son in London was that the matter-of-fact reference to "some business" was, in fact, a reference to Monck's task of proclaiming the creation of the Dominion of Canada on 1 July 1867 in the frontier town of Ottawa. Although crêpe paper was hung in mourning in some Maritime cities, there was a flurry of festivity in the new capital of the new Dominion. At midnight, one hundred and one guns were fired, church bells were pealed, and huge bonfires were lit. Official ceremonies were held at the City Hall and the Privy Council Office, and in the streets there were parades and military marchpasts. The Parliament Buildings were illuminated that evening, and midnight approached with a great blaze of fireworks. John A. Macdonald was the hero of the day: the first prime minister of Canada, a newly created Knight Commander of the Bath. Macdonald had faith in this Confederation, which he expressed in a letter of 3 June 1867: "By the exercise of common sense and a limited amount of that patriotism that goes by the name of self-interest, I have no doubt that the Union will be for the common weal." I have attempted to catch the spirit of Confederation not through the occasional verses that the celebrations in Ottawa or elsewhere inspired but through a poem written two decades later by Sir Charles G.D. Roberts (1860-1943). "A national feeling is awakening quietly but surely," Sir Charles wrote to his cousin Bliss Carman. In the first three months of 1885, Sir Charles was inspired to compose "Collect for Dominion Day." It is reprinted from *In Divers Tones* (1887).

Collect for Dominion Day/*Sir Charles G.D. Roberts*

Father of nations! Help of the feeble hand!
   Strength of the strong! to whom the nations kneel!
   Stay and destroyer, at whose just command
   Earth's kingdoms tremble and her empires reel!
Who dost the low uplift, the small make great,
   And dost abase the ignorantly proud,
   Of our scant people mould a mighty state,
   To the strong, stern,—to Thee in meekness bowed!
Father of unity, make this people one!
   Weld, interfuse them in the patriot's flame,—
   Whose forging on thine anvil was begun
In blood late shed to purge the common shame;
   That so our hearts, the fever of faction done,
   Banish old feud in our young nation's name.

Canada First

"The ink was scarcely dry upon our Constitution when we began to think constitutionally," noted one nationalist about the immediate post-Confederation period. Perhaps George W. Ross, the patriotic superintendent of Ontario's schools, was referring to the Canada First movement, founded in Ottawa in 1868 by a group of enthusiasts who wanted to foster national pride. The movement encouraged a literary flowering—Sir Charles G.D. Roberts, Bliss Carman, W.W. Campbell, Archibald Lampman, and Duncan Campbell Scott are a few of the poets who thrived on national themes—and it produced at least one political bud, Edward Blake's well-known "Aurora Speech" of 1874. George Munro Grant's inspired travelogue, *Ocean to Ocean* (1873), is perhaps the peak of Canada First's influence. The spark glowed for a decade or so and then died out, never to be long rekindled. George Taylor Denison, one of the leaders of the movement, attributes the phrase "Canada First" to Sir James D. Edgar (1841-99), a future speaker of the House of Commons, who is the author of the verse that follows. "This Canada of Ours" won a prize for a Canadian national song in 1874. As Sir Charles G.D. Roberts noted in *Flying Colours* (1942): "This poem was written in 1870. The title has become a household word though the poem itself be undeservedly forgotten." It is reprinted from *This Canada of Ours, and Other Poems* (1893).

This Canada of Ours/*Sir James D. Edgar*

Let other tongues in older lands
    Loud vaunt their claims to glory,
And chaunt in triumph of the past,
    Content to live in story.
Tho' boasting no baronial halls,
    Nor ivy-crested towers,
What past can match thy glorious youth,
        Fair Canada of ours?
            Fair Canada,
            Dear Canada,
        This Canada of ours!

We love those far-off ocean isles
    Where Britain's monarch reigns;
We'll ne'er forget the good old blood
    That courses through our veins;
Proud Scotia's fame, old Erin's name,
    And haughty Albion's powers,
Reflect their matchless lustre on
        This Canada of ours.
            Fair Canada,
            Dear Canada,
        This Canada of ours!

May our Dominion flourish then,
    A goodly land and free,

Where Celt and Saxon, hand in hand,
    Hold sway from sea to sea.
Strong arms shall guard our cherished homes
    When darkest danger lowers,
And with our life-blood we'll defend
        This Canada of ours.
            Fair Canada,
            Dear Canada,
        This Canada of ours!

The Nine-Hour Movement, 1872

"But no suppression of facts, no titles the crown is misled to confer, no Windsor uniforms, no strutting in swords and cocked hats, no declarations and resolutions of Parliament, no blare of party conventions, no lies graven on marble, no statues of bronze can change the truth, that the true makers of Canada were those who, in obscurity and poverty, made it with axe and spade, with plough and scythe, with sweat of face and strength of arms." So wrote Robert Sellar about farm life in Upper Canada. Had he been writing half a century later he would have included among his workers the factory labourers. On 15 May 1872 the workers of Hamilton, Ontario, held a huge demonstration to demand a shorter working week. The Toronto Trades Assembly took up the demand, adopting as its slogan the phrase "Nine-Hour Day." Meetings were held in Montreal, Toronto, Hamilton, Brantford, St. Catharines and elsewhere to demand the nine-hour working day, the fifty-four-hour working week, and so great was the clamour that the movement realized its aims. One Hamilton trade unionist, Alexander Wingfield (1818-96), a mechanic in the boiler shop of the Great Western Railway, wrote "The Nine-Hour Pioneers" which was published in *The Ontario Workman*, May 1872. I have reprinted Wingfield's verse from *The Poetry of the Canadian People: 1720-1920* (1976), edited by N. Brian Davis.

The Nine-Hour Pioneers/*Alexander Wingfield*

Honour the men of Hamilton,
The Nine-Hour pioneers,
Their memory will be kept green,
Throughout the coming years.

And every honest son of toil
That lives in freedom's light
Shall bless that glorious day in May
When might gave way to right.

Your cause was just, your motives pure,
Again, again, again,
You strove to smooth the path of toil
And help your fellow-men.

And Canada will bless your name
Through all the coming years,
And place upon the scroll of fame
The Nine-Hour pioneers.

The Riel Rebellions

"I am the half-breed question," exclaimed Louis Riel (1844-85), the Métis leader who led his people in Manitoba and in Saskatchewan into two unsuccessful uprisings: the Red River Rebellion of 1869-70 and the North-West Rebellion of 1884-85. Seen by the newly created Dominion of Canada as acts of disloyalty, today the rebellions are considered expressions of minority rights against majority encroachments. Both were protests against the expansionist policies of the Dominion and both were put down firmly by Sir John A. Macdonald, who refused to forgive Riel for his role in the rebellions and saw to it that he was duly executed for his crime of high treason. (The section "Records of Our Past" includes an interview with Riel.) The turning point in the North-West Rebellion was the Battle of Batoche, fought 9-12 May 1885. The Métis settlement on the South Saskatchewan River near Prince Albert, Alberta, was Riel's capital, and when it fell under an attack by troops under General Frederick Middleton, Riel fled, only to surrender three days later. Batoche, with its tiny church of Saint-Antoine-de-Padoue, is now a national historic site. What broke the back of the rebels was the Gatling gun, a crank-operated prototype of the modern machine gun, patented in 1862 by Dr. Richard Jordan Gatling and capable of firing five hundred rounds of ammunition a minute. Middleton had one of these under the command of a Lieutenant Howard, an American who demonstrated the "patent murdering machine" against the Métis, who were reduced to stuffing their muzzle-loaders with gravel and nails. "The Man with the Gatling Gun" is an anonymous verse published by Charles Pelham Mulvaney of the Queen's Own Rifles in *The History of the North-West Rebellion of 1885* (1886). Following it is "The Battlefield at Batoche," a meditation on the battle by the contemporary poet Al Purdy (b. 1918), published in *Sex and Death* (1973).

The Man with the Gatling Gun/*Unknown*

Full many a line of expressions fine
    And of sentiments sweet and grand
Have been penned of "our boys" who, from home's
    dear joys,
    Set out for the North-West land.
We've been told how they've fought for the glory sought,
    We've heard of the deeds they've done;
But it's quite high time for some praise in rhyme
    For the man with the Gatling gun.

Music hath charms, even midst war's alarms,
    To soothe the savage breast;
None can hold a candle to that "music by Handel"
    That lulled Riel's "breeds" to rest,
And they sleep that sleep profound, so deep,
    From which shall awaken none;
And the lullabies that closed their eyes
    Were sung by the Gatling gun.

All honour's due—and they have it, too—
    To the Grens. and Q.O.R.
They knew no fear but, with British cheer,
    They charged and dispersed afar
The rebel crew; but 'twixt me and you
    When all is said and done,
A different scene there might have been
    But for Howard and his Gatling gun.

The Battlefield at Batoche/*Al Purdy*

Over the earthworks among slim cottonwood trees
wind whistles a wind tune
I think it has nothing to do with living or dead men
or the price of groceries
it is only wind
And walking in the wooded dish-shaped hollow
that served to protect generals and staff
officers from sniper fire
I hear a different kind of murmur
 — no more than that at least not definitely
the sort of thing you do hear
every now and then in a city never
questioning because it's so ordinary
but not so ordinary here
I ask my wife "Do you hear anything?"
She smiles "Your imagination again?"
"All right then don't you wish you had one?"
"If I did I'd burn your supper..."
the sort of thing she says to annoy me
the unanswerable kind of remark
that needs time to think about
I take my time watching the green curve
of the South Saskatchewan River below
a man riding an inch-long machine a mile distant
that makes dark waves cutting the yellow wheat
I wonder if Gunner Phillips heard the sound
on the day of May 12 in 1885
before the bullet knocked him down
the stairs he spent twenty years climbing?
Did Letendre with his muzzle-loader
clamped under one arm stuffing gun powder
down the barrel and jamming in a bullet
stop remembering great itchy beasts
pushing against log palisades at night
and running the buffalo at Grand Coteau
the Sioux screaming insults from a safe distance

at men from the White Horse Plain?
— all this in dream pantomime
with that sound and nothing else?
And old Ouellette age 90
his hearing almost gone anyway
wiping off river mist from his rifle
listening — ?
Under my feet grass makes small noises
a bright-eyed creature I can't identify
is curious about me
and chitters because it's August
In May the annoyed general eats his lunch
on the cliffs ordering "a reconnaissance in force"
his officers misinterpret as "attack in force"
Midlanders   Winnipeg Rifles   Grenadiers
move out from their own positions
and burst into the Metis rifle pits
with Captain Howard from Connecticut
a demonstrator for the Colt Firearms Company
of Hartford demonstrating
death at 500 rounds a minute
with the borrowed Gatling gun
But it wasn't the sound I hear now
not the dead shifting positions underground
to dodge bullets stopped in mid-earth
here a little way under the black soil
where wheat yellow as a girl's hair blossoms
the Metis nation was born and died
as the last buffalo stumbles to his knees
and felt cold briefly while his great wool
blanket was ripped from bloody shoulders
It is for Parenteau and Desjarlais
Ah-si-we-in of the Woods Crees
for Laframboise and old Ouellette
and dark girls left alone
that such words as mine are spoken
and perhaps also for Gunner Phillips
in his grave above the South Saskatchewan
but most for myself
And I say to my wife, "Do you hear nothing?"
"I hear the poem you're writing" she says
"I knew you were going to say that" I say
In evening listening
to the duplicate rain-sound on the roof
of our camped trailer it seems
that I was wrong about my motives
and the dark girls mourning at Batoche
the dead men in shallow rifle pits
these mean something
the rain speaks to them
the seasons pass
just outside their hearing
but what they died for has faded away
and become something quite different
past justice and injustice
beyond old Ouellette and his youngest grandson

with the larking dog chasing a rabbit
green grass growing
rain falling
on the road cars passing by
Like the child I am/was I say "Me too"
camped on the battlefield of Batoche
just slightly visible in August
me an extension of anything that ever happened
a shadow behind the future
the bullets aimed at me
by Gunner Phillips and old man Ouellette
eighty-five years ago
whispering across the fields of eternity

The Last Spike, 1885

"All I can say is that the work has been done well in every way," conceded Sir William Cornelius Van Horne, general manager and chief builder of the Canadian Pacific Railway, after Donald Smith (later Lord Strathcona) had driven in "the last spike" at Craigellachie, British Columbia, 9:22 A.M., 7 November 1885. Driving the ordinary iron spike home marked the completion of the dream of Confederation: a transcontinental railway. Built at tremendous cost against immense odds over impossible terrain by private enterprise and public capital, it connected Montreal and Vancouver, and points between, with twin rails of steel, welding the country into a single unit. Let me represent the saga of the CPR with "Canadian Railroad Trilogy," the popular song written in 1967 by Gordon Lightfoot (b. 1939).

Canadian Railroad Trilogy/*Gordon Lightfoot*

There was a time in this fair land when the railroad did
     not run,
When the wild majestic mountains stood alone against
     the sun,
Long before the white man and long before the wheel
When the green dark forest was too silent to be real.

But time has no beginnings and history has no bounds,
As to this verdant country they came from all around,
They sailed upon her waterways and they walked the
     forests tall,
Built the mines, the mills and the factories for the good of
     us all.

And when the young man's fancy was turnin' in the
     spring,
The railroad men grew restless for to hear the hammers
     ring,
Their minds were overflowin' with the visions of their day
And many a fortune won and lost and many a debt to
     pay.

For they looked in the future and what did they see,
They saw an iron road runnin' from the sea to the sea,
Bringin' the goods to a young, growin' land
All up from the seaports and into their hands.
"Look away!" said they, "across this mighty land,
From the eastern shore to the western strand!"

"Bring in the workers and bring up the rails,
We gotta lay down the tracks and tear up the trails,
Open her heart, let the life blood flow,
Gotta get on our way 'cause we're movin' too slow,
Get on our way 'cause we're movin' too slow."

"Behind the blue Rockies the sun is declinin',
The stars they come stealin' at the close of the day,
Across the wide prairie our loved ones lie sleepin'
Beyond the dark ocean in a place far away."

"We are the navvies who work upon the railway,
Swingin' our hammers in the bright blazin' sun,
Livin' on stew and drinkin' bad whisky,
Bendin' our backs 'til the long days are done."

"We are the navvies who work upon the railway,
Swingin' our hammers in the bright blazin' sun,
Layin' down track and buildin' the bridges,
Bendin' our backs 'til the railroad is done."

"So over the mountains and over the plains,
Into the muskeg and into the rain,
Up the Saint Lawrence all the way to Gaspé,
Layin' 'em in and tyin' 'em down,
Away to the bunkhouse and into the town,
A dollar a day and a place for my head,
A drink for the livin', a toast to the dead!"

"Oh, the song of the future has been sung,
All the battles have been won,
On the mountaintops we stand,
All the world at our command.
We have opened up the soil
With our teardrops—
And our toil."

For there was a time in this fair land when the railroad
    did not run,
When the wild majestic mountains stood alone against
    the sun,
Long before the white man and long before the wheel,
When the green dark forest was too silent to be real,
When the green dark forest was too silent to be real.
And many are the dead men,
Too silent
To be real.

The Klondike Gold Rush, 1896

It began on 16 August 1896 with a lucky strike on the
bank of Bonanza Creek, a tributary of the Klondike
River, Yukon Territory, and before it was over, four years
later, it had attracted many thousands of prospectors,
miners, gold-seekers, and adventurers from the four corners of the world. Some were lucky, others were not. "The
Klondike experience had taught all these men that they
were capable of a kind of achievement they had never
dreamed possible," Pierre Berton noted in *Klondike*
(1958). "It was this, perhaps, more than anything else,
that set them apart from their fellows." One of those who
benefited from his experiences was Robert W. Service
(1874-1958), an English-born bank clerk who was transferred from Vancouver to Whitehorse in 1904 and then to
Dawson in 1906. Service began to write verses there, and
one of the earliest was "The Spell of the Yukon," which
appeared in his first book, *Songs of a Sourdough* (1907).
His writings made Service financially independent, and
in 1911 he left the Yukon, never to return. For many
years he lived on the Riviera, about as far away from the
Yukon as it is possible to go.

The Spell of the Yukon / *Robert W. Service*

I wanted the gold, and I sought it;
    I scrabbled and mucked like a slave.
Was it fame or scurvy—I fought it;
    I hurled my youth into a grave.
I wanted the gold, and I got it—
    Came out with a fortune last fall,—
Yet somehow life's not what I thought it,
    And somehow the gold isn't all.

No! There's the land. (Have you seen it?)
    It's the cussedest land that I know,
From the big, dizzy mountains that screen it
    To the deep, deathlike valleys below.
Some say God was tired when He made it;
    Some say it's a fine land to shun;
Maybe; but there's some as would trade it
    For no land on earth—and I'm one.

You come to get rich (damned good reason);
    You feel like an exile at first;
You hate it like hell for a season,
    And then you are worse than the worst.
It grips you like some kinds of sinning;
    It twists you from foe to a friend;
It seems it's been since the beginning;
    It seems it will be to the end.

I've stood in some mighty-mouthed hollow
    That's plumb-full of hush to the brim;
I've watched the big, husky sun wallow
    In crimson and gold, and grow dim,
Till the moon set the pearly peaks gleaming,
    And the stars tumbled out, neck and crop;
And I've thought that I surely was dreaming,
    With the peace o' the world piled on top.

The summer—no sweeter was ever;
    The sunshiny woods all athrill;
The grayling aleap in the river,
    The bighorn asleep on the hill.
The strong life that never knows harness;
    The wilds where the caribou call;
The freshness, the freedom, the farness—
    O God! how I'm stuck on it all.

The winter! The brightness that blinds you,
    The white land locked tight as a drum,
The cold fear that follows and finds you,
    The silence that bludgeons you dumb.
The snows that are older than history,
    The woods where the weird shadows slant;
The stillness, the moonlight, the mystery,
    I've bade 'em good-by—but I can't.

There's a land where the mountains are nameless,
    And the rivers all run God knows where;
There are lives that are erring and aimless,
    And deaths that just hang by a hair;
There are hardships that nobody reckons;
    There are valleys unpeopled and still;
There's a land—oh, it beckons and beckons,
    And I want to go back—and I will.

They're making my money diminish;
    I'm sick of the taste of champagne.
Thank God! when I'm skinned to a finish
    I'll pike to the Yukon again.
I'll fight—and you bet it's no sham-fight;
    It's hell!—but I've been there before;
And it's better than this by a damsite—
    So me for the Yukon once more.

There's gold, and it's haunting and haunting;
    It's luring me on as of old;
Yet it isn't the gold that I'm wanting
    So much as just finding the gold.
It's the great, big, broad land 'way up yonder,
    It's the forests where silence has lease;
It's the beauty that thrills me with wonder,
    It's the stillness that fills me with peace.

British Preferential Tariff, 1897

The principle of "British Preference" in matters of trade and tariff was first incorporated in a Liberal budget in 1897 when the newly elected government of Sir Wilfrid Laurier limited preferential rates to imports from Britain and the colonies. By granting a rebate of one-eighth on the general rate of imports from within the British Empire—increased to one-quarter and then to one-third—the government effectively raised the cost of imports from other countries. For almost half a century "British Preference" was an important part of the Canadian tariff

structure. Today we have three levels of tariff, based on country of origin, but there is little essential difference between British Preferential Status (for Commonwealth countries) and Most-Favoured Nations Status (for non-Commonwealth countries), with General Status (the highest) applying to a negligible number of countries. Although these matters may be distant from us today, thinking about them inspired the British writer and imperialist Rudyard Kipling (1865-1936) to set pen to paper and compose "Our Lady of the Snows," which defined Britain's relations with Canada in terms of those of a mother and a daughter. The poem gave us a snowy image we have never been able to shake off. "Our Lady of the Snows" first appeared in the London *Times*, 27 April 1897, and is reprinted from *Rudyard Kipling's Verse: Definitive Edition* (1940, 1966).

Our Lady of the Snows/ *Rudyard Kipling*
(Canadian Preferential Tariff, 1897)

A Nation spoke to a Nation,
A Queen sent word to a Throne:
"Daughter am I in my mother's house,
    But mistress in my own.
The gates are mine to open,
    As the gates are mine to close,
And I set my house in order,"
    Said our Lady of the Snows.

"Neither with laughter nor weeping,
    Fear or the child's amaze—
Soberly under the White Man's law
    My white men go their ways.
Not for the Gentiles' clamour—
    Insult or threat of blows—
Bow we the knee to Baal,"
    Said our Lady of the Snows.

"My speech is clean and single,
    I talk of common things—
Words of the wharf and the market-place
    And the ware the merchant brings:
Favour to those I favour,
    But a stumbling-block to my foes.
Many there be that hate us,"
    Said our Lady of the Snows.

"I called my chiefs to council
    In the din of a troubled year;
For the sake of a sign ye would not see,
    And a word ye would not hear.
This is our message and answer;
    This is the path we chose:
For we be also a people,"
    Said our Lady of the Snows.

"Carry the word to my sisters—
    To the Queens of the East and the South.

I have proven faith in the Heritage
  By more than the word of the mouth.
They that are wise may follow
  Ere the world's war-trumpet blows,
But I — I am first in the battle,"
  Said our Lady of the Snows.

A Nation spoke to a Nation,
  A Throne sent word to a Throne:
"Daughter am I in my mother's house,
  But mistress in my own.
The gates are mine to open,
  As the gates are mine to close,
And I abide by my Mother's House,"
  Said our Lady of the Snows.

Fraser River Strike, 1912

Protesting low pay, bad food, poor living and working
conditions, about eight thousand construction workers
laying track for the Canadian Northern Railway along
the mighty Fraser River near Yale, British Columbia,
went on strike on 27 March 1912. The workers were supported by the Industrial Workers of the World, and there
arrived on the scene the IWW bard, the almost legendary
Joe Hill (1879-1915). At Yale, the Swedish-born American labour organizer composed one of his best-known
songs, "Where the Fraser River Flows," to be sung to the
tune of "Where the Shannon River Flows." By the fall of
1912 the strike was over, with the workers gaining most of
their demands. Three years later, charged with murder
in Utah, Hill was executed. His dying words, "Don't waste
any time in mourning — organize!" are well remembered
in labour history. The story of "the man who never died"
is told by Gibbs M. Smith in *Labour Martyr: Joe Hill*
(1969).

Where the Fraser River Flows/*Joe Hill*

Fellow workers pay attention to what I'm going to mention,
For it is the fixed intention of the Workers of the World.
And I hope you'll all be ready, true-hearted, brave and
  steady,
To gather 'round our standard when the Red Flag is un-
  furled.

Where the Fraser river flows, each fellow worker knows,
They have bullied and oppressed us, but still our Union
  grows.
And we're going to find a way, boys, for shorter hours
  and better pay, boys;
And we're going to win the day, boys; where the river
  Fraser flows.

For these gunny-sack contractors have all been dirty
  actors,

And they're not our benefactors, each fellow worker
  knows.
So we've got to stick together in fine or dirty weather,
And we will show no white feather, where the Fraser river
  flows.

Where the Fraser river flows, each fellow worker knows,
They have bullied and oppressed us, but still our Union
  grows.
And we're going to find a way, boys, for shorter hours
  and better pay, boys;
And we're going to win the day, boys; where the river
  Fraser flows.

Now the boss the law is stretching, bulls and pimps he's
  fetching,
And they are a fine collection, as Jesus only knows.
But why their mothers reared them, and why the devil
  spared them,
Are questions we can't answer, where the Fraser river
  flows.

Where the Fraser river flows, each fellow worker knows,
They have bullied and oppressed us, but still our Union
  grows.
And we're going to find a way, boys, for shorter hours
  and better pay, boys;
And we're going to win the day, boys; where the river
  Fraser flows.

The First World War, 1914-18

Canada entered the Great War as a matter of course
when Great Britain declared war against Germany on 4
August 1914. The armistice was signed 11 November
1918. Canada contributed 626,636 officers and men to
all services, of whom 59,769 lost their lives. The suffering
and slaughter is evoked by cenotaphs in the centre of
towns and cities across the country which bear such place
names as Ypres, Vimy, and Passchendaele. No poem conveys so movingly and for so many the heroism of the war
dead as "In Flanders Fields," which was written by John
McCrae (1872-1918) a medical officer with the First Canadian Contingent. It was composed in twenty minutes on
3 May 1915 during the Second Battle of Ypres, a Flemish
town in Belgium. It is reprinted from McCrae's sole book,
In Flanders Fields and Other Poems (1919), edited by Sir
Andrew Macphail. In stark contrast to "In Flanders
Fields" is a little song which appeared in a keepsake
volume, *With the First Canadian Contingent* (1915),
edited by Mary Plummer and published on behalf of the
Canadian Field Comforts Commission. I have called it
"Five Hundred Thousand Strong" for it is nameless there;
the author is identified only as "Canucas." The ready
patriotism, especially the reference to Flanders, might
make some wince today, yet the ditty conveys something
of the high spirits invoked by the Great War.

In Flanders Fields/ *John McCrae*

In Flanders fields the poppies blow
Between the crosses, row on row,
    That mark our place; and in the sky
    The larks, still bravely singing, fly
Scarce heard amid the guns below.

We are the Dead. Short days ago
We lived, felt dawn, saw sunset glow,
    Loved and were loved, and now we lie
        In Flanders fields.

Take up our quarrel with the foe:
To you from failing hands we throw
    The torch; be yours to hold it high.
    If ye break faith with us who die
We shall not sleep, though poppies grow
        In Flanders fields.

Five Hundred Thousand Strong/ *Unknown*

From Sydney to Esquimalt, from the Lakes to Hudson
    Bay,
Men who never saw you, Mother, those that left you
    yesterday,
We have chucked the tools and ledgers, we have left the
    bench and mine,
We are sailing east to Flanders to join the khaki line!
    (Sign here! S'help you God! Forward—March!)

    We are coming, wild and woolly,
    Hearts and hands are with you fully,
    Pledged to smash the Prussian bully,
    Five hundred thousand strong!

We are coming to our Mother who bore us in her flank,
From the prairie and the backwoods, from the shop and
    mill and bank,
From the orchard and the offing, be the battle brief or
    long,
We are coming, Mother England, five hundred thousand
    strong!
        (Advance! Countersign? Pass—Canada!)

    We are coming, pink and perky,
    Though our drill be quaint and jerky,
    Bound for Sausage-land and Turkey,
    Five hundred thousand strong!

They said that we were softened by the wages and the
    feed,
They said that we were hardened to the kin we used to
    need,
Eager, fit, equipped, and ready—were they right or were
    they wrong?
We are coming, Mother England, five hundred thousand
    strong!
        (Heave ho! Lights out! Farewell, Canada!)

    We are coming, British brother,
    Red War's hellish flames to smother,
    We are off to help our Mother—
    Five hundred thousand strong!
    (Altogether, boys!—"The Maple Leaf Forever!")

The Winnipeg General Strike, 1919

The Winnipeg general strike was the only general strike
ever held in Canada. It was called on 15 May 1919 in support of metal and building-trade workers who were on
strike over issues of union recognition and collective bar-
gaining. Over twenty-two thousand workers responded,
including civic and government employees, initially
paralysing the city. Permits were then issued by the strike
committee to allow essential services to continue. Order
was maintained until the Royal North-West Mounted
Police intervened to separate the strikers and anti-
strikers, and violence ensued. The strike was called off on
26 June. In the aftermath, leaders of the strike committee
were charged with seditious conspiracy, which was
described in Section 98 of the Criminal Code as a
criminal offence for anyone suspected of advocating the
use of force to change society. New legislation hurriedly
introduced into the House increased the maximum
penalty for those found guilty of seditious conspiracy
from two to twenty years' imprisonment, and an amendment to the Immigration Act provided for the immediate
deportation of any New Canadian suspected of sedition,
regardless of citizenship status or length of stay. Both
were repealed in 1936. Of the ten leaders arrested, four
were subsequently elected to the provincial legislature,
and a fifth, J.S. Woodsworth, to the House of Commons.
The verse that follows was written by Edmund Vance
Cooke and appeared in the *Industrial Banner*, 20 March
1920. It is reprinted from *The Poetry of the Canadian
People: 1720-1920* (1976), edited by N. Brian Davis.

"Sedition"/ *Edmund Vance Cooke*

You cannot salt the eagle's tail,
    Nor limit thought's dominion.
You cannot put ideas in jail;
    You can't deport opinion.

If any cause be dross and lies,
    Then drag it to the light;
Out in the sunshine evil dies,
    But fattens on the night.

You cannot make a truth untrue
    By dint of legal fiction.
You cannot prison human view,
    You can't convict conviction.

For though by thumbscrew and by rack,
    By exile and by prison,

Truth has been crushed and palled in black
    Yet truth has always risen.

You cannot quell a vicious thought
    Except that thought be free;
Gag it, and you will find it taught
    On every land and sea.

Truth asks no favour for her blade
    Upon the field with error,
Nor are her converts ever made
    By threat of force and terror.

You cannot salt the eagle's tail,
    Nor limit thought's dominion.
You cannot put ideas in jail,
    You can't deport opinion.

The Great Depression, 1929-39

"The Dirty Thirties! Just put in your book that you met Henry Jacobson and he's seventy-eight years old. Might I say I never took a backward step in my life until that Depression whipped me, took away my wife, my home, a section of good land back in Saskatchewan. Left me with nothing. Write that down." Barry Broadfoot (b. 1926) recorded that testimony and hundreds of others like it in *Ten Lost Years, 1929-1939: Memories of Canadians Who Survived the Depression* (1973). The ten years of hard times corresponded to dust-bowl conditions on the prairies, with Saskatchewan being the hardest hit. Something of the misery and suffering occasioned by the social and psychological conditions of the day may be felt in *The Wind Our Enemy*, the quintessential poem about farming conditions in Canada in the 1930s. It was written by Anne Marriott (b. 1913) and published as a Ryerson Poetry Chap-Book in 1939, just as the country found it could afford the foodstuffs and weaponry required to fight the Second World War.

The Wind Our Enemy/*Anne Marriott*

I

Wind
flattening its gaunt furious self against
the naked siding, knifing in the wounds
of time, pausing to tear aside the last
old scab of paint.

Wind
surging down the cocoa-coloured seams
of summer-fallow, darting in about
white hoofs and brown, snatching the sweaty cap
shielding red eyes.

Wind
filling the dry mouth with bitter dust

whipping the shoulders worry-bowed too soon,
soiling the water pail, and in grim prophecy
greying the hair.

II

The wheat in spring was like a giant's bolt of silk
Unrolled over the earth.
When the wind sprang
It rippled as if a great broad snake
Moved under the green sheet
Seeking its outward way to light.
In autumn it was an ocean of flecked gold
Sweet as a biscuit, breaking in crisp waves
That never shattered, never blurred in foam.
That was the last good year. . . .

III

The wheat was embroidering
All the spring morning,
Frail threads needled by sunshine like thin gold.
A man's heart could love his land,
Smoothly self-yielding,
Its broad spread promising all his granaries might hold.
A woman's eyes could kiss the soil
From her kitchen window,
Turning its black depths to unchipped cups—a silk crepe
    dress—
(Two-ninety-eight, Sale Catalogue)
Pray sun's touch be gentleness,
Not a hot hand scorching flesh it would caress.
But sky like a new tin pan
Hot from the oven
Seemed soldered to the earth by horizons of glare. . . .

The third day he left the fields. . . .

Heavy scraping footsteps
Spoke before his words, "Crops dried out—every-
    where—"

IV

They said, "Sure, it'll rain next year!"
When that was dry, "Well, next year anyway."
Then, "Next—"
But still the metal hardness of the sky
Softened only in mockery.
When lightning slashed and twanged
And thunder made the hot head surge with pain
Never a drop fell;
Always hard yellow sun conquered the storm.
So the soon sickly-familiar saying grew,
(Watching the futile clouds sneak down the north)
"Just empties goin' back!"
(Cold laughter bending parched lips in a smile
 Bleak eyes denied.)

V

Horses were strong so strong men might love them,
Sides groomed to copper burning the sun,
Wind tangling wild manes, dust circling wild hoofs,
Turn the colts loose!   Watch the two-year-olds run!
Then heart thrilled fast and the veins filled with glory
The feel of hard leather a fortune more sweet
Than a girl's silky lips.   He was one with the thunder,
The flying, the rhythm, of untamed, unshod feet!

But now—
It makes a man white-sick to see them now,
Dull—heads sagging—crowding to the trough—
No more spirit than a barren cow.
The well's pumped dry to wash poor fodder down,
Straw and salt—and endless salt and straw—
(Thank God the winter's mild so far)
Dry Russian thistle crackling in the jaw—
The old mare found the thistle pile, ate till she bulged,
Then, crazily, she wandered in the yard,
Saw a water-drum, and staggering to its rim,
Plodded around it—on and on in hard,
Madly relentless circle.   Weaker—stumbling—
She fell quite suddenly, heaved once and lay.
(Nellie the kids' pet's gone, boys.
Hitch up the strongest team. Haul her away.
Maybe we should have mortgaged all we had
Though it wasn't much, even in good years, and draw
Ploughs with a jolting tractor.
Still—you can't make gas of thistles or oat-straw.)

VI

Relief.
"God, we tried so hard to stand alone!"

Relief.
"Well, we can't let the kids go cold."
They trudge away to school swinging half-empty lard-
    pails,
to shiver in the schoolhouse (unpainted seven years),
learning from a blue-lipped girl
almost as starved as they.

Relief cars.
"Apples, they say, and clothes!"
The folks in town get their pick first,
Then their friends—
"Eight miles for us to go so likely we
won't get much—"
"Maybe we'll get the batteries charged up and have
the radio to kind of brighten things—"

Insurgents march in Spain
Japs bomb Chinese
Airliner lost

"Maybe we're not as badly off as some—"

"Maybe there'll be a war and we'll get paid to fight—"
"Maybe—"
"See if Eddie Cantor's on to-night!"

VII

People grew bored
Well-fed in the east and west
By stale, drought-area tales,
Bored by relief whinings,
Preferred their own troubles.
So those who still had stayed
On the scorched prairie,
Found even sympathy
Seeming to fail them
Like their own rainfall.

  "Well—let's forget politics,
    Forget the wind, our enemy!
  Let's forget farming, boys,
  Let's put on a dance to-night!
  Mrs. Smith'll bring a cake.
  Mrs. Olsen's coffee's swell!"

The small uneven schoolhouse floor
Scraped under big work-boots
Cleaned for the evening's fun,
Gasoline lamps whistled.
One Hungarian boy
Snapped at a shrill guitar,
A Swede from out north of town
Squeezed an accordion dry,
And a Scotchwoman from Ontario
Made the piano dance
In time to "The Mocking-Bird"
And "When I Grow too Old to Dream,"
Only taking time off
To swing in a square dance,
Between ten and half-past three.

Yet in the morning
Air peppered thick with dust,
All the night's happiness
Seemed far away, unreal
Like a lying mirage,
Or the icy-white glare
Of the alkali slough.

VIII

Presently the dark dust seemed to build a wall
That cut them off from east and west and north,
Kindness and honesty, things they used to know,
Seemed blown away and lost
In frantic soil.
At last they thought
Even God and Christ were hidden
By the false clouds.

—Dust-blinded to the staring parable,
Each wind-splintered timber like a paint-bent Cross.
Calloused, groping fingers, trembling
With overwork and fear,
Ceased trying to clutch at some faith in the dark,
Thin sick courage fainted, lacking hope.
But tightened, tangled nerves scream to the brain
If there is no hope, give them forgetfulness!
The cheap light of the beer-parlour grins out,
Promising shoddy security for an hour.
The Finn who makes bad liquor in his barn
Grows fat on groaning emptiness of souls.

IX

The sun goes down.   Earth like a thick black coin
Leans its round rim against the yellowed sky.
The air cools.   Kerosene lamps are filled and lit
In dusty windows.   Tired bodies crave to lie
In bed forever.   Chores are done at last.
A thin horse neighs drearily.   The chickens drowse,
Replete with grasshoppers that have gnawed and scraped
Shrivelled garden leaves.   No sound from the gaunt cows.
Poverty, hand in hand with fear, two great
Shrill-jointed skeletons stride loudly out
Across the pitiful fields, none to oppose.
Courage is roped with hunger, chained with doubt.
Only against the yellow sky, a part
Of the jetty silhouette of barn and house
Two figures stand, heads close, arms locked,
And suddenly some spirit seems to rouse
And gleam, like a thin sword, tarnished, bent,
But still shining in the spared beauty of moon,
As his strained voice says to her, "We're not licked yet!
It must rain again—it *will!*   Maybe—soon—"

X

Wind
in a lonely laughterless shrill game
with broken wash-boiler, bucket without
a handle, Russian thistle, throwing up
sections of soil.

God, will it never rain again?   What about
those clouds out west?   No, that's just dust, as thick
and stifling now as winter underwear.
No rain, no crop, no feed, no faith, only
wind.

The Spanish Civil War, 1936-39

The bloody battles in Spain were a full-dress rehearsal for those of the Second World War, in which the forces of democracy fought those of fascism. Some 1,250 Cana-

dians, largely young men, volunteered to join the Popular Front against the Nationalist forces under General Francisco Franco and formed the celebrated Mackenzie-Papineau Battalion of the XVth International Brigade of the Spanish Republican Army. The battalion was known as the "Mac-Paps," after the Patriot leaders William Lyon Mackenzie and Louis-Joseph Papineau. The best known of the volunteers was Norman Bethune (1890-1939), a brilliant and erratic medical doctor who organized the world's first mobile blood-transfusion service at Madrid and raised funds in Canada for the Republican cause. In 1938 he switched battlefields and joined the Eighth Route Army of the Chinese Communists in the hills of Yenan, Northern China, where he formed the world's first mobile medical unit, dying there of an infection picked up while operating under primitive conditions. The verse here, written by Bethune the evening he decided to leave Montreal for Madrid, first appeared in the *Canadian Forum*, July 1937.

Red Moon / *Norman Bethune*

And this same pallid moon tonight,
    Which rides so quietly, clear and high,
The mirror of our pale and troubled gaze,
    Raised to a cool Canadian sky,

Above the shattered Spanish tops
    Last night, rose low and wild and red,
Reflecting back from her illumined shield,
    The blood-bespattered faces of the dead.

To that pale disc, we raise our clenched fists
    And to those nameless dead our vows renew,
"Comrades, who fought for freedom and the future world,
    You died for us, we will remember you."

The Royal Tour, 1939

Members of the Royal Family, including future monarchs, visited the Dominion earlier than 1939, of course, but never before had a reigning monarch toured the country. The first royal visit was made by King George VI and Queen Elizabeth from 17 May to 15 June, 1939. Their Majesties' progress in a royal blue train across the country, with frequent whistlestops along the way, left an indelible impression on those—monarchists and anti-monarchists alike—who took this opportunity to view the couple. The royal blue train did stop at Stratford, Ontario, although not at neighbouring Shakespeare, and this elicited a poem from James Reaney (b. 1926), which was first collected in *The Red Heart* (1949). The text is taken from Reaney's *Poems* (1972), edited by Germaine Warkentin.

The Royal Visit / *James Reaney*

When the King and the Queen came to Stratford
Everyone felt at once
How heavy the Crown must be.
The Mayor shook hands with their Majesties
And everyone presentable was presented
And those who weren't have resented
It, and will
To their dying day.
Everyone had almost a religious experience
When the King and Queen came to visit us
(I wonder what they felt!)
And hydrants flowed water in the gutters
All day.
People put quarters on the railroad tracks
So as to get squashed by the Royal Train
And some people up the line at Shakespeare
Stayed in Shakespeare, just in case —
They did stop too,
While thousands in Stratford
Didn't even see them
Because the Engineer didn't slow down
Enough in time.
And although,
But although we didn't see them in any way
(I didn't even catch the glimpse
The teacher who was taller did
Of a gracious pink figure)
I'll remember it to my dying day.

The Second World War, 1939-45

Canada declared war on Germany on 10 September 1939, seven days following Britain's declaration. The German government surrendered in the French cathedral city of Reims on 5 May 1945, and the Japanese surrender was taken at Tokyo Bay on 2 September 1945. A total of 730,625 Canadians saw service in the army, the navy, and the air force. I have chosen two short poems to represent the Second World War. The first suggests the exhilaration experienced by many of the combatants, the second the sorrow that blighted the lives of those it touched. "High Flight" was written by a young American, John Gillespie Magee Jr. (1922-41), born in Shanghai, who left Yale to enlist with the Royal Canadian Air Force in Montreal in October 1940. He trained with the Royal Air Force in England and was killed in action on 11 December 1941. He wrote the sonnet that follows on the back of a letter addressed to his mother three months before his death. It was chosen as the official poem of the RAF and posted in pilot-training centres throughout the Commonwealth. "This Was My Brother" was written by the sister of an officer who died during one of the great catastrophes of the Second World War. This was the controversial Dieppe raid in which an Allied force of almost five thousand Canadian soldiers and more than a thousand British commandos launched a full-scale attack on the northern French seaport, a German-occupied stronghold. The raid lacked surprise and the invading force withdrew under fire. The Canadians suffered 3,367 casualties, the Germans 333. The failure on "that brave and bitter day" ensured, it was later said, the success of the Normandy invasion of 1944, the turning-point of the war. Perhaps "This Was My Brother" by Mona Gould (b. 1908) will suggest the suffering occasioned by the Dieppe raid and the war itself. It is reprinted from *Tasting the Earth* (1943), where the following note appears: "The poem is for 'Mook' (Lt.-Col. Howard McTavish, Royal Canadian Engineers, killed in action, Dieppe, 1942)."

High Flight / *John Gillespie Magee, Jr.*

Oh, I have slipped the surly bonds of earth
And danced the skies on laughter-silvered wings;
Sunward I've climbed and joined the tumbling mirth
Of sun-split clouds — and done a hundred things
You have not dreamed of — wheeled and soared and swung
High in the sunlit silence. Hov'ring there,
I've chased the shouting wind along and flung
My eager craft through footless halls of air.
Up, up the long delirious, burning blue
I've topped the wind-swept heights with easy grace,
Where never lark, or even eagle, flew;
And, while with silent, lifting mind I've trod
The high untrespassed sanctity of space,
Put out my hand and touched the face of God.

This Was My Brother / *Mona Gould*

This was my brother
At Dieppe,
Quietly a hero
Who gave his life
Like a gift,
Withholding nothing.

His youth . . . his love . . .
His enjoyment of being alive . . .
His future, like a book
With half the pages still uncut —

This was my brother
At Dieppe —
The one who built me a doll house
When I was seven,
Complete to the last small picture frame,
Nothing forgotten.

He was awfully good at fixing things,
At stepping into the breach when he was needed.

That's what he did at Dieppe;

He was needed.
And even death must have been a little shamed
At his eagerness.

The Evacuation of the Japanese, 1942

Although Prime Minister Mackenzie King could rise in
the House of Commons on 4 August 1944 and admit that
the Japanese population of Canada, which had been
principally located on the British Columbia coast, had
committed no act of subversion or sabotage, the country's
treatment of these people was hardly exemplary. Fears of
attack from Japan, fanned by racial prejudice, led to an
order-in-council on 26 February 1942, declaring that all
Japanese, whether naturalized or native, be evacuated
from coastal areas and relocated. Some twenty-two thousand people were resettled in camps located in the
interior of British Columbia. By the end of the war the
Japanese were resettled "east of the Rockies," the majority in Alberta and Ontario. The humiliation and suffering occasioned by this preventative evacuation has found
expression in very few literary works. One in which it does
is a poem of over five hundred lines written for radio and
published in 1950 by the Winnipeg-born poet Dorothy
Livesay (b. 1909). *Call My People Home*, "A Documentary Poem for Radio," is a work of strength. Two se-
quences which give voice to the fears and hopes of the
Nisei (or Canadian-born Japanese, as distinct from the
Issei, those born in Japan) are reprinted here.

Call My People Home/*Dorothy Livesay*

A YOUNG NISEI:
We lived unto ourselves
Thinking so to be free
Locked in the harbour
Of father and mother
The children incoming
The tide inflowing.

Sometimes at remote midnight
With a burnt-out moon
An orange eye on the river
Or rising before dawn
From a house heavy with sleepers
The man touching my arm
Guiding my hand through the dark
To the boat softly bumping and sucking
Against the wharf;
We go out toward misty islands
Of fog over the river
Jockeying for position;
Till morning steals over, sleepy,
And over our boat's side, leaning
The word comes, Set the nets!
Hiding the unannounced prayer

Resounding in the heart's corners:
May we have a high boat
And the silver salmon leaping!

We lived unto ourselves
Locked in the harbour

I remember the schoolhouse, its battered doorway
The helter-skelter of screaming children
Where the old ones went, my sisters
Soberly with books strapped over their shoulders:
Deliberately bent on learning —

(And learned, soon enough, of
the colour of their skin, and why
Their hair would never turn golden.)

But before the bell rang
For me
My turn at becoming
Before the bell rang
I was out on the hillside
Reaching high over my head for the black ones
The first plump berries of summer;
A scratch on the arm, maybe, a tumble
But filling my pail and singing my song
With the bees humming
And the sun burning.

Then no bell rang for me;
Only the siren
Only the women crying and the men running.
Only the Mounties writing our names
In the big book; the stifled feeling
Of being caught, corralled.
Only the trucks and a scramble to find
A jacket, a ball, for the bundle.

My blackberries spilled
Smeared purple
Over the doorway.
Never again did I go
Blackberry picking on the hillside.
Never again did I know
That iron schoolbell ringing.

The children incoming
The tide inflowing

*

CHORUS OF NISEIS:
Home, we discover, is where life is:
Not Manitoba's wheat
Ontario's walled cities
Nor a B.C. fishing fleet.

Home is something more than harbour —
Than father, mother, sons;
Home is the white face leaning over your shoulder
As well as the darker ones.

Home is labour, with the hand and heart,
The hard doing, and the rest when done;
A wider sea than we knew, a deeper earth,
A more enduring sun.

Postwar Immigration

"We are all immigrants to this place even if we were born here: the country is too big for anyone to inhabit completely, and in the parts unknown to us we move in fear, exiles and invaders. This country is something that must be chosen—it is so easy to leave—and if we do choose it we are still choosing a violent duality." This is Margaret Atwood (b. 1939) writing about the experience of "inner immigration," being in exile in one's own country. More widely recognized is the experience of immigration and emigration, the moving of human beings from one country or continent to another country or continent. Since 1945, Canada has benefited immeasurably by having an open-door policy. We have accepted among us no end of immigrants and exiles from Great Britain, Germany, Italy, Hungary, Czechoslovakia, the Caribbean, the United States, Hong Kong, East Africa, Israel, and the Soviet Union. No single New Canadian can possibly represent the range of disillusion and idealism felt by the newcomer, the mixed emotions experienced at settling in, but perhaps some of the feelings are conveyed by Walter Bauer (1904-76), son of German labourers, who left postwar Germany far behind when he arrived in Toronto in 1952. A widely published author in Germany, he became one of the most interesting of Canada's poets, writing first in German and later, towards the end of his life, in English. The two poems that follow come from Bauer's *A Different Sun* (1976), where they appear in the skilful translations of Henry Beissel (b. 1929), himself born in Germany.

My Luggage/*Walter Bauer*

At every border I was asked
How much money I was carrying.
And of course they were able to check my luggage
To make sure that
Apart from suits, clothing, shoes
And a few other necessary personal items
I carried nothing on which duty had to be paid.
But I took along more
Than they could see
At the borders of blind Europe
(I wasn't even asked for it).
Now that I've arrived
And walk on alien soil and live in Canada
I'll make a laughing-stock of the customs officers
And tell you what I took along,
What I found most burdensome to carry:
My desperate love for Europe.

Arrival in Halifax/*Walter Bauer*

I'm no longer young enough
To throw myself on the ground and stammer:
Hail, new land of Canaan!
At the age of 48
You don't come as a scout any more,
Especially not
With such a heritage
Of guilt,
Which I take along everywhere.
My eyes observe coolly now,
Without excessive expectations,
The heart throbs inside.
There's only one thing I ask of you,
Earth of Canada, whose morning greatness I sense:
Don't be too hard on this stranger,
Give him among friendly people
An open sky to breathe.

The Stratford Festival, 1953

"July 13, 1953, was the most exciting night in the history of Canadian theatre," wrote the long-time drama critic Herbert Whittaker. "I doubt if there will ever be another night to match it, for me and for a great many others who were at that opening of the first Stratford Festival." Tom Patterson's vision of a theatre devoted to the production of Shakespeare's plays in the Bard's namesake city in Ontario turned the sleepy town of Stratford into a thriving, theatre-conscious summer tourist centre. It inspired James Reaney (b. 1926), who had the good fortune to be born on a farm just outside Stratford, to write a poetic tribute to the community. *Twelve Letters to a Small Town* (1962) includes "Shakespearean Gardens," in which the townsfolk are seen in the context of the major plays. The text of the poem is reproduced from Reaney's *Poems* (1972).

Shakespearean Gardens/*James Reaney*

The Tempest   The violet lightning of a March thunderstorm glaring the patches of ice still stuck to the streets.

Two Gentlemen of Verona   On Wellington St. an elegant colonel-looking gentleman with waxed white moustachioes that came to tight little points.

Merry Wives of Windsor   The Ladies' Auxiliary of the Orange Lodge marched down the street in white dresses with orange bows on them.

Richard III   At last all the children ran away from home and were brought up by an old spinster who lived down the street.

Henry VIII   Mr. White's second wife was the first Mrs. Brown and the first Mrs. White was the second Mrs. Brown.

Troilus & Cressida   "Well, I haven't been to that old festival yet but since it began I've had ten different boyfriends."

Titus Andronicus   Young Mr. Wood to-day lost his right hand in an accident at the lumber yards.

Romeo & Juliet   Romeo & Juliet Streets.

Timon of Athens   Old Miss Shipman lived alone in a weatherbeaten old cottage and could occasionally be seen out on the front lawn cutting the grass with a small sickle.

Julius Caesar   Antony wore a wrist watch in the Normal School production although he never looked at it during the oration.

Macbeth   Principal Burdoch's often expressed opinion was that a great many people would kill a great many other people if they knew for certain they could get away with it.

Hamlet   A girl at the bakery took out a boat on the river, tied candlesticks to her wrists and drowned herself.

King Lear   Mr. Upas was a silver haired cranky old individual who complained that the meat was too tough at the boarding house.

Othello   At the edge of town there stood a lonely white frame building — a deserted Negro church.

The Merchant of Venice   When my cousin worked for the Silversteins she had her own private roll of baloney kept aside in the refrigerator for her.

Henry V   The local armouries are made of the usual red brick with the usual limestone machicolation.

Springhill Mining Disaster, 1958

The little town of Springhill, Nova Scotia, near the border with New Brunswick, has faced more than its share of disasters. There were coal-mine catastrophes in 1891, 1956, and 1958. The cave-in that occurred on 23 October 1958 resulted in the deaths of seventy-four miners. The Cumberland Mine was closed and the town almost collapsed. The luck of one miner is proverbial. Byron (Barney) Martin, caught in a mineshaft, was suddenly surrounded by rock. He survived nine days and eight nights with no food or drink and was the last to be rescued. When asked to explain his luck, he said, "God must have saved that little hole for me." The spunk of the miners and their melancholy life inspired Ewan MacColl (b. 1915), the British-born folksinger, and Peggy Seeger (b. 1935), his American-born wife, the sister of Pete Seeger, to write their well-known song "The Ballad of Springhill" shortly after the cave-in. The lyrics come from *The Ewan MacColl/Peggy Seeger Song Book* (1970).

The Ballad of Springhill
Ewan MacColl/Peggy Seeger

In the town of Springhill, Nova Scotia,
Down in the dark of the Cumberland Mine,
There's blood on the coal and the miners lie
In the roads that never saw sun nor sky,
Roads that never saw sun nor sky.

In the town of Springhill, you don't sleep easy,
Often the earth will tremble and roll,
When the earth is restless, miners die,
Bone and blood is the price of coal,
Bone and blood is the price of coal.

In the town of Springhill, Nova Scotia,
Late in the year of fifty-eight,
Day still comes and the sun still shines,
But it's dark as the grave in the Cumberland Mine,
Dark as the grave in the Cumberland Mine.

Down at the coal face, miners working,
Rattle of the belt and the cutter's blade,
Rumble of rock and the walls close round
The living and the dead men two miles down,
Living and the dead men two miles down.

Twelve men lay two miles from the pitshaft,
Twelve men lay in the dark and sang,
Long, hot days in the miners' tomb,
It was three feet high and a hundred long,
Three feet high and a hundred long.

Three days passed and the lamps gave out
And Caleb Rushton he up and said:
There's no more water nor light nor bread
So we'll live on song and hope instead.
Live on song and hope instead.

Listen for the shouts of the *bareface miners,*
Listen through the rubble for a rescue team,
Six hundred feet of coal and slag,
Hope imprisoned in a three-foot seam,
Hope imprisoned in a three-foot seam.

Eight days passed and some were rescued,
Leaving the dead to lie alone,
Through all their lives they dug a grave,
Two miles of earth for a marking stone,
Two miles of earth for a marking stone.

In the town of Springhill, Nova Scotia,
Down in the dark of the Cumberland Mine,
There's blood on the coal and the miners lie
In the roads that never saw sun nor sky,
Roads that never saw sun nor sky.

The Centennial of Confederation, 1967

The one song that will evermore evoke the spirit of Centennial Year and express the high hopes Canadians felt for their country on 1 July 1967 is "CA-NA-DA." The words and music of this catchy bilingual song took Canadians by surprise, and its composer, the trumpeter Bobby Gimby (b. 1921), crossed and recrossed the country performing it. Gimby wrote the song as the theme music for *Preview '67*, a Centennial film released in the spring of the previous year. Judy LaMarsh, then the federal minister in charge of the national birthday celebrations, wrote, in *Bird in a Gilded Cage* (1969): "There had been no original intention of selecting a popular Centennial song, but when 'CA-NA-DA' was put forward, it proved to be so bright and sparkly it was quickly accepted. It was the only thing associated with the Centennial Commission, so far as I am aware, that was not chosen by a committee after a contest."

CA-NA-DA/*Bobby Gimby*

CA-NA-DA
One little two little three Canadians
We love Thee
Now we are Twenty Million
CA-NA-DA
Four little five little six little Provinces
Proud and Free
Now we are ten and the Territories Sea to Sea
North, South, East, West
There'll be Happy Times
Church Bells will Ring, Ring, Ring
It's the Hundredth Anniversary of Confederation
Ev'rybody Sing, together
CA-NA-DA
Un petit deux petits trois Canadiens
Notre pays
Maintenant nous sommes vingt millions
CA-NA-DA
Quatre petites cinq petites six petites Provinces
Longue vie
Et nous sommes dix plus les Territoires Longue vie
Hurrah, Vive le Canada!
Three cheers, Hip, Hip, Horray! Le Centenaire!
That's the order of the day
Frère Jacques, Frère Jacques
Merrily we roll along
Together, all the way.

The October Crisis, 1970

"Instead of submitting to history, perhaps at last the hour has struck to begin making it *ourselves*," wrote Pierre Vallières in *White Niggers of America*, his autobiography published in French in 1968 and in English three years later. In not quite the way the Quebec revolutionary and FLQ sympathizer might have anticipated, the hour struck about eight o'clock on the morning of 5 October 1970, when the British trade commissioner James R. Cross was kidnapped from his Westmount home in Montreal. His release was secured on 3 December, with the government guaranteeing his kidnappers—seven FLQ members—safe passage to Cuba. For all that suffering, Cross was luckier than Pierre Laporte, the Quebec minister of labour who was kidnapped by a second FLQ cell and murdered on 17 October, the day following the government's invocation of the War Measures Act. The next day his body was found in the trunk of a car at St. Hubert airport. His murderers were caught and convicted, and the October Crisis passed into history, leaving a foretaste of how dissatisfied many Québécois are with provincial status within Confederation and a taste of how transient are personal liberties. A sense of how events unfolded, almost day by day, is caught in "The Peaceable Kingdom," a poem written at the time by Al Purdy (b. 1918) and reprinted from his book *Sex and Death*(1973). A characteristic of daily news reports is that they are often mistaken in fact or emphasis. Halfway through the poem, where it says Laporte was found "shot in the head," the poet has added a note: "This was a false report. Laporte was strangled." (The reader will find in "Records of Our Past" a reprint of the FLQ Manifesto.)

The Peaceable Kingdom/*Al Purdy*
(In Ottawa, after the War Measures Act is invoked against the F.L.Q.)

Friday, Oct. 16: Along Elgin Street
traffic crawls at four o'clock
attaches with brief cases
of importance on Wellington
expensive mistresses and wives
of diplomats walking dogs
and babies in Rockcliffe Park
two Carleton students with lettered signs
VIVE le F.L.Q. on Parliament Hill
the Mounties don't lay a finger on them
below the Peace Tower
cabinet ministers interviewed on TV
inside the House
orators drone and wrangle as usual
in a way almost reassuring
In Quebec the Fifth Combat Group
from Valcartier occupies Montreal
paratroopers fly in from Edmonton
infantry from the Maritimes
And the P.M.'s comment
on bleeding hearts who dislike guns
"All I can say is go on and bleed
it's more important to keep law and order...."

All this
in the Peaceable Kingdom

Saturday, October 17: No change
the two kidnapped men are still missing
In the House of Commons politicians
turn into statesmen very occasionally
Reilly on CTV news demands Trudeau resign
Eugene Forsey does not agree
Yesterday driving to Ottawa
with my wife
citizens of no Utopia
red autumn leaves on Highway #7
—thinking of the change come over us
and by us I mean the country
our character and conception of ourselves
thinking of beer-drinkers in taverns
with loud ineffectual voices disagreeing
over how to escape their own limitations
men who have lost their way in cities
onetime animals trapped inside tall buildings
farmers stopped still in a plowed furrow
that doesn't match the other straight lines
as a man's life turns right or left from the norm
No change in the news
N.D.P. and P.C. members condemn the government
Creditiste Real Caouette does not
Diefenbaker thunders at the P.M.
a prophet grown old
Police raids continue in Montreal

Sunday, Oct. 18: Pierre Laporte found dead
    in a green Chev
outside St. Hubert shot in the head
hands tied behind his back murdered
A note from James Cross found in a church
asking police to call off the hunt for him
Crowds gather on Parliament Hill
for the same reason as myself
and stand close to the heart of things
perhaps if some were not before
they have become Canadians
as if it were not beneath them
gathered here to mourn for something
we did not know was valuable
the deathbed of innocence
mocked at by foreign writers
the willingness to pretend
our illusions were real
gone now
Soon we shall have refugees escaping the country
expatriates of the spirit and the body politic
and men in prison raving about justice
defectors beyond the reach
of what we had supposed was freedom
and the easy switchers of loyalty
will change ideas and coats and countries

as they do elsewhere and are no loss
Well
I suppose these things are easy to say
and some think sadness is quite enjoyable
I guess it is too
but this is not an easy sadness
like my own youth full of tears and laughter
in tough middle-age when I'm not
listening anymore sings to me sometimes
Beyond the death of Laporte
and the possible death of James Cross
the deathbed of something else
that is worth being mocked
by cynics and expatriate writers
—the quiet of falling leaves perhaps
autumn rains
long leagues of forest and the towns
tucked between hills for shelter
our own unguarded existence
we ransom day by day of our short lives

Driving west from Ottawa
we stop at a roadside park for lunch
beside a swift narrow black river
looped into calm by the park
thinking in this backwater
how the little eddy that is my life
and all our lives quickens
and bubbles break as we join
the mainstream of history
with detention camps and the smell of blood
and valid reasons for writing great novels
in the future the past closing around
and leaving us where I never wanted to be
in a different country from the one
where I grew up
where love seemed nearly an affectation
but not quite
beyond the Peaceable Kingdom

Victory of the Parti Québécois, 1976

"I am sure that I have just experienced, politically, the most beautiful and perhaps the greatest night in the history of Quebec." These sentiments René Lévesque, newly elected premier of Quebec, shared with eight thousand supporters gathered at the Paul Sauvé Arena in Montreal, and via radio and television with millions more Canadians, on the evening of 15 November 1976. That election, many political and social commentators claim, marks the turning point in Quebec's history and, by extension, in Canada's. The exhilaration felt by *les Québécois* was anticipated as early as 1964 when the *chansonnier* Gilles Vigneault (b. 1928) wrote "Mon Pays" (the lyrics of which may be found in the "National Songs" section). In 1976 he wrote "Gens du Pays," with the refrain that includes the line "Your turn has come." It is at the composer's request that both the French and the English versions of the song are included. The translation is by Alexandre L. Amprimoz.

Gens du Pays (Chant d'anniversaire)/*Gilles Vigneault*

*Gens du pays c'est votre tour
De vous laisser parler d'amour*

Le temps que l'on prend pour dire: Je t'aime
C'est le seul qui reste au bout de nos jours
Les voeux que l'on fait, les fleurs que l'on sème
Chacun les récolte en soi-même
Aux beaux jardins du temps qui court

*Gens du pays c'est votre tour
De vous laisser parler d'amour*

Le temps de s'aimer, le jour de le dire
Fond comme la neige aux doigts du printemps
Fêtons de nos joies, Fêtons de nos rires
Ces yeux où nos regards se mirent
C'est demain que j'avais vingt ans

*Gens du pays c'est votre tour
De vous laisser parler d'amour*

Le ruisseau des jours aujourd'hui s'arrête
Et forme un étang où chacun peut voir
Comme en un miroir l'amour qu'il reflète
Pour ces coeurs à qui je souhaite
Le temps de vivre leurs espoirs

*Gens du pays c'est votre tour
De vous laisser parler d'amour*

**People of the Land (Anniversary Song)/
*Gilles Vigneault***

*People of the land your turn has come
To listen to the voice of love*

The time we take to say: I love you
Is all that is left at the end of our days
The wishes we make, the flowers we plant
Each gathers them to himself
In the fair gardens of passing time

*People of the land your turn has come
To listen to the voice of love*

The time to love, the day to declare
Melts like snow in the fingers of spring
Let's feast on our joys, feast on our laughter
These days that reflect our gaze
Tomorrow, I was twenty

*People of the land your turn has come
To listen to the voice of love*

The stream of days stops today
And forms a pond where each can see
As in a mirror the reflection of love
To these hearts I wish
The time to live their hopes

*People of the land your turn has come
To listen to the voice of love*

From the Known to the Unknown

"I have long considered it one of God's greatest mercies that the future is hidden from us," explained Eugene Forsey. "If it were not, life would surely be unbearable." Having journeyed through history like time travellers, we find ourselves standing on the shores of the unfathomable future. We have moved from prehistory to posthistory, and our time machine has come to a halt. There is no shortage of futurologists to predict what is in store for us. Economists do it all the time, and there is even a prophet, the celebrated Nostradamus (1503-66), who, in his collection of mystical stanzas, *Centuries* (1555), made this "Canadian" prediction:

> Du Mont Royal naistra d'une casane,
> Qui duc, & compte viendra tyranniser,
> Dresser copie de la marche Millane.
> Favence, Florence d'or & gens espuiser.

What the French seer meant is not quite clear, although the dark lines may be translated: "Out of Montreal shall be born in a cottage, / One that shall tyrannize over duke and earl, / He shall raise an army in the land of the rebellion, / He shall empty Favence and Florence of their gold." But enough of prophecies. Lacking a poet able to write in human terms about our future, I can do no better than to reprint a verse in which historic figures from our past are made to take cognizance of *us* today. (Perhaps at some future date someone will write similarly about men and women living now.) The poem, by Miriam Waddington (b. 1917) from her book *Driving Home: Poems New and Selected* (1972), is called "Canadians."

Canadians/*Miriam Waddington*

Here are
our signatures:
geese, fish, eskimo
faces, girl-guide
cookies, ink-drawings
tree-plantings, summer
storms and winter
emanations.

We look
like a geography but

just scratch us
and we bleed
history, are full
of modest misery
are sensitive
to double-talk double-take
(and double-cross)
in a country
too wide
to be single in.

Are we real or
did someone invent
us, was it Henry
Hudson Etienne Brûlé
or a carnival
of village girls?
Was it
a flock of nuns
a pity of indians

a gravyboat of
fur-traders, professional
explorers or those
amateur map-makers
our Fathers
of Confederation?

Wherever you are
Charles Tupper Alexander
Galt D'Arcy McGee George
Cartier Ambrose Shea
Henry Crout Father
Ragueneau Lord Selkirk
and John A. — however
far into northness
you have walked —
when we call you
turn around please and
don't look so
surprised.

II
Some Unusual Fiction

"Great literature is any old stuff you can read without disgust," noted Louis Dudek. Although there are many works of fiction written in this country that may be read "without disgust," and indeed with positive enjoyment and enlightenment, the majority of Canadians still turn to their newspapers for reading matter, to the sports page for thrills, to the comic strips for imagination. As Susanna Moodie noted back in 1853, "The standard literature of Canada must be looked for in her newspapers." I have obviously not chosen to represent the mainstream of the Canadian imagination in the four fictional works reprinted here. Rather than anthologize already familiar stories and novel-sections by the country's leading writers (available anyway in short-story anthologies), I have chosen to select some curious works of quality which suggest some of the delights that may be discovered on the tributaries of our literature. I enjoyed reading these pieces, as diverse as they are, and I hope you will too.

Jean-sans-Nom/*Jules Verne*

"I seemed to be listening to a Canadian Homer singing the Iliad of the regions of the North," wrote Jules Verne (1828-1905) of Ned Land, the Canadian harpooner in *Twenty Thousand Leagues Under the Sea* (1870). Ned Land may be Verne's best-known Canadian hero, but Jean-sans-Nom is his most important, for he is the central character in *Famille-sans-Nom* (1889), the French writer's least-known novel. Although the novel dramatizes the Rebellion of 1837 in Upper and Lower Canada, it has never been translated into English. The last two chapters of the book appear here for the first time in an English version prepared by Alexandre L. Amprimoz. Jean-sans-Nom (Nameless Johnny) is a *habitant* who becomes the *éminence grise* of the Patriots. He fights "like a lion" on behalf of the revolutionary ideals of his French-Canadian people. He finances the purchase of the Patriots' weapons. Perhaps such exertions are undertaken to redeem the family name, for his family were traitors.

Then he falls in love with Clary de Vaudreuil, the beautiful daughter of a French aristocrat. What follows is self-explanatory....

EVENING OF DECEMBER 20TH

The bell of the little church in Schlosser rang: it was three in the afternoon. A grey, chilling fog filled the Niagara valley. It was bitingly cold. The sky was covered with heavy clouds that the slightest rise in temperature would have condensed to snow, under the influence of eastern winds.

The rumble of the British guns at Chippewa rent the air. Between volleys, the distant roar of the falls could be heard.

Fifteen minutes after leaving M. de Vaudreuil's house, the Patriots, making their way through the woods, taking cover along hedges and fences, arrived at the left bank of the river.

Already, some had fallen, hit by shell splinters, and were forced to retreat. Others, stretched in the snow, would never rise again. In all, less than two hundred Patriots remained to stave off the attacking Royalists.

From Chippewa, the British artillery had already done a great deal of damage to Navy Island. The grassy banks that would have given cover to the French had been almost entirely destroyed. It became necessary to take up positions at the foot of the bank, among the rocks inundated by the rushing current. From there, the Blue Tuques, led by Jean, would try to stop the landing of the Royalists, so long as their ammunition held out.

Meanwhile, the movement of the Patriots had been observed from the Chippewa camp. Colonel MacNab, having been informed of the enemy manoeuvres by the signals and reports of his spy Rip, redoubled his fire and concentrated it upon the fortified points. Around Jean, upwards of thirty had been struck down by fragments chipped from the rocks by the enemy fire.

Jean, pacing along the bank, observed the enemy manoeuvres, in spite of the cannon balls landing at his feet or cutting the air above his head.

At that moment, great, flat, oar-driven barges set out from the Canadian shore, one by one.

In a final attempt to destroy the Patriots' position, the British fired three or four volleys, which passed over their ships, hurtled into the enemy forces, and ricocheted away.

Jean, uninjured, shouted, "Patriots, be ready!"

The French were waiting for the ships to come within range of their fire.

The British, crouching on board so as to offer less of a target, appeared to be four to five hundred strong, of which half were Loyalist volunteers.

A few moments later, the ships, having reached the middle of the river, were now too close to the island for the Chippewa artillery to continue its bombardment.

Then the first gunshots were fired from behind the rocks. The boats returned a volley immediately, but as the British were very exposed to the fusillade from the banks, they plied their oars vigorously.

A few minutes were sufficient to bring the boats alongside the bank, and both camps prepared for hand-to-hand combat.

Careless of the hail of bullets, Jean continued to give his orders.

"Take cover, Jean," cried Vincent Hodge.

"Me?" he laughed.

And with a stentorian voice, he shouted to the disembarking assailants, "I am Jean-sans-Nom!"

The Royalists were amazed to hear this name, since it was believed that Jean-sans-Nom had been killed at Fort Frontenac.

Rushing towards the first ships, Jean shouted, "Forward, Blue Tuques!. . .Death to the Pink Habits!"

The action became extremely violent. The first British soldiers who landed on the island were pushed back. A few fell overboard and were carried away by the current towards the falls. The Patriots, leaving their rock shelters, invaded the bank and fought with such impetuosity that, for a while, they maintained the advantage. There was even a moment when the ships had to draw off. But soon after, reinforcements arrived and several hundred pink habits were able to set foot on the island. The British forced their way through the ranks of the French, their numbers about to overcome the force of the Patriots' courage.

In fact, due to the enemy's material superiority, the Patriots were forced to abandon the bank, but not without inflicting serious losses upon their assailants and suffering cruel casualties themselves.

Among them, Thomas Harcher and his sons, Pierre and Michel, wounded by bullets, were finished off by the ferocious Loyalists who spared no one. William Clerc and André Farran, both injured, were taken, after having traced a circle around themselves with the blood of the enemy. Without the intervention of an officer, they would have suffered the same fate as Thomas and his two sons. But Colonel MacNab had recommended that the leaders be spared to be court-martialed in Quebec or Montreal. It was only because of this recommendation that Clerc and Farran escaped the massacre.

It was impossible to resist against such a number: the Blue Tuques, after having fought desperately, the Mahogannis, after having defended themselves with that cold courage, the contempt for death, characteristic of Indians of their tribe, were forced to flee through the shrubs of the island, pursued from hedge to hedge, overtaken on their flanks, and crushed from behind. It was a miracle that Lionel escaped death on twenty different occasions, and that Master Nick himself was not slaughtered. As for the Hurons, how many of them would never again see the wigwams of Walhatta!

As they reached de Vaudreuil's house, Master Nick tried to convince Clary to throw herself into one of the ships that were headed for Schlosser.

"As long as my father is on the island," she said, "I will not abandon him!"

Yes, her father! But perhaps Jean also, even though she realized that he had only come back to die!

Around five o'clock in the evening, de Vaudreuil knew that it was impossible to hold their position against the onslaught of the enemy, who now occupied a large part of the island. If the survivors had any intention of saving their lives, they could only do so by taking shelter on the right bank of the Niagara River.

De Vaudreuil, barely able to stand, lacked the strength to return to his house and waiting daughter so as to take one of the ships and cross to Schlosser.

Vincent Hodge tried to carry him. But at that very moment de Vaudreuil was hit squarely in the chest and could scarcely whisper: "My daughter!. . .Hodge!. . .My daughter!"

Jean, who had rushed to their aid, heard him.

"Rescue Clary!" he shouted to Vincent Hodge.

As he cried out, a dozen volunteers jumped on him. They had recognized him. To capture the famous Jean-sans-Nom, to bring him back alive to the Chippewa camp, what luck!

In a last effort, Jean threw off two of the volunteers who were trying to capture him, then disappeared in a volley of gunfire which did not reach its mark.

As for Vincent Hodge, severely wounded, he had been taken near the body of de Vaudreuil.

Where was Jean-sans-Nom going? Did he really want to survive, now that the best Patriots had either been killed or had fallen into the hands of the Royalists?

No! Had not de Vaudreuil's last words been for his daughter. . .?

So! Vincent Hodge was no longer able to rescue her, Jean himself would do it, would force her to flee, lead her to the American shore, and return to his companions who were still fighting.

Clary de Vaudreuil, alone in front of her house, could

hear all the battle sounds—cries of fury, cries of pain, above the rifle-fire.

All this tumult was coming closer and closer, as the sporadic flash of firearms grew brighter.

Already about fifty Patriots, most of them wounded, had thrown themselves into the ships heading for the village of Schlosser.

Only the little steamboat *Caroline* was left, encumbered with fugitives, and already preparing to cross the arm of the Niagara.

Suddenly Jean appeared, covered with blood—Royalist blood. He was alive and well, after having vainly looked for death, after having given it twenty times to the enemy.

Clary threw herself into his arms.

"My father...?" she asked.

"Dead."

Clary must consent to leave the island!

Jean caught her in his arms, unconscious, as the volunteers began to surround the house to cut off his retreat. With Clary in his arms he bounded towards the *Caroline* and left the young woman there; then, standing up:

"Go with God, Clary."

As he put his foot on the gunwale to jump back onto the bank, he was hit by two bullets and thrown back onto the deck, as the *Caroline* left the bank at full steam.

In the light of the shots, Jean had been recognized by the volunteers who had pursued him across the island, and these cries were heard:

"Killed! We killed Jean-sans-Nom!"

The cries brought Clary back to consciousness and she struggled to her knees.

"Dead!..." she whispered, crawling towards him.

A few minutes later, the *Caroline* docked at the quay of Schlosser. There the fugitives believed that they were safe under the protection of American authority.

Some disembarked immediately. However, since the sole inn of the village soon filled up and the hotels of Niagara Falls were three miles down-river, most Patriots decided to spend the night in the cabins of the steamboat.

It was then eight o'clock in the evening.

Jean, lying on the deck, was still breathing. Clary, kneeling, holding his head, spoke to him... but he didn't answer... perhaps he could no longer hear her?

Clary looked around. Where could she find help? Certainly not in this village, crowded with a disarray of fugitives, packed with wounded, without doctors or medicine.

Clary saw her entire life in an instant. Her father, killed for the national cause!... The one she loved dying in her arms, having fought until the final hour. Now she was alone in the world, without family, without homeland, hopeless....

After having covered Jean with a tarpaulin to protect him against the rigours of the cold, Clary, leaning over him, tried to feel if his heart was still beating, if he was still breathing....

In the distance, on the other side of the river, the last gunshots were being fired. One could see their vivid gleam bursting out from between the trees of Navy Island.

A final calm settled over the Niagara, and the valley fell asleep in a gloomy silence.

The young woman murmured incessantly the names of her father and of her beloved, thinking: "Oh, my God, my God...."

And she feared that Jean might have died with the thought that beyond the tomb he would be pursued by the curses of men! And she prayed for her father and for Jean.

Suddenly Jean quivered, his heart beat a little faster. Clary called his name....

No answer.

Two hours passed. Everything was still on board the *Caroline*. No noise could be heard from the cabins or from the deck. Only Clary de Vaudreuil was awake, at the bedside of a dying man, like a sister of charity.

The night was very dark. Heavy clouds were beginning to unfold slowly above the river. Long patches of fog clung to the skeletons of trees, their branches heavy with frost seemed to make faces against the bank.

Nobody saw the four boats that passed round the cape of the island upstream and manoeuvred in order to reach without noise the bank of Schlosser.

These boats carried about fifty volunteers, under the command of Lieutenant Drew of the Royal Militia. On the orders of Colonel MacNab, this officer, in contempt of civil rights, was coming to execute a most revolting act of savageness within American waters.

Among these men there was one MacLeod, whose cruelties would bring about international complications a few months later.

The four boats, silently propelled by their oars, crossed the left arm of the Niagara and docked alongside the *Caroline*.

Upon docking, the volunteers, creeping onto the bridge, rushed down to the cabins to start their frightful slaughter.

The passengers, wounded or asleep, had no chance to defend themselves, and their cries for mercy did not move the Royalists. Nothing could stop the fury of these wretches, among them MacLeod, his pistol in one hand, his axe in the other, howling like a cannibal....

Jean had not regained consciousness. Clary, terrified, quickly pulled the tarpaulin over herself and Jean.

A few Patriots managed to flee, either by jumping onto the quay of Schlosser or by diving overboard in order to reach some point on the bank where MacLeod and his butchers would not dare to follow. The alarm had been given in the village and the inhabitants were already coming out of their houses to rush to the aid of the Patriots.

The massacre lasted only a few minutes, and many Patriots would have been spared if MacLeod had not been at the head of the murderers.

Having brought flammable materials, this wretch ordered it piled on the deck of the *Caroline*. It took only a few seconds for the boat to catch fire.

The moorings having been cut, the boat, pushed away from the bank, caught the current.

The situation was desperate.

Three miles downstream, the Niagara was engulfed in the abyss of its falls.

Five or six pitiful Patriots, panic-stricken, rushed to the flaming rail and flung themselves headlong into the river. It was nearly impossible to reach the bank, the river being full of drift ice.

It was never discovered how many victims were slaughtered by the butchers of Lieutenant Drew or how many drowned in trying to escape the fire.

Meanwhile, the *Caroline* was smoothly floating between the banks of the Niagara, like a fire-ship. The fire was now approaching the stern! Clary, terrified, called for help....

Jean finally heard her, opened his eyes, raised his head, and looked around him.

By the lurid gleam of the fire, the banks moved by faster and faster.

Jean saw the young woman next to him.

"Clary!" he whispered.

If he had had any strength remaining, he would have taken her in his arms, would have dived into the river, would have tried to rescue her!...But, not being able to keep his head up, he fell back on the deck. They were now less than half a mile away, and the angry roar of the falls grew louder and louder.

Death was waiting for her and for him as for the other victims that the *Caroline* was dragging downstream.

"Jean," said Clary, "we are going to die...to die together!...Jean, I love you...I would have been proud to carry your name!...It wasn't God's will!..."

Jean found the strength to squeeze her hand. Then his lips repeated the last word murmured by his mother: "Expiation!...Expiation!"

The boat was now drifting at a frightening pace, passing around Goat Island, which separates the American falls from the Canadian. And then, towards the centre of the horseshoe, where the current deepens and quickens in greenish waters, the *Caroline* teetered on the edge of the abyss and then disappeared in the falls' yawning chasm.

LAST PHASES OF THE INSURRECTION

The crime committed by the British, in violation of civil and human rights, had enormous international repercussions. An inquiry was ordered by the authorities of Niagara Falls. MacLeod had been recognized by a few Patriots who survived both the slaughter and the fire.

Furthermore, it was not long before this wretch began to brag openly about the fact that he "had done his business right under the noses of those damned Yankees!"

However, it was only a request for indemnification that the Americans would make to the British, until, in November 1840, MacLeod was arrested in the streets of New York.

The British representative, Mr. Fox, asked that he be extradited; the American government refused. Then, in the House of Lords, as in the House of Commons, the ministry was informed that MacLeod had acted according to the orders of Her Majesty. The American Congress answered this pretence with the publication of the rights of the State of New York. This report having been considered as veritable *casus belli*, the United Kingdom took appropriate action.

For its part, after having sent the assassin before the assizes, the American Congress voted subsidies. Without a doubt, war would have been declared had MacLeod not pleaded such a dubious alibi. This enabled the British and the Americans to hush up the matter.

This is the way the victims of the horrible crimes of those attacking the *Caroline* were avenged!

After the Patriots' defeat at Navy Island, Lord Gosford was informed that reformists would never again try to revolt against the authorities. Furthermore, their principal leaders had been dispersed or jailed in Quebec or Montreal; as for Jean-sans-Nom, he was dead.

However, in 1838 a few upheavals took place in various parts of the colony.

In March, the first attempt, provoked by Robert Nelson, brother of the man who had led the Patriots at Saint-Denis, failed from the outset.

At Napierville, in a second attempt, two thousand Patriots were dispersed, by an army consisting of six hundred British soldiers of John Colborne, five hundred Indians and four hundred volunteers, during Odelltown's Day.

November saw the third attempt. The reformists of the counties of Chambly, Verchères, Laprairie, L'Acadie, Terrebonne, and Deux-Montagnes, under the command of Brière, the Lorimiers, the Rochons, etc., split into two bands of a hundred men each. The first band attacked a manor, which was defended to no avail by the volunteers. The others took a steamboat at the quay of the important village of Beauharnais. Later, at Châteauguay, Cardinal, Duquet, Lepailleur, Ducharme, began an unsuccessful campaign to force the Indians of Caughnawaga to give up their weapons. Robert at Terrebonne, the two Sanguinets at Saint-Anne, Bouc, Gravelles, Roussin, Marie, Granger, Latour, Guillaume Prévost and his sons organized the last movements of the insurrection of 1837-38.

It was now the hour of retaliation. The British government was about to proceed with such ruthless energy that it could easily have been mistaken for cruelty.

On November 4, John Colborne, who had then full authority, proclaimed martial law and suspended the *habeas corpus* across the entire colony. Once the court martial had been constituted, it began to render judgement of a biased and revolting lightness. This court sent to the scaffold Cardinal, Duquet, Robert, Hamelin, the two Sanguinets, Decoigne, Narbornne, Nicholas, Lorimier, Hindelang, and Daunais, whose names can never be erased from the martyrology of French Canada.

To these names we should add those of several of the characters presented in this account: that of the lawyer Sébastien Gramont and that of Vincent Hodge, who died, as had died his father, with the same courage and for the same cause.

William Clerc did not recover from his wounds and died on American soil. André Farran, who escaped to the United States, seems to have been the only survivor.

Then comes the list of exiles. It contains the names of fifty-eight of the most important Patriots; many years would go by before they would be allowed to return to their motherland.

As for Papineau, the politician whose personality had dominated this period of nationalistic claims, he managed to escape. A long life allowed him finally to see Canada in possession of her autonomy, if not of her complete independence. Papineau finally died as a respected man.

It remains to recount the fate of Catherine Harcher and her family. Of her five sons who had accompanied their father to Saint-Charles and to Navy Island, two only returned to the farm of Chipogan, after a few years of exile. They never again left their land.

As for the Mahogannis, who remained involved up to the end of the insurrection, the government chose to overlook their actions, as it overlooked those of their excellent leader, involved, in spite of himself, in things he really had no taste for.

So, Master Nick, disgusted with the prestige of a public office he had never sought, went back to Montreal, where he took up his old life. And if Lionel went back to his desk of second clerk in Master Nick's law firm on Bonsecours Street, under the iron rod of Sagamore, it was with his heart filled with the memories of a man he would gladly have died for.

Everyone would guard the memory of the Vaudreuil family and that of Jean-sans-Nom, rehabilitated by his death, and one of Canada's legendary names.

However, even though the insurrections failed, they sowed the seeds of freedom. With the progress that time imposes, those seeds would bear fruit. It is never in vain that the blood of patriots is spilled for the rights of others. No country that has the duty to regain its independence should forget that.

The subsequent governors sent to direct the colony—Sydenham, Bagot, Metcalfe, Elgin, Monck—conceded, bit by bit, the claims of the Crown. Then the Constitution of 1867 established on a solid basis the Canadian Confederation. It was at that time that Quebec City was considered as a possible choice for the capital. Finally, it was decided that the capital would be at Ottawa.

Today, the loosening of ties with England is practically complete. Canada is, strictly speaking, a free power, under the name of the *Dominion of Canada*, where the French-Canadian and the English people live in perfect equality. One-third of the five millions of her inhabitants still belong to the French race.

Each year, a touching ceremony gathers the Patriots of Montreal at the foot of the column erected on Côte des Neiges to the political victims of 1837-38. There, on the day of inauguration, a speech was given by Mr. Euclide Roy, president of the institute, and his last words can summarize the moral of our story:

"To glorify dedication is to create heroes!"

The Adventure of the Annexationist Conspiracy/*Jack Batten and Michael Bliss*

There may be occasional references to this country in the various adventures of Sherlock Holmes, the most famous fictional detective of all time, but none of the stories written by Sir Arthur Conan Doyle is set in Canada. This sad situation has been remedied by two Canadian authors, Jack Batten (b. 1932), a journalist, and Michael Bliss (b. 1941), a historian. Together they researched and wrote "The Adventure of the Annexationist Conspiracy," which solves a puzzle that has perplexed Canadian historians for decades. This is a slightly longer version of "Sherlock Holmes' Great Canadian Adventure" which first appeared in *Weekend Magazine*, 28 May 1977.

The story that follows relates the adventure in Canada in the early part of 1891 of the celebrated English detective, Mr. Sherlock Holmes, as it was recorded by his close associate, Dr. John Watson. That fact is remarkable enough, but what is more astounding is that the tale has never until this publication seen print. Indeed its manuscript was uncovered, after almost a century of obscurity, only this year by a young history scholar who was researching a book on the personal life of Sir John A. Macdonald. He happened across the manuscript, mysteriously filed, in a sealed envelope marked "Patronage—Essex South" in Box 429 of the Macdonald papers, apparently one of so many similar envelopes that previous researchers had not bothered to open it.

Accompanying the manuscript was a letter addressed to Macdonald from Dr. Watson, dated April 21, 1891, in which Watson explained, inter alia, that his "publishers think the story of Holmes' service to yourself in February of this year does not constitute much of interest to their English reading public who have little knowledge or much concern with matters in your distant colony. I am

*quite put out of countenance by their decision and can-
not bring myself to destroy a manuscript over which I
have laboured hard. I am therefore placing it in your
hands. Perhaps you will wish to have it published in
Canada or perhaps you will merely care to preserve it
among your valued papers. After all, if I am not putting
too high a gloss on the matter—and I hardly think that to
be the case—it records the historic occasion when my
friend Sherlock Holmes, acting on your behalf, saved
Canada from annexation to the United States of
America."*

When my friend Sherlock Holmes invited me by
messenger to go round to 221B Baker Street on the morning of January 22nd, 1891, I confess that I was perhaps
not at first so sympathetic to the obvious agitation in
which I found him as I might have been. My own heart
and head were filled with my happy marriage, which had
taken me from Baker Street almost two years earlier, and
with my medical practice, which if not flourishing was at
least serving me well. The connections I had with Holmes
and his startling feats of detection had fallen away in the
previous year. Indeed I could account for a mere three
cases that I had recorded throughout all of 1890, The
Adventures of Wisteria Lodge, Silver Blaze, and The
Adventures of the Beryl Cornet. I experienced some guilt
and regret that I was not able to share in more of Holmes'
affairs, and yet at the same time, my own were most
deeply satisfying.

"My dear Watson, it's good of you to come," said
Holmes as I entered the familiar quarters.

"How could I refuse an opportunity to pass a morning
with you, Holmes?"

"It's not about Moriarty, you understand," he said
quickly, giving me the sense that he was labouring to hold
himself in check.

"Moriarty?" I felt genuine perplexity. I had never
heard Holmes mention such a person, but more than
puzzlement over the new name, I became chagrined at
the look of Holmes, paler and thinner than ever and so
obviously caught in some wrenching state of mind.

"There it is!" he cried, walking to and fro. "You have
no knowledge of the man nor has the rest of London, but
for all of that abysmal ignorance, he's the perverted
genius of crime reigning throughout the city. A cunning,
secretive phantom, Watson, a man as intellectually gifted
as myself, but I mean to have him before I rest my
career!"

Holmes spoke these words in an outpouring of pas-
sion, and then as swiftly as the storm had risen, he
affected a calm air and ceased his pacing.

"Put aside Moriarty for now, Watson," he said, offering me a smile of comfort. "It's quite another matter for
which I wished your company on this fine morning,
perhaps something in the spirit of the old days."

"Yes?"

"A Canadian adventure."

"I never knew you to be concerned with the colonies,
Holmes."

"Nor am I now, except that this particular colony may
yield me a respite from the cursed Moriarty business. I
was approached only last evening by letter from Sir
Charles Tupper, Her Majesty's High Commissioner from
Canada, requesting an urgent appointment at eleven
o'clock this morning. He hinted not at his reasons, but I
surmise he supposes that I may be of assistance to the
Canadian government in some secret capacity such as I
have rendered to other foreign governments in the past."

"May it not be a simple criminal matter, Holmes, a
murder or lesser crime that their authorities are unable to
cope with?"

"I think not, Watson. Canada is singularly backward
in the occurrence of murder. There's but a single recent
exception that comes to mind, the Birchall case of last
year. Perhaps you read of it. Reginald Birchall, the son of
an English clergyman, went out to a village called Woodstock in the Canadian province of Ontario where he
passed himself on the locals as a certain Lord Somerset.
Once settled, he placed advertisements in the newspapers
back here in London inviting young men to join him on
the pretext that he would teach to the youths the arts and
labours of farming. In short, Watson, he murdered one
of the applicants, a poor lad named Benwell, for whatever gain he thought he might acquire, and sought to
hide the body in a swamp. Lord Somerset, unmasked as
Birchall, was charged, convicted, and hung on November 11th last. But I think the case, sensationally as it was
received in the international press, was the exception in
Canada. I'm inclined that Tupper's business is governmental, and...ha, this must be him."

A rap on the door from what I recognized as the hand
of Mrs. Hudson, landlady at 221B Baker Street, followed
immediately on Holmes' last sentence, and in a moment,
a short bulldog of a man was ushered into the room. Sir
Charles Tupper, if this were he, wore long white side-
burns and full jowls. He seemed well advanced in middle
age, but he exuded an air of pugnacity and was in his
dogged way a man of appealing handsomeness.

"Sir Charles Tupper, I believe," said Holmes.

"And you are Mr. Sherlock Holmes?"

"I am," said Holmes, inviting the newcomer to turn in
my direction. "May I introduce you to my very good
friend, Dr. John Watson, with whom, if I am not mistaken, you share a profession."

"What?" said Tupper, taken aback but losing none of
his aggressive nature. "It is true that I once practised
medicine, but that occurred a good quarter-century ago,
before I abandoned it in favour of a political life. How
did you know? I've not bruited my background about
London."

"Those ancient scars on your hands, Sir Charles.
Young students of medicine often inflict incisions on

themselves during their early attempt at surgery. Some students, as is the case with yourself, never lose the scars."

"I'd heard of your reputation for sagacity, Mr. Holmes," said Tupper, speaking in a level, almost tenacious tone. "May I prevail upon you to put that quality at the service of my country?"

"Pray take a seat, Sir Charles. I shall be most happy to hear you out."

I could tell that Holmes was intrigued by the prospects that Tupper presented. Whether it was as an antidote to his concern over this man Moriarty or as a problem on its own merits I could not be certain. In any event, Holmes composed himself in his chair, eyes half-closed and fingertips pressed together, and prepared to listen.

"Allow me to read a cable I received yesterday," Tupper began. "It comes from my prime minister, Sir John A. Macdonald, and runs as follows. 'Immediate dissolution almost certain. Your presence during election contest in Maritime provinces essential to encourage our friends. Please come, answer.' I may say, parenthetically, that I have cabled my intention to return by ship tomorrow. My political party, Mr. Holmes, and that of Sir John is the Conservative, and I tell you with pride that we have held power for many years much to Canada's benefit. At the last general election in 1887, we took 123 seats to 92 for our long-time Opposition, the Liberals. But in this coming election, I judge, we find ourselves against a more formidable task. There are unspecified rumblings of discontent in the country, and the Liberal party has at its head a naive but politically attractive young Frenchman from Quebec named Laurier."

"I confess, Sir Charles," Holmes interrupted, "that politics is not my long suit."

"It is not politics that concerns me this morning, Mr. Holmes," Tupper went on, "but matters more sinister. Simultaneously with the cable I have just read to you, I received a second message from Sir John. It came through diplomatic channels and my oath of secrecy forbids me from revealing its exact contents, but I can advise you, Mr. Holmes, that your name lies among its contents. The long and the short of it is that Sir John requests your services. His word to me is that certain underhanded individuals who mean to see the future of Canada betrayed are masking their intentions beneath the usual activities attendant upon a general election. Their machinations threaten the very continuity of the British Empire of which Canada is a most loyal adherent, but they cannot be headed off through normal governmental action. Sir John indicates that the task requires someone, Mr. Holmes, of your self-sufficiency from the police and from politics. I am permitted to say no more."

"You need say no more," Holmes replied, eyes glinting with new life and appearing as a man transformed from the one who had greeted me that morning. "I shall accompany you to Canada, Sir Charles, and I am certain

that I may prevail upon Dr. Watson to join us. For my part, the sooner I vanish from London's streets, the better I shall like it. Tomorrow we sail."

Events moved swiftly in the ensuing twenty-four hours. My wife took the opportunity of my impending absence to depart for an extended visit to relatives in the Cotswold Hills, while a neighbouring physician consented to attend my patients until my return. I packed hurriedly and joined Sir Charles early on the morning of January 23rd at Victoria Station for the train to Southampton. Holmes arrived in our carriage at the last possible instant, muttering that it had been necessary to evade the attentions of "two of Moriarty's rogues," who were apparently lurking outside Baker Street. He appeared none the worse for his exertions, and after a pleasant trip by rail, we boarded a medium-sized ship, the *Cedric*, which was bound for New York City. Canadian ports, I learned from Sir Charles, were beyond our capabilities since Montreal was isolated by the icing-over of the St. Lawrence River and since the suddenness of our departure rendered it too late to obtain bookings to Halifax.

As to myself, our destination became of little consequence for I was immediately overcome by *mal de mer*. The Atlantic pitched and rolled in ferocious winter upheaval, and I passed most of the voyage of seven days reclining in my cabin under woeful duress. Holmes, all this time, devoted his attentions to a fat bundle of newspapers, magazines, and books which he had procured before our departure, all of them from Canada or dealing with that country's social and political life.

"One question provokes me, Sir Charles," Holmes said on an afternoon near the end of our voyage when he and Tupper came to my cabin for tea. "Is your Sir John A. Macdonald a sober man?"

"I can assure you that he is a man changed from previous excesses," Tupper replied with his customary intent manner. "His wife, Lady Macdonald, keeps a solicitous eye on his imbibing habits. Nothing more than an evening glass of port. You need entertain no qualms on that score."

"You set me at ease, Sir Charles," said Holmes, nodding his satisfaction.

The *Cedric* docked in New York City, and we enjoyed two quiet days in that cosmopolitan centre while I regained my equilibrium. We then proceeded by overnight train through wilderness until we reached Montreal, a city that proved a highly agreeable treat. It combined the civilizing aspects of Europe with the outdoor exuberance which I associated with the new continent. Our hostelry, the Windsor opposite Dominion Square, was as sumptuous as any that one might find in Mayfair, and the baronial mansions along Dorchester Street, though they tended to a certain bleakness in the architecture, matched the grandest houses of England.

Montreal's winter recreations, however, struck me as

singularly abandoned in a way that would be unique to any visiting Englishman. I witnessed tobogganing down lengthy and treacherous slides carved into the snow in the city's principal park, Mount Royal. I saw very combative curling matches on the ice of the St. Lawrence River. And on the grounds of a university which drew its name from a Scotsman named James McGill, I beheld a form of hockey played on sheets of ice by two teams of players, equipped with skate blades on their boots and curved sticks in their hands. It was a graceful if fierce sport, carried on at remarkable velocity.

By the afternoon of February 6th, Tupper pressed us on to Ottawa, Canada's capital city, whither we proceeded by train, arriving at night-fall. A carriage waited to hurry us directly to Earnscliffe, Sir John A. Macdonald's official residence. It lay about a mile from the city in a secluded district and, glimpsed in the gathering dark, it seemed a rambling Gothic edifice, as heavily gabled as any house I have ever seen. A maid showed us from the front door to a large and pleasant office which Holmes remarked was of more recent construction than the rest of the building. Tupper was confirming this to be true when a gentleman entered at the door behind us.

"John!" exclaimed Tupper with much warmth. "Old friend, how fine to be with you again." Tupper turned to Holmes and myself. "Gentlemen, may I present the prime minister of Canada, Sir John A. Macdonald."

As Holmes and the Canadian leader greeted one another, I assessed Macdonald and was at first shocked by his obvious great age. The straggly white hair down the sides of his head, the bald dome, and the bushy eyebrows of a startling paleness all emphasized advancing years, just as the bulbous red nose spoke of many past hours at the whisky bottle. And yet there was another quality about the man that a mere physical catalogue could not convey. In my adventures with Holmes, I have had occasion to enter the presence of many men who are accustomed to power. They are a particular and singularly impressive breed. Sir John was one of them.

"I tender apologies for my wife," Macdonald said as he directed us to chairs. "She has retired with a severe fatigue headache and is unable to greet you."

"I understand her weariness, Sir John," said Holmes. "It is no doubt exhausting to care for a daughter whose needs are so acute."

"That's most true, Mr. Holmes," answered Macdonald, fussing slightly. "I wonder that you know of the constant care dear Mary requires. But I expect Tupper told you about her."

"Tupper mentioned nothing, Sir John. It is my own surmise from the tracks on your carpeting. They were undoubtedly left by a wheelchair but they are hardly deep enough to have been indented by a patient of substantial weight. A person comparatively young in years, I judge, and a female if the small bracelet dropped beside the track leading out of the door is a true sign."

"Our daughter Mary is twenty-two, Mr. Holmes," said Macdonald, suddenly sagging in his chair, "but her physical condition places her far behind others of her age."

Macdonald regained himself and offered us refreshments. All took port, and we settled again into our chairs.

"Tomorrow, gentlemen, I announce the dissolution of Parliament and send the country to the polls," began the prime minister. "I believe my friend Tupper has previously described to you the political struggle which we Conservatives face to maintain our government against the Liberals. Now let me enlighten you, Mr. Holmes, as to another struggle that certain members in high standing of the Liberal party are inflicting upon loyal Canadians of every political stripe. Significant Liberal theorizers have long championed a doctrine called Commercial Union or, as they now disguise it, Unrestricted Reciprocity.

"Whatever the designation, its import is to eliminate tariffs and other commercial barriers between our own land and the United States until the two countries arrive at a condition of entire free trade. That, Mr. Holmes, is to me and to all of my clear-thinking countrymen merely a first step towards political union which would result in nothing less evil than the disappearance of Canada, but a tiny morsel, down the giant maw of the United States of America."

"Most threatening, Sir John," Holmes murmured in an abstracted voice. He was slumped in his chair and his eyes had assumed the half-hooded aspect which indicated to me his process of cerebration.

"Treacherous enough," continued Macdonald, his voice taking on an edge of steel that I hardly suspected a man of his age could retain. "But worse is at hand. I have information from a dedicated sub-editor among the loyal Tory press in Toronto that Liberals in that city, Sir Richard Cartwright foremost in their number, are seeking to hasten the move to annexation. Wilfrid Laurier, I may say, is not a party to the plot. He has been gulled through his inexperience. But other and senior Grits are even now negotiating with agents of the American government to arrange Canada's leaving of the Empire and entering into the United States immediately following a Liberal victory, may God forbid, in the election I am on the verge of announcing."

A silence of profound eeriness followed these words. Tupper stared fixedly at the floor. Macdonald's shrewd eyes were upon Holmes who was slowly straightening his long body in the chair to an erect and alert posture.

"You were quite right to approach me, Sir John," said Holmes, breaking at last the quiet of the study.

"I require tangible proof of the plot, Mr. Holmes," said Macdonald, his voice almost at a hush. "I require documents or papers or other evidence that I may present to the Canadian people who will in their repugnance to annexation refute the Grits at the polls and vanquish the threat of betrayal that hangs over us."

"You shall have it, Sir John," Holmes cried with a remarkable intensity of feeling.

"But Holmes," I blurted, fearing that my friend had overstepped himself, "this matter is immense and much beyond your accustomed criminal investigations."

"No matter, my dear Watson," Holmes answered, as he rose from his chair and inserted his hands in the side pockets of his jacket. "The problems, whether civil or criminal, demand similar methods. Ratiocination, as ever."

"Your sentiments offer me hope, Mr. Holmes," Macdonald said.

Holmes turned slowly on his heel. "Farrer, Sir John?" he queried in measured tones. "Am I barking up the right tree if I initiate questions in his direction?"

"I congratulate you, Mr. Holmes," replied Macdonald, whose features registered surprise and pleasure in equal degree. "You are a quick study of our country's nuances."

"Farrer, Holmes?" I asked.

"Edward Farrer, Watson," Holmes said. "A Toronto journalist—and curiously peripatetic according to my readings of the Canadian papers. His byline caught my eye here and there, from the *Mail* of Toronto in the latter years of the past decade and then, as of last summer, at the *Globe* which, if I'm not erring, Sir John, is an organ of your political enemies."

"Scurrilously so, Mr. Holmes," said Macdonald.

"Farrer's writings are clever," Holmes went on, "and he makes no bones about his avowal of annexationism. That alone is not sufficient to arouse suspicion about his involvements, but I am intrigued by Farrer's American connections. In the *Globe* of January 28th, as you no doubt observed yourself, Sir John, he printed a personal interview with James Blaine, who is no less than the American secretary of state. Most intimate associations for a Canadian journalist. Hmm."

The remainder of the evening went by in discussion of Canadian personalities whose names conveyed no meaning to me but seemed familiar enough to Holmes. I found the talk wearying, especially after so much travel in recent days, and was content when, shortly on midnight, Sir John showed Holmes and me to rooms on the second floor of Earnscliffe with assurances that he would arrange transport for us to Toronto on the next day.

Accordingly we were off by train at an early hour, once more passing through primitive wildernesses and reaching Toronto in the evening. I registered a suite at a hotel recommended by Macdonald, the Queen's on Front Street near Yonge. While I did so, Holmes unaccountably hung back on the perimeter of the lobby.

"I'll say *adieu*, Watson," Holmes muttered to me in a low voice.

"What?!"

"Only for a necessary few days, my friend," said Holmes, glancing to either side and over his shoulder.

"Holmes, it's not this Moriarty hobgoblin?"

"I've not given Moriarty a thought since we boarded ship at Southampton," Holmes answered, drawing the collar of his cloak high around his ears. "No, if I'm to be of service to Sir John, I must act swiftly and surreptitiously. I'll be back with you in due course. Meantimes, amuse yourself."

And so I did, a pleasure that was made the easier by the genial hospitality I encountered among Torontonians. Entire strangers, apparently glad of English company, hailed me almost hourly in the lobby of the Queen's and insisted on my joining them for meals and drink. Though the food was well prepared and generous in the extreme, a simple tea providing enough provender for a week and every luncheon and supper being followed by a courtesy cigar, I found my new companions, gentlemen of money and quality as they were, to possess uniformly shabby table manners.

Toronto, I concluded, was a city of conundrums. On my rambles about the precisely laid-out streets, the large number of churches convinced me that the citizens must be a pious lot until I noted that the places of worship were rivalled in quantity only by places of drink. And these many saloons appeared to manufacture drunkenness, disgorging inebriated fellows into the streets at all hours. Then, too, it struck me as paradoxical that the agencies for selling magazines were rife with journals from the very country which Canada, according to Macdonald, was intent on rejecting. I found *Harper's*, the *Atlantic*, *Scribner's Monthly* and others, all of United States origin, but only one local magazine, a lively thing called *Saturday Night*.

I ignored these puzzles and concentrated on visiting the sights of the city, the cavernous Victoria Skating Rink on Huron Street, the hotel maintained on Toronto Island by a retired champion of sculling and most entertaining host named Ned Hanlan, the munificently stocked emporium of Mr. Timothy Eaton, the Grand Opera House on Adelaide Street where I dozed through a performance of the local Philharmonic Society. And one evening I dined at the new house of Mr. George Gooderham, a leading distiller, at the corner of St. George and Bloor Streets on the northern reaches of the city, a handsome and ingenious mansion that included among its equipages a bathtub mounted on railway tracks that wound through much of the second floor.

It was on the late night of my return from the Goodderham residence that I let myself into our rooms at the Queen's and discovered to my astonishment a strange gentleman dressed in white suiting and languidly smoking a cheroot in the sitting room of the suite.

"Sir!" I roared. "As I have committed no error in entering the correct rooms, I must advise you that you are presently in the wrong ones!"

"Ah beg yah pardon, Dr. John Watson," the stranger replied, making no effort to arise. "Ah intended no offence."

"You have the advantage of me, sir," I said, experiencing resentment that this curious though not disagreeable man had availed himself of my name. He was clearly not a Canadian, an American perhaps, since, quite apart from his foreign accent, his drooping white moustaches, long hair of the same shade and his clothes reminded me of photographs of United States citizens who are indigenous to states south of the Mason-Dixon Line. I turned from him, intending to summon the manager of the Queen's.

"My dear Watson," said a familiar voice, "will you not condescend to greet me?"

I whirled around in fresh surprise. The southern gentleman had discarded his cheroot and was peeling the moustaches from his upper lip and lifting a white wig from his head.

"Holmes!" I cried. "You startled me!"

"Drastic steps have been called for, Watson," he said, laughing. "Not to the exclusion of disguise."

"I trust this marks the end of it."

"Not quite, Watson. Take up the pen on the desk over there, would you, and jot down a message for cabling as I dictate."

"Very well, Holmes," I said, moving to follow his instructions.

"These are the words. 'Urgently suggest you dispatch agents to printing plant of Hunter Rose, this city, on night of February 16th. Invest particular heed in document on presses in yellow paper. Signed, Holmes.' That's sufficient."

"To whom do I address it, Holmes?"

"Sir John A. Macdonald. Earnscliffe. Ottawa."

"Macdonald!"

"Yes, Watson," Holmes said, looking merrier than I had seen him in some weeks. "Arrange for the cable this instant, and I promise you that tomorrow we'll put conspiracy behind us for a few days and enjoy the sights of this estimable colony."

I recognized that Holmes had no intention as yet of divulging to me his recent whereabouts, and I acquiesced in the plans for tourism. On the next day we journeyed westward to Hamilton, a city of quite noble dimensions whose most impressive architecture was contained in the asylum for lunatics at the summit of its mountain. Niagara Falls lay several score miles beyond, and when we attained it, I complained mildly that there was less water than I had been led to expect. Holmes, to the contrary, was deeply moved.

"Just as I inferred, Watson," he muttered, "just as I inferred."

I caught his meaning without hesitation. In an earlier case which I recorded in print as "A Study in Scarlet," I included a written declaration of Holmes' that "from a drop of water, a logician could infer the possibility of an Atlantic or a Niagara without having seen or heard of one

or the other." Holmes' theory had apparently been confirmed to his satisfaction.

Our itinerary included Woodstock, the village in which had taken place the Birchall affair, Canada's single murder of international repute as Holmes had told me. We visited various geographical points throughout the village which were, I gathered, connected with the crime, and it was when we were musing about the swamp where the victim's body had been uncovered that a policeman hailed us.

"Is it truly you, Mr. Sherlock Holmes?" asked the officer in awe.

When Holmes confirmed that he was indeed himself, the officer proffered lavish welcome and particularly extended gratitude for what he termed Holmes' "assistance in the matter of the spurious Lord Somerset."

"Good heavens, Holmes!" I exclaimed. "You played a role in the Birchall case?"

"Only by post, Watson," he replied enigmatically.

We returned to Toronto on the morning of Tuesday, February 17th, and over an early dinner at the Queen's, Holmes announced our arrangements for the evening.

"Watson, I promise you a drama at the Academy of Music building," he said.

"And the principal performer in this piece of theatre?"

"Sir John A. Macdonald."

We made our way on foot through cold and snowy streets to the nearby academy and discovered outside the auditorium a jostling crush of men eager to gain admittance.

The interior of the academy was lit by flaring jets and was filled with an air of buoyant expectancy. A small brass band in the orchestra pit favoured the crowd with rousing anthems and march tunes until a group of distinguished gentlemen, nodding and waving to the audience, slowly filed to a row of chairs on the platform. Just as I recognized Macdonald among their number, the band crashed into "For He's a Jolly Good Fellow" and the full hall joined in chorus after chorus while Macdonald smiled his acknowledgments. When at last some semblance of quiet fell on the crowd, our former companion, Sir Charles Tupper, stepped forward to introduce Sir John with great gusto. More cheers ensued, lasting an interminable interval, but ultimately Macdonald began to speak.

Many of the specifics of the early passages of his address were, I'm bound to say, lost on me. But there was no mistaking the gist, nay the core, of his remarks. They concerned loyalty to Canada, a quality that Macdonald proclaimed was peculiar to his Conservatives and alien to the other party, the Liberals.

"There is," Macdonald trumpeted in a most loud and clear voice, "a deliberate conspiracy in which some of the leaders of the Opposition are more or less compromised. I say there is a deliberate conspiracy by force, by fraud or by both to force Canada into the American union!"

This charge excited fierce rumblings in the crowd. Three or four men, apparently Liberals, grew unruly, and at least two bouts of fisticuffs erupted.

"Politics," Holmes remarked to me *sotto voce*, "is Canada's leading participatory sport."

On the platform, meanwhile, Macdonald had removed a sheaf of yellow papers from the inside pocket of his jacket and was displaying them high above his bald dome. The document, he cried, had come into his hands by secret and fortuitous means. It was written by the traitorous journalist of Liberal persuasion, Mr. Edward Farrer, with Sir Richard Cartwright, the Toronto Grit, behind him, and it constituted a manifesto addressed to certain United States politicians instructing them in the most expeditious strategy by which America might absorb its Canadian neighbour. It outlined a programme, Macdonald verily shouted, of betrayal.

He began to read from the papers, the early sections of which were, once again, wholly Greek to me, matters to do with the interfering by the United States with a Canadian railway route to a place called Sault Ste. Marie, the arranging for the withdrawal of Britain's support of Canada and other similar details. All of these, contained in the words of Farrer as Sir John read them to the hushed audience, plainly represented steps in a master plan for the ultimate annexation of Canada by the United States.

"'They would secure the end desired,'" Macdonald read from the yellow sheets which quivered in his hand, "'without leaving the United States open to the charge of being animated by hatred of Canada on which Sir John Macdonald trades. Whatever course the United States may see fit to adopt, it is plain that Sir John's disappearance from the stage is the signal for a movement toward annexation!'"

At this, the floor of the academy broke into such a frenzy as I have never before experienced in a large gathering, the pounding of feet, the hooting of voices, whistling, cries, and tumult.

Macdonald read on, his voice rising to a crescendo. "'The enormous debt of the Dominion, the virtual bankruptcy of all the provinces except Ontario, the pressure of the American tariff upon trade and industry, and the incurable issue of race and the action of the natural forces making for the consolidation of the lesser country with the greater have already prepared the minds of most intelligent Canadians for the destiny that awaits them. And a leader will be forthcoming when that hour arrives!'"

Macdonald put aside the yellow pamphlet, stared into the heart of the crowd and cried, "Who is to be that leader?"

The crowd roared as in a single voice, "Sir Richard Cartwright!"

"Infamy!" Macdonald thundered, and once again the academy veered to the precipices of riot.

"I should think," Holmes said into my ear, "that Sir John is set on the desired path."

"These fellows are united enough, Holmes!" I shouted back. The words were no sooner out of my mouth when the entire auditorium, led by the platform party, broke into song, the words of which came to my ears as "We will hang Ned Farrer on a sour apple tree!"

Holmes and I pushed our way from the stormy mob and made course for the Queen's. En route, we passed close by a building that was surrounded by several dozens of Toronto's constabulary.

"What do you suppose the police are seeking in that place, Holmes?" I asked.

"On the contrary, Watson," Holmes replied in a cool voice. "I rather think their task is the reverse—to prevent outsiders from entering the building."

"What might it house?"

"A newspaper, Watson. The *Globe*."

"By jove, Holmes, isn't that Farrer's journal?"

"Quite so, Watson."

Abruptly on the following morning, Holmes insisted that his work was completed in North America and that, in any event, he could no longer put off his confrontation with the demon Moriarty in London. We packed in a few hours and boarded a train that took us on three days' journey across Canada's eastern limits to the port of Halifax, where we engaged passage on a large, handsome and sturdy ship called the *Lucania*. The ocean, to my not inconsiderable relief, had assumed a placid mood. I passed each afternoon in the ship's lounge with beverage and reading matter, and it was on the third day at sea when, in the lounge, I tossed aside my copy of *The Times* and fell into a brown study.

"You have a point, Watson," Holmes' voice broke into my musings. "It's time I resolved for you the question of my disappearance in Toronto."

"Quite right!" I exclaimed, suddenly realizing that he had gone straight to the bottom of my inmost thoughts. I gathered myself and stared at him in surprise.

"How did you guess, Holmes?" I said. "I was exactly pondering that point."

"Not difficult, my friend," he answered with a smile. "The feature story on the page of the paper you have just discarded blazes one significant word in its headline, 'Conservative.' It hardly matters that *The Times* article deals with the English Conservative party while you and I have been preoccupied with the Canadian party. It was the sight of the word itself—'Conservative'—that caused you to cast down your paper and utter a sigh of distinct anguish. You began idly to stroke that fine hickory cane which you purchased in Toronto, and from that action I discerned the geographical area in which your mind was wandering. When you let out another sigh, this one more of impatience than anguish, it was impatience with whom else but myself and for what other reason than your questioning of my connection with the Farrer pamphlet which served Sir John A. Macdonald so decisively on the evening of February 17th."

"I must admit, Holmes, that this is the case."

"I apologize, my dear Watson," Holmes said, settling himself into the chair opposite mine. "Let me ease your puzzlement now, though I might warn you that, at base, the Canadian case called for little more than some nocturnal excursions on my part."

"I'm always fascinated by the workings of your intellect, Holmes," I said in a quiet voice.

"Well, Watson," Holmes went on, "I should begin by relating that my destination on leaving you after our arrival at the Queen's Hotel was the building of the *Globe* newspaper. Edward Farrer was of course the quarry. You'll recall that I'd early determined on the fellow as my starting point in the affair, and I loitered outside his newspaper until he emerged late in the evening. I recognized Farrer from his photographs in various journals and followed him to his flat off Spadina Avenue. I engaged rooms myself with a window that gave on the entrance to Farrer's residence and took up observation. Tedious work, Watson, but fruitful. His first visitor shortly after noon on the next day was a gentleman whose name you'll recognize as much bandied in the election contest, Sir Richard Cartwright, the senior Liberal. Not long after his departure, two more gentlemen called whom I discerned to be American."

"American, Holmes?" I broke in. "How could you tell?"

"There is a difference, Watson. A pair of sentences from a book by one of our own English journalists, J.E. Ritchie, had struck me, a book recounting the author's travels about North America in which he declared, 'Directly you pass the border you see the difference. There is an astonishing contrast between the healthy Canadians and the lean and yellow Yankees.' I don't wholly subscribe to Ritchie's interpretation, Watson. Lean perhaps the Americans are, and possessed of a looseness in their gait and an air of brashness that Canadians, if they have it, are at pains to conceal.

"In any event, the juxtaposition of Cartwright and the Americans at Farrer's flat set me on a course of action. I abandoned my observation post and accompanied the Americans at a discreet distance to their hotel, the Walker House, where I used a mild subterfuge to obtain the names of the two men. One was of significance — Mr. Benjamin Butterworth, a member of the American Congress in Washington and a leading exponent of the annexation cause."

"A wonderful discovery, Holmes!" I blurted out.

"Quite so, Watson. I satisfied myself that Mr. Butterworth and his companion were leaving Toronto directly, and then retired to a clothing shop and another that specialized in wigs and other adornments, after which I spent some hours in my new rooms cloaking myself in the guise of a gentleman of the American south."

"Most effective it was, too, Holmes."

"I waited until Farrer was at home that evening and immediately presented myself at his door as Colonel Cletis Dawkins from North Carolina and an associate of Congressman Butterworth. Farrer confessed that my name was unknown to him, but he received me warmly nevertheless. He's an Irishman, Watson, and roguish, not at all an unappealing man but one deeply in love with intrigue even for its own sake. At one period earlier in his journalistic career, I happen to know, he edited a town's evening and morning newspapers of opposite politics, thus passing his working days in violent controversy against himself. Given such propensities, it wasn't difficult to persuade him that I, as Colonel Dawkins, required him to enter into a clandestine mission. I was present, I said, under circumstances of secrecy that must not be mentioned beyond Farrer's walls. I told him that I spoke for the highest councils in Washington and that I and they required a reasoned setting-out of the means by which to obtain the results of annexation which would persuade our colleagues in the American capital who were, unlike us, either indifferent to or unaware of the annexation cause. I told him we desired a clear and positive programme addressed to an American audience and I flattered him that he was uniquely qualified to prepare such a delicate document."

"Holmes," I broke in, "am I being offensive if I protest that you were adopting the unaccustomed role of *agent-provocateur* in this matter?"

"Drastic steps, Watson. I suspected from the beginning, as you may have noted, that they might be necessary in the present case as they have been in the past. I should think you recollect your words in the adventure you recorded as 'A Scandal in Bohemia.'"

Indeed I did. On that occasion, Holmes was forced to resort to plans for stealing certain property belonging to Irene Adler. "After all, I thought, we are not injuring her," I wrote at the time. "We are preventing her from injuring another."

"I see your point, Holmes," I said.

"Farrer fell in with the notion of the pamphlet. I hinted that I myself held extensive tobacco interests in my home state and looked forward to expanding into profitable Canadian markets on the successful conclusion of annexation. That information deepened for Farrer his conception of me as a fellow conspirator. He promised that several score pamphlets would be in readiness by February 16th, that Hunter Rose was a reliable and close-mouthed printer, and that, rather as a personal quirk, he would have the job done up on sheets of paper coloured yellow. I swore him once again to secrecy, bid Farrer farewell, and the remainder of the tale you, Watson, were a witness to."

"But, Holmes, won't Farrer now come forward and reveal that the pamphlet was written by him as a result of misrepresentation?"

"Hardly, Watson, since in so doing he would also

reveal that he had been in communication with an American, or someone he willingly took to be an American. He would thereby play further into Macdonald's hands."

"Quite."

I was satisfied, and the rest of the voyage passed for me in blithe contentment. Such was not the case for Holmes who paced the decks incessantly and devoted long hours to sitting in deep contemplation. When our boat train reached Victoria Station, he vanished with scarcely a word, on his way, I felt certain, to confront Moriarty, an adventure I would no doubt be made cognizant of in due course.

As for myself, I quickly became immersed once again in home and practice. Not long after my return, however, the Canadian affair returned to my attention when I chanced upon a report in *The Times* of the election in the Dominion on March 5th. Sir John's Conservatives had held power, winning 123 seats to 92 for Laurier's Liberals, the same margin of victory as that attained in the previous election of 1887.

Ontario, according to the account, had ensured the victory since its voters had almost unanimously subscribed to Sir John's warnings against the Liberal annexationist conspiracy. The correspondent for *The Times* in Canada opined that the Farrer pamphlet had played the key role in persuading the voters to turn back the Liberals. "But," he reported, "the means by which this mysterious document fell so conveniently into the prime minister's hands is not known."

The Women's Parliament
Nellie L. McClung

What follows is a fictional account of a real and fascinating event, the so-called Women's Parliament, which was staged by militant Manitoba feminists, intent on securing the franchise for women, at the Walker Theatre in Winnipeg, 28 January 1914. The packed house saw a broad caricature of the Legislative Assembly of Manitoba, in which all the members are women who are approached by a delegation of men requesting male suffrage. The evening was a great success and the serious skit was presented twice in Winnipeg and once in Brandon. It was a source of revenue for the feminist cause, a contributing factor to the unseating of Sir Rodmond Roblin, a lay Methodist preacher and the Conservative premier for fourteen years, and at least one reason why the women of Manitoba got the vote. This fictional treatment of the event, Chapter XXII called "The Play," comes from *Purple Springs* (1921), a popular novel written by Nellie L. McClung (1873-1951). In her autobiography, *The Stream Runs Fast* (1945), McClung describes how she herself played the part of the premier to perfection.

The Play

"Sorry, sir," said the man in the box-office of the Grand, "but the house has been sold out for two days now. The standing room has gone too."

"Can you tell me what this is all about, that every one is so crazy to see it?" the man at the wicket asked, with studied carelessness. He was a thick-set man, with dark glasses, and wore a battered hat, and a much bedraggled waterproof.

"The women here have got up a Parliament, and are showing tonight," said the ticket-seller. "They pretend that only women vote, and women only sit in Parliament. The men will come, asking for the vote, and they'll get turned down good and plenty, just like the old man turned them down."

"Did the Premier turn them down?" asked the stranger. "I didn't hear about it."

"Did he? I guess, yes—he ripped into them in his own sweet way. Did you ever hear the old man rage? Boy! Well, the women have a girl here who is going to do his speech. She's the woman Premier, you understand, and she can talk just like him. She does everything except chew the dead cigar. The fellows in behind say it's the richest thing they ever heard. The old boy will have her shot at sunrise, for sure."

"He won't hear her," said the man in the waterproof, with sudden energy. "He won't know anything about it."

"Sure he will. The old man is an old blunderbuss, but he's too good a sport to stay away. They're decorating a box for him, and have his name on it. He can't stay away."

"He can if he wants to," snapped the other man. "What does he care about this tommyrot—he'll take no notice of it."

"Well," said the man behind the wicket, "I believe he'll come. But say, he sure started something when he got these women after him. They're the sharpest-tongued things you ever listened to, and they have their speeches all ready. The big show opens tonight, and every seat is sold. You may get a ticket though at the last minute, from some one who cannot come. There are always some who fail to show up at the last. I can save you a ticket if this happens. What name?"

"Jones," said the gentleman in the waterproof. No doubt the irritation in his voice was caused by having to confess to such a common name. "Robertson Jones. Be sure you have it right," and he passed along the rail to make room for two women who also asked for tickets.

The directors of the Women's Parliament knew the advertising value of a mystery, being students of humanity, and its odd little ways. They knew that people are attracted by the unknown; so in their advance notices they gave the names of all the women taking part in the play, but one. The part of the Premier—the star part—would be taken by a woman whose identity they were "not at liberty to reveal." Well-known press women were taking the other parts, and their pictures appeared on the posters, but no clue was given out as to the identity of the woman Premier.

Long before sundown, the people gathered at the theatre door, for the top gallery would open for rush seats at seven. Even the ticket holders had been warned that no seat would be held after eight o'clock.

Through the crowd came the burly and aggressive form of Robertson Jones, still wearing his dark glasses, and with a disfiguring strip of court plaster across his cheek. At the wicket he made inquiry for his ticket, and was told to stand back and wait. Tickets were held until eight o'clock.

In the lobby, flattening himself against the marble wall, he waited, with his hat well down over his face. Crowds of people, mostly women, surged past him, laughing, chattering, feeling in their ridiculous bags for their tickets, or the price of a box of chocolates at the counter, where two red-gold blondes presided.

Inside, as the doors swung open, he saw a young fellow in evening dress, giving out handbills, and an exclamation almost escaped him. He had forgotten all about Peter Neelands!

Robertson Jones, caught in the eddies of women, buffeted by them, his toes stepped upon, elbowed, crowded, grew more and more scornful of their intelligence, and would probably have worked his way out—if he could, but the impact of the crowd worked him forward.

"A silly, cackling hen-party," he muttered to himself. "I'll get out of this—it's no place for a man—Lord deliver me from a mob like this, with their crazy tittering. There ought to be a way to stop these things. It's demoralizing—it's unseemly."

It was impossible to turn back, however, and he found himself swept inside. He thought of the side door as a way of escape, but to his surprise, he saw the whole Cabinet arriving there and filing into the boxes over which the colors of the Province were draped; every last one of them, in evening dress.

That was the first blow of the evening! Every one of them had said they would not go—quite scornfully—and spoke of it as "The Old Maids' Convention"—Yet they came!

He wedged his way back to the box office, only to find that there was no ticket for him. Every one had been lifted. But he determined to stay.

Getting in again, he approached a man in a shabby suit, sitting in the last row.

"I'll give you five dollars for your seat," he whispered.

"Holy smoke!" broke from the astonished seat-holder, and then, recovering from his surprise, he said, "Make it ten."

"Shut up then, and get out—here's your money," said Mr. Jones harshly, and in the hurriedly vacated seat, he sat down heavily.

Behind the scenes, the leader of the Women's Party gave Pearl her parting words:

"Don't spare him, Pearl," she said, with her hand around the girl's shoulder, "it is the only way. We have coaxed, argued, reasoned, we have shown him actual cases where the laws have worked great injustice to women. He is blind in his own conceit, and cannot be moved. This is the only way—we can break his power by ridicule—you can do it, Pearl. You can break down a wall of prejudice to-night that would take long years to wear away. Think of cases you know, Pearl, and strike hard. Better to hurt one, and save many! This is a play—but a deadly serious one! I must go now and make the curtain speech."

"This is not the sort of Parliament we think should exist," she said, before the curtain, "This is the sort of Parliament we have at the present time—one sex making all the laws. We have a Parliament of women tonight, instead of men, just to show you how it looks from the other side. People seem to see a joke better sometimes when it is turned around."

Robertson Jones shrugged his shoulders in disgust. What did they hope to gain, these freaks of women, with their little plays and set little speeches. Who listened or noticed? No one, positively no one.

Then the lights went out in the house, and the asbestos curtain came slowly down and slowly crept into the ceiling again, to re-assure the timorous, and the beautiful French garden, with its white statuary, and fountain, against the green trees, followed its plain asbestos sister, and the Women's Parliament was revealed in session.

The Speaker, in purple velvet, with a sweeping plume in her three-cornered hat, sat on the throne; pages in uniform answered the many calls of the members, who, on the Government side were showing every sign of being bored, for the Opposition had the floor, and the honorable member from Mountain was again introducing her bill to give the father equal guardianship rights with the mother. She pleaded eloquently that two parents were not any too many for children to have. She readily granted that if there were to be but one parent, it would of course be the mother, but why skimp the child on parents? Let him have both. It was nature's way. She cited instances of grave injustice done to fathers from having no claim on their offspring.

The Government members gave her little attention. They read their papers, one of the Cabinet Ministers tatted, some of the younger members powdered their noses, many ate chocolates. Those who listened, did so to sneer at the honorable member from Mountain, insinuating she took this stand so she might stand well with the men. This brought a hearty laugh, and a great pounding of the desks.

When the vote was taken, the House divided along party lines. Yawningly the Government members cried "No!"

Robertson Jones sniffed contemptuously; evidently this was a sort of Friday afternoon dialogue, popular at Snookum's Corners, but not likely to cause much of a flutter in the city.

There was a bill read to give dower rights to men, and the leader of the Opposition made a heated defence of the working man who devotes his life to his wife and family, and yet has no voice in the disposition of his property. His wife can sell it over his head, or will it away, as had sometimes been done.

The Attorney General, in a deeply sarcastic vein, asked the honorable lady if she thought the wife and mother would not deal fairly—even generously with her husband. Would she have the iron hand of the law intrude itself into the sacred precincts of the home, where little cherub faces gather round the hearth, under the glow of the glass-fringed hanging lamp. Would she dare to insinuate that love had to be buttressed by the law? Did not a man at the altar, in the sight of God and witnesses, endow his wife with all his goods? Well then—were those sacred words to be blasphemed by an unholy law which compelled her to give back what he had so lovingly given? When a man marries, cried the honorable Attorney General, he gives his wife his name—and his heart—and he gives them unconditionally. Are not these infinitely more than his property? The greater includes the less— the tail goes with the hide! The honorable leader of the Opposition was guilty of a gross offense against good taste, in opening this question again. Last session, the session before, and now this session, she has harped on this disagreeable theme. It has become positively indecent.

The honorable leader of the Opposition begged leave to withdraw her motion, which was reluctantly granted, and the business of the House went on.

A page brought in the word that a delegation of men were waiting to be heard.

Even the Opposition laughed. A delegation of men, seemed to be an old and never-failing joke.

Some one moved that the delegation be heard, and the House was resolved into a committee of the whole, with the First Minister in the chair.

The First Minister rose to take the chair, and was greeted with a round of applause. Opera glasses came suddenly to many eyes, but the face they saw was not familiar. It was a young face, under iron gray hair, large dark eyes, and a genial and pleasant countenance.

For the first time in the evening, Mr. Robertson Jones experienced a thrill of pleasure. At least the woman Premier was reasonably good looking. He looked harder at her. He decided she was certainly handsome, and evidently the youngest of the company.

The delegation of men was introduced and received— the House settled down to be courteous, and listen. Listening to delegations was part of the day's work, and had to be patiently borne.

The delegation presented its case through the leader, who urged that men be given the right to vote and sit in Parliament. The members of the Government smiled tolerantly. The First Minister shook her head slowly and absent-mindedly forgot to stop. But the leader of the delegation went on.

The man who sat in the third seat from the back found the phrasing strangely familiar. He seemed to know what was coming. Sure enough, it was almost word for word the arguments the women had used when they came before the House. The audience was in a pleasant mood, and laughed at every point. It really did not seem to take much to amuse them.

When the delegation leader had finished, and the applause was over, there was a moment of intense silence. Every one leaned forward, edging over in their seats to get the best possible look.

The Woman Premier had risen. So intent was the audience in their study of her face, they forgot to applaud. What they saw was a tall, slight girl whose naturally brilliant coloring needed no make-up; brilliant dark eyes, set in a face whose coloring was vivid as a rose, a straight mouth with a whimsical smile. She gave the audience one friendly smile, and then turned to address the delegation.

She put her hands in front of her, locking her fingers with the thumbs straight up, gently moving them up and down, before she spoke.

The gesture was familiar. It was the Premier's own, and a howl of recognition came from the audience, beginning in the Cabinet Ministers' box.

She tenderly teetered on her heels, waiting for them to quiet down, but that was the occasion for another outburst.

"Gentlemen of the Delegation," she said, when she could be heard, "I am glad to see you!"

The voice, a throaty contralto, had in it a cordial paternalism that was as familiar as the Premier's face.

"Glad to see you—come any time, and ask for anything you like. You are just as welcome this time as you were the last time! We like delegations—and I congratulate this delegation on their splendid, gentlemanly manners. If the men in England had come before their Parliament with the frank courtesy you have shown, they might still have been enjoying the privilege of meeting their representatives in this friendly way.

"But, gentlemen, you are your own answer to the question; you are the product of an age which has not seen fit to bestow the gift you ask, and who can say that you are not splendid specimens of mankind? No! No! Any system which can produce the virile, splendid type of men we have before us today, is good enough for me, and," she added, drawing up her shoulders in perfect imitation of the Premier when he was about to be facetious, "if it is good enough for me—it is good enough for anybody."

The people gasped with the audacity of it! The impersonation was so good—it was weird—it was uncanny. Yet there was no word of disrespect. The Premier's nearest friends could not resent it.

Word for word, she proceeded with his speech, while the theatre rocked with laughter. She was in the Premier's most playful, God-bless-you mood, and simply radiated favors and goodwill. The delegation was flattered, complimented, patted on the head, as she dilated on their manly beauty and charm.

In the third seat from the back, Mr. Robertson Jones had removed his dark glasses, and was breathing like a man with double pneumonia. A dull, red rage burned in his heart, not so much at anything the girl was saying, as the perfectly idiotic way the people laughed.

"I shouldn't laugh," a woman ahead of him said, as she wiped her eyes, "for my husband has a Government job and he may lose it if the Government members see me but if I don't laugh, I'll choke. Better lose a job than choke."

"But my dear young friends," the Premier was saying, "I am convinced you do not know what you are asking me to do." Her tone was didactic now; she was a patient Sunday School teacher, laboring with a class of erring boys, charitable to their many failings and frailties, hopeful of their ultimate destiny, "you do not know what you ask. You have not thought of it, of course, with the natural thoughtlessness of your sex. You ask for something which may disrupt the whole course of civilization. Man's place is to provide for his family, a hard enough task in these strenuous days. We hear of women leaving home, and we hear it with deepest sorrow. Do you know why women leave home? There is a reason. Home is not made sufficiently attractive. Would letting politics enter the home help matters. Ah no! Politics would unsettle our men. Unsettled men mean unsettled bills—unsettled bills mean broken homes—broken vows—and then divorce."

Her voice was heavy with sorrow, and full of apology for having mentioned anything so unpleasant.

Many of the audience had heard the Premier's speech, and almost all had read it, so not a point was lost.

An exalted mood was on her now—a mood that they all knew well. It had carried elections. It was the Premier's highest card. His friends called it his magnetic appeal.

"Man has a higher destiny than politics," she cried, with the ring in her voice that they had heard so often, "what is home without a bank account? The man who pays the grocer rules the world. Shall I call men away from the useful plow and harrow, to talk loud on street corners about things which do not concern them. Ah, no, I love the farm and the hallowed associations—the dear old farm, with the drowsy tinkle of cow-bells at eventide. There I see my father's kindly smile so full of blessing, hard-working, rough-handed man he was, maybe, but able to look the whole world in the face....You ask me to change all this."

Her voice shook with emotion, and drawing a huge white linen handkerchief from the folds of her gown, she cracked it by the corner like a whip, and blew her nose like a trumpet.

The last and most dignified member of the Cabinet, caved in at this, and the house shook with screams of laughter. They were in the mood now to laugh at anything she said.

"I wonder will she give us one of his rages," whispered the Provincial Secretary to the Treasurer.

"I'm glad he's not here," said the Minister of Municipalities, "I'm afraid he would burst a blood vessel; I'm not sure but I will myself."

"I am the chosen representative of the people, elected to the highest office this fair land has to offer. I must guard well its interests. No upsetting influence must mar our peaceful firesides. Do you never read, gentlemen?" she asked the delegation, with biting sarcasm, "do you not know of the disgraceful happenings in countries cursed by manhood suffrage? Do you not know the fearful odium into which the polls have fallen—is it possible you do no know the origin of that offensive word 'Poll-cat'; do you not know that men are creatures of habit—give them an inch—and they will steal the whole sub-division, and although it is quite true, as you say, the polls are only open once in four years—when men once get the habit—who knows where it will end—it is hard enough to keep them at home now! No, history is full of unhappy examples of men in public life; Nero, Herod, King John—you ask me to set these names before your young people. Politics has a blighting, demoralizing influence on men. It dominates them, hypnotizes them, pursues them even after their earthly career is over. Time and again it has been proven that men came back and voted—even after they were dead."

The audience gasped at that—for in the Premier's own riding, there were names on the voters' lists, taken, it was alleged, from the tomb-stones.

"Do you ask me to disturb the sacred calm of our cemeteries?" she asked, in an awe-stricken tone—her big eyes filled with horror of it. "We are doing very well just as we are, very well indeed. Women are the best students of economy. Every woman is a student of political economy. We look very closely at every dollar of public money, to see if we couldn't make a better use of it ourselves, before we spend it. We run our elections as cheaply as they are run anywhere. We always endeavor to get the greatest number of votes for the least possible amount of money. That is political economy."

There was an interruption then from the Opposition benches, a feeble protest from one of the private members.

The Premier's face darkened; her eyebrows came down suddenly; the veins in her neck swelled, and a perfect fury of words broke from her lips. She advanced threateningly on the unhappy member.

"You think you can instruct a person older than yourself, do you—you, with the brains of a butterfly, the acumen of a bat; the backbone of a jelly-fish. You can tell me something, can you? I was managing governments when you were sitting in your high chair, drumming on a tin plate with a spoon." Her voice boomed like a gun. "You dare to tell me how a government should be conducted."

The man in the third seat from the back held to the arm of the seat, with hands that were clammy with sweat. He wanted to get up and scream. The words, the voice, the gestures were as familiar as his own face in the glass.

Walking up and down, with her hands at right angles to her body, she stormed and blustered, turning eyes of rage on the audience, who rolled in their seats with delight.

"Who is she, Oh Lord. Who is she?" the Cabinet ministers asked each other for the hundredth time.

"But I must not lose my temper," she said, calming herself and letting her voice drop, "and I never do—never—except when I feel like it—and am pretty sure I can get away with it. I have studied self-control, as you all know—I have had to, in order that I may be a leader. If it were not for this fatal modesty, which on more than one occasion has almost blighted my political career, I would say I believe I have been a leader, a factor in building up this fair province; I would say that I believe I have written my name large across the face of this Province."

The government supporters applauded loudly.

"But gentlemen," turning again to the delegation, "I am still of the opinion, even after listening to your cleverly worded speeches, that I will go on just as I have been doing, without the help you so generously offer. My wish for this fair, flower-decked land is that I may long be spared to guide its destiny in world affairs. I know there is no one but me—I tremble when I think of what might happen to these leaderless lambs—but I will go forward confidently, hoping that the good ship may come safely into port, with the same old skipper on the bridge. We are not worrying about the coming election, as you may think. We rest in confidence of the result, and will proudly unfurl, as we have these many years, the same old banner of the grand old party that had gone down many times to disgrace, but thank God, never to defeat."

The curtain fell, as the last word was spoken, but rose again to show the "House" standing, in their evening gowns. A bouquet of American beauty roses was handed up over the foot-lights to the Premier, who buried her face in them, with a sudden flood of loneliness. But the crowd was applauding, and again and again she was called forward.

The people came flocking in through the wings, pleading to be introduced to the "Premier," but she was gone.

In the crowd that ebbed slowly from the exits, no one noticed the stout gentleman with the dark glasses, who put his hat on before he reached the street, and seemed to be in great haste.

The comments of the people around him jabbed him

like poisoned arrows, and seared his heart like flame.

"I wonder was the Premier there," one man asked, wiping the traces of merriment from his glasses, "I've laughed till I'm sore—but I'm afraid he wouldn't see the same fun in it as I do."

"Well, if he's sport enough to laugh at this, I'll say he's some man," said another.

"That girl sure has her nerve—there isn't a man in this city would dare do it."

"She'll get his goat—if he ever hears her—I'd advise the old man to stay away."

"That's holding a mirror up to public life all right."

"But who is she?"

"The government will be well advised to pension that girl and get her out of the country—a few more sessions of the Women's Parliament, and the government can quit."

He hurried out into the brilliantly lighted street, stung by the laughter and idle words. His heart was bursting with rage, blind, bitter choking. He had been laughed at, ridiculed, insulted—and the men, whom he had made—had sat by applauding.

John Graham had, all his life, dominated his family circle, his friends, his party, and for the last five years had ruled the Province. Success, applause, wealth, had come easily to him, and he had taken them as naturally as he accepted the breath of his nostrils. They were his. But on this bright night in May, as he went angrily down the back street, unconsciously striking the pavement with his cane, with angry blows, the echo of the people's laughter in his ears was bitter as the pains of death.

Friends, Romans, Hungrymen/A.M. Klein

In the depths of the Depression, which hit the Canadian West particularly hard, there were many thousands without work. The plight of the unemployed has been given expression by poets and journalists, but there are not that many descriptions of breadlines in serious Canadian fiction. An exception is the nightmarish vision by the distinguished poet and author, A.M. Klein (1909-72), who practised law in Montreal and ran unsuccessfully as a CCF candidate in the 1940s. "Friends, Romans, Hungrymen" first appeared in *New Frontier,* April 1936.

So one day, way back in the time of the fairytales, the boss called me into his cave and said that he was sorry but he was going to lay me off. He said it nicely, like an ogre elocuting fee-fi-fo-fum. He grabbed me, wrapped me up in a little package, and laid me down upon a dusty shelf. Then he stuck out a long tongue, licked the gluey side of a strip of paper, pasted it on me, and read it over: Unemployed.

At night, when I heard no more belches in the cave, I

knew the boss had gone home for a refill of his belching stuff. He is a sick man, he always eats. I wriggled out of the package, and went to the park. I applied for membership in the zoo.

I have been there ever since.

Sometimes I am very hungry. Things in my stomach toy about with my intestines, pulling them out like elastic, and letting them go snap.

At those times, I go through the lanes of the city. I lift the haloes from off the garbage-cans, and always find a tid-bit. Manna. It tastes like whatever one wishes it to taste. I only want it to taste like food.

Once I realized that it would be a long time before I would get a real meal. So I took out my false teeth, polished them on my cuff and wrapped them in a piece of cellophane that I picked up in the street on a cigarette box. Soon I put the teeth back into my mouth. The better to smile with, my child.

I smile to the dames that pass through the park. They look good, and when they are gone, a sweet smell still floats in the air. But they never give me a tumble. I think I am too skinny. They don't like ethereal guys.

It is terrible not to have a roof over your head. All day, white molten lead is poured over me from a big cauldron which somebody on purpose hangs up in the sky.

At night I sleep on a bench in the park. A lot of other bums do the same. Before I fall asleep, I always watch the shadowy cobras, and the prowling leopards coming towards me. In the morning I wake up, and my shoes and cap are wet from the licking of the beasts.

My head is getting duller and duller. It feels like a cage in which mice are scampering about looking for cheese that isn't there. It is because I am getting so stupid that I was nearly run over by Ezekiel's chariot which came rushing at me, stinking like a field of over-ripe radishes, and screaming with the voice of a dinosaur. I was picked up from the gutter, sugared with dust like a Turkish delight.

As I turned a street corner, I met God. I asked Him for a dime for a cup of coffee. He told me He had no small change, but recommended to me a swell flophouse on the Milky Way. Then, as an afterthought He put His hand in His pocket, and took out a couple of cheap comets. Because my pockets are torn, I tied one up in my shirt, lit the other, and strolled down the boulevard, puffing like a plutocrat.

There is nothing like a bit of self-confidence. I went back to the boss who was swathed in many rolls of pork-loins. I asked him for my job. He said: Can't you see that you are lying on a shelf? Go away from here, you are a ghost. I pushed my fingers between my ribs and pulled out my heart, and said: Look, it is going. It's a fake, he answered, you just wound it up.

After that I had to take a drink. I drank at a public fountain. But I did not enjoy it. A creature, with two arms, two legs, a wooden fang, and growing blue wool all over him, kept watching me. And when I stopped to wipe my lips with my sleeve, he said—in English—Move on.

The best is to sit on a bench in the park. There are all kinds of papers lying around, and if you are not tired, you can read them, for nothing. I like to read the menus. Yesterday, I picked up a nifty, and the birds who were looking over my shoulder sang, *Fricassee! Fricassee! Pâté de foi gras!*

But you get rubbed out sitting too much. Some day I will have to sit on my sixteenth vertebra. I look around. There is a sign which says KEEP OFF THE GRASS, but the sign itself breaks the rule. So I lie down on my belly, and watch the ant-hills. I have nothing to do. I give every ant a name, names of fellows who used to work with me in the office. The fat ant is Bill the accountant, the skinny one is the office boy, Fred, and the one with the shaking head is Old Man Harris, the Credit manager. I envy the ants. They all have jobs.

Did you ever come to think that birds and beasts are always employed? They all have jobs. They are always doing something. They are laid off only when they are dead. That's civilization for you.

And the birds that work all summer go to Miami for the winter. Even the squirrels save up their nuts for a snowy day. Perhaps the boss kept something for me, to give me when he laid me off. I went to him, and asked him for my ten kegs of sweat which he was keeping back. The boss pulled up his lips, and showed me his teeth. I heard noises going on in his throat.

That night I dreamed I was up in the sky. I picked bright blueberries out of its floor, and ate them. Then I washed it all down by drinking a bucketful that I pulled up from a well of golden soup.

But in the morning my mouth was dry. A kind lady gave me a sandwich. I took it to the park and ate it. All the bums pointed their fingers at me, singing: Shame! Shame! He's ea-ting! He's ea-ting!

The benchers of the park say that the trouble with the system is that there are not enough coins in circulation. They are going to issue some of their own. They had a fight about whose map to put on the ducats. Big Tom wants his face there, but Sam says he looks nicer. Somebody suggested an Indian's head. Naw, we don't want no foreigners.

Then somebody said that it would be better to have a symbol. No, a face, No, a symbol. Alright, a face and a symbol. So it was decided that we put a skull, anybody's skull, on the coin. Now we have to find the metal.

I have no faith in their plans. I would like to be a sweeper in the mint.

On the park bench I found a newspaper. I noticed one page on which the printer had forgotten to set any type; then in the corner I observed a number of bugs arrayed in a funny combination on the blank paper. They weren't bugs; it said Man Wanted. I went to the place.

The man at the door said: You have a late edition, buddy, that was a month ago.

I scrammed. On the way I met my cousin Gerald. He stopped his car, and undid the top buttons of his pants. It's tough, he said, and caught his breath. I said yes. Why don't you go into business for yourself, he said. That's a good idea, I said. I am going to get a sky-rocket and shoot up to the moon. I will take the moon off its hinges, and hide it somewhere. I will say: You want moonlight, pay. Then I will rent the moon out at so much per night. Cut rates for sweethearts. Then I will organize a company and sell moonbeam shares. Yes, I will go into business for myself. Anyway, give me your paper.

In the paper there was a headline, with a big fat exclamation mark: There is a job! When it came my turn to see the guy who was looking over the candidates, I said: Gotta job? It must have sounded foolish, after me waiting in line for so long. Gotta job? How much am I offered, he said.

I went back to the park. I threw my soul into a thimble which a nursemaid had lost under a bench. I planted the thing in the earth. I spat upon it; I said: Let it grow.

And now, now I want to die. The bums in the park had a long talk about suicide. They said to me: If you want to die so much, why don't you throw yourself from a sky-scraper?

I haven't enough weight to hurt myself, I said.

How about poison?

I *have* eaten in relief joints, I said.

Ah, they said, shooting?

That's to kill healthy men with.

Then they got sore. Go and hang yourself, they said.

I got sore, too. You dumb clucks, I said, can't you see my neck's too thin not to slip out of any knot?

Somebody said, Have you tried starving? when a guy who was eavesdropping on us, jumped on a bench and shouted: Friends, Romans, hungrymen, lend me your tears. Then he threw his arms up in the air, and pushed out his chest, on which his arms landed when they fell. Then he craned his neck this way and that, and asked a lot of questions, and didn't wait for an answer. We lent him our tears, and he wept.

Suddenly there appeared a herd of those same creatures that once mooed me away from the fountain. They were grabbing the boys by their manes, and pushing them into a wagon. One of them bit me over the head with a wooden fang, and dragged me to a station. That is the name of the lair of these creatures.

Then I was stood before a head which was lying on an open code, and the head said that somebody had overheard me talking about suicide. This was a crime, the head said, and screamed numbers at me. My life belonged to the state. I felt very proud because they were making a fuss about me killing myself.

Then the head said that I would be charged in due course with attempt at suicide and disturbing the peace. In the meantime, if I wanted to make a statement, I didn't have to, and if I didn't want to make a statement, I might. Or something like that. Then somebody gave me pen and ink.

That's how I come to write down everything that I have written down. I am very happy because they tell me that I am going to jail. I hear that they have meals there, regular.

And I hear too that they have work. They even make you work. Imagine! Nobody says how much am I offered?

I hope I stay there forever and forever, amen. This is my statement.

III
As We Were Saying

For a number of years now I have spent a good part of my working life collecting, compiling, and collating Canadian quotations, and I am always on the lookout for new remarks about this country and its people by foreigners, as well as for sage observations made about everything under the sun by Canadians themselves. The fruits of my research are *Colombo's Canadian Quotations* (1974) and *Colombo's Concise Canadian Quotations* (1976), not to mention *Colombo's Little Book of Canadian Proverbs, Graffiti, Limericks & Other Vital Matters* (1975); further compilations will follow. Robin Skelton has called me a "Master Gatherer." I am not quite sure what that means, and I know of no one else to whom the phrase has been applied, so I will wear the badge proudly!

Great Canadian Quotations

From my extensive files of over twenty thousand quotations, all by Canadians or about Canada, I have selected these Great Canadian Quotations. These are, in my opinion, the all-time great remarks (with special reference to the last two decades). They illustrate the history and spirit of the country and its people. I limited myself to fifty-two, corresponding to the number of weeks in a year. This is an easy-to-remember number, and I chose it to suggest how arbitrary the selection process is. I could easily have extended the coverage to sixty-six or one hundred and one memorable passages. I think every Canadian worth his salt should be able to identify these remarks.

In fine I am rather inclined to believe that this is the land God gave to Cain.

> Jacques Cartier's description of the north shore of the Gulf of St. Lawrence, today's Labrador and Quebec, and one of the earliest images associated with the country, summer 1534.

We are as near to heaven by sea as by land!

> Dying words of Sir Humphrey Gilbert, Elizabethan explorer, as he and the crew aboard the *Squirrel* sank in the Atlantic on 9 September 1583, returning to England from Newfoundland which he had claimed as England's first overseas colony.

I have no reply to make to your general other than from the mouths of my cannon and muskets.

> Count Frontenac's indignant reply to the envoy of the British admiral, Sir William Phips, who ordered him to surrender Quebec, 15 October 1690.

Are the streets being paved with gold over there? I fully expect to awake one morning in Versailles to see the walls of the fortress rising above the horizon.

> Sentiments attributed to Louis XIV, the French "Sun King," on learning how expensive it was to build Louisbourg, the largest fortress in North America, begun in 1713 and now almost fully restored.

You know that these two nations have been at war over a few acres of snow near Canada, and that they are spending on this fine struggle more than Canada itself is worth.

> Voltaire's oft-quoted quip on the French and English who were fighting over Quebec, in his novel *Candide* (1759).

Gentlemen, I would rather have written those lines than take Quebec tomorrow.

> Major-General James Wolfe, after reciting Gray's "Elegy, Written in a Country Churchyard," 12 September 1759, the evening before he died on the Plains of Abraham securing Quebec for the British.

Now, God be praised, I will die in peace.

> Wolfe's dying words on the Plains of Abraham, upon learning the French were in retreat, 13 September 1759.

Feel towards them as they have caused me to feel. Do not let them perceive that they have changed masters. Be their protector as I have been their father.

> From the last letter of the Marquis de Montcalm, the defeated French leader, dictated to the British victors on his deathbed, 14 September 1759.

Push on, brave boys, Quebec is ours!

> Dying words of Richard Montgomery, brigadier-general of the invading United States army, in a futile attempt to take Quebec, 31 December 1775.

I now mixed up some vermilion in melted grease, and inscribed, in large characters, on the South-East face of the

rock on which we had slept last night, this brief memorial
—"Alexander Mackenzie, from Canada, by land, the twenty-second of July, one thousand seven hundred and ninety-three."

> Famous inscription of Sir Alexander Mackenzie on a rock on the shore of Dean Channel, Bella Coola River, British Columbia, 22 July 1793.

Push on, brave York Volunteers!

> Ringing command of General Sir Isaac Brock and popularly believed to be his dying words, Battle of Queenston Heights, 13 October 1812.

Remember the *Caroline*.

> Slogan of the Patriots in the Rebellion of 1837 when Captain Andrew Drew set on fire and cut adrift the *Caroline*, their supply vessel, which headed for Niagara Falls, 29 December 1837.

I expected to find a contest between a government and a people: I found two nations warring in the bosom of a single state.

> Celebrated observation of Lord Durham in his *Report on the Affairs of British North America*, 1839.

A careful consideration of the general position of British North America induced the conviction that the circumstances of the times afforded the opportunity, not merely for the settlement of a question of personal politics, but also for the simultaneous creation of a new nationality.

> Lord Monck, who with Confederation would become Canada's first governor general, in a Speech from the Throne, Parliament of Canada, Quebec, 19 January 1865. (Authorship of the phrase "a new nationality" is generally credited to Thomas D'Arcy McGee.)

The Maple Leaf, our emblem dear,
  The Maple Leaf forever;
God save our Queen, and Heaven bless
  The Maple Leaf forever.

> The chorus of "The Maple Leaf Forever," written by Alexander Muir, a Toronto schoolteacher, in 1867, and popular for a hundred years.

It shall be lawful for the Queen, by and with the Advice and Consent of the Senate and House of Commons, to make Laws for the Peace, Order, and Good government of Canada....

> From Article 91 of the British North America Act, 1867. The act became effective 1 July 1867. The phrase "Peace, Order and Good government" is frequently contrasted with Thomas Jefferson's words from the Declaration of Independence, 1776: "Life, liberty, and the pursuit of happiness."

They always get their man.

> Unofficial motto of the Royal Canadian Mounted Police, which has been traced back to an observation made in 1877 by J.J. Healy, a whisky trader turned publisher. The official motto of the Force, established in 1873, is "Maintiens le droit" (Uphold the Right).

And that true North, whereof we lately heard....

> A line from the Epilogue to *Idylls of the King* (1873) in which Alfred Lord Tennyson characterized the loyalty of the country. The phrase "true North" was later incorporated by R. Stanley Weir into his English version of "O Canada."

Stand fast, Craigellachie!

> Terse cable sent by George Stephen, president of the CPR, who was in England raising badly needed capital, to his cousin Donald Smith (later Lord Strathcona), a director in Montreal, referring to the mighty rock near their birthplaces in northern Scotland, November 1884.

You'll never die, John A.!

> Unknown Conservative at a rally in Toronto, 17 December 1884, to celebrate the prime minister's forty years in Parliament.

Goods Satisfactory or Money Refunded.

> Famous guarantee of the T. Eaton Co. and associated with the popular mail-order catalogue published from 1884 to 1976.

I say humbly, through the grace of God I believe I am the prophet of the New World.

> Louis Riel in his defence speech in Regina, 31 July 1885.

All I can say is that the work has been done well in every way.

> Impromptu remark made by Sir William Van Horne, general manager of the CPR, to mark the "last spike" ceremony, Craigellachie, British Columbia, 7 November 1885.

As for myself, my course is clear. A British subject I was born—a British subject I will die.

> An affirmation of loyalty from the last electoral address of Prime Minister Sir John A. Macdonald, Ottawa, 7 February 1891.

Splendid isolation.

> A once-familiar phrase that echoed throughout the British Empire, characterizing Great Britain's position in the world, first used by Sir George E. Foster in the House of Commons, 16 January 1896.

The twentieth century belongs to Canada.

> Based on a remark made by Prime Minister Sir Wilfrid Laurier in the course of an address to the Canadian Club of Ottawa, 18 January 1904.

O Canada! Our home and native land!
True patriot-love in all thy sons command.
With glowing hearts we see thee rise,
The True North strong and free,
And stand on guard, O Canada,
We stand on guard for thee.

> First verse of "O Canada," written by R. Stanley Weir in 1908, a version of the French words of Sir Adolphe-Basile Routhier, with music by Calixa Lavallée.

I took possession of Baffin Island for Canada in the presence of several Eskimo, and after firing nineteen shots I instructed an Eskimo to fire the twentieth, telling him that he was now a Canadian.

> Captain J.E. Bernier, Arctic explorer, describing in 1926 how he claimed the Arctic Archipelago for Canada, 1 July 1909.

No Truck Nor Trade with the Yankees.

> Slogan of the Conservative party, which waged an anti-reci-
> procity campaign and defeated the Liberals in 1911; it was
> coined by Sir George E. Foster (who earlier coined the term
> "splendid isolation").

Lord Ronald said nothing; he flung himself from the
room, flung himself upon his horse and rode madly off in
all directions.

> A favourite sentence—the last six words are almost part of
> the language—from "Gertrude the Governess," *Nonsense
> Novels* (1911), by Stephen Leacock.

Let there be no dispute as to where I stand. When Britain's message came then Canada should have said:
"Ready, aye ready; we stand by you."

> To criticize W.L. Mackenzie King's isolationism, the Con-
> servative leader Arthur Meighen invoked the traditional
> British call to arms in a Toronto address, 22 September
> 1922.

He shoots! He scores!

> Foster Hewitt, veteran sports broadcaster, covering a
> Toronto Maple Leaf - Boston Bruin game for a radio audi-
> ence, 4 April 1923.

We live in a fire-proof house, far from inflammable
materials.

> Widely quoted statement of Canadian isolationism made by
> Raoul Dandurand, Canadian delegate to the League of Na-
> tions Assembly, The Hague, 2 October 1924.

The question is, the State or the United States?

> Well-known remark of Graham Spry, enthusiast for na-
> tional broadcasting, appearing before the Parliamentary
> Committee on Broadcasting, 18 April 1932.

My place is marching with the workers rather than riding
with General Motors.

> Aphorism of David A. Croll from his letter of resignation
> from the Ontario ministry at the height of the Oshawa
> strike, 14 April 1937.

Not necessarily conscription but conscription if necessary.

> Highly characteristic expression employed during the Con-
> scription Crisis by Prime Minister Mackenzie King in the
> House of Commons, 10 June 1942.

What's a million?

> C.D. Howe, outspoken Liberal minister, when the expendi-
> tures of his ministry were questioned, House of Commons,
> 19 November 1945.

Co-operation, Yes. Domination, No!

> Celebrated formulation of Canadian labour sovereignty, ex-
> pressed by Percy Bengough, president of the Trades and
> Labour Congress, before the American Federation of
> Labour, March 1949.

Then hurrah for our own native isle, Newfoundland!
Not a stranger shall hold one inch of its strand!
Her face turns to Britain, her back to the Gulf.
Come near at your peril, Canadian Wolfe!

> Last menacing verse of "An Anti-Confederation Song,"

composed 1869 and lustily sung when Newfoundland joined
Confederation in 1949.

We French, we English, never lost our civil war,
endure it still, a bloodless civil bore;
no wounded lying about, no Whitman wanted.
It's only by our lack of ghosts we're haunted.

> Lines from "Can. Lit.," a poem written in 1952 by the poet
> Earle Birney.

A TV franchise is a licence to print money.

> Roy Thomson, later Lord Thomson of Fleet, after he
> acquired the licence to operate a television station in Edin-
> burgh, Scotland, in the fall of 1957.

The grim fact is that we prepare for war like precocious
giants and for peace like retarded pygmies.

> Lester B. Pearson, future prime minister, accepting the
> Nobel Prize for Peace, Oslo, 10 December 1957.

I am the first prime minister of this country of neither
altogether English nor French origin. So I determined to
bring about a Canadian citizenship that knew no hyphe-
nated consideration.

> Prime Minister John G. Diefenbaker in an interview pub-
> lished on 29 March 1958.

The medium is the message.

> The best-known and widest-known quotation of Canadian
> origin today, first used by Marshall McLuhan, the media
> theorist, in Vancouver, 30 July 1959.

The Americans are our best friends whether we like it or
not.

> A popular blooper attributed to Robert Thompson while
> national leader of the Social Credit party in the 1960s.

Geography has made us neighbours. History has made us
friends. Economics has made us partners. And necessity
has made us allies. Those whom nature hath so joined
together, let no man put asunder.

> United States president, John. F. Kennedy, addressing a
> joint sitting of the Senate and the House of Commons, 17
> May 1961.

A nation is a body of people who have done great things
together in the past and who hope to do great things
together in the future.

> Frank Underhill, historian and political commentator, in a
> radio talk, 1964.

Vive le Québec! Vive le Québec libre!

> Charles de Gaulle, president of the French Republic, from
> the balcony of the Montreal City Hall, 24 July 1967.

There's no place for the state in the bedrooms of the nation.

> Pierre Elliott Trudeau, then minister of justice, Ottawa, 22
> December 1967. (The part about "the bedrooms of the na-
> tion" was adapted from an unsigned editorial in the *Globe
> and Mail* written by Martin O'Malley.)

Living next to you is in some ways like sleeping with an
elephant. No matter how friendly and even-tempered is

the beast, if I can call it that, one is affected by every twitch and grunt.

> Prime Minister Trudeau in a widely reproduced address to the National Press Club in Washington, D.C., 26 March 1969.

Fuddle-duddle.

> A genuine Canadianism (and a euphemism) created by Prime Minister Trudeau following some unprintable remarks in the House of Commons, 16 February 1971.

For God's sake, either we have a country or we don't. Let's decide!

> Characteristic remark of Pierre Juneau, chairman of the Canadian Radio-Television Commission, appearing before the Senate Committee on Transportation and Communications, October 1974.

Great Canadian Eloquence

Having chosen the fifty-two Great Canadian Quotations, let me now select the twelve passages in our literature and lore which I personally find eloquent and memorable. These quotations may not be on the tip of everyone's tongue, and they may be of marginal historical importance, yet the words, I feel, are charged with emotion and insight. They have a life of their own and should be savoured and reread.

White people do not know how to live; they leave their houses in small parties; they risk their lives on the great waters, among strange nations who will take them for enemies. What is the use of beaver? Do they make gunpowder of them? Do they preserve them from sickness? Do they serve them beyond the grave?

  We are no slaves! Our fathers were not slaves! In my young days there were no white men, and we knew no wants. We were successful in war; our arrows were pointed with flint, our lances with stone, and their wounds were mortal. Our villages rejoiced when the men returned from war, for of the scalps of our enemies they brought many. The white people came; they brought with them some good, but they brought also the smallpox, and they brought evil liquors. The Indians since diminish, and they are no longer happy.

> Attributed to "The Mandan Chief" in "On the White Man and His Ways," *Canadian Eloquence* (1910), edited by Lawrence J. Burpee.

Ask a Northern Indian, what is beauty? he will answer, a broad flat face, small eyes, high cheek-bones, three or four broad black lines a-cross each cheek, a low forehead, a large broad chin, a clumsy hook-nose, a tawny hide, and breasts hanging down to the belt. Those beauties are greatly heightened, or at least rendered more valuable, when the possessor is capable of dressing all kinds of skins, converting them into the different parts of their clothing, and able to carry eight or ten stone in Summer, or haul a much greater weight in Winter. These, and other similar accomplishments, are all that are sought after, or expected, of a Northern Indian woman.

> Samuel Hearne in *A Journey from Prince of Wales's Fort* (1795), 18 April 1771.

We have here no traditions and ancient venerable institutions; here, there are no aristocratic elements hallowed by time or bright deeds; here, every man is the first settler of the land, or removed from the first settler one or two generations at the furthest; here, we have no architectural monuments calling up old associations; here, we have none of those old popular legends and stories which in other countries have exercised a powerful share in the government; here, every man is the son of his own works.

> Thomas D'Arcy McGee, Legislative Assembly, Quebec, 9 February 1865.

Since we cannot find a comparison on this poor earth emblematic of our future greatness, let us borrow one from the heavens at the risk of losing ourselves in the clouds with the advocates of Confederation; I propose the adoption of the rainbow as our emblem. By the endless variety of its tints the rainbow will give an excellent idea of the diversity of races, religions, sentiments and interests of the different parts of the Confederation. By its slender and elongated form, the rainbow would afford a perfect representation of the geographical configuration of the Confederation. By its lack of consistence—an image without substance—the rainbow would represent aptly the solidity of our Confederation. An emblem we must have, for every great empire has one; let us adopt the rainbow.

> Sir Henri-Gustave Joly de Lotbinière, Legislative Assembly, Quebec, 20 February 1865.

A wise nation preserves its records, gathers up its muniments, decorates the tombs of its illustrious dead, repairs its great public structures, and fosters national pride and love of country, by perpetual references to the sacrifices and glories of the past.

> Joseph Howe, address at Framingham, Massachusetts, 31 August 1871.

To the man who is not a lover of Nature in all her moods the Barren Ground must always be a howling, desolate wilderness; but for my part, I can understand the feeling that prompted Saltatha's answer to the worthy priest, who was explaining to him the beauties of Heaven.

  "My father, you have spoken well; you have told me that Heaven is very beautiful; tell me now one thing more. Is it more beautiful than the country of the musk-ox in summer, when sometimes the mist blows over the lakes, and sometimes the water is blue, and the loons cry very often? That is beautiful; and if Heaven is still more beautiful, my heart will be glad, and I shall be content to rest there till I am very old."

> Attributed to Saltatha, a brave of the Yellowknife tribe and guide to Warburton Pike, the author of *The Barren Ground of Northern Canada* (1892).

A little while and I will be gone from among you, whither I cannot tell. From nowhere we came, into nowhere we go. What is life? It is a flash of a firefly in the night. It is a breath of a buffalo in the winter time. It is as the little shadow that runs across the grass and loses itself in the sunset.

> Dying words of Chief Crowfoot, overlooking the Bow River, Alberta, 25 April 1890.

Strangers have surrounded us whom it is our pleasure to call foreigners; they have taken into their hands most of the rule, they have gathered to themselves much of the wealth; but in this land of Quebec nothing has changed. Nor shall anything change, for we are the pledge of it. Concerning ourselves and our destiny but one duty have we clearly understood: that we should hold fast—should endure. And we have held fast, so that, it may be, many centuries hence the world will look upon us and say:— These people are a race which knows not how to perish.... In the land of Quebec naught shall die and naught change.

> Louis Hémon in the famous peroration of *Maria Chapdelaine* (1921), translated by W.H. Blake.

You young palefaces that are within my heart know well what a path through the forest is, or what a track across the valley means, but the Indian calls these footways "a trail," and some trails are hard to follow. They hide themselves in the wilderness, bury themselves in the swamps and swales, and sometimes a man or a buffalo must beat his own trail where never footstep has fallen before. The Shadow Trail is not of these, and at some time every man must walk it. I was a very small, very young brave when I first heard of it. My grandsire used to tell me, just as I tell you now, of the wonder country through which it led, of the wise and knowing animals that had their lairs and dens beside it, of the royal birds that had their nests and eyries above it, of the white stars that hovered along its windings, of the small, whispering creatures of the night that made music with their cobweb wings. These things all talk with a man as he takes the Shadow Trail; and the oftener they speak and sing to him, the higher climbs the trail; and, if he listens long enough to their voices, he will find the trail has lifted its curving way aloft until it creeps along the summit of the mountains, not at their base. It is here that the stars come close, and the singing is hushed in the great, white silence of the heights; but only he who listens to the wise animals and the eagles and the gauzy-winged insects will ever climb so high. This is the Shadow Trail the wild geese take on their April flight to the north, as, honking through the rain-warm nights, they interweave their wings with the calling wind. They leave no footprints to show whither they go, for the northing bird is wise.

This is the Shadow Trail that countless buffaloes thundered through when, hunted by the white men, they journeyed into the great unknown. Wise men who are nearing the height of the trail say they can hear the booming of myriad hoofs, and see the tossing of unnumbered horns as the herds of bison yet travel far ahead. This is the Shadow Trail the Northern Lights dance upon, shimmering and pale and silvery. We Indians call them the "Dead Men's Fingers," though sometimes they pour out in great splashes of cold blue, of poisonous-looking purple, of burning crimson and orange. We speak of them then as the "Sky Flowers of the North," that scatter their deathless masses along the lifting way.

And this is the Shadow Trail the red man has followed these many, many moons. His moccasined feet have climbed the heights silently, slowly, firmly. He knows it will lead beyond the canyons, beyond the crests; that behind the mountains it merges into a vast valley of untold beauty. We Indians call it "the Happy Hunting Grounds."

Only one person ever returns from the "Shadow Trail," and he comes once a year on this night—Christmas Eve. Stars wake and sing as he passes, the Sky Flowers of the North surround him on his journey from the summits to this valley where we live. He is a little Child, who was born hundreds of years ago in a manger beneath the Eastern stars, in the Land of Morning. Many times I have met him on the Shadow Trail, for I have travelled towards its heights for nearly eighty years. Perhaps I shall see the little Child again to-night, for Indian eyes can see a long way. Indian ears catch oftenest the singing of the stars, and the Indian heart both sees and hears.

> Words put in the mouth of Peter Ottertail, an eighty-year-old Mohawk, by Pauline Johnson in "The Shadow Trail" in the *The Shagganappi* (1913). "And, after gay good wishes and handshakes, the old man went out into the night, perhaps to watch for the Christmas Child coming down the Shadow Trail!"

In the hearts and minds of the delegates who assembled in this room on September 1, 1864, was born the Dominion of Canada.

Providence being their guide
They builded better than they knew.

> Inscription on the bronze plaque unveiled 1 July 1927 to mark the place in the Legislative Chamber, Government House, Charlottetown, Prince Edward Island, where the basis was established for the confederation of the British North American colonies. The last two lines are a powerful pastiche of lines by John Milton and Ralph Waldo Emerson.

When you look north from Quebec, to the north and north-west, your eyes glide over a wide valley, following it up the gentle incline to the Laurentian mountains bounding the horizon. Your gaze is led to the soft undulations of those peaks and remains hovering there in suspense. Boundless space lies beyond, mysteriously hidden and beckoning to us with a vague, enchanting appeal. Before this view we understand the *coureurs de bois*, those who have known already and for all time what leave-taking is—and why tarry now? Why resist this mighty appeal of all space on the other side, space that we do not see and will see? Why not now, our blood already beating to a great initial departure, a clean break, a fresh start with everything before us and nothing behind, why not another departure, why not heed this call, and why not all the departures in the world?

Saint-Denys Garneau, written in 1937 at Fossambault, north of Quebec City, translated by John Glassco in *The Journal of Saint-Denys Garneau* (1962).

Canada is not going to have a national literature in the mode of those European lands where a long history has bound the people together, and where a homogeneous racial inheritance has given them a language, customs, and even a national dress of their own. We are not an externally picturesque people: we are a people of today, upon whom the marks of the nineteenth century are still clearly to be seen. But Canada has at present, and may have in greater measure in the future, a literature fully national in being the work of writers who have made an inner exploration which has taken them to the depths of their innermost being, where they have discovered not only truths about themselves, but truths that are relevant, revelatory, and healing about the people among whom they live. If we hope to understand their work, and make it part of our national heritage, we must take them seriously...we must be prepared to find ourselves discussed in terms which may seem strange, but are not for that reason untrue. For we are the heirs of Jung and Mann, and must recognize that the great literary explorations of the future will be made by the inner journey, and not only on the great waters and the uncharted portions of our land. And these writers will speak not of a single, racially coherent nation, but of a nation that belongs to a constantly growing international community.

We must do what we have until now been reluctant to do in our artistic life. We must forgo our trust and delight in the surface of things. We must explore and sound our depths, and we must embrace our modernity, for only through that can we discover whatever there is about us which belongs to all time and all men.

Robertson Davies, "Canadian Nationalism in Arts and Science," *Transactions of the Royal Society of Canada* (Series IV, Volume XIII, 1975).

IV
Some Dramas

"'Canadian playwright.' The words seem a little incongruous together, like 'Panamanian hockey-player,' or 'Lebanese fur-trapper,'" wrote Julius Novick, the American drama critic, in 1973. Even a Canadian, Merrill Denison, could complain, back in 1929: "I find writing about the Canadian theatre or drama depressingly like discussing the art of dinghy sailing among the Bedouins." But the sixties and seventies witnessed the growth of indigenous dramatic works of imagination and quality, especially those by such playwrights as George Ryga, James Reaney, and Michel Tremblay. I have not tried to represent this recent efflorescence in our drama. Instead, I have chosen to reprint three texts that treat themes that are historical or national. It is interesting to note that two out of the three works presented here owe their existence not to the stage but to radio. National radio broadcasting has played an important role in the development of an indigenous culture, especially in the department of radio drama. "Terror and Erebus" and "Transit through Fire" were originally commissioned by CBC Radio. Only "The Masque of Heritage," the most theatrical of the three, was commissioned by an established theatre company. As well as treating historical or national themes, these three plays are, I believe, highly readable.

Terror and Erebus

The disappearance of Sir John Franklin (1786-1847), the famous Arctic explorer, and of his two ominously named naval vessels, *Terror* and *Erebus*, which were deserted at Lancaster Sound, Northwest Territories, 25 April 1848, held the Victorian world in thrall and sparked some forty search parties, one of which determined that Sir John had discovered the fabled Northwest Passage to the East through the polar ice. The fascination and futility of such quests is the theme of "Terror and Erebus," a "play for voices" by Gwendolyn MacEwen (b. 1941). It was commissioned for CBC Radio by Robert Weaver and subsequently published in *The Tamarack Review,* October 1974.

SPEAKERS: RASMUSSEN, FRANKLIN, CROZIER, QAQORTINGNEQ

Roaring wind which fades out to Rasmussen

RASMUSSEN:
King William Island . . . latitude unmentionable.
But I'm not the first here.
They preceded me, they marked the way
       with bones
White as the ice is, whiter maybe,
The white of death,
       of purity. . . .

But it was almost a century ago
And sometimes I find their bodies
Like shattered compasses, like sciences
Gone mad, pointing in a hundred directions
      at once —
The last whirling graph of their agony.

How could they know what I now know,
A century later, my pockets stuffed with
      comfortable maps —
That this was, after all, an island,
That the ice can camouflage the straits
And drive men into false channels,
Drive men
      into white, sliding traps . . . ?

How could they know, even stand back and see
The nature of the place they stood on,
When no man can, no man knows where he stands
Until he leaves his place, looks back
      and knows.

Ah, Franklin! I would like to find you
Now, your body spreadeagled like a star,
A human constellation in the snow.
      The earth insists
There is but one geography, but then
There is another still —
The complex, crushed geography of men.
You carried all maps within you;
Land masses moved in relation to
      you —

As though you created the Passage
By *willing* it to be.
        Ah, Franklin!
To follow you one does not need geography.

At least not totally, but more of that
Instrumental knowledge the bones have,
Their limits, their measurings.
The eye *creates* the horizon,
The ear *invents* the wind,
The hand reaching out from a parka sleeve
By touch demands that the touched thing
        be.

Music and more wind sound effects, fade out to...

RASMUSSEN:
So I've followed you here
Like a dozen others, looking for relics
        of your ships, your men.
Here to this awful monastery
        where you, where Crozier died,
        and all the men with you died,
Seeking a passage from imagination to
        reality,
Seeking a passage from land to land
        by sea.

Now in the arctic night
I can almost suppose you did not die,
But are somewhere walking between
The icons of ice, pensively
        like a priest,
Wrapped in the cold holiness of snow,
        of your own memory....

Music bridge to Franklin, wind sound effects

FRANKLIN:
I brought them here, a hundred and twenty-nine men,
Led them into this bottleneck,
This white asylum.
I chose the wrong channel and
The ice folded in around us,
Gnashing its jaws, folded in
        around us....

The ice clamps and will not open.
For a year it has not opened
Though we bash against it
Like lunatics at padded walls.

My ships, The Terror, The Erebus
Are learning the meanings of their
        names.
What madman christened them
The ships of Terror and of Hell?
In open sea they did four knots;
Here, they rot and cannot move at all.

Another winter in the ice,

The second one for us, folds in.
Latitude 70N. November 25, 1846.
The sun has vanished.

Music, etc.

RASMUSSEN:
Nothing then but to sit out the darkness,
The second sterile year,
        and wait for spring
And pray the straits would crack
Open, and the dash begin again;
Pray you could drive the ships
Through the yielding, melting floes,
        drive and press on down
Into the giant virginal strait of
        Victoria.

But perhaps she might not yield,
She might not let you enter,
        but might grip
And hold you crushed forever in her stubborn
        loins,
        her horrible house,
Her white asylum in an ugly marriage.

Music, etc.

FRANKLIN:
I told him, I *told* Crozier
The spring is coming, but it's *wrong*
        somehow.
Even in summer the ice may not open,
It may not *open.*
Some of the men have scurvy, Crozier....
        Their faces, the sick ones,
        their faces reflect their minds.
I can read the disease in their souls.
It's a mildewed chart
On their flesh.
        But this is no place
To talk of souls; here
The soul *becomes* the flesh.

Sighs

I may have to send men on foot
To where the passage is,
To prove it, to prove it is there,
That Simpson joins Victoria,
That there is a meaning, a pattern
        imposed on this chaos,
A conjunction of waters,
        a kind of meaning
Even here, even in this place....

RASMUSSEN:
A kind of meaning, even here,
Even in this place.
        Yes, yes,

We are men, we demand
That the world be logical, don't we?

But eight of your men went overland
                and saw it, proved it,
Proved the waters found each other
                as you said,
Saw the one flowing into the other,
Saw the conjunction, the synthesis
                of faith, there
In the white metallic cold.

And returned to tell you, Franklin,
And found you dying in Erebus,
In the hell
                of your body,
The last ship of your senses.

June 11, 1847....

Music and sound effects bridge

RASMUSSEN:
Crozier took command,
A scientist, understanding magnetism
                the pull of elements, but
The laws which attract and as easily repel
Could not pull him from the hell
                of his science.

Crozier, what laws govern
This final tug of war
                between life and death,
The human polarities...?
What laws govern these?
                The ice
Is its own argument.

Music bridge to

CROZIER:
It is September, the end of summer....

Laughs briefly, bitterly

Summer, there was no summer....
Funny how you go on using
                the same old terms
Even when they've lost all meaning.

Two summers, and the ice has not melted.
Has the globe tipped? The axis slipped?
                Is there no sense of season
Anywhere?

September 1847.
We await our *third* winter in the ice.

On the word third *a chilling sound effect*

RASMUSSEN:
But the ice, wasn't it drifting south
Itself, like a ship, a ship within a
Ship?

CROZIER:
The ice is drifting south, but
                not fast enough.
It has time, it has more time than we
                have time;
It has eternity to drift south.
Ice doesn't eat, doesn't get scurvy,
Doesn't die, like my men are dying.

Music to suggest a time lapse

CROZIER:
April 1848. The winter is over.
Supplies to last three months only.
We are leaving the ships for good.

RASMUSSEN:
You went overland, then.
Overland, an ironic word....
How can you call this *land*?
                It's the white teeth
Of a giant saw,
                and men crawl through it
Like ants through an upright comb.
Overland. You set out from the ships
In a kind of horrible birth,
                a forced expulsion
From those two wombs, solid at least,
Three-dimensional, smelling of wood
And metal and familiar things.

Overland....

Music bridge

CROZIER:
April 21, 1848. Good Friday.
Our last day in the ships.
We pray, we sing hymns, there
                is nothing else to do.
We are all of us crucified
                before an ugly Easter.
Civilization...six hundred and seventy miles away.

On the words six hundred and seventy miles away *more chilling sound effects*

CROZIER:
A hundred and five men left. Three months' supplies.
Our Father who art in heaven,
Hallowed be thy name....
                Six hundred and seventy miles to civilization,
Three months' supplies, a hundred and five men....
Give us this day our daily bread
and forgive us....
                scurvy among the men.
                We leave ship tomorrow.
Thy kingdom come, thy will be done....
                Six hundred and seventy miles to
                civilization....

For Thine is the kingdom, and the Power,
And the Glory...
Our Father
Our Father
Our Father

RASMUSSEN:
April 25, 1848. HMS Terror and
Erebus were deserted, having been beset
since the 12th of September 1846.
The officers and crew consisting of a hundred and five
souls under the command of Captain F.R.
Crozier landed here.
The total loss by deaths in the Expedition
has been to this date nine officers and
fifteen men.

So you pushed on, and sun and snow,
          that marriage of agonizing light
Assailed you.

Music bridge

CROZIER:
In the beginning God made the light
And saw that it was good...
          the light...
          and saw that it was good....

Eerie music

My men fall back, blinded,
          clutching their scorched eyes!
Who ever said that Hell was darkness?
What fool said that light was good
          and darkness evil?
In extremes, all things reverse themselves;
In extremes, there are no opposites.

RASMUSSEN:
The naked eye dilates, shrinks,
Goes mad, cannot save itself.
You didn't even have those wooden slits
The eskimos wore
          to censor the sun,
          to select as much light
As the eye can bear.
Some science could have tamed the light
For you,
          not hope, not prayer —
But pairs of simple wooden slits,
Only those, only those ridiculous
          instruments
You need to keep the cosmos out.
I share your irony, Crozier,
That, and your despair....

CROZIER:
Breathing heavily while speaking
To select what we will and will not see,

To keep the cosmos out with layers of cloth
          and strips of leather —
          That's man, I suppose,
          an arrogant beast. Whether
He is right or wrong is —

O Hell! Look, Lord, look how
They fall back behind me!

Music bridge

CROZIER:
I sent thirty men back to the ships,
Thirty good men back to the Terror, the Erebus
          for food, somehow.
We can go blind but we must eat
          in the white waste.
Though all our senses fall apart
          we must eat
          we must still eat....

RASMUSSEN:
Thirty good men.
On the way back all of them but five
          died,
Knelt before the sun for the last time
          and died,
Knelt like priests in the whiteness
          and died,
          on their knees, died,
Or stretched straight out,
Or sitting in a brief stop
          which never ended,
          died.
It does not matter how.

Five made it back to the ships
And there, in the womb, in the
          wooden hulls,
          died.
Five who could not go back,
Who could not a second time
Bear the birth, the going out,
          the expulsion
          into pure worlds of ice.

Music bridge

CROZIER:
The men do not return with food.
We push on, we cannot wait here.
The winds wait, the sun waits,
          the ice waits, but
We cannot wait here;
          to stop is to die
In our tracks,
          to freeze like catatonics
In our static houses of bone.

Already we look like statues,

marbled, white.
The flesh and hair bleaches out;
              we are cast in plaster.
The ice cannot bear the flesh of men,
The sun will not tolerate colouring;
              we begin already
To move *into* the ice, to mimic it.
Our Father who art in heaven,
Our Father
Our Father

Music, wind

One night we saw Eskimos
And they were afraid;
They gave us a seal,
They ran away at night . . . .

More music, wind

CROZIER:

Slowly

We have come two hundred miles from the ships,
We have come two hundred miles.
There are thirty men left.
It is the end, it is
The end . . . .

Wind, bridge to

RASMUSSEN:

Now there was nothing more to do,
              no notes to write and leave in cairns,
              no measurements to take, no
Readings of any temperatures
              save the inner
Agony of the blood.
Now, Crozier, now you come
To the end of science.

CROZIER:

Speaking slowly, painfully

We scattered our instruments behind us,
              and left them where they fell
Like pieces of our bodies, like limbs
We no longer had need for;
              we walked on and dropped them,
              compasses, tins, tools, all of them.
Now we come to the end of science . . . .

Now we leave ciphers in the snow,
We leave our instruments in the snow.
It is the end of science.
What magnet do I know of
Which will pull us south . . . ?
              none,
              none but the last inevitable
              one.

Death who draws
Death who reaches out his pulling arms
And draws men in like filings
              on paper.

This is the end of science.
We left it behind us,
A graph in the snow, a horrible cipher,
              a desperate code.
And the sun cannot read, and the snow
              cannot either.

Music, etc. suggesting death

RASMUSSEN:
No, Crozier, the sun cannot read
And the snow cannot either.
But men can, men like me who come
To find your traces, the pieces
Of your pain scattered in the white
              vaults of the snow.
Men like me who come and stand
              and learn
The agony your blood learned—
              how the body is bleached
And the brain itself turns
              a kind of pure, purged
              white.
And what happened to the ships?
It hurts to talk of it.
              The Eskimo, Qaqortingneq
Knows—
              let him tell of it . . . .

*Wind etc. bridge to Qaqortingneq, who speaks slowly,
falteringly, with language difficulties*

QAQORTINGNEQ:
I remember the day
When our fathers found a ship.
They were hunting seals,
And it was spring
And the snow melted around
The holes where the seals breathed . . . .

Music

Far away on the ice
My fathers saw a strange shape,
A black shape, too great to be seals.
They ran home and told all the men
In the village,
And the next day all came to see
This strange thing . . . .

It was a ship, and they moved closer,
And saw that it was empty,
That it had slept there for a long time.
My fathers had never seen white men,
And my fathers did not know about ships.

They went aboard the great ship
As though into another world,
Understanding nothing;
They cut the lines of the little boat
Which hung from the ship
And it fell broken to the ice;
They found guns in the ship
And did not understand
And they broke the guns
And used them for harpoons....

And they did not understand....

They went into the little houses
On the deck of the ship,
And found dead people in beds
Who had lain there a long time.
Then they went down, down
Into the hull of the great ship
And it was dark
And they did not understand the dark....

And to make it light they bored a hole
In the side of the ship,
But instead of the light,
The water came in the hole,
And flooded, and sank the ship,
And my fathers ran away,
And they did not understand....

Music

RASMUSSEN:
And the papers? Franklin's papers?
The ship's logs, the reports?

QAQORTINGNEQ:
Papers, O yes!
The little children found papers
In the great ship,
But they did not understand papers.
They played with them,
They ripped them up,
They threw them into the wind
Like birds....

Music

RASMUSSEN:

Laughing bitterly

Maybe they were right, —
What would papers mean to them?
　　　cryptic marks, latitudes,
　　　signatures, journals,
　　　diaries of despair,
　　　official reports
Nobody needs to read.
I've seen the real journals
You left us, you Franklin, you Crozier.

I've seen the skulls of your men
　　　in the snow, their sterile bones
Arranged around cairns like
　　　compasses,
Marking out all the latitudes
　　　and longitudes
Of men.

Music

Now the great passage is open,
The one you dreamed of, Franklin,
And great white ships plough through it
Over and over again,
Packed with cargo and carefree men.
It is as though no one had to prove it
Because the passage was always there.
Or...is it that the way was *invented*,
Franklin?
　　　that you cracked the passage open
With the forces of sheer certainty?
　　　—or is it that you cannot know,
Can never know,
Where the passage lies
Between conjecture and reality...?

Music, fade out

Transit Through Fire

Does the good life consist of serving others or of helping oneself? How is it possible for a community, within a matter of years, to move from a purposeless existence to a passionately committed life? These are some of the moral questions answered by William and Joan in an isolated skiing cabin while William is on leave in 1942. These two recent university graduates are the principals in *Transit through Fire*, the first opera ever commissioned by the CBC. The libretto was written by John Coulter (b. 1888) and set to music by Healy Willan (1880-1968). The hour-long opera, produced live from Toronto by John Adaskin, was broadcast Sunday evening, 8 March 1942, with the role of William being sung by Howard Scott and that of Joan by Frances James. The conductor was Sir Ernest MacMillan. Published in broadsheet form in 1942, the libretto has been specially abridged by the playwright for its appearance here. John Coulter has explained that he "proposed to write the retrospective story of one of the millions of young people who had emerged from the universities into the bewildering, hostile world of the nineteen-thirties, the years of the Great Depression which led to the Second World War."

PROLOGUE

WILLIAM
I, Sergeant William Thomson
Master of Arts,
infantryman,
am here to tell in retrospect
my story:
mine, yet a story
common to regimented hosts
of soldiers, sailors, airmen,
youths from factories and farms
and offices and shops and universities.
This is our Odyssey,
our transit through fire
out of the futile nineteen-thirties
into the fighting nineteen-forties:
out of the clanging maze
of life with no meaning,
into the core of quiet,
the sanctuary of peace
in the hearts of men at war,
the fighting men
who, having transcended self
in dedication to a true ideal,
have utterly found themselves
and are at peace
one in community.
I, Sergeant William Thomson,
commend our story.

SCENE I

WILLIAM
Here in this shack
where you and I came skiing
in Varsity days,
how good it is
to spend brief respite
from a world at war,
alone,
together.

JOAN
Alone?

WILLIAM
Surely as utterly alone
as though marooned
upon some uninhabited
frozen planet.

JOAN
Yet I hear voices.

WILLIAM
Voices?

JOAN
Dear, familiar voices.

WILLIAM
Beyond our door no footprints
pattern the white wilderness of snow
lying so still,
so silent,
in the crystalline night
under the sparkle of winter stars.

JOAN
Yet I hear voices
and in the friendly firelight glow
see forms and faces,
familiars of long ago —
our Varsity days in masquerade.

CHORUS
Varsity — let's go!
Rah, rah, rah!

WILLIAM AND JOAN
Varsity.
A sentimental pair
in retrospective mood.

JOAN
We sit and brood and stare,
rhyming that word
as though it were
some old forgotten air
out of our childhood.

WILLIAM
Classes and common-room,
campus and playing-fields,
the grave debates,
the callow co-ed chasings
seem now but scenes we acted out
in some old play —
a juvenile comedy.

JOAN
Do you remember
our graduation day?

WILLIAM
That curtain fell
a thousand years ago.

JOAN
Five years ago, that day.
I can still hear the President
piping his valedictory.

PRESIDENT
Farewell, alumni, ere you pass
beyond our ken. . . .

WILLIAM
Yes, I remember —
fussy old hen
flapping a moulted wing

at an irreverent brood.

PRESIDENT
Your alma mater bids you — farewell.

JOAN
Dear, pompous, sweet old thing.

PRESIDENT
Alma mater, beneficient mother
of your maturing mind and spirit,
having protected you and nurtured you
through these your formative years
now sends you forth, well-armed
each to his Odyssey,
and ever in your journeying
she bids you keep this precept
shining in your souls like a clear beacon:
*Each man must find
his individual good
in seeking first the general good
of the community.*

CHANCELLOR
Convocatio dimissa est.

WILLIAM
That was five years ago, that day.

JOAN
That was a thousand years ago.

SCENE II

WILLIAM
Out of the universities
like rudderless ships
upon uncharted seas
we sailed,
and tried this course and that,
and yet
could follow none with constancy,
having no certainty
of any happy landfall to be made
when voyaging was done,
and the white moon was set
below the glittering wave
edging our bleak horizon.

JOAN
Oh, you do pluck from the past
a thought
as gay as a flower — wrought
in frozen alabaster
on a wintry grave.

WILLIAM
I am no master of cynical irony
to sing a frivolous stave
in celebration

of the desolate years,
the phantom years
when the sounds of day and of night
were the ceaseless knell
of the passing bell
and the mourner's dirge in my ears.

JOAN
Yet there was dancing in those years
and some of us were sometimes merry.

WILLIAM
Sometimes merry —
with the hollow merriment
of an hysterical artifice
to mask from our bewildered minds
importunate fears,
the soul's presentiment
of spectral evils
congregating for catastrophe.

JOAN
You thought so then,
and looked as though you thought so.
Do you remember when you danced
your first reluctant dance with me?

WILLIAM
That dancing class.
The "Lambeth Walk."

JOAN
I still recall your grim unsmiling face
as you paced up and down
or sulked against the wall
watching:
watching the dancing master
herding us round with:
Whoopee!
Slap the knee!
Watch me!
Hoy!

SCENE III

WILLIAM
Cocktails and cocktail chatter
on every topic that didn't matter
were not to my mind:
since I was nigh distraught
thinking how best I might employ
such talent as I brought
from Varsity
to that good end
enjoined upon us
in the President's valedictory.

PRESIDENT
This precept keep in mind:

Each man must find
his individual good
in seeking first the general good
of the community.

JOAN
I do remember
your scalding words of disillusion
when you said,
"We were naive enough
to count that precept
something more
than a pious platitude
hypocritically mouthed
by hard-boiled men-of-the-world:
a farcical Sabbath Day aside
between the predatory acts
of the secular melodrama."

WILLIAM
So I thought:
and in the shock
and catastrophic shattering of faith
which followed,
I looked upon what seemed
a cynical obscene world,
and saw each counter and bench
and desk
as but a butcher's block
where the broken body of this society
was hewn in pieces
amid the stench
of carrion
and the buzz
of carrion flies.

CHORUS
High
low
buying
selling
profit-taking
money-making
new flotation
curb quotation
nine
nine
nine-and-a-half
nine-and-a-quarter
minus a quarter
nine,
all done at nine,
all done.

Hurry
hurry
grab your slice
at beggary's price.

When it rockets
unload for a profit,
yank the dopes
and suckers
into line,
sign,
sign:
the dough
in their pockets
is mine.
All done at nine
all done,
quicker
quicker,
there's so little time,
ever quicker
let the ticker run. . . .
Hullo,
hullo:
what's this? Obituary notice:
"Suddenly, in his office. . . ."

WILLIAM
In that nightmare vision
I thought the banal purpose of life
well caught in the banal phrase,
"to get a position":
a permanent situation
somewhere among
the milling throng
engaged in mutual pocket-picking.

JOAN
"To get a position,"
and not because most fitted
to serve the general good. . . .

WILLIAM
But because of having outwitted
five hundred other competitors
by superior aptitude
at wangling and boot-licking. . .
that cynical time
when clouds of applications
with highest recommendations
brought no reply,
or but this reply:
"No vacancy exists."

That shameful time
when the tightening screw
impelled me
to beg that people I hardly knew
should beg that people
they hardly knew
might use some influence
with a possible employer
to grant me an interview.

JOAN
Influence—
oh the offence of that unctuous word,
"to use some—influence"!

YOUNG GIRL'S VOICE
The manager will see you now.

MANAGER
Good morning, Mr. Thomson.
Very briefly tell me
what you can sell me.

WILLIAM
I would sell my time and my abilities.

MANAGER
Your qualifications?

WILLIAM
I am an honours graduate:
Master of Arts.

MANAGER
Have you had business experience?

WILLIAM
None.

MANAGER
Get some, my son.

WILLIAM
But everyone
must begin, somewhere.

MANAGER
When you've begun elsewhere
apply to us again,
we may have a vacancy then.

WILLIAM
But please . . . do let me say . . . .

MANAGER
I'm busy now. Good day.

CHORUS
Ah, what a shame!
what cruel luck
for the hundredth time
another employer passes the buck!

WILLIAM
Knowing what game
each was compelled to play
by our crazy economy
I had but little individual blame
for this or that employer:
yet in that nadir hour
of bleak humiliation,
oh, I could have plunged
from some high tower

down to the arch-destroyer
in frenzied capitulation.

JOAN
That was a crime
committed by our community:
to have permitted
such wanton maiming
of the aspiring pride and spirit
of the young manhood of the nation.

WILLIAM
It was the cardinal crime
of our dispirited time:
that only by spilling lagoons of blood
could again be stirred
the genius and generosity
of living democracy.

JOAN
I do remember
you strove to make it known
before it were too late,
but pled with pillars of stone.

That radio talk you gave
in nineteen thirty-nine,
when you sombrely pleaded a text
from D.H. Lawrence's words.

WILLIAM
"The next few months
are dark with tragedy:
'A new great wave of generosity
or a great new wave of death'
will deluge the world."

JOAN
Your warning was derided.

WILLIAM
Merely unheeded:
no pessimists were needed.

CHORUS
And songs were sung,
and hymns were sung,
and comics played
their antics at the fair:
and businessmen
stung businessmen,
and parsons prayed
long prayers into the air:
and only poor silly Salvation Billy
was sometimes heard to declare
that the God of Love
in heaven above
looked glum in His golden chair
and soon in His might
should arise and smite

with fire and brimstone and annihilation
a Sodom-and-Gomorrah generation.

WILLIAM
In this prelude to destruction
the President's valedictory
seemed but ironic mockery.

PRESIDENT
Each man must find
his individual good
in seeking first the general good
of the community.

WILLIAM
I had right faithfully sought
this general good
yet had found nought
save a satanic parody
of such community:
the emptiness and desolation
of each-man-for-himself:
the meaningless negation
of all philosophy
and religion.

So for some valid answer
to this importunate question:
How the divided self
could be made whole,
an integrated soul,
one in community?
I turned at last
to this snow-beleaguered place,
and strove to find
through merciless flagellation
of my most secret mind,
my individual salvation.

SCENE IV

WILLIAM
There is a passage into life,
out of limbo masquerading as life,
that mystic way
the spiritual adepts knew:
to which I sought some clue
through fasting and meditation.
Yet found no guidance
and was nigh despair,
when suddenly
through the shuttered air
a wind blew in my face,
a radiance was about me:
I stood in a desolate place
by the foam of an occult tide
where sea-birds circled and cried
of the cabalistic secrets

which only the dead can know,
and in a lull of their crying
it was as though I heard a voice,
the stricken voice
of the Syrian Mystic
who died two thousand years ago.

THE MYSTIC
My son, if you would find salvation,
cast from you all you are and were:
in utter denudation of self
is the self's true consummation.

CHORUS
This mystery
the saints and sages in all ages
do faithfully declare.

WILLIAM
And when those voices ceased
I heard the voice of the Beast.

THE BEAST
My son, do not despise
the hard-boiled wisdom
of the worldly wise.

In our realistic vocabulary
the synonym of sage or saint
is sucker.

Cast away foolish dreams:
all ideals are dope:
which goes for that sucker's hope:
a Christian democracy.

My son, from what you have
give nothing for nothing away,
but every day
add more and always more
even to the overflowing store.

A little greed
is better than great need.

All pious window-dressing aside:
if you would succeed, my son,
by those precepts you must abide.

WILLIAM
I looked and saw
no horns on the head
of the man who spoke those words,
but under a bowler hat
one of the living dead,
one of the blank-faced men
who commute between
a suburban mortuary
and a forty-storey pen.

But again
I heard that stricken voice.

THE MYSTIC
My son, those too you must accept
in true humility
and comprehending charity:
brother with brother
ye are all members one of another.

WILLIAM
And with those words
that truth which I had sought
so diligently,
was in my mind,
transforming to luminous thought
that blacked-out platitude.

PRESIDENT
*Each man must find
his individual good
in seeking first the general good
of the community.*

JOAN
When through the snow
I came and found you here,
a desolating fear
caught suddenly at my heart,
I saw you lying
as stilled and apart
as the dead or the dying.

WILLIAM
I had passed through transforming fire.

JOAN
And when at last
you looked and smiled,
a new serenity—
some spiritual grace—
as hushed and strange
as the grey of dawn,
shone in your face.

WILLIAM
I had found peace.

JOAN
Like a lost child,
hunted and wild,
come home.

WILLIAM
A journey ended,
a journey begun.

JOAN
I came from the past which had ended.

WILLIAM
You came to the future begun.

JOAN AND WILLIAM
A future where love had begun.

And we found in love
future and past transcended,
all living things made one.
And we took wings and ascended
into the spring of the day.
Out of mortality
into the immutable moment
of eternity.

SCENE V

JOAN
In that first September of the war,
do you remember how astounded
people were
on hearing we had carried our affair
so far as to be married?

CHORUS OF WOMEN
Oh my! Bill and Joan married!

FIRST WOMAN
If Joan could but have heard
that Bill had found a job!

SECOND WOMAN
And has Bill found a job?

CHORUS
Yes, Bill has found a job
for the duration.

FIRST MAN
But Bill I should have said
was the last man in the world
to have joined of his own accord.

SECOND MAN
He must have gone queer in the head.

FIRST MAN
But is he so misled
by unreserved acceptance
of the Christian theory
of life in community?
Brother with brother to stand or fall,
since we are all members
one of another.

SECOND MAN
Is that why he joined the army?

ALL
Yes, that's why he joined the army.

CHORUS OF MEN
Men with one purpose
marching together
in foul or fair weather:
not asking whether
when the job is done

reprieved society,
in cynical cupidity
or the stupor of senility,
will turn as once before and say:
"Now we don't need you more,
each one must fend for himself
in the good old way:
thank you,
good day!"

WILLIAM
If that should happen again
assuredly it would be
the final Judas-betrayal
of Christian democracy:
and would blasphemously degrade
to meaningless suicide
the sacrificial death
of democracy's fighting men.

These died
the flower of the race,
with morning in their face.

CHORUS
But we are marching:
and we who are marching today
ourselves shall be
the makers and masters
of tomorrow's community.

And we are marching:
and march for a future
when the voice of the charity of God
shall at last be heard,
the quickening word
in the hearts and councils of men.

SCENE VI

JOAN
And now, how sad to think
this respite
from a world at war
so soon is ended.

WILLIAM
Come, come,
let's greet the end of leave
with a shrug and a wink:
I count it ill to spend it
in further reminiscing by the fire.

JOAN
But Bill. . . .

WILLIAM
Think what we're missing.

JOAN
May I enquire. . .?

WILLIAM
Look, look, the moon has risen,
the snow is so inviting:
Joan — let's go skiing.

JOAN
Come then,
I take the trivial cue from you:
Bill — let's go skiing.

WILLIAM
Oh, how exciting!

JOAN
Splendid!

WILLIAM
The moon.

JOAN
The snow.

WILLIAM AND JOAN
Let's go.

The Masque of Heritage

"I knew I wanted to write a play about Canada, and that
its leading character should be a Prime Minister; far in
the back of my mind I dimly perceived that it should take
place in the Arctic." This is how Robertson Davies (b.
1913) has described the genesis of *Question Time*, which
opened at the St. Lawrence Hall, Toronto, 25 February
1975, from which "The Masque of Heritage" has been ex-
cerpted. In the play, Peter Macadam, the prime minister
of Canada, is stranded in the Far North, and through the
good if perplexing offices of the Shaman and his companion, Arnak, the PM experiences a series of illumina-
tions. In the masque that follows, the final illumination
takes place in "a fantastic evocation of the Commons
Chamber," a mock parliament of sorts. Members of this
strange Commons include: Tim and Marge, an incurious
Canadian couple; the secretary of state and the minister
for external affairs, the PM's rivals for power; the
Shaman and Arnak; Sarah, the PM's grieved wife; and
the PM himself, whose dawning enlightenment is dramatized by the splitting of his personality into complemen-
tary though opposing characters: PM (1), the prime
minister; PM (2), the leader of the Opposition. Then
enter the Herald and the Beaver.

*The SHAMAN nods, but the HERITAGE has already appeared. He
is a very old HERALD, silvery, courteous, and charming, dressed
in the full panoply of his office—silken breeches and stockings, a
cocked hat, and a resplendent tabard; he carries the ornate
baton proper to his office. But there is about him a general shab-
biness, and dustiness, and perhaps even a cobweb or two. He
bows with grave courtesy to the SPEAKER, and then to the House.*

PM(2)   Let us hear our heritage.

HERALD   Symbolically represented. I have, as you see, the Lion and Unicorn, the Lions of Scotland, the Irish Harp, the Lilies of France, the Lilies of Brabant, the Lions of Orange-Nassau, and a fine menagerie of double-headed eagles, hippogryphs, golden suns, and all the wonders of the ancient world, to signify Poland, and Russia, and Italy, and Portugal and — dear me, so many lands that have contributed to this one that I am sure to leave somebody out if I try to name them all. Even my stockings, you observe, are silk, which is a compliment to our large Chinese community. My underclothing is of that healthy variety that comes from the Scandinavian lands. I am as symbolic as it lies in my power to be.

TIM   Yeah, but what the hell do you do?

HERALD   I am a Herald. These are, I assure you, my working clothes.

TIM   But what can you do in that outfit?

HERALD   I am a Remembrancer. I remind you of what you were, so that you may have a clearer idea of what you are, and can therefore decide intelligently what you may become. I am the continuance of history.

TIM   By gollies you haven't got anything to do with me! Nope, I'm through with all that. Look at you! All silk and feathers and fancy crap — continuance of history! Not my history.

HERALD   Are you sure? What is your history?

TIM   My history is made up of all the people who came here with nothing — not a cent — and made their own way.

PM(2)   All honour to them. But only unhappy people emigrate. Where did they come from?

TIM   What do you mean, unhappy? Are you calling me unhappy?

PM(2)   What happiness do I see in your face, fellow-citizen?

TIM   I'll have all the happiness I need when there's been a few changes made. Not before. And what's it matter where my gang came from?

HERALD   Well, it's history; that's why it matters. There are no new beginnings.

TIM   Okay then. They musta come from someplace. But they came to get away from you, and all that fancy junk.

HERALD   Fancy junk?

TIM   The romantic stuff.

HERALD   Oh, my friend, there is no romance so potent as the belief that one can get rid of one's past. So do not, I beg you most sincerely, do not reject the fancy junk, as you call it. If I were to show you the unadorned reality of your past, it would sadden you, and perhaps it might break you. Who are you? I don't know. Were you one of the Scots who were shipped to Canada like cattle because their own chieftains had betrayed them for English money? Were you one of the Irish who came because a gentleman-gambler recouped his fortunes by sending his peasants to Canada, at the price of a pound a head? From what more recent abyss of misery and betrayal do you spring? But you had a past: that is as certain as that you have a present. So I beg you to accept me, absurd as I must sometimes appear, for I am a nourishing, romantic legend.

TIM   You think I can't stand the truth?

PM(2)   Why should you demand only the ugliest part of the truth? This also is part of the truth.

TIM   He don't look like truth to me. He looks like he's on the side of the bigshots.

PM(2)   Well, dismaying though you may find it, the bigshots make history because they have the energy and the ruthlessness and the desire to do so, and there is nothing that you or I can do about it. If you want the unadorned truth, I will strip our Heritage of what you call his fancy junk, and all you will see is a naked old creature, humbled by the loss of his dreams. Not even philosophers can endure that: nations need dreams, and not only dreams of the future.

MINISTER   If I may intervene, I think what our friend here means is that there is nothing about this Heritage that speaks directly of the country we know. And I entirely agree. Surely our symbolism must be home-grown. Let us, in everything, be ourselves. Away, I say, with borrowings. Though I myself can only claim to be a practical politician, in no sense a man of unusual abilities —

[*He pauses for contradiction, but there is none, and he is rather disconcerted.*]

—I am always conscious, when I take my place in the House of Commons, of the great figures who have sat there before me, and from whose shades — if you will permit a flight of fancy — I seem to draw sustenance. Among them, surely, there must be some who give us the heroic inspiration we seek. Indeed, I am convinced of it. If we could but see them —

TIM   Naw! I don't want to see any more guys with feathers in their hats.

PM(2)   This is always the difficulty with national heroes. They ought to be enthroned in the hearts of their people, but what can you do for a people in whose hearts there are no thrones?

TIM   There, you see! Thrones! Haven't you got anything to offer but this feather-and-throne crap?

HERALD   Oh, certainly. I am infinitely accommodating. Many countries do very well with a totem-figure, often an animal—

PM(2)   Wait! Wait! I beg you to be careful with animals—

SHAMAN   So you *are* capable of learning something new, Mr. Macadam? Well done, man, well done!

PM(2)   Better to let the animal choose you!

MINISTER   But it has! Why didn't I think of that before? The Beaver!

HERALD   Oh, my dear fellow, I entreat you—not the Beaver.

MINISTER   What's wrong with the Beaver?

HERALD   Will it suffice if I say that no country can hope to rise above mediocrity if it lacks a mystique of the courage, the humour, and also the cunning and roguery of its people—

MINISTER   Exactly, and I repeat—what's wrong with the Beaver?

[*The BEAVER has joined them; he is a sleek and in every respect admirable fellow, whose white shirt, highly polished shoes, neat blue serge suit of conservative cut, and beautifully brushed hair seem wholly in his favour. He has, unfortunately, rather prominent upper front teeth and almost no forehead, but his smile speaks of unlimited self-satisfaction. If his figure has a fault, it is a heaviness about the hips and a shortness of leg, and when he speaks, he occasionally emphasizes a point by smacking his hands together with a damp Splat! that suggests some large flat object striking water.*]

BEAVER   Nothing whatever wrong with the Beaver, I can assure you. Busy, busy, busy. But never too busy to be of help. Now—how can I be of assistance?

MINISTER   We were speaking of you as a national symbol.

SECRETARY   Something that unites. Something everybody agrees to love and respect.

ARNAK   A totem animal for an old country with new people.

BEAVER   Well—well, I don't like to push myself forward. But I have been spoken of in that way. It would be false modesty to deny it.

TIM   I don't know that I like this fellow, either. He's got a managerial look about him.

BEAVER   No, no, no. I can roll up my sleeves, but only after I've thought and planned. Make haste slowly—

but not too slowly, eh? Keep everlastingly at it, eh? Stick-to-itiveness is what wins, eh?

TIM   What did I tell ya? A stakhanovite! Naw! You won't do. Give me the Maple Leaf any day.

BEAVER   All right, I can give you the Maple Leaf any day, any hour, almost any minute. Crrrunch! Crunch-crunch-crunch-crunch! Timber! Wham! And I've laid it at your feet. Your Maple Leaf is a johnny-come-lately compared with me. If it hadn't been for jealousy in high places I'd be on the flag. Industry. That's how we build a modern nation.

MINISTER   I certainly can't find fault with that.

TIM   Naw! Only on the condition that industry ensures a paradise for the worker.

BEAVER   Certainly! A big beaver lodge with everybody snug and dry inside it—after the day's work is done. I like you. I particularly like the way you keep saying Gnaw! That's how we'll build the Worker's Paradise: gnaw, gnaw, gnaw.

MARGE   You got him wrong. He's a great union man. He doesn't say Gnaw. He just says Naw.

BEAVER   No problem. A little remedial work on his front teeth will fix that. Then you'll hear him say Gnaw.

TIM   The hell you will!

BEAVER   Oh yes. Remember that there was at least one great civilization in this country before any of you arrived. It was the beaver's civilization. Fraternally organized. Lodges everywhere. Lumbering on an extraordinary scale. Everybody happy. Happy, happy beavers. Now I'm sure this gentleman in the fancy pinafore has been telling you about the advantages of giving proper heed to your past. You might very well give a thought to that beaver civilization. We had no problems.

TIM   Commie bastards!

BEAVER   Co-operative, certainly; not bastards. Industry and morality went hand in hand. We mated monogamously and we coddled our kits—

MINISTER   Of course our national interests have expanded since that idyllic time. We now have to work with other nations—

BEAVER   Ah, yes; but we have a formula for that. The Honest Broker, eh?

MINISTER   That's what we've been called, certainly. The Honest Broker. A proud name.

BEAVER   And you've done it according to the Beaver Formula.

MINISTER   I've never heard that.

BEAVER   Oh, yes.

HERALD   Oh, wretched animal! I knew this would happen!

BEAVER   What's the matter with you?

HERALD   You and your Beaver Formula. You are invited to appear as a national totem, and you talk of your disgraceful Formula!

BEAVER   It's always worked, hasn't it?

HERALD   But at what a cost! Honour sacrificed! More than honour!

SHAMAN   What formula is under discussion?

HERALD   I ask your pardon, Mr. Speaker. But the Beaver Formula robs me of all sense of propriety.

PM(2)   Will you define it for us?

BEAVER   Surely I should do that?

SHAMAN   The Herald has the ear of the House.

HERALD   How am I to phrase it? I speak, you know, for the wisdom of the past. Sometimes my office, and my attitude toward life, is spoken of as medieval. I don't mind. There was great wisdom in the Middle Ages. The people in those times were very strong on symbols, and to every animal they attributed a symbolic significance. Thus, the Pelican, which fed its young with its own blood, stood for piety; the Ox stood for patience; but the Beaver stood for a certain sort of diplomacy. Must I go on?

SHAMAN   Is it the will of the House?

EVERYBODY   Aye! Aye!

HERALD   As you wish, then. The Beaver's industry and goodwill were conceded by everyone. [BEAVER: Thank you, thank you.] Arguing somebody else's cause the Beaver was eloquent and fair. [BEAVER: Very kind of you.] But if, in an argument with any greater animal—be it the Lion, the Eagle, the Bear, or what you will—the greater animal spoke to the Beaver in a sufficiently loud and hectoring tone, the Beaver would make a peace-offering to his opponent by biting off and offering—his own testicles. [BEAVER: But—but—but—] This made the Beaver the mockery of the animal kingdom; quite small animals with loud voices would leap out from hiding and shout "Boo!" just to see the Beaver roll over and put into effect its policy of appeasement.

[*The BEAVER is whistling feebly.*]

You see, it never developed a good voice. The Lion offered to teach it to roar; the Eagle proposed a short course in screaming; even the Hyena suggested that it might learn to laugh. But the Beaver was true to its own nature, and never produced any sound greater than a short whistle. Now I put it to you, Mr. Speaker, with all the emphasis that inheres in my traditional office, is this the kind of diplomacy you wish to embrace? Is this the example you wish to present to a nation? Is this the creature you would exalt to the dignity of a national totem?

[*Pause while they think. BEAVER whistles intermittently.*]

SECRETARY   You have to watch your step with the big fellows.

MINISTER   Appeasement, allied to goodwill and intelligence, is not an ineffective policy.

HERALD   No, gentlemen, no! The sacrifice the Beaver makes for what it calls peaceful co-existence is irreversible. It is a simple fact of sovereignty: when the orbs are gone, the sceptre is unavailing! No!

SARAH   And I say no!

MARGE   Me too!

EVERYONE   No! No!

[*Uproar*]

CLERKS   Order! Order!

SHAMAN   The decision seems to be against you.

EVERYBODY   Out! Out! Out!

CLERKS   Order! order!

[*The cries of "No! No!" mount and the BEAVER loses his composure completely. In desperation he produces a large pair of scissors and offers them to his opponents; his whistles are pitiful. The SHAMAN rises and everyone who is not already standing rises with him.*]

SHAMAN   Take away that Beaver!

[*The SERGEANT-AT-ARMS, with drawn sword, approaches the BEAVER, who collapses utterly, falling on his back in an obliging position. With the help of the CLERKS he is dragged from the scene, uttering plaintive whistles.*]

MINISTER   I'm sorry about that. But how was I to know? He seemed such a nice fellow.

SECRETARY   But an extremist.

TIM   Jeez, what some people will do to get their faces on a stamp!

MINISTER   How did he get as far as he did?

PM(2)   Because people like you want a pet, not a totem. If anyone can pet your totem or order it to kennel you may be sure they'll do the same to you.

SHAMAN   [*In an undertone*] Yes, you do learn, Mr. Macadam, and there's hope for you yet.

V   Records of Our Past

"It is about time that Canada entered history," observed Charles de Gaulle a few years before making his historic "Vive le Québec Libre" speech in Montreal. The truth is that long before it was a country this land had entered world history, and that if the world at large did not realize this, it was the fault of Canadians themselves who had failed to appreciate the fact and draw it to the world's attention. The reader will find in this section a gallimaufry of essays, articles, reports, memoirs, speeches, interviews, and manifestos. What better way to represent the variety and contrariety of the Canadian experience than through a mosaic of documents written, for the most part, by participants in the historic events and movements and issues of the past? Not all the principal happenings or crucial ideas are represented here, but there should be enough to yield the reader a panoramic view of the memorable moments in our collective experience, part of both our past and our present. Some of these records will be familiar to the general reader, some will be familiar only to the specialist. In my opinion all of them are well worth reading, rereading, and pondering.

The Great Peace / 1390

Unmatched among the world's great constitutions for poetic power must be that of the Iroquois Confederacy established by the Five (later Six) Nations Indians. The constitution of the confederacy takes the form of a traditional narrative which was transmitted orally from generation to generation until 1910 when a transcription and a translation were made at the Six Nations Reservation in southern Ontario. It is known to the Iroquois as the Great Binding Law or the Great Peace or the Code of Dekanawidah, and it is said to date back to 1390 when the semi-legendary culture hero Dekanawidah first addressed the Indian lords (or chiefs), among whom was an Onondagan "firekeeper" (or custodian) named Adodarhoh (better known as Hiawatha). This meeting took place on land north of Onondaga Lake in present-day New York State. It effectively united the Mohawk, Seneca,

Cayuga, Oneida, Onondaga (and about 1722 the Tuscarora), and includes an elaborate apparatus for the election of officials and the maintenance of law and order. Of impressive poetic appeal is the symbol of "the Tree of the Great Peace," for the Iroquois saw themselves establishing not just a local peace but a universal peace for all the tribes of man. In its day, the Iroquois Confederacy was the chief power east of the Mississippi; by allying itself with the British against the French, it cast a deciding vote in determining the fate of the North American continent. The two passages that follow appear in "The Council of the Great Peace" included by Arthur C. Parker in *Parker on the Iroquois* (1968), edited by William N. Fenton.

I am Dekanawidah and with the Five Nations' Confederate Lords I plant the Tree of the Great Peace. I plant it in your territory, Adodarhoh, and the Onondaga Nation, in the territory of you who are Firekeepers.

I name the tree the Tree of the Great Long Leaves. Under the shade of this Tree of the Great Peace we spread the soft white feathery down of the globe thistle as seats for you, Adodarhoh, and your cousin Lords.

We place you upon those seats, spread soft with the feathery down of the globe thistle, there beneath the shade of the spreading branches of the Tree of Peace. There shall you sit and watch the Council Fire of the Confederacy of the Five Nations, and all the affairs of the Five Nations shall be transacted at this place before you, Adodarhoh, and your cousin Lords, by the Confederate Lords of the Five Nations.

Roots have spread out from the Tree of the Great Peace, one to the north, one to the east, one to the south and one to the west. The name of these roots is The Great White Roots and their nature is Peace and Strength.

If any man or any nation outside the Five Nations shall obey the laws of the Great Peace and make known their disposition to the Lords of the Confederacy, they may trace the Roots to the Tree and if their minds are clean and they are obedient and promise to obey the wishes of the Confederate Council, they shall be welcomed to take shelter beneath the Tree of the Long Leaves.

We place at the top of the Tree of the Long Leaves an Eagle who is able to see afar. If he sees in the distance any evil approaching or any danger threatening he will at once warn the people of the Confederacy.

*

I, Dekanawidah, and the Union Lords, now uproot the tallest pine tree and into the cavity thereby made we cast all weapons of war. Into the depths of the earth, down into the deep underearth currents of water flowing to unknown regions we cast all the weapons of strife. We bury them from sight and we plant again the tree. Thus shall the Great Peace be established and hostilities shall no longer be known between the Five Nations but peace to the United People.

The Heroic Deeds
of Madeleine de Verchères / 1692

Madeleine de Verchères (1678-1747) was but fourteen years old and virtually defenceless when the Iroquois raided the family seigniory on the St. Lawrence River, eight leagues from Montreal, 22 October 1692. Her energetic defence of the fort for eight days and seven nights guarantees her a permanent place among the heroes and heroines not only of New France but also of Canada. In 1726, for the newly appointed governor of New France, the Marquis de Beauharnois, who had first heard of Madeleine's heroic deeds in the French court, she penned the following account of her experience. The narrative is taken from the *Supplement to the Report of the Public Archives of Canada for 1899* (1901) where Edouard Richard wrote: "The day is not far distant when the painter, the sculptor and the writer of romance, will accomplish the patriotic work of enshrining more deeply in our memory and crowning with a bright halo of glory, the brow of the national heroine, Marie-Madeleine de Verchères."

Narrative of the heroic deeds of Mlle Marie-Madeleine De Verchères, aged fourteen years, against The Iroquois.

I was five arpents away from the fort of Verchères, belonging to Sieur De Verchères, my father, who was then at Kebek by order of M. Le Chevalier De Callières, governor of Montreal, my mother being also in Montreal. I heard several shots without knowing at whom they were fired. I soon saw that the Iroquois were firing at our settlers, who lived about a league and a-half from the fort. One of our servants called out to me:

"Fly, mademoiselle, fly! the Iroquois are upon us!"

I turned instantly and saw some forty-five Iroquois running towards me, and already within pistol shot. Determined to die rather than fall into their hands, I sought safety in flight. I ran towards the fort, commending myself to the Blessed Virgin, and saying to her from the bottom of my heart: "Holy Virgin, mother of my God, you know I have ever honoured and loved you as my dear mother; abandon me not in this hour of danger! I would rather a thousand times perish than fall into the hands of a race that know you not."

Meantime my pursuers, seeing that they were too far off to take me alive before I could enter the fort, and knowing they were near enough to shoot me, stood still in order to discharge their guns at me. I was under fire for quite a time, at any rate I found the time long enough! Forty-five bullets whistling past my ears made the time seem long and the distance from the fort interminable, though I was so near. When within hearing of the fort, I cried out: "To arms! To arms!"

I hoped that someone would come to help me, but it was a vain hope. There were but two soldiers in the fort and these were so overcome by fear that they had sought safety by concealing themselves in the redoubt. Having reached the gates at last, I found there two women lamenting for the loss of their husbands, who had just been killed. I made them enter the fort, and closed the gates myself. I then began to consider how I might save myself and the little party with me, from the hands of the savages. I examined the fort, and found that several of the stakes had fallen, leaving gaps through which it would be easy for the enemy to enter. I gave orders to have the stakes replaced, and heedless of my sex and tender age, I hesitated not to seize one end of the heavy stake and urge my companions to give a hand in raising it. I found by experience that, when God gives us strength, nothing is impossible.

The breaches having been repaired, I betook myself to the redoubt, which served as a guard-house and armoury. I there found two soldiers, one of them lying down and the other holding a burning fuse. I said to the latter:

"What are you going to do with that fuse?"

"I want to set fire to the powder," said he, "and blow up the fort."

"You are a miserable wretch," I said, adding: "Begone, I command you!"

I spoke so firmly that he obeyed forthwith. Thereupon putting aside my hood and donning a soldier's casque, I seized a musket and said to my little brothers:

"Let us fight to the death for our country and for our holy religion. Remember what our father has so often told you, that gentlemen are born but to shed their blood for the service of God and the king!"

Stirred up by my words, my brothers and the two soldiers kept up a steady fire on the foe. I caused the cannon to be fired, not only to strike terror into the Iroquois and show them that we were well able to defend ourselves, since we had a cannon, but also to warn our own soldiers, who were away hunting, to take refuge in some other fort.

But alas! what sufferings have to be endured in these awful extremities of distress! Despite the thunder of our guns, I heard unceasingly the cries and lamentations of some unfortunates who had just lost a husband, a brother, a child or a parent. I deemed it prudent, while the firing was still kept up, to represent to the grief-stricken women that their shrieks exposed us to danger, for they could not fail to be heard by the enemy, notwith-standing the noise of the guns and the cannon. I ordered them to be silent and thus avoid giving the impression that we were helpless and hopeless.

While I was speaking thus, I caught sight of a canoe on the river, opposite the fort. It was Sieur Pierre Fontaine with his family, who were about to land at the spot where I had just barely escaped from the Iroquois, the latter being still visible on every hand. The family must fall into the hands of the savages if not promptly succoured.

I asked the two soldiers to go to the landing place, only five arpents away, and protect the family. But seeing by their silence, that they had but little heart for the work, I ordered our servant, Laviolette, to stand sentry at the gate of the fort and keep it open, while I would myself go to the bank of the river, carrying a musket in my hand and wearing my soldier's casque. I left orders on setting out, that if I was killed, they were to shut the gates and continue to defend the fort sturdily. I set out with the heaven-sent thought that the enemy, who were looking on, would imagine that it was a ruse on my part to induce them to approach the fort, in order that our people might make a sortie upon them.

This is precisely what happened, and thus was I enabled to save poor Pierre Fontaine, with his wife and children. When all were landed, I made them march before me as far as the fort, within sight of the enemy. By putting a bold face upon it, I made the Iroquois think there was more danger for them than for us.

They did not know that the whole garrison, and only inhabitants of the fort of Verchères, were my two brothers aged 12 years, our servant, two soldiers, an old man of eighty, and some women and children.

Strengthened by the new recruits from Pierre Fon-taine's canoe, I gave orders to continue firing at the enemy. Meantime the sun went down and a fierce north-easter accompanied by snow and hail, ushered in a night of awful severity. The enemy kept us closely invested and instead of being deterred by the dreadful weather, led me to judge by their movements that they purposed assault-ing the fort under cover of the darkness.

I gathered all my troops — six persons — together, and spoke to them thus: "God has saved us to-day from the hands of our enemies, but we must be careful not to be caught in their snares to-night. For my part, I want to

show you that I am not afraid. I undertake the fort for my share, with an old man of eighty, and a soldier who has never fired a gun. And you, Pierre Fontaine, with La Bonté and Galhet (our two soldiers), will go to the redoubt, with the women and children, as it is the strong-est place. If I am taken, never surrender, even though I should be burnt and cut to pieces before your eyes. You have nothing to fear in the redoubt, if you only make some show of fighting."

Thereupon, I posted my two young brothers on two of the bastions, the *youth* of 80 on a third bastion and myself took charge of the fourth. Each one acted his part to the life. Despite the whistling of the northeast wind, which is a fearful wind in Canada, at this season, and in spite of the snow and hail, the cry of "All's well," was heard at close intervals, echoing and re-echoing from the fort to the redoubt and from the redoubt to the fort.

One would have fancied, to hear us, that the fort was crowded with warriors. And in truth the Iroquois, with all their astuteness and skill in warfare were completely deceived, as they afterwards avowed to M. De Callières. They told him they had held a council with a view to assaulting the fort during the night, but that the increas-ing vigilance of the guard had prevented them from accomplishing their design, especially in view of their losses of the previous day (under the fire maintained by myself and my two brothers).

About an hour after midnight, the sentinel at the gate bastion, cried out:

"Mademoiselle! I hear something!"

I walked towards him, in order to see what it was, and through the darkness, aided by the reflection from the snow, I saw a group of horned cattle, the remnant escaped from the hands of our enemies.

"Let me open the gates for them," said the sentry.

"God forbid," I answered, "you do not know all the cunning of the savages; they are probably marching behind the cattle, covered with the hides of animals, so as to get into the fort, if we are simple enough to open the gates."

I saw danger everywhere, in face of an enemy so keen and crafty as the Iroquois. Nevertheless, after adopting every precaution suggested by prudence under the cir-cumstances, I decided that there would be no risk in opening the gate. I sent for my two brothers, and made them stand by with their muskets loaded and primed, in case of a surprise, and then we let the cattle enter the fort.

At last the day dawned, and the sun in scattering the shades of the night seemed to banish our grief and anxi-ety. Assuming a joyful countenance I gathered my garri-son around me and said to them:

"Since, with God's help, we have got through the past night with all its terrors, we can surely get through other nights by keeping good watch and ward and by firing our cannon hour by hour, so as to get help from Montreal, which is only eight leagues off."

I saw that my address made an impression on their minds. But Marguérite Antiome, the wife of Sieur Pierre Fontaine, being extremely timorous, as is natural to all Parisian women, asked her husband to take her to another fort, representing to him that while she had been lucky enough to escape the fury of the savages the first night, she had no reason to expect a like good fortune for the coming night; that the fort of Verchères was utterly worthless, that there were no men to hold it, and that to remain in it would be to expose one's self to evident danger, or to run the risk of perpetual slavery or of death by slow fire. The poor husband, finding that his wife persisted in her request and that she wanted to go to Fort Contrecoeur, three hours distant from Verchères, said to her: "I will fit you out a good canoe, with a proper sail, and you will have your two children, who are accustomed to handle it. I myself will never abandon the fort of Verchères, so long as Mademoiselle Magdelon (this was the name I went by in my childhood) holds it."

I spoke up firmly then, and told him that I would never abandon the fort; that I would sooner perish than deliver it up to our enemies; that it was of the last importance that the savages should never enter one of our French forts; that they would judge of the rest by the one they got possession of, and that the knowledge thus acquired could not fail to increase their pride and courage.

I can truthfully say that I was on two occasions, for twenty-four hours without rest or food. I did not once enter my father's house. I took up my station on the bastion, and from time to time looked after things on the redoubt. I always wore a smiling and joyful face, and cheered up my little troop with the prospect of speedy assistance.

On the eighth day (for we were eight days in continual alarms, under the eyes of our enemies and exposed to their fury and savage attacks), on the eighth day, I say, M. De La Monnerie, a lieutenant detached from the force under M. De Callières, reached the fort during the night with forty men. Not knowing but the fort had fallen, he made his approach in perfect silence. One of our sentries hearing a noise, cried out: "Qui vive?"

I was dozing at the moment, with my head resting on a table and my musket across my arms.

The sentry told me he heard voices on the water. I forthwith mounted the bastion in order to find out by the tone of the voice whether the party were savages or French. I called out to them:

"Who are you?"

They answered: "French! It is La Monnerie come to your assistance."

I caused the door of the fort to be opened and put a sentry to guard it, and went down to the bank of the river to receive the party.

So soon as I saw the officer in command I saluted him, saying:

"Sir, you are welcome, I surrender my arms to you."

"Mademoiselle," he answered, with a courtly air, "they are in good hands."

"Better than you think," I replied.

He inspected the fort and found it in a most satisfactory condition, with a sentry on each bastion. I said to him:

"Sir, kindly relieve my sentries, so that they may take a little rest, for we have not left our posts for the last eight days."

I was forgetting one circumstance which will give an idea of my confidence and tranquility. On the day of the great battle, the Iroquois who were around the fort, were sacking and burning the houses of our settlers and killing their cattle before our eyes, when I called to mind, about one o'clock in the afternoon, that I had three sacks of linen and some quilts outside the fort. I asked my soldiers to take their guns and accompany me while I went out for the clothes; but their silence and sullen looks convinced me of their lack of courage, so I turned to my young brothers and said to them:

"Take your guns and come with me! As to you," I said to the others, "keep your fire against the enemy while I go for my linen."

I made two trips, in sight of the enemy, in the very place where they had so narrowly missed taking me prisoner, a few hours before. They must have suspected some plot under my proceedings, for they did not venture to try to capture me, or even to take my life with their guns. I felt then that when God overrules matters, there is no danger of failure....

This is a simple and truthful account of the adventure which secured for me His Majesty's favour, and which I would not have undertaken to put in writing had not M. Le Marquis De Beauharnais, our governor, whose one care is to protect our colony against the incursions of the barbarians, and to promote therein the glory of France, by rendering the name of her illustrious monarch formidable to all her enemies and respected and loved of all his subjects, induced me to prepare this detailed narrative.

Our governor, in his wisdom, is not content with constraining all the tribes by whom we are surrounded to hold us in respect and fear, and keeping the enemies of the state at a distance of four or five hundred leagues. His indefatigable devotion to the most weighty matters is interrupted only by the attention he gives to the more striking events which have occurred since the establishment of this colony, using them on occasion with the goodness and distinction of manner which are natural to him, in order to encourage every subject of His Majesty to seek distinction by performing heroic deeds, whensoever the opportunity presents itself.

The Life of a Montagnais Missionary/1697

"Not a cape was turned, not a river entered, but a Jesuit led the way," wrote the American historian George Bancroft. Members of the Society of Jesus not only sought converts among the original inhabitants of North America but also described their experiences, their successes and failures both, in their Reports, or Relations. These were written from 1611 to 1768 and addressed to their superiors in Quebec and in France. The accounts were published annually to promote the Jesuit missions abroad. Today they comprise a vast storehouse of irreplaceable information about ways of life that have all but disappeared. R.G. Thwaits, secretary of the State Historical Society of Wisconsin, edited in the original French and in English translation seventy-three volumes of *The Jesuit Relations and Allied Documents* between 1896 and 1901. "The Life of a Montagnais Missionary," written by François de Crespieul (1639-1702), who spent thirty years in Montagnais territory, may be found there or in the convenient one-volume edition, *The Jesuit Relations and Allied Documents* (1954), edited by Edna Kenton.

Presented to His Successors in the Montagnais Mission for Their Instruction and Greater Consolation by Father François de Crespieul, Jesuit, and an Unprofitable Servant of the Missions of Canada from 1671 to 1697, which completes the 26th wintering in the Service of the Tadoussac Mission, and the 4th at the Mission of St. Xavier at Chicoutimi, April 21, 1697.

The life of a Montagnais missionary is a long and slow martyrdom:

Is an almost continual practice of patience and of mortification:

Is a truly penitential and humiliating life, especially in the cabins, and on journeys with the savages.

1. The cabin is made of poles and birch-bark; and fir-branches are placed around it to cover the snow and the frozen ground.

2. During nearly all the day, the missionary remains in a sitting or kneeling position, exposed to an almost continual smoke during the winter.

3. Sometimes he perspires in the day-time and most frequently is cold during the night. He sleeps in his clothes upon the frozen ground, and sometimes on the snow covered with fir-branches, which are very hard.

4. He eats from an ouragan (dish) that is very seldom cleaned or washed, and in most cases is wiped with a greasy piece of skin, or is licked by the dogs. He eats when there is anything to eat, and when some is offered to him. Sometimes the meat is only half-cooked; sometimes it is very tough, especially when smoked (dried in the smoke). As a rule, they have a good meal only once — or, when

provisions are abundant twice; but it does not last long.

5. The savage shoes, or the dogs' hairy skins, serve him as napkins, as the hair of the savage men and women serves them.

6. His usual beverage is water from the streams or from some pond — sometimes melted snow, in an ouragan that is usually quite greasy.

7. He often scorches his clothes, or his blanket, or his stockings during the night — especially when the cabin is small or narrow. He cannot stretch himself, but he curls himself up, and his head rests upon the snow covered with fir-branches; this chills his brain, and gives him tooth-ache, etc.

8. He always sleeps with his clothes on, and takes off his cassock and his stockings only to protect himself against vermin, which always swarm on the savages, especially the children.

9. Usually when he wakes he finds himself surrounded by dogs. I have sometimes had 6, 8, or 10 around me.

10. The smoke is sometimes so strong that it makes his eyes weep; and when he sleeps he feels as if some one had thrown salt into his eyes; when he awakes, he has much difficulty in opening them.

11. When the snow thaws, while he is walking upon lakes or long rivers, he is so dazzled for 4 or 5 days by the water that drops continually from his eyes that he cannot read his breviary. Sometimes he has to be led by the hand. This has happened to Father Silvy, to Father Dalmas, and to myself; while on the march I could not see further than the edge of my snowshoes.

12. He is often annoyed by little children, by their cries, their weeping, etc.; and sometimes he is made ill by the stench of those who have scrofula, with whom he even drinks out of the same kettle. I have spent more than 8 days in the cabin of Kawitaskawat, the chief man among the Mystassins, and have slept near his son, who was troubled with that disease; and the stench from him often caused me nausea, both by day and night. I have also eaten and drunk from his ouragan.

13. He is sometimes reduced to drinking only water obtained from melted snow, which smells of smoke and is very dirty. For 3 weeks I have drunk nothing else, while I was with strangers in the region of Peokwagamy. I have never seen savages dirtier than these, as regards eating, drinking and sleeping. Among them the meat was often covered with moose-hairs or sand. An old woman, with her long nails, gathered up handfuls of grease in the kettle into which snow had been thrown, and then offered it to us to eat, in a very dirty ouragan: and all drank broth out of the same kettle.

14. In the summer-time, while travelling, especially on the Saguenay and on the great River, he often drinks the very dirty water obtained from ponds. During 3 days, while detained by contrary winds, we drank no other water. Sometimes the wind compels him to take refuge in

places where there is none at all. This has happened to me more than once — indeed, more than 3 times. I have even been obliged to drink from ponds in which I saw toads, etc.

15. In most cases during the winter, while on long and difficult journeys, he does not find a drop of water wherewith to quench his thirst, although exhausted with toils and fatigues.

16. He suffers greatly from cold and from smoke, before the cabin is finished, for 2 or 3 hours when the weather is very severe in winter. His shirt, which is wet with perspiration, and his soaked stockings, render him benumbed with cold; he suffers also from hunger, because in most cases he has had nothing but a piece of dried meat, eaten before the camp was struck.

17. Suffering and hardship are the appanages of these holy but arduous missions. Faxit Deus ut iis diu immoretur et immoriatur Servus Inutilis Missionum Franciscus, S.J. (God grant that in them may long remain and die the Useless servant of the missions, François, S.J.).

The Coureur de Bois/1700s

Coureurs de bois is French for "runners of the woods," the unlicensed fur traders who journeyed by canoe from New France to the trading posts in the West, often living for long periods of time with the Indians and assuming their ways. They were later called voyageurs or "voyagers." A celebrated passage in The Fur Hunters of the Far West (1855), written by Alexander Ross (1783-1856), an employee of the Hudson's Bay Company, catches the buoyant spirit of these canoemen who were the mainstay of the fur trade that was so important to the economic life of early Canada.

One day while in a jocular mood the old man began to talk over his past life. It was full of adventure, and may appear amusing to others as it did to us. I shall give it as nearly as I can in his own words. "I have now," said he, "been forty-two years in this country. For twenty-four I was a light canoeman. I required but little sleep, but sometimes got less than I required. No portage was too long for me; all portages were alike. My end of the canoe never touched the ground till I saw the end of it. Fifty songs a day were nothing to me. I could carry, paddle, walk and sing with any man I ever saw. During that period I saved the lives of ten bourgeois, and was always the favourite because when others stopped to carry at a bad step and lost time, I pushed on — over rapids, over cascades, over chutes; all were the same to me. No water, no weather ever stopped the paddle or the song. I have had twenty wives in the country; and was once possessed of fifty horses and six running dogs trimmed in the first

style. I was then like a bourgeois, rich and happy. No bourgeois had better-dressed wives than I; no Indian chief finer horses; no white man better-harnessed or swifter dogs. I beat all the Indians at the race, and no white man ever passed me in the chase. I wanted for nothing; and I spent all my earnings in the enjoyment of pleasure. Five hundred pounds twice told have passed through my hands, although now I have not a spare shirt to my back nor a penny to buy one. Yet, were I young I should glory in commencing the same career. I would spend another half-century in the same fields of enjoyment. There is no life so happy as a voyageur's life; none so independent; no place where a man enjoys so much variety and freedom as in the Indian country. Huzza, huzza pour le pays sauvage!"

After this cri de joie he sat down in the boat and we could not help admiring the wild enthusiasm of the old Frenchman. He had boasted and excited himself till he was out of breath and then sighed with regret that he could no longer enjoy the scenes of his past life.

The Deaths of Wolfe and Montcalm/1759

Like Homer, Francis Parkman (1823-93) was blind or nearly sightless by the time he had completed his epic. Between 1851 and 1892, the great American historian finished his eight-volume masterwork to which he gave the general title "France and England in the New World." Although the modern scholar has access to sources of information unavailable to Parkman, no historian before or since has yet attained the degree of psychological penetration or the sheer narrative power of the master story-teller. Sir Arthur Conan Doyle referred to Parkman as "one of the very greatest historians who ever lived." The brief excerpt below captures a crucial event in Canadian history, the conquest of Quebec, which took place on the Plains of Abraham, 13 September 1759. It comes from Montcalm and Wolfe (1884), considered by many to be the copestone of the author's work.

Wolfe was everywhere. How cool he was, and why his followers loved him, is shown by an incident that happened in the course of the morning. One of his captains was shot through the lungs; and on recovering consciousness he saw the general standing at his side. Wolfe pressed his hand, told him not to despair, praised his services, promised him an early promotion, and sent an aide-de-camp to Monckton to beg that officer to keep the promise if he himself should fall.

It was towards ten o'clock when, from the high ground on the right of the line, Wolfe saw that the crisis was near. The French on the ridge had formed themselves into three bodies, regulars in the centre, regulars and Canadians on the right and left. Two field-pieces, which had been dragged up the heights at Anse du Foulon, fired on them with grape-shot, and the troops, rising from the ground, prepared to receive them. In a few moments more they were in motion. They came on rapidly, uttering loud shouts, and firing as soon as they were within range. Their ranks, ill ordered at the best, were further confused by a number of Canadians who had been mixed among the regulars, and who, after hastily firing, threw themselves on the ground to reload. The British advanced a few rods; then halted and stood still. When the French were within forty paces the word of command rang out, and a crash of musketry answered all along the line. The volley was delivered with remarkable precision. In the battalions of the centre, which had suffered least from the enemy's bullets, the simultaneous explosion was afterwards said by French officers to have sounded like a cannon-shot. Another volley followed, and then a furious clattering fire that lasted but a minute or two. When the smoke rose, a miserable sight was revealed: the ground cumbered with dead and wounded, the advancing masses stopped short and turned into a frantic mob, shouting, cursing, gesticulating. The order was given to charge. Then over the field rose the British cheer, mixed with the fierce yell of the Highland slogan. Some of the corps pushed forward with the bayonet; some advanced firing. The clansmen drew their broadswords and dashed on, keen and swift as bloodhounds. At the English right, though the attacking column was broken to pieces, a fire was still kept up, chiefly, it seems, by sharpshooters from the bushes and cornfields, where they had lain for an hour or more. Here Wolfe himself led the charge, at the head of the Louisbourg grenadiers. A shot shattered his wrist. He wrapped his handkerchief about it and kept on. Another shot struck him, and he still advanced, when a third lodged in his breast. He staggered, and sat on the ground. Lieutenant Brown, of the grenadiers, one Henderson, a volunteer in the same company, and a private soldier, aided by an officer of artillery who ran to join them, carried him in their arms to the rear. He begged them to lay him down. They did so, and asked if he would have a surgeon. "There's no need," he answered; "it's all over with me." A moment after, one of them cried out: "They run; see how they run!" "Who run?" Wolfe demanded, like a man roused from sleep. "The enemy, sir. Egad, they give way everywhere!" "Go, one of you, to Colonel Burton," returned the dying man; "tell him to march Webb's regiment down to Charles River, to cut off their retreat from the bridge." Then, turning on his side, he murmured, "Now, God be praised, I will die in peace!" and in a few moments his gallant soul had fled.

Montcalm, still on horseback, was borne with the tide of fugitives towards the town. As he approached the walls a shot passed through his body. He kept his seat; two soldiers supported him, one on each side, and led his horse through the St. Louis Gate. On the open space within, among the excited crowd, were several women, drawn, no doubt, by eagerness to know the result of the fight. One of them recognized him, saw the streaming blood, and shrieked, *"O mon Dieu! mon Dieu! le Marquis est tué!"* "It's nothing, it's nothing," replied the death-stricken man; "don't be troubled for me, my good friends."*("Ce n'est rien; ne vous affligez pas pour moi, mes bonnes amies.")*

Mrs. Secord's Trek/1813

As the wry joke goes, if it had not been for Mrs. Secord's trek through the woods to alert the British forces that an American attack was pending, we would all be eating Fanny Farmer chocolates today. There is no question that Laura Secord (1775-1868), the United Empire Loyalist lady who, at thirty-eight, in the dead of night, walked nineteen miles through the woods between Queenston and Beaver Dam in the Niagara region, 21-22 June 1813, was a brave and loyal woman and a genuine heroine of the War of 1812. There is some question of the strategic importance of the trek, for Lieutenant James FitzGibbon, the British commander she warned, had been forewarned by the Indians. Yet the commander on at least two occasions recognized her dedication and her role in the American defeat. Historians, like J. Mackay Hitsman in *The Incredible War of 1812* (1965), have been less kind: "Caughnawaga Indians fought the battle, the Mohawks got the plunder and FitzGibbon got the credit.... Legend, however, has placed the credit elsewhere." Mrs. Secord's trek, which did not become common knowledge for some forty years, was not officially recognized until 1860 when the Prince of Wales, later King Edward VII, visiting Niagara Falls, learned of her heroism and sent her his personal cheque for one hundred pounds. The following passage by Laura Secord is taken from *The Anglo-American Magazine*, November 1853.

I shall commence at the battle of Queenston, where I was at the time the cannon balls were flying around me in every direction. I left the place during the engagement. After the battle I returned to Queenston, and then found that my husband had been wounded; my house plundered and property destroyed. It was while the Americans had possession of the frontier, that I learned the plans of the American commander, and determined to put the British troops under FitzGibbon in possession of them, and, if possible, to save the British troops from capture, or, perhaps, total destruction. In doing so, I found I should have great difficulty in getting through the American guards, which were out ten miles in the country. Determined to persevere, however, I left early in the morning, walked nineteen miles in the month of June, over a rough and difficult part of the country, when I came to a field belonging to a Mr. Decamp, in the neighbourhood of the Beaver Dam. By this time daylight had left me. Here I found all the Indians encamped; by moonlight the scene was terrifying, and to those accustomed to such scenes, might be considered grand. Upon advancing to the Indians they all rose, and, with some yells, said "Woman," which made me tremble. I cannot express the awful feeling it gave me; but I did not lose my presence of mind. I was determined to persevere. I went up to one of the chiefs, made him understand that I had great news for Capt. FitzGibbon, and that he must let me pass to his camp, or that he and his party would all be taken. The chief at first objected to let me pass, but finally consented, after some hesitation, to go with me and accompany me to FitzGibbon's station, which was at the Beaver Dam, where I had an interview with him. I then told him what I had come for, and what I had heard — that the Americans intended to make an attack upon the troops under his command, and would, from their superior numbers, capture them all. Benefiting by this information, Capt. FitzGibbon formed his plans accordingly, and captured about five hundred American infantry, about fifty mounted dragoons, and a field-piece or two was taken from the enemy. I returned home next day, exhausted and fatigued. I am now advanced in years, and when I look back I wonder how I could have gone through so much fatigue, with the fortitude to accomplish it.

Billy the Scout/1813

"In Billy Green the Scout, who has been called the Paul Revere of Canada, have we not a local hero worthy of belated recognition?" The answer to that question, asked by Mabel W. Thompson in her article "Billy Green, The Scout" in *Ontario History*, October 1952, is Yes. She reproduces the youthful hero's own account of how, with pluck and invention, he helped the British regiments and Canadian volunteers ward off the American invaders, who, more than anything, feared an engagement with the Indians. Thus Billy Green (1794-1877), a native of Saltfleet, near Stoney Creek, played a small yet significant role in the Battle of Stoney Creek, fought on 5 June 1813, an important engagement in the War of 1812. The account reproduced here was written down six years after the battle. It has been suggested that the "countersign" Billy obtained was "Will-Hen-Har," a nonsense phrase until it is remembered that the name of the American general was William Henry Harrison.

I was the first white child born at Stoney Creek, being born February 4, 1794, and at the time of the Battle of Stoney Creek I was 19 years old, my home being in Stoney Creek up to that time. My father, brothers and sisters lived there also.

We heard that the American army were camping down east below the Forty [Forty Mile Creek, now Grimsby, Ontario], so my brother Levi and I went down the road on top of the Mountain about 6 o'clock in the morning on June 5. We got to the Forty and stayed out on the Peak of the Mountain above the Forty until noon, when we espied the troops marching up the road. We stayed there until all the enemy but a few had passed through the village. Then we yelled like Indians. I tell you those simple fellows did run. Then we ran along the Mountain and took down to the road that the Americans had just passed over. Levi ran across a soldier with his boot off, putting a rag on his foot. The soldier grabbed for his gun, but Levi was too quick for him, hitting him with a stick until he yelled with pain and some of the scouts fired at us.

We made our way to the top of the Mountain again. I whooped like an Indian and Levi answered. By this time the settlers came out to the brow of the Mountain to see what was going on. Among them were the Lee brothers who lived near the brow of the Mountain at that time. They went home and the rest of us went to brother Levi's place on the side of the Mountain. When we heard them [the enemy] coming through the village of Stoney Creek, we all went out on the brow of the hill to see them. Some of them espied us and fired at us. One ball struck the bars where Tina, my brother Levi's wife, was sitting holding Hannah, her oldest child, on her arm. We all went back to the Mountain to one of Jim Stoney's trapping huts. Tina went to the house with Hannah, her child.

Not long after, two American officers came up to the house and asked her if she had seen any Indians around there. She said there was a band of Indians on the Mountain. The officers left, and Tina came out to where we were hiding and whistled. I answered her and told them I would go down to Isaac Corman's. When I got there I whistled and out came Keziah, my sister [Corman's wife]. I asked her where Isaac was, and she said the enemy had taken him prisoner and taken the trail to the beach.

I asked her how she knew. She said Alf had followed them to the swamp. [Alf was their oldest son.] I asked, "Where is Alf?" and she said he was in the cellar with Becky and Jane, his two sisters. I went down to the cellar and Alf told me where to go to find his father. I started and ran; every now and then I would whistle until I got across the creek. When I heard Isaac's hoot like an owl, I thought the enemy had him there, but he was coming back alone. I was going to raise an Indian war-whoop to scare them when I saw Isaac coming. I asked him how he got away and he said, "The major and I got a-talking, and he said he was second cousin to General Harrison. I said I was first cousin to General Harrison and came from Kentucky. After talking a little longer a message came for the major; he said, 'I must go; you may go home, Corman.' I said I couldn't get through the lines. 'I will give you the countersign,' and he did."

Isaac gave the countersign to me; I got it and away I came. When I got up the road a ways I forgot it and didn't know what to do; so I pulled my coat over my head and trotted across the road on my feet and hands like a bear.

I went up the hill to Levi's house and got Levi's old horse "Tip" and led him along the Mountain side until I could get to the top. Then I rode him away around by the gully, where I dismounted and tied old Tip to the fence and left him there, making my way on foot to Burlington Heights.

When I got there they took me for a spy, and I had to tell them all I knew before they would believe me. It was about 11 o'clock p.m. I explained to Colonel Harvey where and how the American army were encamped near Stoney Creek. He suggested a night attack on the enemy. After Colonel Harvey had a short interview with General Vincent, it was decided to start at once for Stoney Creek, and they commenced to hustle.

We got started about 11.30 p.m. Colonel Harvey asked me if I knew the way, and I said, "Yes, every inch of it." He gave me a corporal's sword and told me to take the lead. Sometimes I would get away ahead and go back to hurry them up. I told them it would be daylight before we got there if we did not hurry. Someone said that would be soon enough to be killed.

We got down the east side of the Red Hill Creek, near William Davis', when three sentries fired at us, and then ran over to the south side of the creek. Then we came on more carefully after that. I espied a sentry leaning against a tree. I told the man behind to shoot him, but Colonel Harvey said, "No, run him through!" and he was dispatched. The next sentry was at the church. He discharged his gun and demanded a pass. I commenced to give him the countersign and walked up to him. I grabbed his gun with one hand and put my sword to him with the other. His old gun had no load in it. He had shot the ramrod away.

Then we could see the camp fires; we cut across and got in Lewis' lane, when the order was given to "Fix flint! Fire!" and we fired three rounds and advanced about one hundred yards. Then we banged away again. There was a rush in our middle flank. Their south flank charged, then came orders for our flank to charge. This is where we lost most of our men. We got bunched right down under them. The centre rank captured two of their guns, then the general order was given to charge and we drove them back. We could hear them scampering. We were ordered to fire and we shot all our powder away. When it commenced to get daylight we could see the enemy running in all directions.

In the flat just across the creek near Lewis' Lane about five hundred American soldiers were encamped in advance of their artillery, which was situated on a hill

directly in front of the road that our troops must pass. The five hundred on our left were the first that were discovered excepting those that were taken prisoners in the church. Two thousand of their men were on the hill to the right and about one thousand on the hillside just east of the James Gage house. They were burning James Gage's fence rails for their camp fires.

Major Plenderleath, with thirty men of the 49th, and Major Ogilvie, with the 8th or King's Regiment, charged and captured four field pieces in very gallant style. Generals Chandler and Winder were captured near their cannon. Our General Vincent came in the rear of his army to Stoney Creek that night, and somehow got lost in the bushes and the dark foggy night. He was found in the morning after the battle, down near Van Wagner's. He had lost his hat. Seth White and George Bradshaw found him.

We lost about eighty killed and one hundred and forty wounded. Their loss was two hundred killed and two hundred and forty wounded. The settlers helped to scare the enemy by giving war-whoops from the top of the hill. After the battle was over we got William Gage's oxen and stoneboat and his son Peter, John Lee, John Yeager, I and several others buried the dead soldiers on a knoll near the road where the enemy had placed their guns and where the road then turned south towards the Gage house; the road then went south of the Gage house and south of the cemetery, also north of Red Hill past William Davis' house. William kept a hotel there at the time, and it was used as a hospital for some of the wounded soldiers after the battle was over. The old Dr. Case homestead, near Hamilton, was also used for the same purpose. John Brady kept hotel at Stoney Creek at the time of the war of 1813, and the Americans refreshed themselves and their horses at his expense and did not leave his premises until they had eaten and drunk all that they could find around his place.

Uncle Tom's North Star/1830

"Among all the singular and interesting records to which the institution of American slavery has given rise, we know of none more striking, more characteristic and instructive than that of Josiah Henson." This sentence comes from Harriet Beecher Stowe's foreword to the autobiography of Josiah Henson (1789-1883). The most famous of all fugitive slaves, Henson was born in Maryland and served as an overseer on a Kentucky plantation until 1830, when with his wife and four young children he was able to board "the underground railroad" and find freedom in Upper Canada. Henson became a farmer and a founder of the Dawn Institute, a co-operative settlement for former slaves and their families. He met Harriet Beecher Stowe in Boston in 1848 and she made some use of his character and experiences in her depiction of the central character in *Uncle Tom's Cabin* (1852), which must be one of the most influential books of all time. Henson is buried near the two-storey tulipwood house that is part of Uncle Tom's Cabin Museum, opened in 1948 in Dresden, Ontario. As Robin W. Winks noted in *The Blacks in Canada: A History* (1971): "Henson thus became the best known of all Negro Canadians, his narratives the most frequently used sources, his life the archetypical fugitive experience." Winks went on to caution Canadians and answer in the affirmative the following question: "If Uncle Tom came to Canada, could conditions need improving?" The three passages that follow come from *An Autobiography of the Rev. Josiah Henson ("Uncle Tom"),* edited by John Lobb and published in 1881.

During the bright and hopeful days I spent in Ohio, while away on my preaching tour, I had heard much of the course pursued by fugitives from slavery, and became acquainted with a number of benevolent men engaged in helping them on their way. Canada was often spoken of as the only sure refuge from pursuit, and that blessed land was now the desire of my longing heart. Infinite toils and perils lay between me and that haven of promise, enough to daunt the stoutest heart; but the fire behind me was too hot and fierce to let me pause to consider them. I knew the North Star — blessed be God for setting it in the heavens! Like the Star of Bethlehem, it announced where my salvation lay. Could I follow it through forest, and stream, and field, it would guide my feet in the way of hope. I thought of it as my God-given guide to the land of promise far away beneath its light. I knew that it had led thousands of my poor, hunted brethren to freedom and blessedness. I felt energy enough in my own breast to contend with privation and danger; and had I been a free, untrammelled man, knowing no tie of father or husband, and concerned for my own safety only, I would have felt all difficulties light in view of the hope that was set before me. But, alas! I had a wife and four dear children; how should I provide for them? Abandon them I could not; no! not even for the blessed boon of freedom. They, too, must go. They, too, must share with me the life of liberty.

*

The next evening we reached Buffalo, but it was too late to cross the river that night. "You see those trees," said the noble-hearted captain, next morning, pointing to a group in the distance; "they grow on free soil, and as soon as your feet touch that, you're a *mon.* I want to see you go and be a freeman. I'm poor myself, and have nothing to give you; I only sail the boat for wages; but I'll see you across. Here, Green," said he to a ferryman, "what will you take this man and his family over for — he's got no money?" "Three shillings." He then took a dollar out of

his pocket and gave it to me. Never shall I forget the spirit in which he spoke. He put his hand on my head and said, "Be a good fellow, won't you?" I felt streams of emotion running down in electric courses from head to foot. "Yes," said I; "I'll use my freedom well; I'll give my soul to God." He stood waving his hat as we pushed off for the opposite shore. God bless him! God bless him eternally! Amen!

It was the 28th of October, 1830, in the morning, when my feet first touched the Canada shore. I threw myself on the ground, rolled in the sand, seized handfuls of it and kissed them, and danced around, till, in the eyes of several who were present, I passed for a madman. "He's some crazy fellow," said a Colonel Warren, who happened to be there. "Oh no, master! don't you know? I'm free!" He burst into a shout of laughter. "Well, I never knew freedom make a man roll in the sand in such a fashion." Still I could not control myself. I hugged and kissed my wife and children, and, until the first exuberant burst of feeling was over, went on as before.

*

There was not much time to be lost, though, in frolic even, at this extraordinary moment. I was a stranger in a strange land, and had to look about me at once for refuge and resource. I found a lodging for the night, and the next morning set about exploring the interior for the means of support. I knew nothing about the country or the people, but kept my eyes and ears open, and made such inquiries as opportunity afforded. I heard, in the course of the day, of a Mr. Hibbard, who lived some six or seven miles off. He was a rich man, as riches were counted there, had a large farm, and several small tenements on it, which he was in the habit of letting to his labourers. To him I went immediately, though the character given him by his neighbours was not, by any means, unexceptionally good. But I thought he was not, probably, any worse than those I had been accustomed to serve, and that I could get along with him, if honest and faithful work would satisfy him. In the afternoon I found him, and soon struck a bargain with him for employment. I asked him if there was any house where he would let me live. He said, "Yes," and led the way to an old two-storey sort of shanty, into the lower storey of which the pigs had broken, and had apparently made it their resting-place for some time. Still, it was a house, and I forthwith expelled the pigs, and set about cleaning it for the occupancy of a better sort of tenants. With the aid of hoe and shovel, hot water and a mop, I got the floor into a tolerable condition by midnight, and only then did I rest from my labour. The next day I brought the rest of the Hensons, the only furniture I had, to *my house,* and though there was nothing there but bare walls and floors, we were all in a state of great delight, and my wife laughed and acknowledged that it was better than a log cabin with an earth-floor. I begged some straw of Mr.

Hibbard, and confining it by logs in the corners of the room, I made beds of it three feet thick, upon which we reposed luxuriously after our long fatigues.

Another trial awaited me which I had not anticipated. In consequence of the great exposures we had been through, my wife and all the children fell sick; and it was not without extreme peril that they escaped with their lives.

My employer soon found that my labour was of more value to him than that of those he was accustomed to hire; and as I consequently gained his favour, and his wife took quite a fancy to mine, we soon procured some of the comforts of life, while the necessaries of life, food and fuel, were abundant. I remained with Mr. Hibbard three years, sometimes working on shares, and sometimes for wages; and I managed in that time to procure some pigs, a cow, and a horse. Thus my condition gradually improved, and I felt that my toils and sacrifices for freedom had not been in vain. Nor were my labours for the improvement of myself and others, in more important things than food and clothing, without effect. It so happened that one of my Maryland friends arrived in this neighbourhood, and hearing of my being here, inquired if I ever preached now, and spread the reputation I had acquired elsewhere for my gifts in the pulpit. I had said nothing myself, and had not intended to say anything of my having ever officiated in that way. I went to meeting with others, when I had an opportunity, and enjoyed the quiet of the Sabbath when there was no assembly. I could not refuse to labour in this field, however, when afterwards desired to do so; and I was from this time frequently called upon, not by blacks alone, but by all classes in my vicinity — the comparatively educated, as well as the lamentably ignorant — to speak to them on their duty, responsibility, and immortality, on their obligations to themselves, their Saviour, and their Maker.

I am aware it must seem strange to many that a man so ignorant, unable to read, and having heard so little as I had of religion, natural or revealed, should be able to preach acceptably to persons who had enjoyed greater advantages than myself. I can explain it only by reference to our Saviour's comparison of the kingdom of heaven to a plant which may spring from a seed no bigger than a mustard-seed, and may yet reach such a size, that the birds of the air may take shelter therein. Religion is not so much knowledge as wisdom; and observation upon what passes without, and reflection upon what passes within a man's heart, will give him a larger growth in grace than is imagined by the devoted adherents of creeds, or the confident followers of Christ, who call Him "Lord, Lord," but do not the things which He says.

The "Cutting-out" of the *Caroline* / 1837

"Now, as the *Caroline* will live in history, it seems a duty on my part to give a faithful and authentic account of an event which has been much exaggerated and misrepresented," explained Andrew Drew (1792-1878), a retired naval officer who commanded the Provincial Marine during the Rebellion of 1837. He was in charge of the party that set fire to and "cut-out" the *Caroline* on the night of 29 December 1837. An American steamer, the *Caroline* was pressed into service by the Upper Canadian Rebels to transport men and supplies from the American shore of the Niagara River to the Rebel camp on Navy Island, above Niagara Falls, where William Lyon Mackenzie had established his provisional government following the failure of the uprising. This is Drew's own account of how he crossed to Schlosser's Landing, where the *Caroline* was moored, and set it on fire and sent it adrift to go flaming over the brink of the falls. Despite the description of "the splendid sight" in *A Narrative of the Capture and Destruction of the Steamer "Caroline"* (1864), there is some doubt as to whether more than the vessel's figurehead and planks were swept over the falls.

I directed the boats to move their oars as gently as possible, just enough to stem the current, and not to talk, or even whisper. Being able to expend half an hour here unseen was a great event for us, to allow it to become darker, as everything depended upon our being able to reach the vessel unseen. At last I judged it dark enough, and we dropped silently down upon our prey literally without moving an oar until we were close alongside of her. These were anxious moments for me, knowing how hazardous it is to climb a vessel's side and make good a footing upon the deck without being knocked on the head; however, in this, as in everything else, fortune favoured us. When within a boat's length of the vessel, one of the watch (who had apparently just awoke out of a sleep) cried out, "Boat, ahoy! boat, ahoy!" "Give us the countersign," I answered, in a low tone of voice. "Silence, silence! Don't make a noise, and I'll give you the countersign when we get on board." I then mounted the vessel's side, which I had some difficulty in doing for want of a ladder, and when fairly on deck I drew my sword, and found three men lounging over the starboard gangway unarmed, and quite unconcerned. I said to them, "Now I want this vessel, and you had better go ashore at once." She was laying alongside a wharf, to which she was secured. I waved my sword over their heads to make them go, and I do not think that until this moment they fairly understood their position. Then they moved leisurely over to the port-side, I thinking they were going on shore; but as they saw none of my party on the deck but myself they took up their fire-arms, which it appeared had been left on that side the deck, and the foremost man fired his loaded musket at me. Not more than a yard from him, how the ball missed me I do not know; but he was too close to take aim, and it passed me. I thought this an act of treachery, and that I need show him no mercy, so with the full swing of my arm I gave him a cut with my sword over the left temple, and he dropped at my feet. In another second one of the other men put a pistol close to my face and pulled the trigger; fortunately it flashed in the pan, or I should not have been here to have told the tale. Why I was so lenient with this man I do not know, for he deserved death at my hands as much as the other; but I merely gave him a sabre-cut on the inside of the right arm, which made him drop his pistol, and he was unarmed. The other man I disarmed, and drove them both over the side; but as they did not seem to move as fast as I thought they ought, I gave them about an inch or two of the point of my sword, which quickened their pace wonderfully.

All this did not appear to have taken up more than a minute of time, and we were in complete possession of the after-part of the vessel. Three of the boats boarded forward, where there was a good deal of firing going on, and, as the quarter-deck was clear, I mounted the paddle-box and gave orders for the firing to cease immediately, fearing from the darkness of the night we might take friends for foes; and Lieutenant MacCormick had already received a desperate wound.

The vessel was now entirely in our possession, and, to guard against an attack from the shore, I directed Lieutenant Elmsley to head a small party as an advanced guard, to warn us should an attack be meditated. We then roused everybody out of their beds and sent them on shore, a considerable number of persons having been sleeping on board. After this the vessel was set on fire in four different places, and soon began to burn. The next thing was to cast her off from the jetty, which at one time I feared we should have had great difficulty in doing, as she was made fast with chains under water, or rather under ice — for this was the middle of a Canadian winter, where water freezes to the thickness of a foot in a very short time; but a young gentleman of the name of Sullivan, understanding the difficulty, seized hold of an axe, jumped down upon the ice, and in a short time cleared the chain and set the vessel adrift.

This done, and the vessel in flames fore and aft, I ordered everyone to the boats, which became the more necessary as the enemy had opened a fire of musketry from the shore, and some shot came disagreeably near to me standing on the paddle-box. The order was soon obeyed, for it was also getting too hot to stand upon the deck. I did not give any particular orders to the officer of my own boat; but I intended to be the last person out of the vessel, and naturally thought they would wait for me, and, when just ready to embark, I saw a man coming up the fore hatchway. I went forward to ascertain whether it was likely anyone else was down below; but the man said

it was not possible, for it was so hot he could not have lived there another minute. I then went to get into my boat, when to my horror I found that every boat had left the vessel. I cannot describe my feelings at that moment, nor shall I ever forget the sensation that came over me: the vessel in flames and fast drifting down the stream. I looked around, and could just see one boat in the distance; another minute would have been fatal to me. I hailed her to come back, calling out as loud as I could that they had left me behind; fortunately, they heard me, and returned and took me and the man on board.

Having now accomplished our object, we had only to find our way safely back; and when we rounded the point of the island before named we saw a tremendous blazing fire on the Canadian shore, not only enough to guide us, but almost to light us on our way back. It was most welcome, for by this time it had become quite dark. Not caring about discovery now, and as little for shot from Navy Island, we kept much closer to it, and felt safe in so doing. We landed between two and three o'clock in the morning at the spot from whence we started, and found hosts of people to receive us with good hearty British cheers. Sir Allan Macnab was most particularly cordial in his welcome, and candidly acknowledged he never expected to see me again, but that our success had far exceeded his most sanguine expectations.

By this time the burning vessel was fast approaching the Canadian shore, and not far distant. Of all the marvels attending this novel expedition, the course which the steamer took of her own accord was the most wonderful. When free from the wharf at Fort Schlosser, her natural course would have been to follow the stream, which would have taken her along the American shore and over the American Falls; but she acted as if she was aware she had changed owners, and navigated herself right across the river, clearing the Rapids above Goat Island, and went as fairly over the centre of the British Falls of Niagara as if she had been placed there on purpose.

There were hundreds of people on the banks of the river to witness the splendid sight, for it was perfectly beautiful, and the descent took place within a quarter of an hour after our landing; and no human ingenuity could have accomplished what the vessel had so easily done for herself.

An Open Letter to the Chief Justice of Upper Canada/1838

This moving appeal, written in the form of an open letter addressed to John Beverley Robinson, the chief justice of Upper Canada, was composed by Elizabeth Lount and published in the *Pontiac Herald,* a Michigan newspaper, on 12 June 1838, two months after her husband Samuel Lount was hanged, alongside Peter Matthews, on 12

April 1838 for taking part in the Rebellion of 1837. She wrote on behalf of those Reformers who were in exile. Clemency was a long time in coming and an amnesty was not proclaimed until 1849. According to Mary Holmes in *New Frontiers*, Summer 1954, where the appeal was first published, after the death of her husband, Mrs. Lount "and her children left Canada and settled in the western United States, where she lived to a very old age. One source dates her death about 1883."

Pontiac, June 12, 1838

SIR:

Woman cannot redress her wrongs. Her feeble arm is powerless; even were justice to be reached with certainty through fatigues in the tented field, and liberty be given to an oppressed, enslaved and insulted people, 'tis not woman who should lead the way. It belongs to the "lion heart and eagle eye" of your sex, sir, to lead in war, to maintain a people's rights, to do or die on redressing their wrongs, to save their country from oppression and slavery. But to you, sir, Canada can never look for assistance. It has been said by an eminent author that every man has his price, and however unjust the remark is with regard to others, I conceive it well applies to yourself.

In this letter, intended as a partial exposé of the sufferings of myself and family, and of the execution for treason of my beloved husband, Samuel Lount, M.P., I would remark that my husband was born in the state of Pennsylvania, in the year 1791, and emigrated to Canada when about 23 years of age. He had taken the oath of allegiance, and had become an adopted citizen of the Province. He was a reformer and a loyal subject. He had become familiar with the constitution and the laws of Great Britain, and where they were regarded and justly administered it always gave him pleasure. During his lifetime he had frequently been requested by his fellow citizens to become a candidate for a seat in the Provincial Parliament, but refused repeatedly. At length, however, he was taken up and elected.

While in Parliament he became acquainted with the leading men of the country, and being a liberalist in his opinions, united his political fortunes with Doctor Rolph, Mr. Mackenzie, and other distinguished gentlemen, who beheld with regret the corruptions of the government. They saw a rich and fertile country, almost prostrate and ruined — a hopeful people possessed of the feelings and sympathies of men, trampled upon by the mercenary wretches, whose places in office gave them power. Year after year Canadian grievances became more alarming, until almost the entire population groaned for relief — groaned beneath the yoke of their bondage. This, sir, no one knows better than yourself. And while seated upon the judicial bench, enjoying one of the highest offices in Canada, you, together with others, conceived the noble thought of working a civil revolution in the Province, to

give liberty to a people whose chains you have, since the outbreak of that war, most diligently labored to rivet yet closer upon them. He whom you have been instrumental in consigning to the grave, and whose spirit is pure as the angels in heaven, testifies to your guilt — a guilt despicable and most horrid — as *friend, co-patriot, traitor* and *Judge!*

True it is that my dear husband, whom your laws have torn from me and from his helpless children, espoused sincerely the cause of reform. Had their plans succeeded, that reform would have been obtained — the Governor secured — and the Province freed without shedding of a drop of human blood. Had not the mistake been made for the rally, the arms of the Province would have been seized by the patriots, Toronto would have been taken by consent and Sir Francis held in their power to answer for his oppressions.

Those with whom my husband acted were moved by the impulses of noble and generous sympathies. They panted not for offices, for those they enjoyed — they thirsted not for blood, for Canadians were their brothers — they were determined to drive a Nero from his throne, to rid Canada of a tyrant, and to effect a civil revolution that would give happiness and prosperity to the country. Had they been successful, Canadians to the latest posterity would have blest them.

But, sir, all is not over yet. No government whose only acts are those of violence and cruelty, whose statute book is stained with the blood of innocent sufferers, and whose land is watered by the tears of widows and orphans, can long stand contiguous to a nation abounding in free institutions.

O Canada, my own country, from which I am now exiled by a party whose mercy is worse than death — I love thee still. Destruction has overtaken thy brightest ornaments, and the indignant feelings of thy sons burn their hearts, but they dare not give utterance to their thoughts. How many mothers have suffered, like me, the loss of a home and all that could make that home pleasant. This, however, could have been borne. They who love liberty, and prize their independence above all earthly things, regard not the loss of property. I do not write to excite your sympathy, for that I neither respect or covet. I write that Canada may know her children will not silently submit to the most egregious outrages upon private property, and even life itself.

Sir, it beggars description, and is beyond my competency to relate my sufferings while a subject of Canada. For the generous acts of a brave and noble hearted man I have seen his son taken before his mother's eyes, tied like a galley slave and driven to prison as a felon — aye, more, I have seen the innocent youth covered with wounds received from a drunken and brutal soldiery whose election it was to do the work of the officials. I have seen my husband's house pillaged, and his parlor made a soldier's camp, his property confiscated, and his heartbroken wife and six children cast upon the charity of the cold world. I have beheld the husband and father in prison, condemned to death without the least shadow of a crime proved against him. I ask in the name of my country, are acts like those to be tolerated by an English Government, or is there on this earth an Englishman who does not blush at the recital of such acts of cruelty?

Sir, the officers of the government of Canada, civil and military, are placed over the people without their consent. They form a combination too powerful for the prayers of an humble citizen to move. Be their acts however corrupt, the law is by themselves administered, and consequently they are beyond its reach; while if the private citizen offend he is neither safe in his property or person. If these things are so, I ask you, sir, how long will the people of Canada tamely submit? Will they not soon rise in their strength, as one man, and burst asunder the chains that bind them to the earth and revolutionize and disenthrall Canada from the grasp of tyrants?

Sir, savage nations respect my sex, and their female captives are treated with kindness. Your Governor and his Council, together with a majority of your party during the late difficulties neither respected private property nor harmless unoffending women. With him and his minions all were fit subjects upon whom to practise cruelty.

After my lamented husband had been convicted, I learned that Governor Arthur had visited the prison and it was hoped that mercy had called him thither. But there was no mercy in his obdurate heart — cruelty is the reigning demon of his passions. When Mr. Lount was arrested and carried bound to Toronto, I immediately repaired there, but was not allowed by the Governor to see him. He told me that my husband "looked well." This I afterwards found to be false as he had suffered much. Captain Fuller finally obtained a pass for me, and I was allowed to go with him and once more see my husband. I found him a shadow, pale and debilitated. Poor man! here I beheld him in prison, not that he had burned a city, for he had saved Toronto from flames — not that he had taken the lives of his enemies, for he was opposed to the shedding of blood. But he opposed himself to the oppressors of his countrymen — and for this was doomed to suffer death, which sentence was pronounced by Your Honor, and on which occasion, I am informed, you trifled with his feelings and acted the demon.

When I learned the result of the trial I was again permitted to see my husband. Learning that the Governor had been to see him, I was anxious to know the result of the interview. He told me "it would give me no satisfaction to know." I asked him if the Governor spoke kindly? He said "No, he spoke harsh and only added insult to injury." The day before my husband was executed, I, in company with a lady of Toronto, visited the Governor. On entering the room he requested me to sit down — but my errand was of importance. I told him I was the wife of Samuel Lount, and had come before him to plead for mercy. He appeared obstinate, and refused my petition. Thirty-five thousand of his subjects also asked him to interpose his power and save my husband from the sentence of the law. I then kneeled before him in behalf of my husband. With an air of disdain he told me "not to kneel to him, but to kneel to my God!" I replied that I was kneeling in prayer to the Almighty that he would soften his heart. I told him that my husband did not fear to die — that he was prepared for death, but it was his wife and children asking for his life to be spared. To this he sneeringly replied "that if he was prepared for death he might not be so well prepared at another time!" O monster that he was to rule a virtuous people. He said they did not condemn my husband because he was guilty — "I do think," said he, "if Rolph and Mackenzie were here mercy would be shown to them. Two lives were lost at Montgomery's and two must now suffer."

At another time he said "there were others concerned in the rebellion," and intimated that if my husband would expose them he might yet go clear; but my husband always said he would never expose others or bring them into difficulty — the cause they enlisted in was a good one, and before he would expose Mackenzie's Council he would himself be sacrificed.

Thus far neither prayer nor petitions could subdue the hard heart of the Governor, and I gave up my husband as lost to me and Canada. The sad morning came — the victim was led forth — and the endearing husband and father fell a martyr in the cause of Canadian reform. Though thousands had petitioned for his respite that his case might be laid before the Home Government, all was of no avail. Petitions moistened by virtuous tears, nor the humble supplications of an almost heartbroken wife at the feet of the Canadian Governor could touch his heart or move his compassion. Did the law of honor or of justice require this useless flow of blood then I could not censure him. Everything high and honorable, all that was generous and great in Canada, called upon Sir George Arthur to interpose his power and rescue the life of a citizen whom thirty-five thousand Canadians had petitioned to save. Call you this English humanity? Call you him a fit Governor to rule Canada?

Sir, could a tale of human suffering lead you to feel another's woe, I would relate a series of hardships brought upon me and my orphaned children by you, and others of the tory party in Canada, that would call the full grown tears to manly eyes.

Was it for fear of an enraged and insulted people that Governor Arthur refused a defenceless woman the corpse of her murdered husband? No, for that people had no arms to defend themselves with. Why then when upon my bended knee I begged the body of my husband, did he send me from his presence unsatisfied? The wrongs of Canada, and the blood of that innocent man continually preyed upon his mind, and he, like a coward and a tyrant, dared not let my husband's friends behold the iniquitous work he had done. He feared that, when they saw the manly corpses of Lount and Matthews, the generous sympathies of a noble people, who have been too long ruled by threats, might rise, and in retributive justice fall with tenfold force upon himself and those who were his chief advisers.

But, sir, this painful relation is sickening and heart-rending, and I shall close my letter to you that I may draw my mind from the horrible subject. Canada will do justice to his memory. Canadians cannot long remain in bondage. They will be free. The lion will give way, and a bold star will eventually ornament the Canadian standard sheet. Then will the name of Canadian martyrs be sung by poets and extolled by orators, while those who now give law to the bleeding people of Canada will be loathed or forgotten by the civilized world.

And now, by the cruelty of the government, I find myself a widow, driven from home and kindred and a stranger in a strange land. I shall close this letter by saying that my husband, just before his tragic death, said "that he freely forgave them (the tories) for their cruelty, and that he was prepared to meet his God in peace."

Elizabeth Lount

The Fathers of Confederation/1866

The concluding conference of the three held to decide the nature of the legislative union of the British North American provinces met in London, England. It was attended by sixteen delegates of the Province of Canada (today's Ontario and Quebec) and the provinces of Nova Scotia and New Brunswick, who met at the Westminster Palace Hotel on 4 December 1866 and for well over a month deliberated on the wording of the constitution inherited from the Charlottetown Conference and the Quebec Conference. It was at the London Conference, chaired by Sir John A. Macdonald, the future prime minister, that the name "Dominion of Canada" was chosen for the new country. The delegates worked so well together that the BNA Act, completed in January of 1867, was passed by the British Parliament on 8 May 1867, to take effect on 1 July, without a single dissenting vote. One of the principal participants at the London Conference was Hector-Louis Langevin (1826-1906), a cabinet minister in Sir John A.'s administration, later Sir Hector. Langevin was an able administrator, a lawyer, and a former journalist whose career was almost wrecked on a number of occasions by scandal and controversy. On the evening of the opening day of the conference, Langevin penned the following letter to his brother Jean in Quebec City. It paints a vivid picture of the attendant personalities. The passage appears in Andrée Désilets's biography *Hector-Louis Langevin: Un père de la Confédération canadienne* (1969). The translation is by an

unknown hand. For the record, I am including the full names of those Fathers of Confederation who attended the London Conference whom Langevin depicts, with the government each represents, herewith: John A. Macdonald (Canada), George-Étienne Cartier (Canada), Hector-Louis Langevin (Canada), Alexander Tilloch Galt (Canada), William P. Howland (Canada), William McDougall (Canada), Charles Tupper (Nova Scotia), Adams G. Archibald (Nova Scotia), Jonathan McCully (Nova Scotia), William A. Henry (Nova Scotia), John M. Johnson (New Brunswick), Samuel Leonard Tilley (New Brunswick), Charles Fisher (New Brunswick), R.D. Wilmot (New Brunswick), Peter Mitchell (New Brunswick). The one "whose name I have forgotten for the moment" is John W. Ritchie (Nova Scotia). Sixteen of the thirty-six Fathers of Confederation attended the London Conference. A list of all the Fathers may be found in the section "Some Facts, Some Figures."

Macdonald is a sharp fox. He is a very well informed man, ingratiating, clever and very popular. He is *the man* of the conference.

Cartier and I, we are Nos. 2 and 3.

Galt is a clever financier, but too headstrong and too yielding. He is not stable.

Howland is a second-class man, but prudent to excess, he is even timid; he is very slow to make up his mind.

McDougall is capable, he gathers information constantly, but he is frankly lazy, possessed with great ambition and little frankness.

Mr. Tupper, of Nova Scotia, is capable, but too incisive; he makes many bitter enemies for himself; he is ambitious and a gambler.

Mr. Archibald, also of Nova Scotia, is a good man of the law; calm, capable, respected and respectable and represents the opposition with McCully.

McCully is a headstrong man, but has a good heart; he is a good writer and a good advocate.

Henry, of Nova Scotia, is a man of six feet one inch, popular, ugly, has the gout, a good heart, loves pleasure and politics which he has followed for twenty-two years; he is a man of many gifts.

Johnson is a distinguished advocate, brusque, and pleasure-loving; he is said to be eloquent. He will play only a *moderate* part in the conference.

New Brunswick is represented by Tilley, a deft trimmer, clever and adroit. He is one of the most distinguished men of the Maritimes. He has four companions: Fisher, a good fellow who talks a good deal and has only a mediocre capacity; Wilmot, a mediocre man, more capable none the less than Fisher, but very ugly; Mitchell, Prime Minister by accident, a good fellow, wordy, with a swelled head, aware of his own importance. There is another whose name I have forgotten for the moment.

Letter on Our Literature / 1867

The author of the letter that follows is Octave Crémazie (1827-79) who has been called "the father of French-Canadian poetry." Crémazie's writings are of literary and historical interest for he wrote well and worked to instil in his readers a pride in the past accomplishments of the French race in North America. He would have contributed much more had not the bookshop he managed in Quebec City, which was a gathering place for professionals and writers, failed in 1862. Disillusioned, Crémazie left for France, where he changed his name, published no further poetry, and died. Although not inspired to write more poems, he felt compelled to set forth his views on the futility of cultural pursuits in Quebec in a series of letters which give readers today a clear view of Quebec culture prior to Confederation. The recipient of a number of these letters was Henri-Raymond Casgrain (1831-1904), a priest who because of ill health was able to devote much of his time to historical and literary pursuits. Casgrain had already edited two periodicals of cultural interest and had helped found the Mouvement Littéraire de Québec, which did much to stimulate national sentiments, when he received Crémazie's letter of 29 January 1867. Portions of the letter have been freshly translated by Ernest DeWald from Crémazie's *Oeuvres: II, Prose* (1976), edited by Odette Condemine.

This is the way it has to be for the Canadian writer. After renouncing without regrets his beautiful dreams of resounding glory, he must then consider himself amply rewarded for his efforts if he can instruct and charm his compatriots, if he can assist in maintaining the old French nationality on the young soil of America.

*

It must be said that when it comes to poetry in our country our taste is not very subtle. Rhyme *gloire* with *victoire* a few times, and then *dieux* with *glorieux*, and *France* with *expérance*, and mix these rhymes with a few sonorous words like *notre religion, notre patrie, notre langue, nos lois, le sang de nos pères*, simmer all these on the flames of patriotism, and serve them up hot. Everybody will say it is magnificent.

*

One does not base poems and certainly not legends on everyday events.

*

We have too many pagan authors forced down our throats when we are in college. Why do they only teach Greek mythology? The Scandinavian gods, and the dreaded Hindu trinity are, it seems to me, much more poetic and above all less immoral than this Olympus populated by thieves and harlots.

*

In my works I have never talked about myself, about my own joys and sorrows, and perhaps the little success I have achieved is due to this impersonal treatment.

*

I believe that literary taste in Canada would soon become more refined if readers could be nourished at those sources from which contemporary genius has found such inspiration. The novel, even as it aspires to be religious, is always a secondary genre. It is like the sugar word to coat pills, that is, it helps to get down a certain number of ideas, be they good or bad. But if ideas can endure the scrutiny of people of education and taste, why cover them with tinsel and affectation? It is in the nature of great artists to give their ideas a clarity and charm that enlightens a whole era, and genius does not need that gaudy outward appearance commonly produced by mediocre minds at any period of time. Do you not think that it would be better to withhold novels from your readers (I am talking about continental France because our own literature will by necessity impose the novel on you) and thus accustom them to accept ideas without the admixture of theatrics? I may be wrong, but I am convinced that the sooner we get rid of novels, even religious ones, the better it will be for everyone. But I realize that I am chattering on and on and that you are going to answer me: "What you are saying there is all well and good, but to take such a course in contemporary literature, one would first have to buy a number of works and then pay an editor to pick over the best of the harvest; but you know that we scarcely have enough money to pay a printer. Therefore please do not burden me with your lofty enterprises!"

Instead let us pretend that I did not say a word, and talk about other things.

The more I dwell on the future of Canadian literature the less I am inclined to believe that it will leave its mark in history. What is lacking in Canada is a language of its own. If we spoke Iroquois and Huron our literature would be alive. Unfortunately we speak and write the language of Bossuet and Racine, and really quite pitifully at that. Whatever we say and do, as far as literature is concerned we will always be a simple colony, and even if Canada were to become an independent nation and fly its flag among those of other nations, we would still remain simple literary colonials.

Look at Belgium where the same language is spoken. Is there a Belgian literature? Unable to compete with France in beauty of style, Canada could have found its place in the literature of the Old World if it had counted among its children a writer who, in advance of Fenimore Cooper, had conveyed to Europe the grandeur of our forests and the legendary exploits of our trappers and voyageurs. If today there were to be found amongst us a talent as powerful as the author of *The Last of the*

Mohicans, his work would not produce any reaction in Europe because he would have committed the unforgivable sin of being second, that is of being too late. I repeat: if we spoke Huron or Iroquois, the labour of our writers would attract the attention of the Old World. These sensitive and yet masculine languages, born in the American forest, would have the naive poetic quality that so delights the foreigner. People would swoon before a novel or a poem translated from the Iroquois but they would not take the trouble to read a text written in French by a colonial from Quebec or Montreal.

For twenty years translations of Russian, Scandinavian, and Romanian novels have been published annually in France. Suppose these same books were written in French by their authors; they would not even find fifty readers. Translations have this advantage: if a work does not live up to its reputation, the reader always has the consolation of telling himself that it must be magnificent in the original language.

But how important is it anyhow that works by Canadian authors are not destined to cross the Atlantic? Are we not a million Frenchmen on the banks of the St. Lawrence forgotten by the mother country? Is this not enough to encourage all those who hold a pen to know that this small population will grow and that it will always remember the name and memory of those who helped to preserve intact that most valuable of all treasures: the language of our ancestors?

An Interview with Louis Riel / 1885

Nicholas Flood Davin (1843-1901) was a brilliant and erratic journalist who donned clerical garb to gain admission to the Regina prison in which Louis Riel (1844-85), the leader of two Métis uprisings, was being held. There he conducted this remarkable interview — an exclusive — on the eve of Riel's execution. It was published in the Regina *Leader,* the newspaper Davin had founded, on the day of Riel's death, 16 November 1885. "Interview with Riel: His Parting Message to Mankind" is reprinted from *A Century of Reporting: The National Press Club Anthology* (1967), edited by Lucien Brault, Jean-Louis Gagnon, Wilfred Kesterton, D.C. McArthur, Frank Underhill, and Christopher Young.

The reporter of the Leader having received the orders of its proprietor to see Riel before his death and have an interview with him, waited on Captain Deane who was suffering from a severe accident, and who said he would be most happy to oblige the Leader, but he doubted if he could do so were he in charge, but his superior officer was here and he had no authority to act without his orders.

"Who is he?" asked the reporter.

"Col. Irvine."

Reporter: "I fear Col. Irvine is not friendly to the Leader, which, in the public interest has felt bound to criticize him. However I must not enlarge on that head with you. My marching orders were to 'See Riel,' who it was understood desired to see the reporter of the Leader with whom during his trial he frequently communicated." Believing it to be useless to wait on the gallant Col. I repaired to the Queen City of the plains and went to my lodgings where I had the "Materials" with which I had long been armed in preparation for this crisis. When first the officer in command of the Leader said "An interview must be had with Riel if you have to outwit the whole police force of the North-West," I revolved various schemes. I reflected what great things had been done by means of the fair sex, and I thought, suppose I enlist on my side the fair "Saphronica" and get her to put the "Come hither" on Irvine's susceptible fancy, and let her represent the Leader. Saphronica was willing. A young lady of undoubted charms and resolute will, she essayed the officer in command, and, strange to say, his sense of duty or his fears of the Government, were stronger than his gallantry and Saphronica utterly failed. To corrupt the guard? But on this the Editor in Chief frowned. At last I hit on a plan of my own. Accordingly on the evening of my refusal by Deane, I repaired to my lodgings, put on a *soutane,* armed my chin with a beard, put on a broad brimmed wide-awake, and stood M. Bienveillée, the *ancien confesseur* of the doomed Riel. I hung at my bosom an enormous silver crucifix and now, speaking French, presented myself at the Barracks.

The guard made no difficulty, and I believe they took me for Père André. Entered his cell, I looked round and saw that the policeman had moved away from the grill. I bent down, told Riel I was a Leader reporter in the guise of a *prêtre,* and had come to give his last message to the world. He held out his left hand and touching it with his right said: "Tick! Tick! Tick! I hear the telegraph, *ah, ça finira."* "Quick," I said, "have you anything to say? I have brought pencil and paper — Speak."

Riel: "When I first saw you on the trial I loved you.

"I wish to send messages to all. To Lemieux, Fitzpatrick, Greenshields. I do not forget them. They are entitled to my *reconnaissance.* Ah!" he cried, apostrophizing them, "You were right to plead insanity, for assuredly all those days in which I have badly observed the Commandments of God were passed in insanity *(passé dans la folie).* Every day in which I have neglected to prepare myself to die, was a day of mental alienation. I who believe in the power of the Catholic priests to forgive sins, I have much need to confess myself according as Jesus Christ has said, 'Whose sins you remit they are remitted.' "

Here he stopped and looked in his peculiar way and said:

"Death comes right to meet one. He does not conceal himself. I have only to look straight before me in order to see him clearly. I march to the end of my days. Formerly I saw him afar. (Or rather "her" for he spoke in French). It seems to me, however, that he walks no more slowly. He runs. He regards me. Alas! he precipitates himself upon me. My God!" he cried, "will he arrive before I am ready to present myself before you. O my God! Arrest it! By the grace, the influence, the power, the mercy divine of Jesus Christ. Conduct him in another direction in virtue of the prayers ineffable of Marie Immaculate. Separate me from death by the force the intercession of St. Joseph has the privilege to exercise upon your heart, O my God! Exempt me lovingly by Jesus, Marie and Joseph, from the violent and ignominious death of the gallows, to which I am condemned.

"Honorables Langevins, Caron, Chapleau, I want to send them a message, let them not be offended if a man condemned to death dares to address them. Whatever affairs hang on you don't forget, 'What shall it profit a man to gain the whole world and to lose his soul?'

"Honorable Messrs. Blake and Mackenzie, I want to send them a message. For fifteen years you have often named me, and you have made resound the echoes of your glorious province, in striking on my name as one strikes on a tocsin. I thank you for having contributed to give me some celebrity. Nobly take from me an advice nobody else will dare to give you. Prepare yourself each day to appear before your God.

"The Vice-Regal throne is surrounded with magnificence. He who occupies it is brilliant, and my eyes cannot fix on him without being blinded. Illustrious personages the qualities with which you are endowed are excellent. For that reason men say 'Your Excellency.' If the voice of a man condemned to death will not appear impertinent to you; it vibrates at the bottom of the cells of Regina to say to you: Excellencies! you also, do not fail to hold yourself in readiness for death, to make a good death, prepare yourself for death!

"Sir John Macdonald! I send you a message. I have not the honour to know you personally. Permit me nevertheless to address you a useful word. Having to prepare myself for death I give myself to meditation and prayer. Excuse me Sir John. Do not leave yourself be completely carried away by the glories of power. In the midst of your great and noble occupations take every day a few moments at least, for devotion and prayer and prepare yourself for death.

"Honorable and noble friends! Laurier, Laflamme, Lachlaelle, Desjardins, Taillon, Beaubien, Trudel, Prud'homme, I bid you adieu. I demand of God to send you the visit of Death only when you shall have long time desired it, and that you may join those who have transformed death into joy, into deliverance and triumph.

"Honorable Joseph Dubuc, Alphonse, C. Lariviere, Marc. A. Girard, Joseph Royal, Hon. John Norquay, Gov. Edgar Dewdney, Col. Irvine, Captain Deane, I would invite them to think how they would feel if they had only a week to live. Life here below is only the preparation for another. You are good Christians, think of eternity. Do not omit to prepare yourself for death.

"O my God! how is it death has become my sweetheart with the horror I feel towards her? And how can she seek me with an attention proportioned to the repugnance she inspires. O Death! the Son of God has triumphed over your terrors! O Death I would make of thee a good death!

"Elezear de la Grinodière! Roger Goulet, and you whom I regard as a relative, Irené Kérouak, prepare yourself for death. I pray God to prolong your days. Louis Schmidt, I ask of the good God to enable you to come to a happy old age. Meanwhile prepare yourself for death. Listen to the disinterested advice of one condemned. We have been placed in this world of pain only for the purpose of probation.

"And you whom I admire and respect, glorious Major General Middleton, you were kind to me, you treated me nobly. Pray see in my words the desire to be as little disagreeable as possible. Life has been smiling and fortunate for you, but alas! it will also finish for you. General, if there is one thing I have appreciated more than being your prisoner of war it is that you chose as my guard Captain Young, one of the most brave and polite officers of your army. Captain Young! Be not surprised that I send you a message through the Leader newspaper which I understand with *reconnaissance* has not called out against me, prepare yourself all your days. Death also disquiets himself about you. Do not sleep on watch. Be ever well on your guard.

"And you whom death spares and does not dare to approach and you whom I cannot forget, Ancien Preacher of Temperance, Chinuiquy, your hairs are white. God who has made them white slowly, wishes to make your heart white right away *(tout d'un coup)*. O be not angry at the disinterested voice of a man who has never spoken to you, to whom you have never given pain, unless it be in having abandoned regrettably the amiable religion of your fathers. The grace of Marie waits for you. Please come."

The prisoner paused, and in the pause one heard the skirr of the spurred heel of the Mounted Policeman and the neighing of one of the horses in the stables hard by, and I said: — "Is this all? Have you no more to say?"

"No more," replied Riel, "Father André has been here. He has told me there is no hope, that he has a letter from my good friend Bishop Grandin. I have made my confession. I have taken the Sacraments. I am prepared. But yet the Spirit tells me, told me last night I should yet rule a vast country, the North-West, with power derived direct from heaven, look!" and he pointed to the vein in his left arm, "there the spirit speaks, 'Riel will not die until he has accomplished his mission' and — "

He was about to make a speech and I left him with some sympathy and no little sadness. I felt that I had been in the presence of a man of genius *manqué*, of a man who, had he been gifted with judgment might have accomplished much; of one who, had he been destitute of cruelty might even command esteem, and as I rode over the bridge and looked down on the frosty creek, and cast my eye towards the Government House where happy people were perhaps at dinner at that hour, I said to myself, "Why did he murder Scott? Why did he seek to wake the bloody and nameless horrors of an Indian massacre? Why did he seek the blood of McKay and his fellow peacemakers? Unhappy man, there is nothing for it. You must die on Monday."

Here as I passed near the trail going north-west the well-known voice of a home-returning farmer saying "Good night" woke me from my reverie. In twenty minutes I was seated at dinner. I joined in the laugh and the joke, so passing are our most solemn impressions, so light the effect of actual tragedy. Our emotions are the penumbras of rapid transitions of circumstances and vanishing associations and like clouds we take the hue of the moment, and are shaped by the breeze that bloweth where it listeth.

Laurier and the Larger Canada/1886

To represent the spirit of French-Canadian liberalism and nationalism, I have chosen to reproduce translations of excerpts from two important addresses made by Sir Wilfrid Laurier (1841-1919), the seventh man and the first French Canadian to become prime minister of Canada. The first address, in which Sir Wilfrid defined political liberalism and stated his opposition to party division along linguistic and religious lines, was delivered by the Liberal member of Parliament at the Club Canadien, Montreal, 26 June 1877. The second address, with its magnificent image of the "uniting" of the Ottawa and the St. Lawrence, was delivered the year before he became leader of the Liberal party (and ten years before becoming prime minister) to the Toronto Young Men's Liberal Club, 10 December 1886. Both are reproduced from *Wilfrid Laurier on the Platform: 1871-1890* (1890), edited by Ulric Barthe. The slogan used as the section head above comes from a party rally of 1904.

But I address myself to all my fellow countrymen without distinction and I say to them:

We are a free and happy people; and we are so owing to the liberal institutions by which we are governed, institutions which we owe to the exertions of our forefathers and the wisdom of the mother country.

The policy of the Liberal party is to protect those institutions, to defend and spread them, and, under the sway of those institutions, to develop the country's latent resources. That is the policy of the Liberal party and it has no other.

Now, to properly estimate all the value of the institutions by which we are ruled to day, let us compare the present state of the country with what it was before they were granted to us.

Forty years ago the country was in a state of feverish commotion, a prey to an agitation which, a few months later, broke out in rebellion. The British crown was only maintained in the country by the force of powder and ball. And yet what were our predecessors seeking? They were asking for nothing more than the institutions which we have at present; those institutions were granted to us and loyally applied; and see the result; the British flag floats over the old citadel of Quebec; it floats to-night over our heads, without a single English soldier in the country to defend it, its sole defence resting in the gratitude, which we owe it for our freedom and the security which we have found under its folds.

Where is the Canadian who, comparing his country with even the freest countries, would not feel proud of the institutions which protect him?

Where is the Canadian who, passing through the streets of this old city and reaching the monument raised a few steps from here to the memory of the two brave men, who died on the same field of battle while contending for empire in Canada, would not feel proud of his country?

In what other country, under the sun, can you find a similar monument reared to the memory of the conquered as well as of the conqueror? In what other country, under the sun, will you find the names of the conquered and the conqueror equally honored and occupying the same place in the respect of the population?

Gentlemen, when, in that last battle which is recalled by the Wolfe and Montcalm monument the iron hail was spreading death in the ranks of the French army; when the old heroes, whom victory had so often accompanied, saw at last victory snatched from them; when, stretched on the ground with their life-blood fast ebbing away, they saw, as the result of their defeat, Quebec in the hands of the enemy and the country forever lost; no doubt, their last thought was of their children, whom they were leaving without protection and without defence; no doubt, they pictured them as persecuted, enslaved, and humiliated, and then, it is reasonable to believe, they drew their last breath with a cry of despair. But, if, on the other hand, Heaven had lifted the veil of the future from their dying eyes and enabled them for an instant, before these closed forever, to pierce what was hidden from their sight; if they could have seen their children free and happy, marching proudly in all spheres of society; if they could have seen, in the old cathedral, the seat of honor of the French governors occupied by a French governor; if they could have seen the church steeples rising in every valley from the shores of Gaspé to the prairies of the Red River; if they could have seen this old flag, which recalls the finest of their victories, carried triumphantly in all our public ceremonies; in fine, if they could have seen our free institutions, is it not permissible to think that their last breath would have been exhaled in a murmur of gratitude to Heaven and that they would have died consoled?

If the shades of these heroes still hover over this old city, for which they laid down their lives; if their shades hover to-night over the hall in which we are now assembled, it is free for us, Liberals, to think — at least we cherish the fond illusion, — that their sympathies are all with us.

*

You see, gentlemen, this is the extent of my imputation. I fully admit that the English language is bound to be the language of this country, and no man in his senses will deny it. For I simply confine myself to say that we are the French race and have certain duties, and have to fulfil those duties and nothing more. Certainly there is nothing in this to which any Canadian can take exception. I will say this, that we are Canadians. Below the island of Montreal the water that comes from the north from Ottawa unites with the waters that come from the western lakes, but uniting they do not mix. There they run parallel, separate, distinguishable, and yet are one stream, flowing within the same banks, the mighty St. Lawrence, and rolling on toward the sea bearing the commerce of a nation upon its bosom — a perfect image of our nation. We may not assimilate, we may not blend, but for all that we are the component parts of the same country. We may be French in our origin — and I do not deny my origin — I admit that I pride myself on it. We may be English, or Scotch or whatever it may be, but we are Canadians; one in aim and purpose; and not only Canadians, but we are also members of the same British Empire. This fact, that we are all Canadians, one in our objects, members of the British Empire, proud of being British subjects and Canadian, is evidence that we can keep pride of race without any detriment to the nation. As Canadians, we have feelings in common with each other that are not shared by our fellow-countrymen on the other side of the water. As Canadians, we are affected by local and national considerations, which bind us together and so we are led to look back to the land of our ancestors and feel, with all that, to be no less good Canadians. These are the feelings of the race to which I belong, and on this question I am true to my race, I am true to Canada. I am true to England, and last, and for this, I have often been reproached with being a traitor. I am above all true to the cause of liberty and justice.

Literature in Canada / 1899

The author of the amusing excerpt that follows, Robert Barr (1850-1912), was a Scottish-born, Ontario-educated journalist and novelist, who at the age of thirty-one, wishing to make a name for himself in the Anglo-American literary world, settled permanently in England. Barr returned to Canada for the occasional visit ("Toronto will recognize the successful Canadian writer when he comes back from New York or London, and will give him a dinner when he doesn't need it"), contributing the occasional article on our philistinism ("The bold truth is that Canada has the money, but would rather spend it on whisky than on books"). The excerpt here comes from "Literature in Canada: Part Two," *Canadian Magazine,* December 1899. Although Barr does not recall letter-perfect Robert Southey's once-popular poem, "The Cataract of Lodore," what he has to say about Canadians knowing little of themselves is dead on. The entire article has been reprinted in a new edition of Barr's novel, *The Measure of the Rule* (1906), edited by Louis K. MacKendrick in 1973.

As a boy I worked my way from Detroit on a schooner to the Welland Canal. The schooner was the *Olive Branch,* and I believe her bones now lie exposed to the winds on the shore near Toronto. My objective point was the Niagara Falls, and as soon as I got off the schooner I tramped from the canal to the cataract, one hot, dusty summer's day. I sat and looked at the Falls, but was bitterly disappointed with them. No reality can ever equal the expectation of a boy's lurid fancy. However, I consoled myself by saying, "Never mind, some day I shall have money enough to go to England and see the Falls of Ladore." In the third, or fourth, or the fifth book, which was then used in all schools throughout Canada, Southey's poem, the "Falls of Ladore," was given:

Recoiling, turmoiling and toiling and boiling,
And steaming, and beaming, and gleaming, and
    streaming,
And dashing, and flashing, and splashing, and
    clashing.
All at once and all o'er, with a mighty uproar,
And this way the water comes down at Ladore!

Naturally I thought such a cataract must be the greatest downpour in the world; and sure enough, neither money nor opportunity being lacking, I had a chance of viewing the wonder of nature which inspired Southey's muse. I landed one summer evening at a lakeside town two miles from Ladore. My impatience would not admit of my waiting till daylight, so I started on foot along the beautiful well-made road which skirts the lake, then almost as light as day under a full harvest moon. After I had tramped about two miles I began to fear I had lost my way, for pausing every now and then, I could hear no sound of water, so I sat down on the rocks by the wayside until some belated passerby should happen along and give me more definite direction. At last a countryman came slowly down the road and I hailed him.

"Can you tell me where the Falls of Ladore are?" I asked. The man paused in astonishment.

"Why sir," he said finally, "you're a-sittin' in 'em."

The fact was the falls had gone temporarily out of commission because of the dryness of the summer. Now, however picturesque the surroundings of a cataract may be, I maintain that a little water is necessary as well, and yet, thanks to our Canadian school books, I had waved Niagara contemptuously aside for this heap of dusty stones!

Canada always underestimates her own. . . .

Constable Pedley's Patrol / 1904-5

In the days when the RCMP was known as the Royal North-West Mounted Police, there occurred numerous deeds of endurance and daring little known at the time and barely better known in the decades to follow. One such deed was the extraordinary patrol of Constable Pedley, who was charged with accompanying a mental patient from Fort Chipewyan to Fort Saskatchewan during the winter of 1904-5. Albert Pedley (1878-1959), an English-born farmer in Manitoba who joined the Force in Regina in 1900, conveyed his prisoner, a crazed missionary, by dogteam, over four hundred miles of snow across northern Alberta. Pedley was credited with saving the missionary's life, but that was not the end of it. On the exhausting trek back, Pedley himself lapsed into madness and had to be hospitalized in Brandon, Manitoba. Happily, he completely recovered, returned to active duty, rose to sergeant, and retired after twenty-four years of service. He died in Salisbury, England, at the age of eighty-one. His son also served with the Force. In 1952, Hollywood produced a film, *The Wild North,* reportedly based on the patrol, but it was false to the details and spirit of the endeavour. The account that follows, partly in Pedley's own words, is from the *Annual Report of 1905,* Sessional Paper No. 28, prepared by Aylesworth Bowen Perry, commissioner of the Force. Further details appear in *RCMP Quarterly,* October 1959. It is interesting to note that while constables were dying of exposure in western Canada, government officials in Quebec City were planning the festivities that would mark three hundred years of Quebec's history: the Tercentenary of Quebec in 1908, the subject of the next document.

Constable A. Pedley, stationed at Fort Chipewyan, was detailed to escort an unfortunate lunatic from that place to Fort Saskatchewan. He reports as follows: —

"I left Chipewyan in charge of the lunatic on December 17, 1904, with the interpreter and two dog trains. After travelling for five days through slush and water up to our knees, we arrived at Fort McKay on December 22.

"Owing to the extreme cold, the prisoner's feet were frost bitten. I did all I could to relieve him, and purchased some large moccasins to allow more wrappings for his feet.

"I travelled without accident until the 27th, reaching Big Weechume lake. Here I had to lay off a day to procure a guide, as there was no trail.

"I arrived at Lac La Biche on the 31st, and secured a team of horses to carry me to Fort Saskatchewan. I arrived on January 7, 1905, and handed over my prisoner.

"During the earlier part of the trip the prisoner was very weak and refused to eat, but during the latter part of the trip he developed a good appetite and got stronger."

The unfortunate man was transferred to a Calgary guard room. Assistant Surgeon Rouleau reports that it was a remarkable case.

"He was badly frozen about his feet, and the exposure to the cold had caused paralysis of the tongue for several days. Every care and attention was given him at the hospital (to which he was transferred), with the result that he was discharged on February 23 with the loss only of the first joint of a big toe. His mind and speech were as good as ever. His life was saved."

Constable Pedley commenced his return trip to Fort Chipewyan. When he left Fort Saskatchewan he was apparently in good health, but at Lac La Biche he went violently insane as a result of the hardships of his trip, and his anxiety for the safety of his charge. He was brought back to Fort Saskatchewan and then transferred to Brandon Asylum. I am glad to say that after spending six months there he recovered his mind and returned to headquarters. He was granted three months' leave, and is now at duty as well as ever.

In spite of all, he has recently re-engaged for a further term of service.

The Tercentenary of Quebec / 1908

"The Quebec Tercentenary was the greatest work of art ever conceived, prepared and carried out in Canada. It was the flower of the national life brought to perfection by the skill of many minds, exactly at the propitious moment." So wrote Sir Arthur G. Doughty, the Dominion Archivist, of the flurry of festivities that took place in Quebec City between 19 July and 31 July 1908, to mark the passing of three centuries from the founding of Quebec by Samuel de Champlain. There were street arches, fêtes, historical pageants, parades, war vessels, military drills, bands, banquets, and the inevitable speeches. By general acclaim, among the best of the speeches was the address delivered by Adélard Turgeon (1863-1930) at the foot of the Champlain Monument, Dufferin Gate, on 23 July, in the presence of the Prince of Wales, the future George V. A former Quebec cabinet minister and a member of the National Battlefields Commission, Turgeon was an orator of note and spoke in the two official languages of the country, moved by a spirited patriotism and a love of effect no longer fashionable, if indeed acceptable. As Frank Carrel explained in *The Quebec Tercentenary Commemorative History* (1908), "The last speaker, Hon. Adélard Turgeon, speaking on behalf of Canada, delivered a speech redounding with beautiful rhetorical phrases describing the grandeur of the Dominion." Turgeon was rewarded for his eloquence. The president of the French Republic conferred on him a knighthood of the Legion of Honour, and the Prince of Wales then and there raised him as Commander of the Royal Victorian Order.

May it please Your Royal Highness, Ladies and Gentlemen: —

This monument, this rock, this grand river, this incomparable panorama of Beaupré, unfolding its succession of beautiful hill-sides, this island resting on the surface of the water like a basket of verdure, those heights of Lévis, whose very name rings like a clarion blast, these plains, these fields and moats — the scenes and witnesses of century-old struggles for the supremacy of a world — all this sublime landscape charm, appeals to our imagination to give it a soul and recalls a heroic age of noble dreams and valiant deeds.

What hour, what place, could be more solemn and more propitious for evoking the memory of him whom the voice of history and the gratitude of peoples have honored with the two-fold title of founder of Quebec and of the Canadian nation. And — as if the setting back of the hand of Time and majestic decorations were not sufficient for such an apotheosis — through concerted kindness for which we are indebted to the generous initiative of our well-beloved Sovereign, the three countries that have in turn, and at times concurrently, mingled in our national life, bring him the tribute of their respect and admiration. The spectacle of three nations assembled at the foot of this monument, animated with the same spirit of peace, of harmony and civilization, on the very soil where in days of old they strove to decide their destinies by the sword on blood-stained battlefields, is surely unique in the annals of the human race.

The presence of the Heir-Apparent to the Throne imparts a special significance to the participation of the metropolis which we cannot misinterpret. The high consideration enjoyed by our country, and the important place it occupies among the aggregation of peoples that make up the British Empire, could not have been better demonstrated. Your Royal Highness will permit me here, on behalf of Canada, to tender the respectful tribute of our devotedness and loyalty to the person of our Sovereign and to the institutions whereof he is the incarnation. And among all Canadians whose voices swell the concert of acclamations that welcomes you, none are more enthu-

siastic or more sincere than those of the descendants of the companions and fellow laborers of Samuel de Champlain.

Our thanks are also due to the great Republic, our neighbor, which shares in the glory of the founder of Quebec, since the field of his action extended beyond our frontiers, and since, with his immediate successors, he left on the North American continent, from East to West, from South to North, from Newfoundland to the Rocky Mountains, from Hudson's Bay to the Gulf of Mexico, an imprint that political revolutions have been powerless to efface. Thus, at the head of all the great lakes, at the bends of all the rivers, and at the strategic points of the valleys, one can see at once, by their French names, that our distinguished ancestors were once there.

As to France, she could not help being here. Without her this memorial celebration would have been somewhat incomplete, as when in family gatherings an empty chair tells of mourning for one who has gone away. It was right that she should once more bend over the cradle of the colony which for a century and a half lived its life as a scion of France, watered by the purest of her blood and wherein, despite political storms, her language, her traditions, her mode of thought, all the flowers of her national originality still flourish.

The glory of France lies in the fact that, through Cartier and Champlain, she stands at the head of those captains, discoverers and missionaries who — roaming under every latitude and penetrating into the remotest solitudes of the North and West, into the forests full of mystery and dread legends — were the pioneers of civilization and Christianity, and left on their surroundings everywhere the impression of the manners, customs, tastes and ideas of their native land. Under whatever ethnical name they reveal themselves, those brilliant flashes have not been lost to the Canadian nation, and the first rays of our history still warm and vivify our national body. Why then should we not love France, when the purest French blood flows in our veins? We love her ardently, disinterestedly, for no political "arrière-pensées" mingles with our love. We love her naturally and without effort because she was the cradle of our infancy, the land of our fathers, "imagines majorum," and because a whole world of memories, of traditions, of struggles, of glories and of mourning, links us to the past.

But, how can such affection be reconciled with our loyalty and profound attachment to the British Isles? Thanks be to God, the hour of tentative effort and experiment has passed and the problem has long since been solved. It has been solved by the sound political sense of our statesmen, by the broadmindedness of our English-speaking fellow countrymen, by the clearsightedness and liberality of the metropolis and its representatives. The fact has been realized that the preservation of the French element and language is not a source of danger, but a pledge of greatness, of progress, and also of security; that the Canadian Confederation is like the beehive whereof Marcus Aurelius said that what is good for the bee benefits the whole hive; that national dualism, according to Lord Dufferin's happy expression, is not an obstacle to the development of a young nation that has everything to gain from the preservation of the literary and social inheritance it has received from the two greatest peoples of Europe. Such a conception is a true one, for what is a nation? Does "nation" mean but one language? The modern nation is made up of divers elements. We have but to look at England, France, Switzerland and Belgium. Each of those countries has been a vast crucible wherein its constituent elements have become fused under the action of time and ambient influences. There is something above language, and that is: will, moral unity of mind, harmony of views, possession of the same ideal aspirations, devotedness to the same works of progress. Each element, each ethnical group, can develop itself solely by developing its natural gifts and its own qualities. Seek not to separate it from its past, to give it another soul as it were, because then you will have naught but uprooted trees, according to a justly celebrated expression.

Animated with that spirit, Canada pursues her way towards the highest destinies. She has barely emerged from the mists of the unknown, and already the older civilization, like the Wise Men in days of yore, are asking who is that child born in the West, whose name fills the world? Westward the star of empire holds its way. The Mediterranean was long the centre of commercial and political activity; then the discoveries of the 15th and 16th centuries gave the preponderance to the Atlantic. In our time the greatest human currents are changing their course, and some day the Pacific Ocean will infallibly play the most important role in the general life of the human race. Cast an eye on the map and tell me if Canada does not occupy a privileged position? The dream of Champlain and of Jacques Cartier is realized. Midway, and by the shortest route between Europe and Asia, our country is the true "road to Cathay," the true road to China, which discoverers sought and which was their fixed idea by day, their dream at night.

O Canada! land of valor and of beauty, I would that my voice were as far-reaching as Roland's magic horn to carry the accents of my love and pride into the homes of all! Land that thrills with life, with its lakes and springs, its rivers fertilizing the plains or mirroring the trees of the great forests on their banks! Land rocked to sleep by the melody of torrents and the songs of streams, irridescent with the powdery spray of cascades, watered by the St. Lawrence, "of all famous rivers, the only one unchangeably pure" (Reclus). Land invigorated by our winters that breathe powerful energy and gaiety over fields bespangled with sparkling crystals, sheltered by splendid mountain tops, and rich in the glowing health of its plains! Land wherein memories sleep and hopes are at rest! Land redolent with the poetry of fields, stars and souls! While

still in the bloom of thy virgin energies, well might thine immortal founder utter in admiration that exclamation never yet surpassed and that we repeat to-day: "It may be said that the country of New France is a new world, and not a kingdom, beautiful in every perfection." (Champlain.)

Of that land, we love not only its natural beauty, but also its moral features, the complexity of its soul, diversity of its races mingling their mutual virtues in a permanent entente-cordiale, love of civil and political liberty, force of tradition, poetry of effort, chivalrous generosity, thirst for justice and for the ideal. We love it, in a word, because it is our country, that so well expresses all the sweetness of one's fatherland.

A Magyar's Prairie Home/1910

"The history of the West is a chronicle of voyages, a ceaseless ebb and flow from east to west and west to east of human beings in search of fur, buffalo, land, wealth, salvation. The quest never ends." So wrote Heather Robertson of the settlement of western Canada. The quest did end for one nameless Hungarian family whose fate so haunted the memory of one ten-year-old farmer's son that sixty-six years later, and a farmer himself, that son recalled the fate of the family. The Hungarians, like hundreds of thousands of other East and West Europeans, were attracted by the cheapest land in the world and took part in one of the greatest migrations in history. What happened to this one Hungarian family and their linen of "the very purest white" will never be known. The memory was collected by Barry Broadfoot (b. 1926) who calls himself "a chronicler, a gatherer of stories, a collector of reminiscences — before it is too late." "Two Pumpkins for the Hungarians" originally appeared in his oral history, *The Pioneer Years, 1895-1914: Memories of Settlers who Opened the West* (1976).

These are the stories I tell my grandchildren. You never find them in the history books and I think they should know.

Once when I was 10 my father decided I would move into town, Whitewood, to be with his brother because he had plans for making a doctor of me. He nearly succeeded, but that's another story. Anyway, he wanted me to board in town where he felt I'd get a better education.

It was 50 miles and halfway along the horse went lame and as we had to stop somewhere, Dad pulled in to this farmyard. It was, believe it or not, a Magyar's home. Imagine, a Hungarian and his family on the bald prairie, and he wasn't doing so well. I always associate Hungarians with riches, wealth, big houses, dashing horses, bright and snappy uniforms, and waxed mustaches. Too many books. This fellow wasn't doing so well but he invited us in. The usual thing. Poplar logs, a chimney made of mud and prairie rocks. Saskatchewan style or Saskapoosh plaster, as we called it. But inside, let me tell you it was another world. This was the world he came from.

There were carpets on the floor. There were tapestries on the log walls. There were lamps, the kind that are so thin that you can see through but it is still china. Translucent would be the word. And bookcases made of planed logs and filled with books, sets of books. All leather bound. Oiled and dusted, and you can see that those books were read. A big table of oak and six chairs. You would have thought the inside of that shack was a castle. At my age it made a fantastic impression. I'm 76 now and I've seen a lot and did a lot, but I can't remember anything that has impressed me quite as much.

Here was a family who had spent a lot of money bringing some of their best things out from the Old Country and they were living like paupers. Oh, I guess they could have sold some of these lovely things, but there are people and then there are people and the old ways. The old things were important to them.

The husband spoke fair English. Not good. He and Dad stabled the horse and I looked at his two kids and they looked at me but that was as far as it went. It was suppertime and so we were asked to stay. Sowbelly. Have you ever eaten sowbelly? Two inches of greasy fat and a sliver of meat. Boiled. Boiled potatoes. The man said they came from their garden. Sowbelly and boiled potatoes, four people's share divided among six of us, and Dad and I were so hungry we could have eaten the arse off a skunk. And the table. Linen. The very purest white. China, straight from the Austro-Hungarian Empire's greatest days. Who was it? Yes, fit for the Emperor Ferdinand. And silver cutlery. But sowbelly so bad it practically made you gag and potatoes. Okay, potatoes were fine. It's the Hollywood movie business maybe but I think it might have been reasonable to expect a string quartet to be playing in the background, over in the corner where there was a heavy drapery. Behind their bed.

How did we know they were Hungarians? Oh, the man told us. He was proud of his being Hungarian. Magyar, he called himself. Proud as a peacock and next morning Dad, I could see, was thinking, "Now how much can I pay this fellow so his proudness won't tear my head off?" It was ticklish, I know, but finally he figured cash money wasn't the thing. Payment in kind. He went to the wagon and brought in two huge pumpkins that he had brought along for my uncle in town. He put them on the stoop outside the door and he didn't say anything. Then he brought out a sack with five pounds of pork sausage in it that my mother had made. That was for my uncle too. I half expected him to go off the deep end and bring out the crocked butter and eggs that my mother had given him to swap at the Whitewood store, but he didn't.

He shook hands and I shook hands with the boy and the girl and then we got up on the wagon seat and Dad said, "Hrrrup, hup!" and away we went. Down the road Dad said, "Feel sorry for that chap. He can't last."

When my uncle drove me home for the Christmas holidays, I used part of my allowance to buy a big bag of hard candy for the man's two kids. I was going to get my uncle to pull off the road and I'd give it to them. When we got close I could see the snow drifted up over the steps and there was a place where a wolf or some coyotes had peed on the corner by the door and I knew I was too late. The family had gone, with all their nice furniture and white tablecloth.

For Valour (I)/1916

It is barely possible to comprehend the magnitude of suffering and slaughter occasioned by the Great War. Of the 626,636 Canadian officers and men from all services who fought in the First World War, 59,769 lost their lives. According to observers, these men fought with a special "dash," and it is not surprising that many were singled out to receive the Victoria Cross, the Commonwealth's highest decoration. Of the many brave men who were awarded the Victoria Cross "For Valour" during the First World War, I find particularly moving the citation and description that accompanied the posthumous award to Piper Richardson. The details appear in Volume VI of *Canada in the Great World War* (1921) and *Valiant Men: Canada's Victoria Cross and George Cross Winners* (1973), edited by John Swettenham.

PRIVATE (Piper) JAMES RICHARDSON

BORN: Bellshill, Lanark, Scotland, November 25th, 1895
Unit: 16th Battalion, Canadian Expeditionary Force
DIED: Regina Trench, The Somme, France, October 8, 1916. V.C.: Awarded Posthumously

For most conspicuous bravery and devotion to duty when, prior to attack, he obtained permission from his commanding officer to play his company "over the top." As the company reached the objective, it was held up by very strong wire, and came under intense fire, which caused heavy casualties and demoralized the formation for the moment. Realizing the situation, Piper Richardson strode up and down outside the wire, playing his pipes with the greatest coolness. The effect was instantaneous. Inspired by his splendid example, the company rushed the wire with such fury and determination that the obstacle was overcome and the position captured. Later, after participating in bombing operations, he was detailed to take back a wounded comrade and prisoners. After proceeding about two hundred yards, Piper Richardson remembered that he had left his pipes behind. Although strongly urged not to do so, he insisted on returning to recover his pipes. He has never been seen since, and death has been presumed accordingly, owing to lapse of time.

*

The situation on the centre and left of the Battalion front, where the wire was totally uncut, at the time Richardson started to play was desperately critical. Not a 16th man had got over the wire. . . . It seemed as if the attacking troops to a man would become casualties.

Richardson, at this moment, took the lead and according to the evidence of different men, played up and down in front of the wire for fully ten minutes.

Piper Richardson was only eighteen years old. He was not originally detailed for the attack. He asked to be paraded before the Commanding Officer; and there pleaded so earnestly to be allowed to go into action, that Colonel Leckie finally granted him his wish.

[A Company Sergeant-Major reported:] Piper Jimmy Richardson came over to me at this moment and asked if he could help, but I told him our Company Commander was gone. Things looked very bad and then it was that the piper asked if he could play his pipes — "Wull I gie them wund [wind]?" was what he said. I told him to go ahead and as soon as he got them going I got what men I could together, we got through the wire.

Our Northern Heritage/1926

Speeches and addresses in their published form seldom give one a sense of the occasion of their delivery. In striking contrast is the address I have included here. "Our Northern Heritage" is the speech delivered by Captain Joseph-Elzéar Bernier (1852-1934) before the Empire Club of Canada, Toronto, 7 October 1926. The talk, in its present form, accomplishes three things. It introduces the reader to the distinguished speaker who explored the Arctic region and claimed the Arctic Archipelago for Canada on 1 July 1909. It presents the north as a vast land of opportunity which requires of us all our determination and common sense. And it documents an institution popular in this country, the businessmen's luncheon-club address, in this instance one that the speaker has illustrated with a "slide show." The address is reprinted from *Empire Club of Canada: Addresses Delivered to the Members during the Year 1926* (1927).

COL. ALEXANDER FRASER, Vice-President of the Club, introduced the Speaker, who illustrated his talk with lantern slides.

CAPTAIN BERNIER

Gentlemen, I do not come before you as a representative of the Government, but as a member of the Government Service for 22 years, during which I have taken possession of all the Arctic Islands that belonged to England, some of them having been surveyed by Franklin, Horne, Maclure, McClintock and many others. When I spoke here some 17 or 20 years ago I was greatly assisted by firms like Christie, Brown & Co., who gave us biscuits that were cached in the north, and they kept alive other explorers who found them 17 years afterwards. The Maclaren Cheese Company also furnished us with food supplies, and Mason & Risch gave us a piano to help our enjoyment during the long dark nights in the north. To all these people I tender our most sincere thanks.

It would be impossible for me to give anything like a comprehensive view of such an immense subject, but I will endeavor to touch the high spots briefly as the pictures are shown.

When I was two years old I went with my father who had shipped a cargo of naval goods for the Crimean war. We went up the Bosphorus, and they bombarded Sebastopol, when we were ordered to go back to Malta to discharge our cargo. After sailing for five more years I went to school, and after leaving school at 12 years of age I shipped as a boy on my father's vessel, and I did my own work and did not trust to other people, and in three years I was a master, and my father told me I could go. Since then I have commanded a ship almost continuously, and have made in the neighborhood of 260 voyages in all parts of the world. I am now 75 years old, but am still going strong. I pity those who have nothing to do. I am now preparing for another voyage, which will be a private commercial venture. My pictures to-day will show you the amount of energy I have spent in conquering all those islands in the north, assisted with the certain knowledge that I got from others. No credit is due to me, more than that I followed the eminent explorers whose records I found, which are our titles. What they said was true.

Here you see me in my study; while Governor of Quebec Jail for four years I studied in this quiet spot. Here I made charts, and worked constantly at the problems connected with the North. I learned by experience that if you work with Nature you are bound to succeed; otherwise you are sure to fail.

In order to navigate the north, the first requisite is a good ship. The Canadian Government bought this ship, the *Arctic,* and I made 12 trips to the north with her. With a good ship and proper men, and working in accordance with Nature, you can succeed; there is no other way. In regard to the ice in Northern waters, it is the same as in the Atlantic and has to be managed in the same way. This ship came from Germany. She has full sail, and an engine of 87 horse power. This picture shows her going before the wind, with ice on the quarter-bow. We keep clear of ice as well as we can, but when she is going full speed ahead we have to be careful. We are near Baffin Land; this island you see was given to us by Great Britain in 1880, and to-day I call it Canadian territory. These natives you see are no longer Eskimos; they are

Canadians, and we have to look after them.

I first took possession of Baffin Land for Canada in the presence of several Eskimo, and after firing 19 shots I instructed an Eskimo to fire the 20th, telling him that he was now a Canadian. A similar ceremony was observed on July 1st, 1909, when I took possession of the whole Arctic Archipelago between Canada and 90th degree of north latitude. I erected a tablet on a rock Peary, the Explorer, had engraved with his initials, in order to commemorate the acquisition of this northern territory for Canada. The event was celebrated on the 1st of July, Confederation Day. This slide shows us taking possession of those islands, so, as I say, we hold a vaster land than has been. I have always taken the position that the Arctic up to the Pole belongs to Canada. That north land used to be a kind of air-route for aviators but in future we shall collect $50 for a permit from them. Our northern limit, according to me, is 90 degrees north. We take the whole Arctic Archipelago from Baffin Land as far north as 82 degrees. This is not a place of desolation, as my hearers might regard it, but is a territory of great value to the Dominion of Canada.

The reason we ran our line was to secure our fishing rights. So far America has not claimed anything, or said anything. We have been friendly with our neighbors in Greenland; we go there every year to pay our respects, and we tell them that we have given strict orders for any of our people to give help in Greenland if wanted, and that we desire and expect the same treatment from them. Formerly we allowed the Americans to go through the whole of this land and hunt and fish, but now we ask them to pay $50, and we will give them a permit. In the past Canada has been a fairway for American fishermen and hunters, but in 1922 the *Arctic* on her trip posted police, who protect the Dominion hunting and fishing rights. It might be asked what was the use of making American fishermen pay toll. Well, when the question of ownership came up in the courts it was said that as the Americans had paid dues to Canada for fishing there, the land evidently belonged to Canada.

This slide shows a house that was built in 1923 for the police. Since 1922 we have been supporting police on these islands in order to maintain our rights, and I must congratulate the Government for that action. The time has come when we have to secure this territory for our children, because it is teeming with wealth, like the northern part of Ontario and Quebec. We have already established our claim to a vast area of land rich in large deposits of coal, iron and copper, and with a possibly large revenue from fishing, whaling and trapping. As we get towards Hudson Bay we find there is a great deal of wealth, and every month of the year we hear of ore being found, gold mines and copper mines.

In the place shown in this picture I found English money. It had been deposited in a cache during the voyage of McClintock. This next picture shows the piano,

and me coming down from the bridge as they are playing "God Save the King," while waiting for others to come to the table. This picture shows the Maclaren cheese and the Christie-Brown biscuits. I am giving natives the biscuits. Now comes the Doctor, and he is waiting to draw teeth of the natives, and I am keeping them in good humour.

I did not know that I would be asked to speak about Hudson Bay, but I will say a few words. Going to Hudson Bay would be the natural thing. The best plan would be for the Government to charter a suitable ship and take engineers and other experts for a trip through the Bay, so that they might see for themselves. With the ships sailing at the proper time, in charge of competent engineers, we could get great wealth from that region. Ships can get out of the Bay during three months, July 15th to October 15th, and they could make two or three trips in the Summer, and could use the coal that is to be had up there, which would be a saving. No ship could stand battling with the ice that comes down in the Spring from Baffin Bay, unless the ship is specially prepared for that work.

This slide shows a chart I made of my own accord, the original. If we ran our line due north to 90 degrees parallel we would be able to say to other people, "Keep away from here; you are fishing in Canada; if you want to fish here you must have a license." Many millions have been taken from the northern islands, and when I was there in 1904 and 1905 we put up notices to prevent fishing by those who had no right to do so.

(Films were then shown illustrating the icebergs, Eskimo children, and various scenes in the northland. The instrument was placed at such a distance from the sheet that the views were not clear, and the Chairman announced that something had gone wrong with the machine and that the operator had sent word that he could not improve matters, therefore the films were called off.)

Capt. Bernier then continued his talk. He told how the natives were invited to the ceremony of taking possession of the islands. They were given luncheon on board the *Arctic,* and he told them that they had become Canadians, and were now the same as himself, and were his brothers. He suggested that they make up their requisition for anything they wanted, and he would see what could be done for them. He promised to buy from them what he wanted, and give value for what he bought. When they came to luncheon they thought it was a good thing to be a Canadian. During and after the meal the Captain got the Eskimos one by one, especially the old heads, and gave them pencil and paper and asked them to mark down where they came from and what they had seen. The Eskimos would put down a dot and would say, through the interpreter, "There is an island here, and plenty of salmon; then there is a nice little bay here, then another island." Then after an hour's time the Captain would see the Eskimo sweating, and he would say, "Now, we will have a cup of tea or a smoke," and after that the

Eskimo would work at the chart till he finished. Thus the Captain got charts made by all the old heads. The Eskimo trackings are not like ours; they always go on a straight line, but on questioning them through the interpreter the direction according to the sun was found, and also how fast they travelled. The way to ascertain the latter point was to find the number of dogs used. In the Summer, with a kyack, they make five miles per dog; when they go on a hunting trip, if they have 10 dogs they make 10 miles; if 5 dogs, 5 miles. In that way the Captain got knowledge of places which he had not visited.

When the Eskimos got through with their charts the Captain would ask the interpreter to find out whether the natives found any copper or other ore, and asked them to bring it in. Sometimes they brought baskets full, and sometimes they found iron, and they would say, "It is nice; it glitters." Sometimes they would bring in a piece of copper pyrites; sometimes a piece of coal; then they would show on the chart where it was found, and the explorers' men would go and find surface coal, and on trial some of it would burn readily like lignite, and it was used on the boat, and was similar to Sydney coal. The coal was frozen to a depth of 9 or 10 feet, and when it came in big pieces it would crumble when put in the sun. In these ways the explorers got knowledge of every place where they had wandered for 8 years, and thus gathered a great deal of information.

The speaker said that the rivers were teeming with salmon weighing from 10 to 15 pounds, and when this fish is properly prepared it makes delicious eating. He added that he had taken a considerable number of bears and foxes, and there were thousands of seals. During the Winter the seals come out on the islands past Baffin Land and past Labrador, towards Newfoundland, and the Gulf of St. Lawrence. The value of the seal is about $45. From Newfoundland they have taken 27,000,000 since 1865, and the numbers do not seem to diminish. A seal gains 10 pounds every day when with its mother.

As to whaling, in the old times Americans made lots of money. America has no Northern waters, the waters are all Canadian. The same remark applies to the Alaska side. It is a common thing for a boat to come out with $1,000,000 worth of seals and furs.

Here in Canada we have a rich country, and we should develop every part of it. We want more help, and we will get it when we give the necessary inducements. Look at our mines. Who would have thought 25 years ago that there would be so much wealth on that Transcontinental Railway, which was thought at first to be a white elephant? As you go north it is the same thing; so if the road is opened to Hudson Bay some more territory will be developed, and will bring sufficient revenue to open up that new country. I admit it is very cold up north, but so it is here when you are not properly clothed and fed; but I have been out every day, and have not had a finger frozen.

Gentlemen, I am sorry that I could not have given you more to-day, but I am at your service tomorrow if you need me, or I will answer any questions you like to put in regard to our northern country.

HON. MR. McCREA, Ontario Minister of Mines, voiced the thanks of the Club to Capt. Bernier for his interesting address.

The Diamond Jubilee of Confederation / 1927

The year 1927 marked the Diamond Jubilee of Confederation, which celebrated sixty years of nationhood. It was a time of national stocktaking, and Canada was not found wanting. There were parades down the King Streets and Queen Streets of the cities, and in the towns and villages of the country, and on Parliament Hill the festive proceedings were broadcast live on a new contraption — radio. The keynote speech was delivered by Prime Minister William Lyon Mackenzie King (1874-1950), then in his early fifties, and it is notable in that it expresses so fully in stately rhetoric the sentiments of the day, so distant from us as we approach the Second Diamond Jubilee of Confederation. "Canada at the Celebration of the Diamond Jubilee of Confederation, Parliament Hill, Ottawa, 1st July, 1927," is reprinted from *The Message of the Carillon and other Addresses* (1927).

FOUR hundred years ago, Canada, from ocean to ocean, was a primeval forest, unknown to the civilized world. Its verdant grandeur lay mirrored in mighty rivers and inland seas. The boundless plains, concealed within its depths, rivalled in their sweep vast stretches of mountain range, unsurpassed in immensity, and unparalleled in antiquity. Through these ancient solitudes the Indian roamed, the lord of the forest, the monarch of all he surveyed.

In the perspective of history it would seem that our country has been well and truly named. Canada, when discovered, was the home of the Indian. Legend has it that the name, Canada, is derived from the Indian word, *Kanata,* which means a group of huts. If we are to go back to the beginning of things, where shall we find a truer picture of the primitive than that afforded by a group of huts?

The Confederation of Canada, the Diamond Jubilee of which we celebrate to-day, was the culmination of a two-fold undertaking, the task of settlement and of government which began more than three centuries ago.

Settlement and government of themselves are not sufficient to make a country. They must be continuous and combined. When, at the close of the fifteenth century, John Cabot, under royal charter from Henry VII, planted on the Canadian mainland the banner of England and the first cross, and when, early in the following century,

Jacques Cartier erected a great cross, on which were the *fleur de lis,* and the words "Long live the King of France," these intrepid mariners bequeathed their names to our country as its discoverers. It can hardly be said that they were its founders. They established no authority, they set up no colony. Their presence at the dawn of our history was, however, strangely prophetic of the two great races that were to develop settlement and government in our midst. Whilst a settlement was begun at Port Royal by Champlain and De Monts in 1605, it was not until Champlain in 1608 erected a small fort at Quebec, felled trees and planted wheat, that order and permanency, the essentials of nationhood, had their beginnings. That day, our Canada, daughter of the woods and mother of the fields, was born.

From a group of huts to a group of provinces, such was the development of Canada in the period that intervened between the founding of our country and Confederation. It was a period of combined settlement and government, continuous over some two hundred and sixty years. In settlement and government alike there were, during this period, mighty developments and transitions. At the end of a century and a half, Canada passed from a French to a British possession. Quebec, grown from a tiny fort to a rock fortress, reappears, at the moment of transition, as the corner-stone of the new national edifice. The monument erected at Quebec to the honour and memory of Montcalm and Wolfe is a fitting symbol of the spirit which has made our nation; a spirit which, in preserving the heroisms, has buried the animosities of the races which have shaped its destiny.

Throughout the seventeenth century, colonization along the St. Lawrence and in the interior was largely French. In 1621, James I granted a charter to Sir William Alexander in the lands now included in the Maritime Provinces. This was the beginning of Scottish settlement in Canada. In the first half of the eighteenth century, the French colonists continued to out-number the English, but in the second half, especially after the conquest, it was the other way. In the nineteenth century, English colonization increased very considerably and settlers began to come in numbers from other lands. The most significant contribution was the influx, following the war of American Independence, of United Empire Loyalists into Nova Scotia and the western portion of what was then the province of Quebec, as defined in 1774. As a result of this influx of new settlers, the Province of New Brunswick was established in 1784. What formerly had been one colony, largely French, was, by the Constitutional Act of 1791, divided into two provinces, Upper Canada and Lower Canada, corresponding, though in lesser outline, to the Ontario and Quebec of to-day. By the Atlantic, in addition to Nova Scotia and New Brunswick, was the colony of Prince Edward Island. British Columbia, as yet under another name, was a lone colony by the Pacific.

In matters of government, during this period, control passed by degrees from autocratic governors and nominated councils to the elected representatives of the people under a system of responsible self-government. To Nova Scotia belongs the distinction of having led the way in representative institutions. The first Legislative Assembly met at Halifax in 1758. In Nova Scotia and the other Maritime Provinces, representative government of a restricted character was succeeded in the course of a normal evolution by responsible self-government. In the Provinces of Lower and Upper Canada, however, it was not without open revolt that responsible self-government was finally established. The rebellion of 1837-38 was, in reality, not an uprising against British authority in Canada; it was an effort to bring the governments of Upper and Lower Canada more into accord with principles already recognized and established under British parliamentary practice. It was a rebellion claiming British rights for British citizens; a rebellion which failed on the field of battle, but which won on the field of principle.

As settlement in the provinces increased, and representative institutions in government paved the way for responsible self-government, the desire for wider political union manifested itself. In 1841 Upper and Lower Canada were united. In 1864 the Maritime Provinces held a Conference at Charlottetown to consider the possible union of the British colonies by the Atlantic. It was to this Conference that, in September of that year, delegates from Upper and Lower Canada repaired in order to suggest a larger idea, the idea of a confederation of all the provinces of British North America. They began to talk about a Nation to which all would belong, a Nation that one day might extend from sea to sea. The idea made its appeal. A conference to bring this project into being was decided upon. Charlottetown thus became "the cradle of Confederation."

Once more, however, Quebec was the historic centre. There, in the October following, the official conference was held. At the Quebec Conference assembled thirty-three delegates, men of diverse temperaments, racial origins, religious and political faiths, but all animated by one supreme purpose. They adopted seventy-two important resolutions which became the basis of the British North America Act, subsequently passed at Westminster. Under its provisions, the Dominion of Canada came into being on July 1, 1867. Thus, in the place of its beginnings, was completed the first epoch in the task of settlement and government, begun two hundred and sixty years before.

History has given to the leaders who assembled at Quebec the title of "Fathers of Confederation." It has been well said they were "the first flowering of responsible Government, fitted by experience for their great task and responsibility."

With Confederation on July 1, 1867, the centre of our

national stage shifts from Quebec to Ottawa. Here sixty years ago, on November 6, the first parliament of the Dominion of Canada met on the hill where we to-day are assembled.

The Canada of 1867 was, however, vastly different from the Canada of 1927, the Canada of to-day. In the light of what many of us have lived to witness, it would appear that, with Confederation, the work of settlement and government had just begun. The Great West had still to be acquired, most of it still to be explored. The record of its development is a history in itself. British Columbia, at the time of Confederation, remained in splendid isolation, a British colony by the Pacific. Prince Edward Island, despite its historic setting, continued, by the Atlantic, to enjoy a like isolation. Manitoba, Saskatchewan, and Alberta, save as Territories, were as yet unknown; as Provinces they were as yet unborn. The transformation of colonies into autonomous provinces, and of combined provinces into a self-governing nation became the larger task of settlement and of government. To settlement and to government there remained also the task of creating new provinces and of widening the country's bounds, that there might be one Dominion from sea to sea.

The sixty years which have intervened since Confederation constitute an era of unprecedented expansion. Manitoba in 1870, British Columbia in 1871, Prince Edward Island in 1873, became a part of the Dominion. Saskatchewan and Alberta, newly created in 1905 out of the Middle West, brought to completion the federation of Provinces from coast to coast.

If the period prior to Confederation marked the development of Canada from a group of huts to a group of provinces, it is equally true that the period succeeding Confederation has witnessed Canada's transition from a group of colonies to a nation within a group of nations, and her transition from a group of provinces to a nation among the nations of the world.

A land of scattered huts and colonies no more
But a young nation, with her life full beating in her
  breast,
A noble future in her eyes — the Britain of the West.

As Canada has developed in settlement and government, so has the great Empire of which Canada is a part. From a parent State with colonial possessions, the British Empire has become a community of free nations "in no way subordinate one to another in any aspect of their domestic or external affairs." They are "united by a common allegiance to the Crown, and freely associated as members of the British Commonwealth of Nations." Such is the position and mutual relation of Great Britain and the Dominions, as defined at the Imperial Conference of 1926. As one of the nations of the British Commonwealth of Nations, though of her own accord, Canada shared in the sacrifices of the world's war; as a nation, Canada par-

ticipated in the terms of a world's peace. In the larger Councils of Empire her position has been increasingly acknowledged; it has been accorded the highest recognition in the League of Nations as well. At no previous period of her history has Canada's status as a nation been so clearly defined, and at no time in her history have her relations, intra-imperial and international, been happier than they are to-day. Thus has been realized, far beyond their dreams, the vision of the Fathers of Confederation.

As we view in retrospect our country's history, what impresses us most is the very brief time within which so much has been achieved. Even to-day we have not lost traces of the earliest Canada. In the background of the present, there remain the Indian habitations — the little groups of huts, silhouetted against the forest depths, content to remain within its shadows that the larger Canada, emerging from obscurity and shade, may take her place in the sun among the powers of the world.

Coming then to our own day, how shall we, who have the responsibilities of the present, play our part? As nation-builders, as Empire-builders, our opportunities are even greater than those of our forefathers. To the problems of nationhood and Empire have been added world problems, problems intimately related to the world's progress and the world's peace. A nation, like an individual, to find itself must lose itself in the service of others.

First and foremost we must strive to be worthy of our past. And to be worthy of our past we must come to have a more intimate knowledge of its history. In the annals of the world there is no more illuminating and inspiring history than the history of Canada. Take whichever phase you will, the economic, the political, the constitutional, where will you find within so small a compass so complete an evolution, and so many factors of world significance? Let us hope that the interest created by the present anniversary will give us a greater pride in our country's past, and mark a place of new beginnings in the importance to be attached to Canadian history in our universities and schools. Let it be a study not from some prejudiced, partisan, or favoured point of view, but a simple record of the truth. There will be sufficient there to reveal the working of Providence through the years.

Next let us strive to build wisely in the present; to make the present, if we can, even more wonderful than the past, knowing that other generations will follow our own, and that our day, too, will be weighed in the balances of Time. "The House Beautiful" — that would seem to be our particular task. Much of the rough and heavy work has been done by those whom we have most in mind to-day — the pioneers in settlement and government who have given us the house in which we dwell. As they laboured, their thought was less of themselves than of their children, and of their children's children. To bequeath to them a freedom, an education which they themselves had been denied, that was what made the hard struggle worth while. What Canadian home has not witnessed that sacrifice of parent for child? What privation and toil has there not been that, in the end, the rough places might be made smooth?

To the builders of our nation, we owe much for what in the way of adornment they have added to utility. The flowering geranium in the cottage window, the tree planted by the wayside, the spire on the village church, all these speak of the love of beauty in the human heart. To the powerful corporations of our land, we owe much for a kindred service. Our railways, our banks, our insurance and investment companies, many of our industrial concerns, have had an eye to the beautiful as well as to dividends. While furthering its economic development in different ways, they have given to our country some noble pieces of architecture and taught many a lesson in artistic design. Our municipalities and governments have done much to educate popular taste in seeking to express a true feeling of form and proportion and to give a befitting dignity and artistic quality to public buildings and other public works. They have done much in the way of establishing parks and public squares and in them of worthily commemorating great personages and great events in our history. My own view is that those in authority cannot have too high a regard for national memorials, nor do too much in the way of beautification of our land. Industry and commerce have robbed our country of much of its natural beauty. We shall not greatly err if, in different ways, we seek to restore what in this respect has been lost.

I am glad that in this year of Diamond Jubilee we have witnessed on the part of parliament and the city of Ottawa, a readiness to share in the permanent improvement of the capital of our Dominion. Let us always remember, it is not the Ottawa or the Canada of to-day that we at this hour are called upon to consider, nor the Ottawa or the Canada of a few years hence; it is the capital of our country as it will exist through generations to come. Already we condemn the failure which has denied us a fitting approach to these beautiful buildings and their magnificent setting. As years go by the extent of that failure will be increasingly felt. With all my heart I hope that the great event in our history which we celebrate to-day may be commemorated in this capital by a means of access to the Houses of Parliament worthy of their great dignity and beauty, worthy of the vision which brought them into being and which placed them here, and in keeping with the place which they hold in our national life. Such an approach we all but have in the improvement already under way in the very heart of the city. Let us bring that splendid work to its obvious completion. Confederation Park, dedicated to the Fathers of Confederation, would be a worthy memorial to this historic occasion. It is a memorial which the Canada of to-day, but even more the Canada of future years, would, I believe, loudly acclaim.

In seeking to be worthy of our past, to build wisely in the present, how can we do better than to remain true to the spirit of those whom we honour to-day; not the Fathers of Confederation alone, but that long procession of discoverers and explorers, pioneers and settlers, sailors and soldiers, missionaries and traders; the men and women who have hewn their homes from the forests, who have developed our resources, fashioned our industries, extended our commerce; the moulders of thought and opinion and ideals in the realm of letters and art and government; that vast unnumbered company, long since gathered to their fathers and now resting from their labours, whose courage and daring, whose heroic purpose and steadfast endurance, whose vision and wisdom, manifested in a multitude of ways, have created a record of achievement unequalled in the romance, and unsurpassed in the pageantry of history.

In the Legislative Buildings at Prince Edward Island there was erected on the fiftieth anniversary of the event, a bronze mural tablet which commemorates the meeting at Charlottetown on September 1, 1864. It reads:

> In the hearts and minds of the
>   delegates who assembled
> in this room on Sept. 1st, 1864
> was born the *Dominion of Canada*
>
> Providence being their guide
> They builded better than they knew.

As I reflect upon our country's past, I come to believe more and more in the profound truth of that inscription. Only I would give to it a wider application. I would have it include all who by service and sacrifice have made Canada what it is to-day. One cannot but be impressed with the sublime faith and the spirit of reverence which in the humblest and the highest have been so generally apparent. From every side they seem to have caught glimpses of "The Vision Splendid." *"He shall have Dominion also from sea to sea."* It would almost seem that this ideal had been present to the hearts and minds of all, and that they had worked together from the beginning to this great end. Can we do better than to find in these words a like inspiration, remembering always *"Where there is no vision the people perish,"* and that *"His truth endureth to all generations."*

Does Shirley Temple Know?/1929

No single document, no two documents, can do justice to the suffering and hardship occasioned by the Great Depression. From the stockmarket crash of October 1929 to the outbreak of the Second World War in September 1939, there was a decade of high unemployment in the cities and unprecedented drought conditions on the prairies (hence the phrase "the dirty thirties"). Most Canadians simply dreamed of better things (and resisted the impulse to hand out free Shirley Temple dolls, as in the excerpt that follows), but a few sat down and planned the means to a more workable and equitable social order (as in the "Manifesto of the LSR," which follows this excerpt). The Shirley Temple excerpt is based on a tape-recorded interview with a female clerk who worked in Eaton's toy department in Toronto one Christmas season during the 1930s. "Through all the horror and despair of real life, the Hollywood tinsel world twinkled brightly," noted Barry Broadfoot in *Ten Lost Years, 1929-1939: Memories of Canadians Who Survived the Depression* (1973). "All over Canada people of all ages scraped together enough money to enter the escapist world of the movies, where stars like Shirley Temple were huge box-office successes."

Shirley Temple. That's what I remember about the Thirties. Shirley Temple dolls. One year they were the rage, everything, everybody was talking about Shirley Temple, going to see her movies, reading stories about her in the newspapers and in the fan magazines. Shirley Temple, Shirley Temple, Shirley Temple.

Eaton's used to turn a big part of their store into a toyland at Christmas and that year, the Shirley Temple year, they had these dolls along one end of the toyland. There must have been hundreds of these dolls, and they weren't cheap. Nine to about sixteen dollars, I'd say, and sixteen dollars was a lot more than some families got in a month for relief. You could rent a cottage at Grand Beach for two weeks in July for that.

They moved girls from all over the store down to toyland for about six weeks before Christmas and I was one that year. We worked, well we had to be there at eight-thirty, door opened at nine, and sometimes we were on our feet for fourteen hours a day except for half an hour lunch and if we had to go to the women's room. For seven dollars a week. They really didn't give us anything for nothing. I never knew a girl who wasn't glad to leave that place. Girls used to marry fellows they didn't even care for, to be free of Eaton's.

Oh yes, these dolls. I'd stand there and watch the faces of those little girls, from about four or five right up to about eleven. Some used to come at opening time and just stand there looking at those pink-cheeked, golden-haired lovely Shirley Temples. Little faces, they needed food. You could see a lot who needed a pint of milk a day a thousand times more than they needed a Shirley doll. They'd stare for hours. We tried to shush them away but it didn't do any good. They'd go once around toyland and be back. This, mind you, went on day after day, day after day, until some of the girls thought they would go crazy. One girl had a crying fit just over that, those hundreds of poor kids who would never own a Shirley Temple in a hundred years. They were lucky if they had breakfast that morning, or soup and bread that night.

The kids weren't the only ones, but the mothers too, and the hopeless look on their faces and trying to shush the little girls away, knowing they only had a dollar or two to buy gifts for the whole family. One day I had this crazy notion that I would give Shirley dolls away to the kids, here, little girl, this is for you, and here's one for you, and this big one is for you, darling. That sort of thing. I thought I'd do it until I was caught and then I'd plead insanity. I never did, of course.

Those six weeks with those goddam dolls were the worst I ever put in, easy at first but sheer torture at the end, all those big and yearning eyes staring at you. I wonder if Shirley Temple ever realized the misery those dolls must have caused children all over the world? I suppose she's never even thought of it.

Manifesto of the LSR / 1932

To represent the programme of the Left in Canada, I have chosen the Manifesto of The League for Social Reconstruction. The LSR, a highly influential group of "unattached critical spirits" (in Kenneth McNaught's phrase), first met in Toronto in the depths of the Great Depression, in February 1932, and formed "a kind of Canadian Fabian Society," in the words of its guiding spirit, Frank Underhill (1889-1971), the principal author of its manifesto, which is reprinted from *The Canadian Forum*, April 1932. Before the LSR was dissolved on the eve of the Second World War, it published *Social Planning for Canada* (1935, 1975), a thoroughgoing critique of the country along socialist and reformists lines. Contributors to that volume included Eugene Forsey, F.R. Scott, Graham Spry, and F.H. Underhill.

Accepting the invitation of J.S. Woodsworth, the honorary president of the LSR who became the first leader of the Co-operative Commonwealth Federation, Underhill went on to write the first draft of the celebrated Regina Manifesto, which was adopted at the First National Convention of the CCF in Regina, July 1938. I would have reprinted the entire Regina Manifesto except that it is a document of some length and is readily available elsewhere — in Kenneth McNaught's *A Prophet in Politics: A Biography of J.S. Woodsworth* (1959), for instance. The LSR acted as a "ginger group" within the CCF, now the New Democratic Party, and the NDP has acted as a "ginger group" within Canada ever since.

The League for Social Reconstruction is an association of men and women who are working for the establishment in Canada of a social order in which the basic principle regulating production, distribution and service will be the common good rather than private profit.

The present capitalist system has shown itself unjust and inhuman, economically wasteful, and a standing threat to peace and democratic government. Over the whole world it has led to a struggle for raw materials and markets and to a consequent international competition in armaments which were among the main causes of the last great war and which constantly threaten to bring on new wars. In the advanced industrial countries it has led to the concentration of wealth in the hands of a small irresponsible minority of bankers and industrialists whose economic power constantly threatens to nullify our political democracy. The result in Canada is a society in which the interests of farmers and of wage and salaried workers — the great majority of the population — are habitually sacrificed to those of this small minority. Despite our abundant natural resources the mass of the people have not been freed from poverty and insecurity. Unregulated competitive production condemns them to alternate periods of feverish prosperity, in which the main benefits go to speculators and profiteers, and of catastrophic depression, in which the common man's normal state of insecurity and hardship is accentuated.

We are convinced that these evils are inherent in any system in which private profit is the main stimulus to economic effort. We therefore look to the establishment in Canada of a new social order which will substitute a planned and socialized economy for the existing chaotic individualism and which, by achieving an approximate economic equality among all men in place of the present glaring inequalities, will eliminate the domination of one class by another.

As an essential first step towards the realization of this new order we advocate:

(1) Public ownership and operating of the public utilities connected with transportation, communications, and electric power, and of such other industries as are already approaching conditions of monopolistic control.
(2) Nationalization of Banks and other financial institutions with a view to the regulation of all credit and investment operations.
(3) The further development of agricultural cooperative institutions for the production and merchandising of agricultural products.
(4) Social legislation to secure to the worker adequate income and leisure, freedom of association, insurance against illness, accident, old age, and unemployment, and an effective voice in the management of his industry.
(5) Publicly organized health, hospital, and medical services.
(6) A taxation policy emphasizing steeply graduated income and inheritance taxes.
(7) The creation of a National Planning Commission.
(8) The vesting in Canada of the power to amend and interpret the Canadian constitution so as to give the federal government power to control the national economic development.
(9) A foreign policy designed to secure international

cooperation in regulating trade, industry and finance, and to promote disarmament and world peace.

The league will work for the realization of its ideal by organizing groups to study and report on particular problems, and by issuing to the public in the form of pamphlets, articles, lectures, etc., the most accurate information obtainable about the nation's affairs in order to create an informed public opinion. It will support any political party in so far as its programme furthers the above principles, and will foster cooperation among all groups and individuals who desire in Canada the kind of social order at which the League aims.

Dedication of the Vimy Memorial/1936

"Canada's most impressive tribute overseas to her sons who fought and gave their lives in the First World War is the majestic and inspiring Vimy Memorial, which overlooks the Douai Plain from the highest point of Vimy Ridge, about five miles northeast of Arras," explained Colonel G.W.L. Nicholson. The twin white pylons of the Vimy Memorial, decorated with the maple leaf and the fleur-de-lis, recall that Easter Monday, 9 April 1917, when the four divisions of the Canadian Corps, fighting together for the first time under commander Lieutenant-General Sir Julian Byng (1862-1935), succeeded in capturing the strategic French ridge from the German occupation forces and holding it. Three thousand Canadians died in the battle and four Victoria Crosses were awarded to Canadians for acts of heroism. The Vimy Memorial remains the country's best-known monument to the fallen. Its design was selected in competition won by the Toronto sculptor Walter S. Allward (1876-1955), who maintained that the concept came to him in a dream. Allward's description of the monument is quoted by Nicholson in *We Will Remember* (1973):

> At the base of the strong impregnable walls of defence are the Defenders, one group showing the Breaking of the Sword, the other the Sympathy of the Canadians for the Helpless. Above these are the mouths of guns covered with olive and laurels. On the wall stands an heroic figure of Canada brooding over the graves of her valiant dead; below is suggested a grave with a helmet, laurels, etc. Behind her stand two pylons symbolizing the two forces — Canadian and French — while between, at the base of these, is the Spirit of Sacrifice, who, giving all, throws the torch to his Comrades. Looking up they see the figures of Peace, Justice, Truth and Knowledge, etc., for which they fought, chanting the hymn of Peace. Around these figures are the shields of Britain, Canada and France. On the outside of the pylons is the Cross.

More than ten thousand Canadians attended the dedication service, held on 26 July 1936 under the auspices of the Canadian Legion. One speaker to address the multitude was the Hon. Lieutenant-Colonel the Reverend George Oliver Fallis (1885-1952), C.B.E., E.D., B.D., D.D., who had served as chaplain in the First World War and had been mentioned in dispatches and would be so again in the Second World War. Fallis, who sounded the human and spiritual depths of the Vimy engagement, was followed by the Prince of Wales (1894-1972), later the Duke of Windsor, who addressed his first words, in French, to Albert Lebrun, the last president of the Third French Republic, and then spoke in English to the gathering to dedicate the memorial. At the conclusion of his address, the prince released the folds of the Union Jack which enveloped the figure of Canada Mourning Her Dead. A great hush fell over the vast throng and "The Last Post" was sounded. Fallis's speech, which follows, is reprinted from *The Epic of Vimy* (1937), edited by W.W. Murray for the Canadian Legion.

Here have we come, 10,000 strong, to Vimy Ridge. Today, standing in the shadow of this noble Memorial, we link ourselves to the universal heart that has always noted the passing of its heroes. Long years ago the writer of the Book of Hebrews inspired his day by rehearsing the heroic accomplishments of his people. He saw that faith in ideals and ideas created the spirit of adventure. In describing the exploits of his native heroes he makes Faith the source of their power. No other word more truly gives explanation of Canadian history. By Faith goodly men and women crossed the seas, arrived in Canada, hewed down the forests, built their log cabins, erected their schoolhouses, colleges, universities and churches, educated their children in wisdom, manners and morals; by Faith they developed industry and commerce, built great railways, mined precious metals, erected mills, and fished the depths of the sea. By Faith they explored the great West, travelling by ox-cart into a land they knew not, transforming the unshorn fields of the prairies into a land of golden grain. By Faith they faced the Rocky Mountains, scaled snow-capped peaks, forded turbulent rivers, and passed through narrow defiles of yawning canyons. By Faith they ran the Thompson, Fraser, Mackenzie and Yukon. By Faith they gazed upon the Pacific. By Faith they carved out of the wilderness a native land filled with beauty and plenty, builded a goodly nation, pursuing peace, loving industry, jealous of none and respectful of all.

Into this atmosphere of peace, industry, and goodwill, war clouds suddenly loomed. A storm broke and there burst upon the world the most startling challenge in human history. Leaders in Church and State, the Press, University and College, held high ideals of service to King, Empire and Humanity, and called forth the noblest in youth. Never in the history of Canada were

such ideals held up so vividly. Everywhere the cry went forth "a war to end war." Into the souls of the young Canadians came the compulsion of a vision that at once disturbed and lured them. It laid high obligations upon them. It was a vision of things as they ought to be against the darker vision of what they were and might be. To follow its light became an imperial duty. Suddenly they realized that they must be ready to die for a cause.

By Faith they faced the vision and from Cape Race to Nootka Sound answered the call. By Faith the First Division sailed, by Faith battalion after battalion and brigade after brigade in vast ships passed out of sight. By Faith they faced the perils of the sea, submarines and mines; by Faith they reached the Motherland, trained in English camps; in Faith they received the good-bye blessings of a noble sovereign, the late King George the Fifth; by Faith they went to France and Belgium; by Faith they lived in trenches, faced poison gas, barbed wire, machine guns and shrapnel. By Faith they died at Givenchy, Festubert, Ypres, Sanctuary Wood, Maple Copse, the Somme, Vimy Ridge, Hill 70, Passchendaele, Amiens, Arras, Drocourt Quéant, Canal du Nord, Bourlon Wood, Cambrai, Valenciennes, and Mons. And what I shall more say, for time would fail to tell of Alderson, Byng and Currie, of privates, corporals, sergeants, lieutenants, captains, majors, colonels and generals, who through Faith wrought victories, obtained successes and stopped the oncoming of enemies.

They were shot, bayoneted, gassed, slain with artillery, shrapnel and machine guns, bombed from the skies. They wandered about in gas masks, living in dugouts and ditches, being tormented with vermin. They were thirsty. They were hungry. They were cold and frost-bitten. They were imprisoned. They were separated from their loved ones. And these all having given a good report, through Faith died not having reached their glorious goals, God having provided that we should finish their task and make real their vision of a world swayed by peace and brotherhood.

Without us their vision fades. Today on these slopes of Vimy a deathless army urges us on. To us they throw the torch. This Monument is a fresh pledge that we shall not break faith. Wherefore seeing we also are compassed about with so great a cloud of witnesses, let us set aside every weight and the sin which doth so easily beset us and run with patience the race that is set before us looking into Jesus, the Author and Finisher of our Faith.

The United Church of Canada would bid me, as one of her ministers, pray: Lord of the worlds, with strong eternal hand, hold us in honour, truth and self-command; the loyal heart, the constant mind, the courage to be true, our wide extending Empire bind, and all the earth renew. Thy name be known through every zone; Lord of the worlds, make all the lands thine own.

O risen Lord, O shepherd of our dead, whose Cross has bought them, and whose star has led, in glorious hope their proud and sorrowing land, commit her children to thy gracious hand.

I'll Stay in Canada/1936

"A cold wind blows across the landscape. That's retirement." So wrote Stephen Leacock (1869-1944), who experienced the feeling at sixty-five, McGill University's mandatory retirement age, when he was asked to leave behind him the Department of Economics, where from January 1901 to May 1936 he had so happily taught generations of students. But "I'll Stay in Canada" is not about retirement so much as it is about a stocktaking in 1936 of the country Leacock lived in. When this essay first appeared in *Funny Pieces: A Book of Random Sketches* (1936), Leacock prefaced it with the following explanation: "Note: This article was written at the suggestion of an English editor who asked whether I should not come 'home' to England (where I was born) now that I have finished my work at McGill University. The wide circulation and the very kind reception that the article received encourage me to reproduce it as the closing chapter of this book."

You are kind enough to suggest that I might, being now free from work, come home to England. But no, no, don't tempt me. It wouldn't work. I know it wouldn't. It sounds fine. But there are all kinds of difficulties, things you wouldn't think of at first — questions of language and manners; a lot of them. Honestly, I don't think I'd better try it.

You see, it's been sixty years, this early spring, since I came out from England as a little boy of six, so wise that I knew all about the Trojan War and which Gods fought for which side, and so ignorant that I had never seen a bark canoe or a bob-sleigh and didn't know what a woodchuck was. We crossed the Atlantic, which I recall as continuous ice; were in river steamers for four days; then in a train with a queer little engine that threw hemlock sparks all over the bush; and then thirty miles in a lumber wagon — and we were *there*.

After that my brothers and I never saw a railway train again for three years, till someone built a railway to Lake Simcoe and the "cars" came. There followed another three years, and then we went away to school and to the world. But the "stamp" I carry is that of the farm in Georgina Township and my predilection is for the soil and the Canadian bush. Forever, I like the sunrise.

I worked at teaching. I taught for three months, in training, eighteen years old, at the old Strathroy High School with General Sir Arthur Currie, our greatest Canadian, as my pupil.

Then I taught for a year at Uxbridge High School. Then I taught ten years at Upper Canada College. Then I

got quite a good job at McGill University and held it for thirty-five years. My life has been as simple as one of Xenophon's Marches. But at least my jobs grew longer. The next, I think, will be what you'd call permanent.

But now, as you say, I am free to do as I please; and, if I like, after sixty years I could come "home." Certainly it sounds tempting. Yet, as I say, there are difficulties. The first is the question of language. When I left Hampshire I spoke English. But I've lost it, and it might be too late to pick it up again. You see, we speak differently here. I don't mean uneducated people, I mean educated men, like my friends at my club (The University Club, Montreal — you can't miss it; it's just opposite McGill University).

We used to be ashamed of our Canadian language, before the war, and try to correct it and take on English phrases and say, "What a ripping day," instead of "What a peach of a morning," and "Ah you thah?" instead of "Hullo Central," and "Oh, rather!" instead of "O-Hell-yes." But now, since the Great War put Canada right on a level with the Portuguese and the Siamese and those fellows who came from — ah! one forgets the names, but it doesn't matter — I mean, made Canada a real nation — we just accept our own language and are not ashamed of it. We say "yep!" when we mean "yep!" and don't try to make out it's "yes," which is a word we don't use; and if we mean "four" we say so and don't call it "faw."

So you see, there's the question of language. Then there's the difference of education. I don't mean that we are not educated — us fellers in the University Club — because we are: only in a different way. At first sight you English people would not think we were educated because we learned different things. Any member of the club knows what a kilowatt is, and you don't; but on the other hand, our members would think that a "perfect aorist" is either a vacuum cleaner or an Italian trombone player.

It is just that difference. I remember a few years ago a distinguished English bishop, speaking at our club, said that he felt that Greek had practically made him what he was; we felt exactly the same about him and thought it very manly and British of him to admit it straight out.

Then, there's the question of manners. There it would be pretty hard for me or for any of my friends here to "get by." You see, we are not just quite what you call gentlemen. Not quite. In the dark and if we don't talk, you could hardly tell us. But when we begin to feel easy and at home the thing comes out. I don't just know what it consists of: I think we are a little too unrestrained and we have a way of referring to money, a thing of which you never definitely speak in England.

I remember, in making conversation with that bishop, I asked him if his salary went right on while he was out here, and when he said, "I beg your pardon," all I could say was, "Forget it." Of course, the bishop didn't know that in Canada we never feel at ease with a man till we know what his salary is, and which of the gold mines he bought shares in last.

All this means we lack "class." There isn't a sufficient distinction between us and those lower down in money. Personally I can go bass fishing with a taxi driver and a Toronto surgeon and an American tourist and the "feller that rents the boat" and can't see any difference. Neither can they. There isn't any.

That brings me to the Americans! There's another reason for not wanting to leave Canada for England. I'd hate to be so far away from the United States. You see, with us it's second nature, part of our lives, to be near them. Every Sunday morning we read the New York funny papers, and all week we read about politics in Alabama and Louisiana, and whether they caught the bandits that stole the vault of the national bank, and — well, you know American news — there's no other like it. And the Americans come-and-go up here, and we go-and-come down there, and they're educated just as we are and know all about kilowatts but quit Latin at the fourth declension.

Their colleges are like ours and their clubs are like ours and their hotels are like ours and Rotaries and Lions and Kiwanis like ours. Honestly, you can't tell where you are unless you happen to get into a British Empire Society; and anyway, they have those in Boston and in Providence, and the Daughters of the American Revolution is practically a British organization — so all that is fifty-fifty.

Our students go and play hockey with their stoodents and our tourists going out meet their towrists coming in. The Americans come up here and admire us for the way we hang criminals. They sit in our club and say, "You certainly do hang them, don't you!" My! they'd like to hang a few! The day may be coming when they will. Meantime, we like to hang people to make the Americans sit up.

And in the same way we admire the Americans for the way they shovel up mountains and shift river-courses and throw the map all round the place. We sit in the club, fascinated, and listen to an American saying, "The proposal is to dam up the Arkansas River and make it run backward over the Rockies." That's the stuff! That's conversation.

There you are again — conversation. It would be hard for me or any Canadian to learn to "converse" in England. You see, English conversation turns upon foreign politics and international affairs. It runs to such things as — "But don't you think that the Singapore Base would have been better if it had been at Rangoon or at least on the Irrawaddy?" "Ah, but would that really control Hoopow, or, for that matter, Chefoo?"

Now, we don't talk about that. Listen to us in my club and you hear, "He told me that in Central Patricia, they were down to the second level and that there was enough stuff *right in sight* to make it a cinch. I bought 100 at 2.30 and yesterday it had got to three dollars. . . ."

That's real talk. And that's our country, anyway — our unfailing interest, for all of us, in its vast development, its huge physical future. In this last sixty years — since I've known it — we have filled it in and filled it in like a huge picture lying in a frame from the frozen seas to the American line, from Nova Scotia to the Pacific. What the English feel about the Armada and the Scottish about Bannockburn, the Canadian, consciously or not, feels about the vast geography of Canada.

There is something inspiring in this building of a new country in which even the least of us has had some part. I can remember how my father went — from our Lake Simcoe farm — to the first Manitoba boom of over fifty years ago — before the railway. He had an idea that what the West needed was British energy and pluck. He came back broke in six months. Then Uncle Edward went; he had a gifted mind and used to quote to us that "the Star of the Empire glitters in the West." He did better. He came back broke only after four years.

Then my brothers Dick and Jim went. Dick was in the Mounted Police and then worked in a saloon and came home broke. Jim got on fine but he played poker too well and had to leave terribly fast. Charlie and George and Teddy went — they all went but me. I was never free to go till now, but I may start at any time. Going West, to a Canadian, is like going after the Holy Grail to a knight of King Arthur. All Canadian families have had, like mine, their Western Odyssey.

It's the great spaces that appeal. To all of us here, the vast unknown country of the North, reaching away to the polar seas, supplies a peculiar mental background. I like to think that in a few short hours in a train or car I can be in the primeval wilderness of the North; that if I like, from my summer home, an hour or two of flight will take me over the divide and down to the mournful shores of the James Bay, untenanted till yesterday, now haunted with its flock of airplanes hunting gold in the wilderness. I never have gone to the James Bay; I never go to it; I never shall. But somehow I'd feel lonely without it.

No, I don't think I can leave this country. There is something in its distances and its isolation and its climate that appeals forever. Outside my window as I write in the dark of early morning — for I rise like a farm hand — the rotary snow ploughs on the Côte des Neiges Road are whirling in the air the great blanket of snow that buried Montreal last night. To the north, behind the mountain, the Northern Lights blink on a thousand miles of snow-covered forest and frozen rivers.

We are "sitting pretty" here in Canada. East and west are the two oceans far away; we are backed up against the ice cap of the pole; our feet rest on the fender of the American border, warm with a hundred years of friendship. The noise and tumult of Europe we scarcely hear — not for us the angers of the Balkans, the weeping of Vienna and the tumults of Berlin. Our lot lies elsewhere — shoveling up mountains, floating in the sky to look for gold, and finding still the Star of Empire in the West.

Thank you, Mother England, I don't think I'll "come home." I'm "home" now. Fetch me my carpet slippers from the farm. I'll rock it out to sleep right here.

For Valour (II)/1944

A total of 730,625 men and women saw service in the Canadian Army, the Royal Canadian Navy, and the Royal Canadian Air Force during the Second World War. The total casualties were 41,992. Many Canadian officers and men were awarded the Victoria Cross, the Commonwealth's ranking decoration "For Valour." Especially moving and dramatic is the citation posthumously awarded to Pilot Officer Mynarski. Details appear in *Valiant Men: Canada's Victoria Cross and George Cross Winners* (1973), edited by John Swettenham. (Since 1972, the Canadian government has awarded its own decorations, these being the Cross of Valour, the Star of Courage, and the Medal of Bravery.)

PILOT OFFICER ANDREW CHARLES MYNARSKI

BORN: Winnipeg, October 14, 1916
SERVICE: Royal Canadian Air Force
DIED: Near Cambrai, France, June 12, 1944
V.C.: Awarded Posthumously.

Pilot Officer Mynarski was the mid-upper gunner of a Lancaster aircraft detailed to attack a target at Cambrai in France, on the night of 12th June, 1944. The aircraft was attacked from below and astern by an enemy fighter.... Fire broke out...and the captain ordered the crew to abandon the aircraft....Mynarski left his turret and went towards the escape hatch. He then saw that the rear gunner was still in his turret and apparently unable to leave it....

Without hesitation...Mynarski made his way through the flames in an endeavour to reach the rear turret and release the gunner. Whilst so doing, his parachute and his clothing, up to the waist, were set on fire. All his efforts to move the turret and free the gunner were in vain. Eventually the rear gunner clearly indicated to him that there was nothing more he could do and that he should try to save his own life. Pilot Officer Mynarski reluctantly went back through the flames to the escape hatch. There, as a last gesture to the trapped gunner, he turned towards him, stood to attention in his flaming clothes and saluted, before he jumped out of the aircraft....He was found eventually by the French, but was so severely burnt that he died from his injuries.

[The rear gunner miraculously survived the crash.]

The Ascetic in a Canoe/1944

The canoe, whether of the birchbark or the Peterborough variety, comes close to being the quintessential Canadian vehicle. (Its only rival is the skidoo, also a Canadian invention.) Pierre Berton once quipped, "A Canadian is somebody who knows how to make love in a canoe." To Pierre Elliott Trudeau (b. 1919), the canoe is a vehicle of self-knowledge. This remarkable essay, originally published in French in *Jeunesse Étudiante Catholique*, November 1944, and first published in English as "Exhaustion and Fulfilment: The Ascetic in a Canoe" in *Wilderness Canada* (1970), edited by Borden Spears, was written by the future prime minister of Canada when he was twenty-five years old.

I would not know how to instil a taste for adventure in those who have not acquired it. (Anyway, who can ever prove the necessity for the gypsy life?) And yet there are people who suddenly tear themselves away from their comfortable existence and, using the energy of their bodies as an example to their brains, apply themselves to the discovery of unsuspected pleasures and places.

I would like to point out to these people a type of labour from which they are certain to profit: an expedition by canoe.

I do not just mean "canoeing." Not that I wish to disparage that pastime, which is worth more than many another. But, looked at closely, there is perhaps only a difference of money between the canoeists of Lafontaine Park and those who dare to cross a lake, make a portage, spend a night in a tent and return exhausted, always in the care of a fatherly guide — a brief interlude momentarily interrupting the normal course of digestion.

A canoeing expedition, which demands much more than that, is also much more rewarding.

It involves a starting rather than a parting. Although it assumes the breaking of ties, its purpose is not to destroy the past, but to lay a foundation for the future. From now on, every living act will be built on this step, which will serve as a base long after the return of the expedition...and until the next one.

What is essential at the beginning is the resolve to reach the saturation point. Ideally, the trip should end only when the members are making no further progress within themselves. They should not be fooled, though, by a period of boredom, weariness or disgust; that is not the end, but the last obstacle before it. Let saturation be serene!

So you must paddle for days, or weeks, or perhaps months on end. My friends and I were obliged, on pain of death, to do more than a thousand miles by canoe, from Montreal to Hudson Bay. But let no one be deterred by a shortage of time. A more intense pace can compensate for a shorter trip.

What sets a canoeing expedition apart is that it purifies you more rapidly and inescapably than any other. Travel a thousand miles by train and you are a brute; pedal five hundred on a bicycle and you remain basically a bourgeois; paddle a hundred in a canoe and you are already a child of nature.

For it is a condition of such a trip that you entrust yourself, stripped of your worldly goods, to nature. Canoe and paddle, blanket and knife, salt pork and flour, fishing rod and rifle; that is about the extent of your wealth. To remove all the useless material baggage from a man's heritage is, at the same time, to free his mind from petty preoccupations, calculations and memories.

On the other hand, what fabulous and undeveloped mines are to be found in nature, friendship and oneself! The paddler has no choice but to draw everything from them. Later, forgetting that this habit was adopted under duress, he will be astonished to find so many resources within himself.

Nevertheless, he will have returned a more ardent believer from a time when religion, like everything else, became simple. The impossibility of scandal creates a new morality, and prayer becomes a friendly chiding of the divinity, who has again become part of our everyday affairs. (My friend, Guy Viau, could say about our adventure, "We got along very well with God, who is a damn good sport. Only once did we threaten to break off diplomatic relations if he continued to rain on us. But we were joking. We would never have done so, and well he knew it. So he continued to rain on us.")

The canoe is also a school of friendship. You learn that your best friend is not a rifle, but someone who shares a night's sleep with you after ten hours of paddling at the other end of a canoe. Let's say that you have to be towed up a rapid and it's your turn to stay in the canoe and guide it. You watch your friend stumbling over logs, sliding on rocks, sticking in gumbo, tearing the skin on his legs and drinking water for which he does not thirst, yet never letting go of the rope; meanwhile, safely in the middle of the cataract, you spray your hauler with a stream of derision. When this same man has also fed you exactly half his catch, and has made a double portage because of your injury, you can boast of having a friend for life, and one who knows you well.

How does the trip affect your personality? Allow me to make a fine distinction, and I would say that you return not so much a man who reasons more, but a more reasonable man. For, throughout this time, your mind has learned to exercise itself in the working conditions which nature intended. Its primordial role has been to sustain the body in the struggle against a powerful universe. A good camper knows that it is more important to be ingenious than to be a genius. And conversely, the body, by demonstrating the true meaning of sensual pleasure, has been of service to the mind. You feel the beauty of animal pleasure when you draw a deep breath of rich morning air right through your body, which has been carried by the cold night, curled up like an unborn child. How can you describe the feeling which wells up in the heart and stomach as the canoe finally rides up on the shore of the campsite after a long day of plunging your paddle into rain-swept waters? Purely physical is the joy which the fire spreads through the palms of your hands and the soles of your feet while your chattering mouth belches the poisonous cold. The pleasurable torpor of such a moment is perhaps not too different from what the mystics of the East are seeking. At least it has allowed me to taste what one respected gentleman used to call the joys of hard living.

Make no mistake, these joys are exclusively physical. They have nothing to do with the satisfaction of the mind when it imposes unwelcome work on the body, a satisfaction, moreover, which is often mixed with pride, and which the body never fails to avenge. During a very long and exhausting portage, I have sometimes felt my reason defeated, and shamefully fleeing, while my legs and shoulders carried bravely on. The mumbled verses which marked the rhythm of my steps at the beginning had become brutal grunts of "uh! uh! uh!" There was nothing aesthetic in that animal search for the bright clearing which always marks the end of a portage.

I do not want you to think that the mind is subjected to a healthy discipline merely by worrying about simplistic problems. I only wish to remind you of that principle of logic which states that valid conclusions do not generally follow from false premises. Now, in a canoe, where these premises are based on nature in its original state (rather than on books, ideas and habits of uncertain value), the mind conforms to that higher wisdom which we call natural philosophy; later, that healthy methodology and acquired humility will be useful in confronting mystical and spiritual questions.

I know a man whose school could never teach him patriotism, but who acquired that virtue when he felt in his bones the vastness of his land, and the greatness of those who founded it.

Refus Global/1948

"Perhaps the single most important social document in Quebec history, and the most important aesthetic statement a Canadian has ever made" is the art curator Dennis Reid's description of *Refus global* (Global refusal), the manifesto issued by the famous painter Paul-Émile Borduas (1905-60). Although only four hundred copies of the mimeographed booklet appeared on 9 August 1948, the publication of the French text had an immediate response: Borduas was dismissed from his teaching post at the École du Meuble in Montreal. He moved to New York and then to Paris, where his painting gained for him international acclaim. Ten years after drafting the manifesto, Borduas was asked by Maurice Beaulieu if he would sign his own manifesto again. And Borduas replied, in *Situations,* February 1959: "In full flood, I wrote and signed *Refus global* without knowing too clearly why. Maybe solely because it was necessary to my inner equilibrium in its relationship with the outside world, which demanded correction of the unbearable forms of a world arbitrarily imposed. Writing today, without denying its essential value (which still remains), I would set it in an entirely different atmosphere: more impersonal, less naive, and, I am afraid, even more cruel to breathe." The English translation is reprinted from *French-Canadian Nationalism: An Anthology* (1969), edited by Ramsay Cook.

We are the offspring of modest French-Canadian families, working-class or lower-middle-class, who, ever since their arrival from the Old Country, have always remained French and Catholic through resistance to the Conquest, through arbitrary attachment to the past, by choice and sentimental pride, and out of sheer necessity.

We are the settlers who, ever since 1760, have been trapped in the fortress of fear — that old refuge of the vanquished — and there abandoned. Our leaders set sail to sell themselves to a higher bidder, a practice they have continued to follow at every opportunity.

We are a small people sheltering under the wing of the clergy — the only remaining repository of faith, knowledge, truth, and national wealth; isolated from the universal progress of thought with all its pitfalls and perils, and raised (since complete ignorance was impossible) on well-meaning but grossly distorted accounts of the great historical facts.

We are a small people, the product of a Jansenist colony, isolated, defeated, left a powerless prey to all those invading congregations from France and Navarre that were eager to perpetuate in this holy realm of fear (fear-is-the-mother-of-wisdom!) the blessings and prestige of a Catholic religion that was being scorned in Europe. Heirs of papal authority, mechanical, brooking no opposition, past masters of obscurantist methods, our educational institutions had, from that time on, absolute control over a world of warped memories, stagnant minds, and crooked intentions.

We are a small people, who yet grew and multiplied in number, if not in spirit, here in the north of this huge American continent; and our bodies were young and our hearts of gold, but our minds remained primitive, with their sterile obsession about Europe's past glories, while the concrete achievements of our own oppressed people were ignored.

It seemed as if there were no future for us.

But wars and revolutions in the outside world broke the spell, shattered the mental block.

Irreparable cracks began to appear in the fortress walls.

Political rivalries became bitterly entrenched, and the clergy unexpectedly made mistakes.

Then came rebellions, followed by a few executions, and the first bitter cases of rift between the clergy and a few of the faithful.

Slowly the breach widened, then narrowed, then once again grew wider.

Foreign travel became more common, with Paris as the centre of attraction. But the distance being almost prohibitive, and the city too active for our timid souls, the trip was often no more than an opportunity for a holiday spent in improving a retarded sexual education or in acquiring, through the prestige of a long stay in France, the necessary authority whereby better to exploit the masses on one's return home. With a very few exceptions, the behaviour of members (travelled or not) of our medical profession, for instance, tends to be scandalous (how-else-is-one-to-finance-these-long-years-of-study?).

Revolutionary publications, if they ever attracted any attention at all, were considered as the virulent outpourings of a group of eccentrics. With our usual lack of discernment we condemned such publications as devoid of any academic merit.

Travel was also, at times, an unhoped-for opportunity for a new awakening. Minds were growing restless, and everywhere the reading of forbidden books brought a little hope and soothing comfort.

Our minds were enlightened by the *poètes maudits* who, far from being monsters of evil, dared to give loud and clear expression to those feelings that had always been shamefully smothered and repressed by the most wretched among us, in their terror of being swallowed up alive. New vistas were opened to us by those literary innovators who were the first to challenge the torments of the soul, the moral turpitude of modern life. How stirring was the accuracy, the freshness of their answers, and how different from the hackneyed old lectures delivered in Quebec and in seminaries the world over.

We began to aspire to greater expectations.

We giddily watched the worn and tattered boundaries of our old horizons vanishing into space. Instead of the humiliation of perpetual slavery there came new pride in the knowledge that freedom could be won.

To hell with Church blessings and parochial life! They had been repaid a hundredfold for what they originally granted.

We had our first burning contact with the brotherhood of man to which Christianity had barred the door.

And fear in all its facets no longer ruled the land.

Its facets were legion, and in an attempt to expel them from memory, I shall enumerate them:

fear of prejudice — fear of public opinion, of persecution, of general disapproval
fear of being abandoned by God and by a society that invariably leaves us to our lonely fate

fear of oneself, of one's brothers, of poverty
fear of the established order — fear of absurd laws
fear of new acquaintances
fear of the irrational
fear of needs to be met
fear of opening the flood-gates of our faith in man —
    fear of the society of the future
fear of the unsettling experience of love
deadly fear — holy fear — paralysing fear: so many
    links to our chains

Gone were the days of debilitating fear as we entered the era of anguish.

It would take an iron constitution to remain indifferent to the sadness of those who grimly assume an artificial gaiety, of the psychological reactions to the refinements of cruelty that are but the transparent cellophane wrappings to our current anguished despair. (How can one stop screaming upon reading the account of that horrible collection of lampshades pieced together out of tattooed skin stripped from the flesh of wretched prisoners on the request of some elegant lady; how can one stifle one's groans at the long list of concentration-camp tortures; how can one stop one's blood from curdling at the description of those Spanish prison cells, those meaningless reprisals, those cold-blooded acts of vengeance?) How can one fail to shudder at the cruel lucidity of science?

And now, after the reign of overpowering mental anguish, comes the reign of nausea.

We have been sickened by man's apparent inaptitude to remedy such evils, by the futility of our efforts, by the shattered vanity of our past hopes.

For centuries the many sources of poetic inspiration have been doomed to total failure in a society that tossed them overboard, and then tried to retrieve them and force them into the mould of integration, of false assimilation.

For centuries lusty, seething revolutions have been crushed after one brief moment of delirious hope during their fatal fall:

    the French revolutions
    the Russian Revolution
    the Spanish Revolution

all ended in international confusion, despite the vain hopes of countless simple souls throughout the world.

There again, fatality was stronger than generosity.

It is nauseating that fat rewards should be handed out to practitioners of gross cruelty, to liars, to forgers, to those who manufacture abortive projects, to the plotters of intrigue, to the openly self-seeking, to the false counsellors of humanity, to those who pollute the fountain of life.

It is nauseating to realize our own cowardice, our helplessness, our weakness, our bewilderment.

Our ill-starred loves. . . .

And the constant cherishing of vain delusions rather than enigmatic realities.

Where is the cause for man's self-imposed efficacy for evil to be found, if not in our stubborn purpose to defend a civilization that ordains the destinies of our leading nations?

The United States, Russia, England, France, Germany, Italy, and Spain: all of them heirs to the same Ten Commandments, to the same gospel.

The religion of Christ has dominated the world. See what has been made of it: a communal faith exploited for the satisfaction of personal ambitions.

Abolish the individual thirst for competition, natural riches, prestige, authority, and these countries will be in perfect agreement. But whichever of them were to gain total supremacy over the world, the general result would be the same.

Christian civilization has reached the end of its tether.

The next world war will cause its total collapse, when international competition is no longer possible.

Its moribund condition will strike those who are still blind to it.

The least sensitive natures will be nauseated at the sight of the gangrene that has been setting in since the fourteenth century.

The despicable way they have been exploited so effectively, for so many centuries and at the cost of life's most precious values, will at last become obvious to its countless victims, to all of its submissive slaves who, the more wretched they were, the more they strove to defend it.

But there will be an end to torture.

The downfall of Christianity will drag down with it all the people and all the classes that it has influenced, from the first to the last, from the highest to the lowest.

The depth of its disgrace will be equal to the height of its success in the thirteenth century.

In the thirteenth century, once man's spiritual awareness of his relations with the universe had been allowed to develop within permissible limits, intuition gave way to speculation. Gradually the act of faith was replaced by the calculated act. Exploitation fed on the very heart of religion by turning to its own advantage the limitations of man's reasoning powers; by a rational use of the holy texts for the maintenance of its easily-won supremacy.

This systematic exploitation spread slowly to all levels of social activity, expecting maximum returns for its investment.

Faith sought refuge in the heart of the populace and became their last hope, their only consolation. But there, too, hope began to fade.

Among the learned the science of mathematics took over from the outmoded tradition of metaphysical speculation.

The process of observation followed that of transfiguration.

Method paved the way toward the elimination of restrictions. Decadence became convivial and necessary, prompting the advent of agile machines moving at frightening speeds, enabling us to harness our riotous rivers pending the day when the planet will blow itself up. Our scientific instruments are wonderful devices for the study and control of size, speed, noise, weight, or length. We have unlocked all the gates of the world with our rational thinking; but it is a world where we are no longer united.

The growing chasm between spiritual and rational powers is stretched almost to breaking-point.

Through systematically controlled material progress — the privilege of the affluent — we were able, with the help of the Church (and later without it), to secure political progress; but we have not been able to renew our basic sensibility, our subconscious impulses; nor have we been capable of seizing our only chance of emancipation from the grip of Christianity by allowing for a free development of man's true feelings.

Society was born through faith, but will perish through reason: A DELIBERATE PROCESS.

The fatal disintegration of collective moral strength into strictly individual self-indulgence has lined the formidable frame of abstract knowledge with a patchwork quilt under which society is snuggling in concealment for a leisurely feasting on its ill-gained prize.

It required the last two wars to achieve this absurd result. The horror of the third war will be decisive. We are on the brink of a D-day of total sacrifice.

The European rat-race has already started across the Atlantic. But events will catch up with the greedy, the gluttonous, the sybarites, the unperturbed, the blind, the deaf.

They will be swallowed up mercilessly.

And a new collective hope will dawn.

We must make ready to meet it with exceptional clear-sightedness, anonymously bound together by a renewed faith in the future, faith in a common future.

The magical harvest magically reaped from the field of the Unknown lies ready for use. All the true poets have worked at gathering it in. Its powers of transformation are as great as the violent reactions it originally provoked, and as remarkable as its later unavailability (after the more than two centuries, there is not a single copy of Sade to be found in our bookshops; Isidore Ducasse, dead for over a century, a century of revolution and slaughter, is still, despite our having become inured to filth and corruption, too powerful for the queasy contemporary conscience).

All the elements of this treasure as yet remain inaccessible to our present-day society. Every precious part of it will be preserved intact for future use. It was built up with spontaneous enthusiasm, in spite of, and outside, the framework of civilization. And its social effects will only be felt once society's present needs are recognized.

Meanwhile our duty is plain.

The ways of society must be abandoned once and for all; we must free ourselves from its utilitarian spirit. We must not tolerate our mental or physical faculties' being wittingly left undeveloped. We must refuse to close our eyes to vice, to deceit perpetrated under the cloak of imparted knowledge, of services rendered, of payment due. We must refuse to be trapped within the walls of the common mould — a strong citadel, but easy enough to escape. We must avoid silence (do with us what you will, but hear us you must), avoid fame, avoid privileges (except that of being heeded) — avoid them all as the stigma of evil, indifference, servility. We must refuse to serve, or to be used for, such despicable ends. We must avoid DELIBERATE DESIGN as the harmful weapon of REASON. Down with them both! Back they go!

MAKE WAY FOR MAGIC! MAKE WAY FOR OBJECTIVE MYSTERY!

MAKE WAY FOR LOVE!

MAKE WAY FOR WHAT IS NEEDED!

We accept full responsibility for the consequences of our total refusal.

Self-interested plans are nothing but the still-born product of their author.

While passionate action is animated with a life of its own.

We shall gladly take full responsibility for the future. Deliberate, rational effort can only fashion the present from the ashes of the past.

Our passions must necessarily, spontaneously, unpredictably forge the future.

The past must be acknowledged at birth — but it is far from sacred. We have paid our debt to the past.

It is naïve and unsound to consider famous men and events in history as being endowed with a special quality unknown to us today. Indeed, such quality is automatically achieved when man follows his innermost inclinations; it is achieved when man recognizes his new role in a new world. This is true for any man, at any time.

The past must no longer be used as an anvil for beating out the present and the future.

All we need of the past is what can be put to use for the present. A better tomorrow will emerge imperceptibly from the present.

We need not worry about the future until we come to it.

The Final Squaring of Accounts

The social establishment resents our dedication to our cause, our uninhibited expression of concern, our going to extremes, as an insult to their indolence, their smugness, their love of gracious living (the meaning of a rich, generous life, full of hope and love, has been lost).

Friends of the prevailing political system suspect us of

being promoters of the "Revolution." Friends of the "Revolution" suspect us of being downright rebels: ". . . we protest against the established order of things, but reform is our sole objective, not complete change."

However tactfully it may be worded, we believe we understand what they are getting at.

It is all a matter of class.

It is being conjectured that we are naïvely trying to "change" society by substituting other, similar men for those currently in power. If that were the case, then why not keep the present ones?

Because they are not of the same class! As if a difference in class implied a difference in civilization, a difference in aspirations, a difference in expectations!

They dedicate themselves, at a fixed salary plus a cost-of-living allowance, to organizing the proletariat; they are absolutely right. The only trouble is that once they have strengthened their positions, they will want to add to their slender incomes, and, at the expense of that self-same proletariat, they will always be demanding more and more, ever and always in the same manner, brooking no rebuttal.

Nevertheless, we recognize that they follow a time-honoured tradition. Salvation can only come after an unbearable exploitation.

These men will be the excess.

They will inevitably become so without anyone's assistance. Their plunder will be plentiful. We shall want none of it.

That is what our "guilty abstention" will consist in.

We leave the premeditated carnage to you (premeditated like everything else that belongs to complacent decadence). As for us, give us spirited action, and the full responsibility of our total refusal.

(We cannot help the fact that various social classes have superseded each other at government level without any of them being able to resist the compelling pull of decadence. We cannot help the fact that history teaches that only through the full development of our faculties, and then through the complete renewal of our sources of emotional inspiration, can we ever hope to break the deadlock and make way for the eager passage of a new-born civilization.)

All those who hold power or are struggling for it would be quite happy to grant our every wish, if only we were willing to confine our activities to the cramping limitations of their cunning directives.

Success will be ours if we close our eyes, stop up our ears, roll up our sleeves, and fling ourselves pell-mell into the fray. We prefer our cynicism to be spontaneous and without malice.

Kindly souls are apt to laugh at the lack of financial success of joint exhibitions of our work. It gives them a feeling of satisfaction to think they were the first to be aware of its small market-value.

If we do hold countless exhibitions, it is not with the naïve hope of becoming rich. We know that there is a world of difference between us and the wealthy, who are bound to suffer something of a shock from their contact with us.

It is only through misunderstanding that such sales have, in the past, brought in big profits.

We hope this text will avoid any such misunderstandings in the future.

If we work with such feverish enthusiasm, it is because we feel a pressing need for unity.

Unity is the road to success.

Yesterday we stood alone and irresolute.

Today we form a group with strong, steady, and already far-reaching ramifications.

We must also share the glorious responsibility of preserving the valuable treasure that history has bequeathed to us.

Its tangible values must constantly be reinterpreted, be compared and considered anew. Such interpretation is an exacting, abstract process that requires the creative medium of action.

This treasure is the poetic source of supply, the fountain of youth for our creative impulses that will inspire the generations of the future. It must be ADAPTED to suit circumstances if it is to serve its rightful purpose.

We urge all of those who are moved by the spirit of adventure to join us.

Within a foreseeable future, man will be able to develop, untrammelled, his own individual skills, through impassioned, impulsive action and glorious independence.

Meanwhile we must work without respite, hand in hand with those who long for a better life; together we must persevere, regardless of praise or persecution, toward the joyful fulfilment of our fierce desire for freedom.

Paul-Emile BORDUAS

Magdeleine ARBOUR, Marcel BARBEAU,
Bruno CORMIER, Claude GAUVREAU,
Pierre GAUVREAU, Muriel GUILBAULT,
Marcelle FERRON-HAMELIN, Fernand LEDUC,
Thérèse LEDUC, Jean-Paul MOUSSEAU,
Maurice PERRON, Louise RENAUD,
Françoise RIOPELLE, Jean-Paul RIOPELLE,
Françoise SULLIVAN.

But You Said We Won/1949

Newfoundland, Britain's oldest colony, joined Confederation on 31 March 1949. At least that is what the history books tell us. But the Great Island is still an island, and the Newfoundlanders remain as fiercely independent and as wary of the Mainlanders as ever. It is these sentiments that are explored in "But You Said We Won," an imaginary (but not too imaginary) dialogue with an oldie, written by Ray Guy (b. 1939), the Leacock Award-winning humorist who was born at Come By Chance and lives outside St. John's. The piece comes from *You May Know Them as Sea Urchins, Ma'am* (1975).

A conversation with an older person who passed away in August, 1943, out Home.

DO ENGLAND STILL STAND?

Oh, yes, sir. And our Sovereign sits yet at her castle at Windsor . . . as they say.

OH, THEY NEVER HAD A BOY, THEN, AFTER.

No, sir. They never had a boy.

WELL, WE WON, THEN.

Oh, yes, sir. We won. It was a bit ticklish in spots but we made it.

UM. AND HOW WAS THE FISH LAST YEAR? MUCH GOT?

Well, yes and no, sir. There was and there wasn't.

There was a good sign of the first of it but it dwindled off. But lobsters were plenty and a good price.

IS THERE MANY CANNING THEM NOW BESIDES MANUEL AND ABBY AND HENRY ALFRED?

No, sir. They passed on, you know. They don't can them any more. The ice came last year.

ICE? COME IN? MUCH?

More than was ever seen since back in your time, sir, they said.

I ONLY SEEN IT TWICE. NO, THREE TIMES. NO, IT WAS ONLY TWICE I SEEN IT. I THINK IT WAS ONLY TWICE. NO DIFFERENCE. DID BILLY LAST LONG?

Oh, yes, sir. He rallied after that and he was great and smart and only passed away, I think it was, the year before . . . no, in the summer . . . two years before Confederation. They put his pipe and a bottle of rum in the box along with him.

EH, MY SON?

His pipe, sir and a bottle. They put it in with him. It was his wish.

CONFEDERATION?

Oh, that came about in 1949. We were joined on to Canada.

CONFEDERATION?

Yes, Confederation. Joined on to Canada. It was in 1949. April Fool's Day. You know, upalong. Canada. We were joined on.

YOU SAID WE WON.

But that was the war, sir. This was after. I can't mind too much about it. I was a boy then.

THE COMMISSION DONE IT.

I don't think so, sir, altogether. I'm going by what I'm told. I believe we were more or less on our own again, then.

THEN HOW MANY WAS THERE KILLED?

So far as I know, sir, there was no one killed. There was only a lot of talk all the time, and swearing. When it came about they put the flag down to half-mast but there was no one killed.

NO ONE?

No, sir. No one . . . so far as I know.

NO ONE.

The ground is sold, sir, but your house is still there and son John's. They rose the roof on it a long time ago, and they put the water in.

All the flakes are gone now, sir, and they got what they call a fish plant across from the Dock Garden below Uncle Walter's. They don't make fish at all, now, sir.

Do you mind Uncle Walter's saying, sir? "Things will rise and things will fall." I don't, sir, but I hear them talk about it.

They say that you and Uncle Abby and Uncle Walter would have something to say if you could only see the television. Or, that's what they used to say first when the television came in.

That's what they said when the men was put on the moon, too. They said you and Uncle Abby and grandfather and them would have something to say about it if you were here now.

It must be hard to believe, sir, all these things. There was a vessel came in through the Bay to the Foxhead last year, sir, longer than The Great Eastern.

They have a thing down there for oil. All the people came down, you know, a few years back, to the Cove. There's nothing up on the Islands now. Wareham's left Harbour Buffett and I was up and saw the church falling down at Merasheen myself.

It must sound wonderful odd to you, sir, but I'm not telling any lies. What, sir?

THERE WASN'T NO ONE KILLED?

A New Vision/1958

It is more difficult to find a document to define the Conservative view of Canada than it is to locate one that defines the Liberal view. The Liberal Party of Canada has issued statements more or less regularly, but the Progressive Conservative Party finds itself less able or less willing to codify its beliefs, no matter how deeply based these may be. It took a new leader, John G. Diefenbaker (b. 1895), to find a new focal point for Conservatism in Canada. As the first Conservative prime minister (from 1957 to 1963) in twenty-two years, he made a series of electrifying speeches which won his party the largest majority ever obtained by a prime minister (208 out of 265 seats in the House of Commons). Here are excerpts from the opening speech in that campaign, taken from the address delivered at the Civic Auditorium, Winnipeg, 12 February 1958. The prime minister addressed an audience five thousand strong — the largest political rally in the prairie provinces in thirty years. The address is reprinted from *Canadian History in Documents, 1763-1966* (1966), edited by J. Michael Bliss.

Ladies and gentlemen, we started in the last few months, since June the 10th, to carry out our promises, and I can tell you this, that as long as I am Prime Minister of this country, the welfare of the average Canadian will not be forgotten.

We intend to launch for the future, we have laid the foundations now, the long-range objectives of this party. We ask from you a mandate; a new and a stronger mandate, to pursue the planning and to carry to fruition our new national development programme for Canada. For years we raised that in the House of Commons, and those in authority ridiculed it. Day before yesterday, Mr. Pearson came out in favour of a national development policy. Why didn't they do it when they were in power?

This national development policy will create a new sense of national purpose and national destiny. One Canada. One Canada, wherein Canadians will have preserved to them the control of their own economic and political destiny. Sir John A. Macdonald gave his life to this party. He opened the West. He saw Canada from East to West. I see a new Canada — a Canada of the North. What are these new principles? What are our objectives? What do we propose? We propose to assist the provinces, with their co-operation, in the financing and construction of job-creating projects necessary for the new development, where such projects are beyond the resources of the provinces. We will assist the provinces with their co-operation in the conservation of the renewable natural resources. We will aid in projects which are self-liquidating. We will aid in projects which, while not self-liquidating will lead to the development of the national resources for the opening of Canada's northland. We will open that northland for development by improving transportation and communication and by the development of power, by the building of access roads. We will make an inventory of our hydro-electric potential.

Ladies and gentlemen, we now intend to bring in legislation to encourage progressively increasing processing of our domestic raw materials in Canada, rather than shipping them out in raw material form. We will ensure that Canada's national resources are used to benefit Canadians and that Canadians have an opportunity to participate in Canada's development. We have not discouraged foreign investment, but we will encourage the partnership of the foreign investors with the Canadian people. . . .

Canadians, realize your opportunities! This is only the beginning. The future programme for the next five to seven years under a Progressive Conservative Government is one that is calculated to give young Canadians, moti-

vated by a desire to serve, a lift in the heart, faith in Canada's future, faith in her destiny. We will extend aid to economically sound railway projects, such as the Pine Point Railroad to Great Slave Lake. That was promised day before yesterday in the Liberal platform. Why didn't they do it then?

Yes, we will press for hydro-electric development of the Columbia River, which now awaits completion of an agreement with the United States. I mentioned the South Saskatchewan. These are the plans.

This is the message I give to you my fellow Canadians, not one of defeatism. Jobs! Jobs for hundreds of thousands of Canadian people. A new vision! A new hope! A new soul for Canada. . . .

As far as the Arctic is concerned, how many of you here knew the pioneers in Western Canada. I saw the early days here. Here in Winnipeg in 1903, when the vast movement was taking place into the Western plains, they had imagination. There is a new imagination now. The Arctic. We intend to carry out the legislative programme of Arctic research, to develop Arctic routes, to develop those vast hidden resources the last few years have revealed. Plans to improve the St. Lawrence and the Hudson Bay route. Plans to increase self-government in the Yukon and Northwest Territories. We can see one or two provinces there.

Taxation adjustments to place Canadians on a more equal footing with foreign investors. Encourage foreign investors to make equity stock available to Canadians for purchase, to appoint Canadians to executive positions, to deny the present plan of certain American companies that do not give to Canadian plants their fair share of the export business. Those are some of the things we want to do.. . .

It is for those things that I ask a mandate, not giving you tonight the whole picture at all, by any means but giving you something of the vision as I see it. The reason that I appeal to the Canadian people, a mandate for a clear majority. You set a pace for Manitoba last time. Give us a few more, this.

We need a clear majority to carry out this long-range plan, this great design, this blueprint for the Canada which her resources make possible.

I want to see Canadians given a transcending sense of national purpose, such as Macdonald gave in his day. To safeguard our independence, restore our unity, a policy that will scrupulously respect the rights of the provinces, and at the same time build for the achievement of that one Canada, is the major reason why 35 of our 113 members in the House of Commons are sufficiently young to belong to the Young Progressive Conservatives. They caught that vision. I am not here to condemn others. I am here for the purpose, as a Canadian, to give you a picture of the kind of Canada the long-range plans that we have in mind will bring about. . . .

This party has become the party of national destiny. I

hope it will be the party of vision and courage. The party of one Canada, with equal opportunities to all. The only party that can give to youth an Elizabethan sense of grand design — that's my challenge.

The faith to venture with enthusiasm to the frontiers of a nation; that faith, that assurance that will be provided with a government strong enough to implement plans for development.

To the young men and women of this nation I say, Canada is within your hands. Adventure. Adventure to the nation's utmost bounds, to strive, to seek, to find, and not to yield. The policies that will be placed before the people of Canada in this campaign will be ones that will ensure that today and this century will belong to Canada. The destination is one Canada. To that end I dedicate this party.

The Canadian Bill of Rights/1960

"There are some who contend that freedom cannot be assured by a written document. In part that is true, for when the spirit of freedom dies in the hearts of people, statutes cannot preserve it. But the ideal of freedom is kept before the people in a declaration of their rights," declared John G. Diefenbaker (b. 1895) in 1948. It was not until he became prime minister that the prairie lawyer was able to ensure that the basic freedoms Canadians enjoy were enshrined in a Bill of Rights. The document, a simple statute and not a constitutional amendment, is seen by many as Prime Minister Diefenbaker's crowning achievement. Arthur R.M. Lower, the historian, wrote: "It may be fifty years before it begins to influence Canadian life very much, but little by little it will make its way." The text is reproduced from *One Canada: Memoirs of the Right Honourable John G. Diefenbaker: The Years of Achievement, 1957-1962* (1976).

THE CANADIAN BILL OF RIGHTS: An Act for the Recognition and Protection of Human Rights and Fundamental Freedoms. Statutes of Canada 1960, 8-9 Elizabeth II, Chapter 44, assented to 10th August 1960.

The Parliament of Canada, affirming that the Canadian Nation is founded upon principles that acknowledge the supremacy of God, the dignity and worth of the human person and the position of the family in a society of free men and free institutions;

Affirming also that men and institutions remain free only when freedom is founded upon respect for moral and spiritual values and the rule of law;

And being desirous of enshrining these principles and the human rights and fundamental freedoms derived from them, in a Bill of Rights which shall reflect the respect of Parliament for its constitutional authority and which

shall ensure the protection of these rights and freedoms in Canada:

THEREFORE Her Majesty, by and with the advice and consent of the Senate and House of Commons of Canada, enacts as follows:

PART I   Bill of Rights

1. It is hereby recognized and declared that in Canada there have existed and shall continue to exist without discrimination by reason of race, national origin, colour, religion or sex, the following human rights and fundamental freedoms, namely,

a) the right of the individual to life, liberty, security of the person and enjoyment of property, and the right not to be deprived thereof except by due process of law;

b) the right of the individual to equality before the law and the protection of the law;

c) freedom of religion;

d) freedom of speech;

e) freedom of assembly and association; and

f) freedom of the press.

2. Every law of Canada shall, unless it is expressly declared by an Act of the Parliament of Canada that it shall operate notwithstanding the *Canadian Bill of Rights*, be so construed and applied as not to abrogate, abridge or infringe or to authorize the abrogation, abridgment or infringement of any of the rights or freedoms herein recognized and declared, and in particular, no law of Canada shall be construed or applied so as to

a) authorize or effect the arbitrary detention, imprisonment or exile of any person;

b) impose or authorize the imposition of cruel and unusual treatment or punishment;

c) deprive a person who has been arrested or detained

(i) of the right to be informed promptly of the reason for his arrest or detention,

(ii) of the right to retain and instruct counsel without delay, or

(iii) of the remedy by way of *habeas corpus* for the determination of the validity of his detention and for his release if the detention is not lawful;

d) authorize a court, tribunal, commission, board or other authority to compel a person to give evidence if he is denied counsel, protection against selfcrimination or other constitutional safeguards;

e) deprive a person of the right to a fair hearing in accordance with the principles of fundamental justice for the determination of his rights and obligations;

f) deprive a person charged with a criminal offence of the right to be presumed innocent until proved guilty according to law in a fair and public hearing by an independent and impartial tribunal, or of the right to reasonable bail without just cause; or

g) deprive a person of the right to the assistance of an interpreter in any proceedings in which he is involved or in which he is a party or a witness before a court, commission, board or other tribunal, if he does not understand or speak the language in which such proceedings are conducted.

3. The Minister of Justice shall, in accordance with such regulations as may be prescribed by the Governor in Council, examine every proposed regulation submitted in draft form to the Clerk of the Privy Council pursuant to the *Regulations Act* and every Bill introduced in or presented to the House of Commons, in order to ascertain whether any of the provisions thereof are inconsistent with the purposes and provisions of this Part and he shall report any such inconsistency to the House of Commons at the first convenient opportunity.

4. The provisions of this Part shall be known as the *Canadian Bill of Rights.*

"I am a Canadian, a free Canadian, free to speak without fear, free to worship God in my own way, free to stand for what I think right, free to oppose what I believe wrong, free to choose those who shall govern my country. This heritage of freedom I pledge to uphold for myself and all mankind."

The Right Honourable John G. Diefenbaker, Prime Minister of Canada, House of Commons Debates, 1 July 1960.

Liberalism/1962

"Liberalism in Canada is a national political creed, but it transcends nationalism," wrote Lester B. Pearson (1897-1972). "Liberalism encompasses the story of man's universal yearning for freedom and security. It shows him how to achieve, and to reconcile, these ideals." These words appear in Pearson's Introduction to J.W. Pickersgill's *The Liberal Party* (1962). The excerpt below constitutes the greater part of that Introduction. To many, Pearson was the very image of Liberalism (or "gliberalism," as John Diefenbaker would have it). Recipient of the Nobel Peace Prize in 1957, Pearson was prime minister from 1963 to 1968. The party he headed from 1957 until his retirement in 1968, the Liberal Party of Canada, knew what it was to govern, for the Liberals have held federal power since 1921 for all but ten years, or since 1935 for all but five years. Its apologist, Jack Pickersgill, even called it "the party of government," with the Progressive Conservative Party by default becoming "the party of opposition." One of the strengths of the Liberal Party has been its ability to corner the progressive spirit and describe it skilfully, as Pearson's practised prose shows.

What, then, are the principles that have inspired and guided the Liberal Party in its service to the Canadian people? The fundamental principle of Liberalism, the foundation of its faith, is belief in the dignity and worth of the individual. The state is the creation of man, to protect and serve him; and not the reverse.

Liberalism, therefore, believes in man; and that it is the first purpose of government to legislate for the liberation and development of the human personality. This includes the negative requirement of removing anything that stands in the way of individual and collective progress.

The negative requirement is important. It involves removal and reform: clearing away and opening up, so that man can move forward and societies expand. The removal of restrictions that block the access to achievement; this is the very essence of Liberalism.

The Liberal Party, however, must also promote the positive purpose of ensuring that all citizens, without any discrimination, will be in a position to take advantage of the opportunities opened up; of the freedoms that have been won.

Progress consists in more than the building of an unobstructed and well-paved highway for man's progress. It also provides for the movement of people on that highway, steady movement in the right direction which will avoid the pitfalls of extremism on the right or the left side of the road. Liberalism is the political principle that gives purpose and reality to this kind of progress.

Liberalism stands for the middle way: the way of progress. It stands for moderation, tolerance, and the rejection of extreme courses, whether they express themselves in demands that the state should do everything for the individual, even if it means weakening and destroying him in the process, or in demands that the state should do nothing except hold the ring so that the fittest survive under the law of the jungle.

In other words, Liberalism accepts social security but rejects socialism; it accepts free enterprise but rejects economic anarchy; it accepts humanitarianism but rejects paternalism.

The Liberal Party is opposed to the shackling limitations of rigid political dogma, or authoritarianism of any kind, which is so often the prelude to oppression and exploitation. It fights against the abuse of power either by the state or by persons or groups within the state. It recognizes the special danger of such abuse in an age of massive concentration of wealth and economic power and of "bigness" of all kinds. Liberalism must protect the right of every man to live his own life, in creative freedom, in the midst of all this "bigness" and the pressures that follow from it.

That is why government, while accepting new obligations to assist and protect the individual, must do so in a way that also respects the individual's right to manage his own affairs; and to hold his own convictions, speak his own mind, and advance his own ideas, even against the policies of a government whose purpose it is to serve him.

Liberalism, also, while insisting on equality of opportunity, rejects any imposed equality which would discourage and destroy a man's initiative and enterprise. It sees no value in the equality, or conformity, which comes from lopping off the tallest ears of corn. It maintains, therefore, that originality and initiative should be encouraged, and that reward should be the result of effort.

For instance, Liberalism can exist only with freedom. But how can freedom, guaranteed politically and legally, be made meaningful in the face of today's industrial and economic pressures? Government must keep pace with the changing needs of the times and accept greater responsibilities than would have been acceptable to a Liberal a hundred years ago. That is why the Liberal Party favours social and economic planning which will stimulate and encourage private enterprise to operate more effectively for the benefit of all.

Liberalism must always remember that responsibility is the other side of freedom. If the individual uses his democratic power and freedom to make irresponsible demands on those he has chosen to govern him, progress may turn into retreat; freedom may be lost in insistence on unwise measures to make it secure.

In short, freedom and welfare must be kept in a healthy balance or there will be trouble. This essential balance can be achieved by applying, to every proposal for further intervention by the state, the question: will it truly benefit the individual; will it enlarge or restrict his opportunity for self-expression and development?

The Liberal purpose remains the creation of opportunity for men and women to become self-directing, responsible citizens. This means, as we have seen, the simultaneous pursuit of freedom and welfare or, if you prefer, of welfare as an element of freedom. It is because welfare has come to be dissociated from freedom, or even set in opposition to it, that freedom has lost so much of its appeal in certain societies and that statist and authoritarian parties have gained in power and prestige. A dynamic, modern, responsible Liberalism need not fear this challenge to its position any more than it need fear the challenge of reaction from the right.

The principles of Liberalism are concerned, however, not only with the individual and his freedom and welfare. They are concerned also with the development of the Canadian people as a nation in the world.

In Canada this has meant growth from a dependent colony to a free state, respected in the world not only for the way it has pushed back the frontiers and built up a strong and stable nation at home, but for the manner in which it has discharged its international responsibilities, in peace and in war. The Liberal Party can take satisfaction out of the contribution it has made through Liberal governments to both national development and international co-operation.

For the progress Canada has made, and will make,

national unity has been essential. The necessity for doing everything possible to maintain and strengthen this unity has been the cornerstone of Liberal policy from the very beginning of its history. Moreover, Liberalism has understood that national unity must be based on two races, cultures, traditions, and languages; on a full and equal partnership of English- and French-speaking Canadians. Liberals have rejected any other kind of unity, which would have been artificial and unenduring.

This view is consistent with the Liberal doctrine of service to *all* the people; with policies which must be beneficial to all classes, all sections, all groups. If others appeal in different ways to different parts and peoples of Canada, Liberals must say the same things at the same time to all Canadians.

National unity, however, based on the principles above, must be reconciled with the fact that Canada is a federal state in which the constitutional and historic rights of the provinces must be preserved. It is important also that the provinces must not be separated by economic inequality which would make national unity difficult, if not impossible. The Liberal Party, therefore, considers it a duty of the federal government to help equalize the distribution of income and wealth and development among the provinces, but in such a way that there will be no interference with the constitutional rights and privileges of the provinces.

The Liberal Party has recognized, not only the interdependence of provinces within Canada, but also the interdependence of nations in a shrinking nuclear world. It has shown this recognition by pursuing when in office an active policy of international co-operation and the acceptance of international responsibilities, at the United Nations, in the Commonwealth, and in the North Atlantic Treaty Organization. Under Liberal governments, after the Second World War, Canada achieved a position of respect and influence in the councils of the world, and in the effort to ensure peace against forces, such as communist imperialism, which threatened it.

The Liberal Party must continue staunchly to support international co-operation and the peaceful negotiation of international problems. It accepts the fact that nuclear war means global destruction; that now the only defence is peace. Nevertheless, it also recognizes that power is necessary on the side of freedom, if freedom and peace are to be preserved. For this reason, nations must band together and unite their strength for deterrence and defence in organizations like NATO, until the day comes when the United Nations will be able to ensure peace under law on a global basis.

The Liberal Party, then, seeks to promote security and welfare, not only for individual Canadians, but also for the Canadian nation and for all men.

It knows, however, that material progress towards these objectives is not enough for a nation. It cherishes for Canada the maintenance and strengthening of those values without which no people can be great, or truly free.

Liberalism must strive to foster all those forces in a nation which will make for true development in other than material ways: the willingness to work and serve and sacrifice to achieve ends that are outside of self; appreciation of the beautiful and the good in life; understanding that bread and circuses are not the ultimate objective of existence, either national or personal; recognition that a society is only as strong as its adherence to moral values.

It is in these fundamental things that Liberal principles must be rooted. If they are, and if those roots are deep, Liberal policies will be strong enough to withstand opposing forces.

Those policies must always look forward. For the very essence of Liberalism is to work for the future.

The Liberal Party has served Canada honourably and well in the past. It is now putting forward new programs for the problems of Canada today, in the conviction that it will have the responsibility of making these effective for Canada tomorrow.

Canada's National Flag/1965

"If our nation by God's grace endures a thousand years, this day will always be remembered as a milestone in Canada's national progress." Lester B. Pearson spoke these words at noon on Parliament Hill in Ottawa at the official raising of Canada's National Flag, 15 February 1965. The new maple-leaf flag was no easy achievement, replacing as it did the traditional Red Ensign, the last in a long line of British and French flags and banners. The House of Commons voted to adopt the new flag after 308 speeches and thirty-seven days of debate in the House, and the fifteen-man Commons committee deliberated for fifty-four sessions to consider some two thousand submitted designs. The final vote was taken, upon closure to prevent filibuster, on 15 December 1964. The prime minister rose in the House and said: "This is the flag of the future. It does not dishonour the past." The new banner is officially described as "a red flag of the proportions two by length and one by width, containing in its centre a white square the width of the flag, bearing a single red maple leaf, or, in heraldic terms, described as Gules on a Canadian pale Argent a maple leaf of the first." The actual design, based on the historic flag of the Royal Military College, was suggested by the RMC historian George F.G. Stanley. The procedures which follow are reprinted from *Etiquette for Canada's Flag*, a brochure issued by the Secretary of State in 1972.

Canada's National Flag. The national flag, adopted by Parliament and proclaimed by Her Majesty the Queen, was inaugurated on February 15, 1965, at ceremonies in Ottawa and throughout Canada as well as at Official Canadian posts abroad.

It is a distinctive symbol which identifies Canada in all parts of the world. Canadians at home wishing to fly the flag may do so at any time and in any place, as long as they treat the flag with the respect that such a symbol warrants. The generally established customs for official use may be taken as a guide.

Flying the Flag. Officially, the flag is flown on land only in daylight hours, being raised at sunrise and lowered at sunset.

There is no official statute concerning a salute to the flag in Canada as in some countries. When the flag is raised it is customary for civilian males to stand and remove their hats. Women also stand.

The flag may be flown at night on special occasions, when it should be illuminated.

With Other Flags. When more than one flag is flown and it is impossible to hoist or lower them at the same time, the Canadian flag should be hoisted first and lowered last.

Territorial flags flown together — for example, the flag of another country or a provincial flag along with the Canadian flag — should be flown on separate staffs. They should be approximately the same size and flown at the same height.

Non-territorial flags — for example, Centennial flags — may be flown beneath the national flag when physical arrangements make it impossible for them to be flown separately. But no flag, banner or pennant should be flown above the Canadian flag.

Position of Honour. When the national flag is flown with a second flag, the maple leaf flag occupies the staff on the left, from the viewpoint of the audience facing the flags. The two flags should be flown side by side and at the same height. They should also be of the same size.

When three flags are flown together, the national flag occupies the centre staff and the flag of the country being honoured is on the left-hand staff, from the viewpoint of the audience facing the flags.

When more than three flags are flown, the national flag may be at the left, or there may be one Canadian flag at each end of a line of flags if several countries are being represented.

If a number of flags are carried in a procession or parade, the Canadian flag should be in the position of honour at the marching right or at the centre front.

Displayed on a Wall. If a flag is displayed flat against a wall, it is normally hung horizontally or vertically.

If the national flag is displayed vertically, the top point of the maple leaf should be to the left and the stem to the right, as seen by spectators.

There is no limit to the number of flags which may be displayed at one time as long as the display is in good taste. This is especially true for large open areas, banquet rooms and convention halls.

During a Speech or Meeting. If the national flag is displayed on a staff placed on a platform, stage or dias, it should be to the right of the speaker.

It should not be used to cover the speaker's table or draped in front of the platform, nor should it be allowed to touch the floor.

If displayed flat against the wall at the back of the platform, the flag should be above and behind the speaker.

On Ships and Boats. The Canadian flag is designated as the proper national colours for all Canadian ships and boats, including pleasure craft.

Foreign vessels may fly the Canadian flag as a "courtesy flag" when in a Canadian port.

Other Customs. The flag is used as a drape only on a casket of the dead or in the unveiling of a monument.

When the flag is flown at half-mast, it should be hoisted first to the masthead, then lowered so that the centre of the flag is exactly half-way down the staff.

When the flag becomes faded or worn, it should be disposed of by burning. This should be done quietly and without ceremony. It is not considered an act of disrespect to burn an unserviceable flag.

The flag is never used for commercial advertising purposes.

Colours and Emblems. White and red, the colours of the flag, are the colours for Canada. They were so declared and appointed officially by King George V on November 21, 1921, in a proclamation of Canada's Coat of Arms recommended to His Majesty by the Canadian Government.

The maple leaf has long been emblematic of Canada. Research undertaken by a former president of the Royal Society of Canada led him to conclude that "the maple leaf was looked upon as a fit emblem for Canadians as early as 1700 if not before." Maple leaves were used widely by Canadians for decorating purposes in Toronto and elsewhere when the Prince of Wales visited Canada in 1860. Eight years later they appeared in the Coats of Arms granted by Queen Victoria to Ontario and Quebec, and in 1921, a similar sprig of maple leaves was used as the distinctively Canadian symbol in the new Coat of Arms mentioned above.

The national flag is described as a red flag of the proportions two by length and one by width, containing in its centre a white square the width of the flag, with a single red leaf within the square.

Lament for Confederation / 1967

"The jubilant crowd of thirty-two thousand was silenced by the moving — and bitter — soliloquy," wrote one reporter, describing the effect of Chief Dan George (b. 1899), the elected chief of the Co-Salish Indians, reading his "Lament for Confederation" in Vancouver's Empire Stadium on 1 July 1967, the centennial of Confederation. He brought to this performance the same dignity and authority he invested in the character of Ol'Antoine on CBC-TV's *Cariboo Country* and of Old Lodge Poles in the Hollywood film *Little Big Man*. A note to the publication of this "Lament" in *Playboard*, November 1967, explains that *seelanum* is "a Squamish Indian word meaning 'lunar months.'"

How long have I known you, Oh Canada? A hundred years? Yes, a hundred years. And many many *seelanum* more. And today, when you celebrate your hundred years, Oh Canada, I am sad for all the Indian people throughout the land.

For I have known you when your forests were mine; when they gave me my meat and my clothing. I have known you in your streams and rivers where your fish flashed and danced in the sun, where the waters said come, come and eat of my abundance. I have known you in the freedom of your winds. And my spirit, like the winds, once roamed your good lands.

But in the long hundred years since the white man came, I have seen my freedom disappear like the salmon going mysteriously out to sea. The white man's strange customs which I could not understand pressed down upon me until I could no longer breathe.

When I fought to protect my land and my home, I was called a savage. When I neither understood nor welcomed this way of life, I was called lazy. When I tried to rule my people, I was stripped of my authority.

My nation was ignored in your history textbooks — they were little more important in the history of Canada than the buffalo that ranged the plains. I was ridiculed in your plays and motion pictures, and when I drank your fire-water, I got drunk — very, very drunk. And I forgot.

Oh Canada, how can I celebrate with you this Centenary, this hundred years? Shall I thank you for the reserves that are left to me of my beautiful forests? For the canned fish of my rivers? For the loss of my pride and authority, even among my own people? For the lack of my will to fight back? No! I must forget what's past and gone.

Oh God in Heaven! Give me back the courage of the olden Chiefs. Let me wrestle with my surroundings. Let me again, as in the days of old, dominate my environment. Let me humbly accept this new culture and through it rise up and go on.

Oh God! Like the Thunderbird of old I shall rise again out of the sea; I shall grab the instruments of the white man's success — his education, his skills, and with these new tools I shall build my race into the proudest segment of your society. Before I follow the great Chiefs who have gone before us, Oh Canada, I shall see these things come to pass.

I shall see our young braves and our chiefs sitting in the houses of law and government, ruling and being ruled by the knowledge and freedoms of *our* great land. So shall we shatter the barriers of our isolation. So shall the *next* hundred years be the greatest in the proud history of our tribes and nations.

The FLQ Manifesto/1970

The document that follows is presumably the work of the Québécois terrorists, the self-styled *Front de Libération du Québec* (Quebec Liberation Front), who at 8:30 A.M. on 5 October 1970 kidnapped James Cross from his Westmount home in Montreal, thereby initiating the October Crisis. One of the kidnappers' least-onerous conditions for the release of the British trade official was the broadcasting and publishing of their manifesto. The government authorized CBC Radio and CBC-TV to read the entire text on 8 October, and newspapers across the country published it the following day. This slight success emboldened a second, unrelated cell of separatist sympathizers, for two days later Pierre Laporte, a Quebec cabinet minister, was kidnapped. The federal government responded by invoking the War Measures Act, on 16 October. This in turn led to the murder of Laporte, whose body was discovered two days later. Mass arrests and interrogations followed, and the combined police forces of the federal and Quebec governments succeeded in locating Cross's kidnappers, who released him in exchange for deportation to Cuba (and subsequent asylum in France), and in tracking down the murderers of Laporte who were duly tried and sentenced. "The FLQ Manifesto" has been reprinted from Marcel Rioux's *Quebec in Question* (1971), translated by James Boake. It gives the English-speaking reader an unexpected sense of the simmering resentments felt by the young and partly educated terrorists who wrote it, and the sense of frustration and alienation experienced by many other lower and middle-class Québécois.

The people in the *Front de Libération du Québec* are neither Messiahs nor modern-day Robin Hoods. They are a group of Quebec workers who have decided to do everything they can to assure that the people of Quebec take their destiny into their own hands, once and for all.

The *Front de Libération du Québec* wants total independence for Quebeckers; it wants to see them united in a free society, a society purged for good of its gang of rapacious sharks, the big bosses who dish out patronage and

their henchmen, who have turned Quebec into a private preserve of cheap labour and unscrupulous exploitation.

The *Front de Libération du Québec* is not an aggressive movement, but a response to the aggression organized by high finance through its puppets, the federal and provincial governments (the Brinks farce, Bill 63, the electoral map, the so-called "social progress" [sic] tax, the Power Corporation, medical insurance — for the doctors, the guys at Lapalme...).

The *Front de Libération du Québec* finances itself through voluntary (sic) taxes levied on the enterprises that exploit the workers (banks, finance companies, etc....).

"The money powers of the status quo, the majority of the traditional tutors of our people, have obtained from the voters the reaction they hoped for, a step backwards rather than the changes we have worked for as never before, the changes we will continue to work for" (René Lévesque, April 29, 1970).

Once, we believed it worthwhile to channel our energy and our impatience, in the apt words of René Lévesque, into the *Parti Québécois*, but the Liberal victory shows that what is called democracy in Quebec has always been, and still is, nothing but the "democracy" of the rich. In this sense the victory of the Liberal party is in fact nothing but the victory of the Simard-Cotroni election-fixers. Consequently, we wash our hands of the British parliamentary system; the *Front de Libération du Québec* will never let itself be distracted by the electoral crumbs that the Anglo-Saxon capitalists toss into the Quebec barnyard every four years. Many Quebeckers have realized the truth and are ready to take action. In the coming year Bourassa is going to get what's coming to him: 100,000 revolutionary workers, armed and organized!

Yes, there are reasons for the Liberal victory. Yes, there are reasons for poverty, unemployment, slums, for the fact that you, Mr. Bergeron of Visitation Street, and you too, Mr. Legendre of Ville de Laval, who make $10,000 a year, do not feel free in our country, Quebec.

Yes, there are reasons, the guys who work for Lord know them, and so do the fishermen of the Gaspé, the workers on the North Shore; the miners who work for Iron Ore, for Q-UeBEC Cartier Mining, for Noranda know these reasons too. The honest workingmen at Cabano, the guys they tried to screw still one more time, they know lots of reasons.

Yes, there are reasons why you, Mr. Tremblay of Panet Street and you, Mr. Cloutier who work in construction in St. Jérôme, can't afford "Golden Vessels" with all the jazzy music and the sharp decor, like Drapeau the aristocrat, the guy who was so concerned about slums that he had coloured billboards stuck up in front of them so that the rich tourists couldn't see us in our misery.

Yes, Madame Lemay of St. Hyacinthe, there are reasons why you can't afford a little junket to Florida like

Symbols of Sovereignty

By such symbols as The Arms of Canada do we define and govern
ourselves as a people. The Arms *(above)* are more properly described
as "Armorial Bearings of Dominion and Sovereignty and of General
Purpose of Her Majesty the Queen in Right of Canada." "The design
is traditional, and its inspiration patent," explained Conrad Swan,
the York Herald of Arms. "As the great majority of Canadians are of
English, Scottish, Irish, and French descent, the arms long associated
with those four countries are included in the first four divisions of the
shield." The Latin motto, A MARI USQUE AD MARE, is translated in
French as "D'un océan à l'autre" and in English as "From Sea to Sea."

ii

The symbols of sovereignty include not only The Arms of
Canada but also the arms and armorial bearings of the
provinces and territories that comprise Canada. The symbols of the ten provinces and two territories appear on
these pages along with the years the arms and armorial
bearings were assigned by royal warrant. Much of the
symbology is traditional and predates the year of assign-
ment, being taken from earlier crests, seals, and flags
authorized by fur-trade companies and other institutions.

Armorial Bearings of Ontario, 1868

Armorial Bearings of Newfoundland, 1637

Arms of Manitoba, 1905

Armorial Bearings of Nova Scotia, 1868

Arms of Saskatchewan, 1906

iii

Arms of Quebec, 1868

Arms of British Columbia, 1906

Arms of Alberta, 1907

Armorial Bearings of
the Yukon Territory, 1956

Arms of Prince Edward Island, 1905

Arms of New Brunswick, 1868

Armorial Bearings of
the Northwest Territories, 1956

The flags of a great many monarchs of many countries have flown over Canadian soil in the past, but until 1965 it could be said Canada had no official national flag. The situation was irrevocably altered on 15 February 1965 when, on the advice of Parliament, Queen Elizabeth II proclaimed the National Flag of Canada: "Gules, on a maple leaf of the first." Such is the well-weathered language of heraldry. The flag is popularly known as "The Maple Leaf" and "The Pearson Pennant" (this to acknowledge the role played by Lester B. Pearson, the prime minister of the day, in its adoption). On these pages will be found other flags associated with Canada, with their dates of official sanction, although sometimes such dates trail behind actual usage.

National Flag of Canada (Maple Leaf), 1965

The Queen's Personal Canadian Flag, 1921

Flag of the Governor General, 1931

The Union Banner (or Jack), 1606; Flag of Newfoundland, 1931

Flag of Prince Edward Island, 1905

The Canadian Red Ensign, 1924 Flag of Ontario, 1965

Flag of Nova Scotia, 1929

Flag of Quebec, 1948

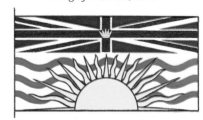

Flag of British Columbia, 1960

Flag of New Brunswick, 1965

Flag of Manitoba, 1966

Flag of Alberta, 1967

Flag of Saskatchewan, 1969

Flag of the Yukon Territory, 1967

Flag of the Northwest Territories, 1969

The Head of State

The representative of the Crown in a self-governing Dominion (like Canada) and the Head of State is called the Governor General, who is symbolic of national unity and the continuity of institutions and national life. The office dates back to 1786, and in its modern form from 1867. Until 1952, the incumbent was invariably a titled (and distinguished) Britisher. Since then, the Queen's appointees have been native-born Canadians of achievement. These are the men who "made the Crown Canadian."

Vincent Massey, 1952-59

Georges Vanier, 1959-67

D. Roland Michener, 1967-74

Jules Léger, 1974-

The Head of Government

The Prime Minister is the head of the federal government in a self-governing Dominion and in practice the leader of the party in power in the lower house of the legislature. Since Confederation, fifteen men have served in this capacity. The first two were born in Scotland; Sir John Abbott was the first native-born Prime Minister. Sir Wilfrid Laurier was the first French Canadian to attain that office. Portraits of all appear here, with party allegiance (C, Conservative; L, Liberal) and dates of office.

Sir John A. Macdonald (C),
1867-73, 1878-91

Alexander Mackenzie (L), 1873-78

Sir John Abbott (C), 1891-92

Sir John Thompson (C), 1892-94

Sir Mackenzie Bowell (C), 1894-96

Sir Charles Tupper (C), 1896

Sir Wilfrid Laurier (L), 1896-1911

Sir Robert Borden (C), 1911-20

Arthur Meighen (C), 1920-21, 1926

*W.L. Mackenzie King (L),
1921-26, 1926-30, 1935-48*

R.B. Bennett (C), 1930-35

Louis St. Laurent (L), 1948-57

John G. Diefenbaker (C), 1957-63

Lester B. Pearson (L), 1963-68

Pierre Elliott Trudeau (L), 1968-

The Centre Block and the Peace Tower.
At midday and at midnight.

Parliament Buildings

The seat of government is the Parliament Buildings, located on Parliament Hill, a promontory overlooking the Ottawa River in downtown Ottawa. There are three of these Gothic structures: the East Block (which includes the Cabinet Chamber), the West Block (now largely offices), and the imposing Centre Block (which holds the Senate Chamber, the Commons Chamber, the Speaker's Chamber, and the Library of Parliament). Soaring above the Centre Block is the Peace Tower, with its Memorial Chamber and its fifty-three-bell carillon, the most symbolic of images. The flanking buildings date back to the 1860s; the Centre Block (destroyed in the Great Fire of 1916) was rebuilt in 1916-24. The Peace Tower was dedicated by the Prince of Wales in an imposing ceremony in 1927.

Above right:
A view of the East Block.

Below right:
A view of the West Block.

In the Centre Block are the Main Corridor (above), *the Senate Chamber* (upper left), *the Commons Chamber* (centre left), *the Speaker's Chamber* (lower left), *and the Library of Parliament* (below).

Provincial Parliaments

Each province has its own parliament or legislative
building. The American writer John Updike called these
"brick valentines posted to a distant dowager queen."
The description fits some of the legislative seats more
than others, of course! Here they are from coast to coast.

Confederation Building, St. John's, Newfoundland

Province House, Halifax, Nova Scotia

Legislative Building, Charlottetown, Prince Edward Island

Legislative Building, Fredericton, New Brunswick

National Assembly Building, Quebec City, Quebec

Legislative Building, Toronto, Ontario

Legislative Building, Winnipeg, Manitoba

Legislative Building, Regina, Saskatchewan

Legislative Building, Edmonton, Alberta

Legislative Building, Victoria, British Columbia

Statues of Greatness

We are in debt to sculptors like Louis-Philippe Hébert and Walter S. Allward for creating such images as these, in metal and stone, which stand so erect in our parks and public places. Statues like these materialize for all time the spirit of those public figures who inspired them. Every park and public place in the country should have as its centrepiece a statue or a bust of some person of vision or achievement in the form of a work of art by a sculptor of talent.

I

II

III

IV

I *Jacques Cartier, navigator*
Being erected in Quebec

II *Samuel de Champlain, colonist*
Couchiching Beach Park, Orillia, Ont.

III *Jean de Brébeuf, missionary*
Park Brébeuf, Val-Tétreau, Que.

IV *Madeleine de Verchères, heroine*
Verchères, on the St. Lawrence, Que.

V *Evangeline, Acadian heroine*
Grand Pré National Historic Park, N.S.

VI *Sir Isaac Brock, general*
Queenston Heights Park, Ont.

V

VI

VII

VIII

IX

X

XI

XII

XIII

XIV

VII *Robert Baldwin & L.-H. Lafontaine, statesmen Parliament Hill, Ottawa*

VIII *Sir George-Etienne Cartier, statesman Parliament Hill, Ottawa*

IX *Sir John A. Macdonald, prime minister Parliament Hill, Ottawa*

X *Louis Riel, Métis leader Wascana Centre, Regina*

XI *Sir Wilfrid Laurier, prime minister Parliament Hill, Ottawa*

XII *Sir Robert Borden, prime minister Parliament Hill, Ottawa*

XIII *W.L. Mackenzie King, prime minister Parliament Hill, Ottawa*

XIV *Louis St. Laurent, prime minister Supreme Court Building, Ottawa*

Death & Life

It is hard to think of the War Dead and not think of the Spirit of Youth. So many of those who died on battlefields far and near were so youthful, full of high ideals and stern endeavour.

Confederation Square in Ottawa is the site of the National War Monument (I), which takes the form of a gigantic stone arch under which passes an army of men and horses cast in bronze. This tribute to the dead of the Great War, designed by Vernon March, was dedicated by King George VI and Queen Elizabeth in May 1939, four months prior to the outbreak of the Second World War.

One of the world's great monuments to the war dead is the Vimy Memorial (II), which rises dramatically from the chalk ridge above the Douai Plain to overlook the village of Vimy in northern France, the scene of great slaughter yet a signal Canadian victory, Easter Monday, 9 April 1917. This Canadian tribute, with its twin pylons (likened to "a gate leading to a better world"), was unveiled by Edward VIII on 26 July 1936.

The Spirit of Eternal Youth is symbolized by Golden Boy (III), the gilded bronze figure of a young man carrying a torch in one hand and a sheaf of wheat in the other. He is perched so high no one can see him, except at a distance, for he stands on one foot on the dome of the Manitoba Legislature in Winnipeg, which opened in 1920. The novelist Jack Ludwig noted: "Golden Boy seems eternal, almost immortal."

A favourite statue in Ottawa is that of Sir Galahad (IV), the brave knight of the Round Table, which stands at the foot of Parliament Hill. It commemorates the death of Henry Albert Harper, a young civil servant who drowned in 1901 in a vain attempt to rescue a little girl who was skating. W.L. Mackenzie King, at its unveiling in 1905, delivered a notable address in which he observed that "the secret of heroism...lies in the life of self-sacrifice."

I

II

III

IV

I

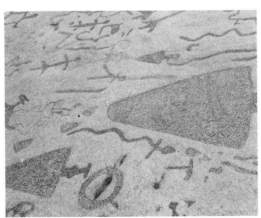

II

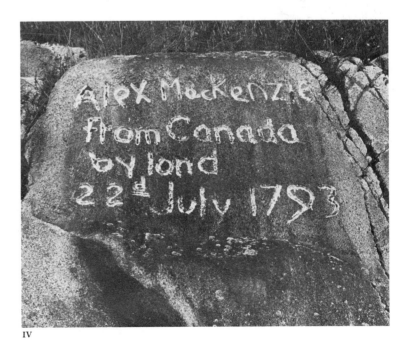

III

IV

Assertions in Stone

From time immemorial the Inuit have erected *inukshuks* (I), human statues in stone. These awesome creations are standing in the Northwest Territories. Anthropologists may debate their purpose, but to Farley Mowat, the Arctic traveller and writer, they have a specific role: "They were created as the guardians of living men against a loneliness which is immeasurable."

The Indians asserted their presence in other ways, especially through "rock art," a term that covers both their pictographs (II) and their petroglyphs (III). Reddish-brown figures, like this galloping horseman, drawn on the side of a cliff in Agawa Bay, north shore of Lake Superior, are centuries old. Longfellow mentions them in *Hiawatha* (1855) but they were only rediscovered in 1958 by naturalist and art historian Selwyn Dewdney. At Petroglyphs Provincial Park, opened in 1972, lies an outcropping of limestone on which 900 images of debatable significance have been engraved. The images were carved by Algonkian Indians between A.D. 900 and 1400. The Park is near Peterborough, Ontario.

Today whitewash brightens the actual letterforms (IV) that Sir Alexander Mackenzie painted with a mixture of vermilion and grease on a rock on the shore of the Bella Coola River, Dean Channel, where he first saw the Pacific Ocean. He was the first man to cross the American continent north of Mexico. This "brief memorial," now carved in rock and filled in red cement, reads "Alex MacKenzie from Canada by land 22d July 1793."

Residences of Renown

Rideau Hall, the popular name of Government House, is the official residence of the Governor General in Ottawa. As the head of state, the Governor General has his own flag, which flies above the main building, erected in 1838. Rideau Hall is located almost across the street from the residence of the Prime Minister.

The Prime Minister resides at 24 Sussex Drive, discreetly named after its street location, like No. 10 Downing Street, the residence of the Prime Minister of the United Kingdom. The grey stone mansion, built in the year of Confederation, came into official use with Louis St. Laurent, the twelfth P.M., in 1951.

Stornoway is the official residence of the leader of the opposition. The two-storey mansion in Rockcliffe Park, built in 1914 and named after a town in the Outer Hebrides, was acquired by a group of public-spirited citizens for this purpose in 1948. The government has since 1970 assumed the responsibility for Stornoway.

History, technology and literature are honoured in three Ontario homes, all open to the public.

In the living-room of her frame house at Queenston Heights in the Niagara Peninsula, Laura Secord overheard occupying American officers planning their attack on Beaver Dam. This occasioned her historic trek in June 1813. The Laura Secord candy company restored the building in 1969 and turned it into a museum.

Alexander Graham Bell, then in his twenties, lived in the attractive Bell Homestead, Tutela Heights, Brantford. It was here in 1874 that Bell conceived the principle of the telephone, which instrument he built the following year at his workshop in Boston, Mass.

The summer home of Stephen Leacock on Old Brewery Bay, Lake Couchiching, preserves the famous humorist's library and is the focal point of the annual banquet at which is awarded the Leacock Medal for Humour. Clearly visible is the sundial in the rear yard, with its inscription suitable for a writer of humour, "I Mark Only the Sunny Hours."

To Encourage Excellence

The awards and the honours conferred by private and public bodies help us to draw attention to excellence and thereby set new and higher standards for all. Here are the best known and the most picturesque of the awards and honours conferred on Canadians of standing and achievement.

The Grey Cup, awarded annually to the best professional football team in eastern or western Canada, dates back to 1909 when the governor general, Lord Grey, donated this silver drinking cup to encourage the game. Since 1966, the custodian of the coveted trophy has been the Canadian Football League.

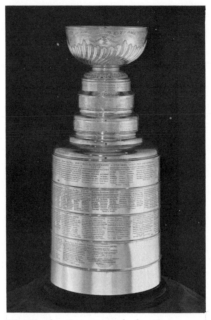

The Stanley Cup, named after Governor General Lord Stanley who donated it in 1893, is the highest award in professional hockey. Since 1946 the sterling bowl has been associated with the National Hockey League. It is symbolic of The World's Hockey Championship.

Nellie is the nickname of the ACTRA Award, given annually by the Association of Canadian Television and Radio Artists to encourage excellence in Canadian broadcasting and film production. First given in 1971, the Nellie is a statuette of a chubby nude sculpted by William McElcheran.

The Leacock Medal for Humour, engraved by Emmanuel Hahn with Stephen Leacock's smiling features, is awarded to the author of the best book of humour published the previous year. It was established by the Stephen Leacock Associates in 1946.

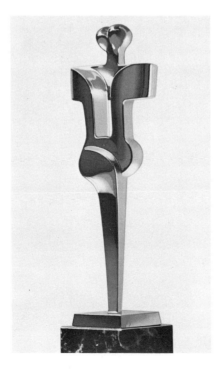

"They Desire a Better Country" is the English translation of the Latin motto on the Seal of the Order of Canada (above), established 1 July 1967 to honour Canadians for outstanding achievement and service to their country or to humanity. The Etrog (left), awarded annually since 1968, recognizes outstanding achievement in Canadian films. The statuette is named after its sculptor, Sorel Etrog.

A People's Symbology

By Symbols Struck

If you have a coin of the realm in your pocket, you possess a symbol of that realm. Although the first coins were minted here as early as 1670, not until 1931 was the Royal Canadian Mint founded to strike them for us. Among the Mint's most memorable images are these nine, reproduced from the reverse sides of Canadian coins.

I

II

III

IV

V

VI

Sovereigns from Stamps

I   *Two images of Queen Victoria (as a young princess and as the Dowager Empress) appear on the Diamond Jubilee Stamp of 1897.*

II   *King Edward VII and Queen Alexandra stare serenely from their cartouches on the Quebec Tercentenary Issue of 1908.*

III   *King George V and Queen Mary, while still H.R.H. The Prince and Princess of Wales, appear on the Quebec Tercentenary Issue of 1908.*

IV   *King Edward VIII, as H.R.H. The Prince of Wales, is depicted in solitary splendour on the Ottawa Confederation Issue of 1932.*

V   *King George VI and Queen Elizabeth stare straight ahead on the Royal Visit Issue of 1939.*

VI   *Queen Elizabeth II and Prince Philip look very young as H.R.H. Princess Elizabeth and the Duke of Edinburgh on the Commemoratives of 1951.*

An Inventory of Images

The look of Canada — the land, the water, the skies, the fauna, the flora — has been documented by topographers, artists, and photographers from the earliest of times to the present. Less consistently documented has been the range of artistic and corporate imagery that Canadians take for granted. Each image has a story to tell, has something to tell us about ourselves. Here are some familiar images from our almost exhaustless inventory.

I *The Martyrdom of Saints Jean de Brébeuf and Gabriel Lalemant at the Hands of the Iroquois Indians* was painted in a stark manner in 1812-14 by Francisco de Goya, the great Spanish artist.

II *The Death of General Wolfe*, a neo-classical treatment of a never-to-be-forgotten scene in Canada's history, was captured in oil by Benjamin West, an American artist, in 1779.

III *The Fathers of Confederation at the Quebec Conference, 1864*, painted by Robert Harris in 1884, was reconstructed following the loss of the original canvas in the Great Fire that destroyed the Parliament Building in 1916.

IV The Coat of Arms of the Hudson's Bay Company, founded as a fur-trade company in 1670, bears the Latin motto which translates "For a skin a skin" (or less literally, "For the pelts which we collect we risk our skins").

V The Great Seal of Canada, authorized for use by Queen Elizabeth II on 15 November 1955, is shown here in a rubber cast. The official keeper of the Great Seal is the Governor General.

VI *Arrival of Loyalist Volunteers at Parliament Bldgs., Toronto, Dec. 1837* is the title of C.W. Jefferys' pen-and-ink caricature of the Rebellion of 1837, executed between 1942 and 1950.

VII *Driving the Last Spike*, the celebrated photograph, was taken at 9:20 a.m., 7 Nov. 1885, at Craigellachie, B.C., showing Donald A. Smith, hammer in hand, driving home the last CPR iron spike.

VIII The RCMP Badge identifies the famed civilian police force, founded in 1873, given its present name in 1920. The French motto of the Royal Canadian Mounted Police is officially translated "Uphold the Right."

I

II

III

IV

V

VI

VII

VIII

IX

X

IX "Karsh of Ottawa," one of the most evocative of phrases, was made famous the world over by the Armenian-born, Ottawa-based Yousuf Karsh, portrait photographer and image-maker *par excellence*. (Karsh, Ottawa)

x *At the Crease*, painted in egg tempera by Ken Danby in 1972, depicts a masked goal-keeper, but moves beyond hockey to evoke the mystery and foreboding of a medieval jouster.

XI The CN Symbol, designed by Allan Fleming, was unveiled 15 December 1960. It graphically identifies Canadian National which, as the Canadian National Railways (CNR), dates back to 1919.

XI

XII

XII The CP Logo has identified Canadian Pacific Limited since 17 June 1968. The privately owned corporation, formed in 1971, was founded in 1881 as the Canadian Pacific Railway (CPR).

XIII The Air Canada Logo came into official use on 1 January 1965 when the government-owned corporation, created as Trans-Canada Air Lines in 1937, became Air Canada. The distinctive orange-red colour is known as "Air Canada Red."

XIII

XIV

XV

XIV The Igloo Tag, attached to a Canadian Eskimo carving, guarantees its authenticity and uniqueness. The Department of Indian and Northern Affairs has used the trademark since 1958.

XV The Stretched Beaver Pelt is the trademark that appears on tags affixed to authentic Indian arts and crafts. The tag was developed by the Department of Indian and Northern Affairs in 1968 for the National Indian Arts and Crafts Corporation.

XVI

XVII

XVI The CBC Symbol, designed by Burton Kramer, has appeared on CBC-TV since 10 December 1974. It evolves from the letter "C" for Canada, and represents the Canadian Broadcasting Corporation, the largest in the world, created in 1936.

XVII The CTV Logo, introduced at the beginning of the 1975-76 television season, identifies the CTV Television Network Ltd., the "second" or private network formed in 1961.

Our Fair Domain

I have called this section "Our Fair Domain," knowing full well that only older readers will recall the phrase's origin. Few younger readers will have heard the words "Canada's fair domain" or ever sung the once-popular anthem "The Maple Leaf For Ever" (of which Alexander Muir's stirring lyrics are included elsewhere in this volume). Yet the country, despite the myriad problems that beset it, remains fair in the dictionary's sense of the word: lovely, desirable. I have attempted to illustrate this by selecting full-colour photographs to illustrate the scenic splendours, the sites of human habitation, and the historical roots of the world's second-largest country. In twenty-five photographs, it is obviously impossible to do more than hint at the range and richness of the country. To impose some order on the selection, I have given equal representation to the three main regions of Canada — Eastern, Central, Western — and added a view of the fourth, the often-overlooked Northland.

I *Stones mark the site of the first Viking settlement at L'Anse aux Meadows, Newfoundland.*

II *Fishing is the mainstay of Lark Harbour, a Newfoundland outport not far from Corner Brook.*

III *The Fortress of Louisbourg, for two hundred years nothing but rubble, rises again on Cape Breton Island.*

IV *Another historical reconstruction is Port Royal, first permanent white settlement founded in 1605, at Annapolis Royal, Nova Scotia.*

V *For rugged splendour there is no more scenic drive than the Cabot Trail which skirts 184 miles of Nova Scotia's Cape Breton coastline.*

VI *The traditional values of Maritime life are suggested by this view of Fredericton from across the Saint John.*

VII *No tourist to Prince Edward Island misses Green Gables, near Cavendish, which was once the home of L.M. Montgomery, author of* Anne of Green Gables.

VIII *The Château Frontenac, with its mansard roof, dominates Upper Town and Lower Town, Quebec City.*

I

II

III

IV

V

VI

VII

VIII

IX

X

XI

XII

XIII

XIV

XV

XVI

XVII

IX Montreal, the second-largest French-speaking city in the world, is seen to best advantage from the slopes of Mount Royal.

X This small farmhouse at Pointe Rouge, on the North Shore, with its outbuildings and roadside cross, illustrates the traditional values of rural Quebec.

XI The Parliament Buildings tower over the Rideau Canal which, during the Ottawa winter, becomes the world's longest skating rink.

XII Clouds of mist and a rainbow rise above Niagara Falls. Indians named the cataract "The Mighty Thunderer."

XIII The CN Tower and a ferry boat complement the Toronto skyline, as seen from Centre Island in Lake Ontario.

XIV The Trans-Canada Highway, completed in 1962, skirts Nipigon Bay in the heavily wooded Lake Superior area of Ontario.

XV Lower Fort Garry, an important Hudson's Bay Company post, has been reconstructed at Selkirk, Manitoba.

XVI No sight is more characteristic of Saskatchewan than these grain elevators, along the railroad line at Gainsborough, unless it be a field of wheat.

XVII Edmonton, the capital of Alberta and the Gateway to the North, is reflected at night in the North Saskatchewan River.

XVIII   *Banff, with its famous Banff Springs Hotel, is nestled in a valley amid the Rocky Mountains of Alberta.*

XIX   *"Splendour Undiminished" is the motto of Vancouver, British Columbia, seen here from Coal Harbour.*

XX   *Victoria's Legislative Building, located on the Inner Harbour, is agreeably illuminated at night.*

XXI   *The stark features of the Thunderbird, a being of immense power to the Indians, appear on this totem pole in Thunderbird Park, Victoria, B.C.*

XXII   *The city of Dawson, at the confluence of the Yukon and Klondike rivers in the Yukon Territory, boasted a population of 25,000 in 1896.*

XXIII   *This inukshuk, raised out of rock by the Inuit, stands like a sentinel at Repulse Bay, Northwest Territories.*

XXIV   *Alert, the world's most northern settlement, is on the northern tip of Ellesmere Island, N.W.T., 518 miles from the North Pole.*

XXV   *Man has yet to scratch the snow-covered surface of Baffin Island, N.W.T., a scene symbolic of "the true North."*

XVIII

XIX

XX

XXI

XXII

XXIII

XXIV

XXV

the rotten judges and members of Parliament who travel on our money.

The good workers at Vickers and at Davie Shipbuilding, the ones who were given no reason for being thrown out, know these reasons; so do the guys at Murdochville that were smashed only because they wanted to form a union, and whom the rotten judges forced to pay over two million dollars because they had wanted to exercise this elementary right. The guys of Murdochville are familiar with this justice; they know lots of reasons.

Yes, there are reasons why you, Mr. Lachance of St. Marguerite Street, go drowning your despair, your bitterness, and your rage in Molson's horse piss. And you, the Lachance boy, with your marijuana cigarettes. . . .

Yes, there are reasons why you, the welfare cases, are kept from generation to generation on public assistance. There are lots of reasons, the workers for Domtar at Windsor and East Angus know them; the workers for Squibb and Ayers, for the Quebec Liquor Commission and for Seven-up and for Victoria Precision, and the blue collar workers of Laval and of Montreal and the guys at Lapalme know lots of reasons.

The workers at Dupont of Canada know some reasons too, even if they will soon be able to express them only in English (thus assimilated, they will swell the number of New Quebeckers, the immigrants who are the darlings of Bill 63).

These reasons ought to have been understood by the policemen of Montreal, the system's muscle; they ought to have realized that we live in a terrorized society, because without their force and their violence, everything fell apart on October 7.

We've had enough of a Canadian federalism which penalizes the dairy farmers of Quebec to satisfy the requirements of the Anglo-Saxons of the Commonwealth; which keeps the honest taxi drivers of Montreal in a state of semi-slavery by shamefully protecting the exclusive monopoly of the nauseating Murray Hill, and its owner — the murderer Charles Hershorn and his son Paul who, the night of October 7, repeatedly tore a .22 rifle out of the hands of his employees to fire on the taxi drivers and thereby mortally wounded Corporal Dumas, killed as a demonstrator. Canadian federalism pursues a reckless import policy, thereby throwing out of work the people who earn low wages in the textile and shoe industries, the most downtrodden people in Quebec, and all to line the pockets of a handful of filthy "money-makers" in Cadillacs. We are fed up with a federalism which classes the Quebec nation among the ethnic minorities of Canada.

We, and more and more Quebeckers too, have had it with a government of pussy-footers who perform a hundred and one tricks to charm the American millionaires, begging them to come and invest in Quebec, the Beautiful Province where thousands of square miles of forests full of game and of lakes full of fish are the exclusive property of these all-powerful lords of the twentieth century. We are sick of a government in the hands of a hypocrite like Bourassa who depends on Brinks armoured trucks, an authentic symbol of the foreign occupation of Quebec, to keep the poor Quebec "natives" fearful of that poverty and unemployment to which we are so accustomed.

We are fed up with the taxes we pay that Ottawa's agent in Quebec would give to the English-speaking bosses as an "incentive" for them to speak French, to negotiate in French. Repeat after me: "Cheap labour is *main d'oeuvre à bon marché* in French."

We have had enough of promises of work and of prosperity, when in fact we will always be the diligent servants and bootlickers of the big shots, as long as there is a Westmount, a Town of Mount Royal, a Hampstead, an Outremont, all these veritable fortresses of the high finance of St. James Street and Wall Street; we will be slaves until Quebeckers, all of us, have used every means, including dynamite and guns, to drive out these big bosses of the economy and of politics, who will stoop to any action however base, the better to screw us.

We live in a society of terrorized slaves, terrorized by the big bosses, Steinberg, Clark, Bronfman, Smith, Neopole, Timmins, Geoffrion, J.L. Lévesque, Hershorn, Thompson, Nesbitt, Desmarais, Kierans (next to these, Rémi Popol the Nightstick, Drapeau the Dog, the Simards' Simple Simon and Trudeau the Pansy are peanuts!).

We are terrorized by the Roman Capitalist Church, though this is less and less true today (who owns the square where the Stock Exchange was built?); terrorized by the payments owing to Household Finance, by the advertising of the grand masters of consumption, Eaton's, Simpson's, Morgan's, Steinberg's, General Motors. . .; terrorized by those exclusive clubs of science and culture, the universities, and by their boss-directors Gaudry and Dorais, and by the vice-boss Robert Shaw.

There are more and more of us who know and suffer under this terrorist society, and the day is coming when all the Westmounts of Quebec will disappear from the map.

Workers in industry, in mines and in the forests! Workers in the service industries, teachers, students and unemployed! Take what belongs to you, your jobs, your determination and your freedom. And you, the workers at General Electric, you make your factories run; you are the only ones able to produce; without you, General Electric is nothing!

Workers of Quebec, begin from this day forward to take back what is yours; take yourselves what belongs to you. Only you know your factories, your machines, your hotels, your universities, your unions; do not wait for some organization to produce a miracle.

Make your revolution yourselves in your neighbourhoods, in your places of work. If you don't do it yourselves, other usurpers, technocrats or someone else, will replace the handful of cigar-smokers we know today and everything will have to be done all over again. Only you are capable of building a free society.

We must struggle not individually but together, till victory is obtained, with every means at our disposal, like the Patriots of 1837-1838 (those whom Our Holy Mother Church hastened to excommunicate, the better to sell out to British interests).

In the four corners of Quebec, may those who have been disdainfully called lousy Frenchmen and alcoholics begin a vigorous battle against those who have muzzled liberty and justice; may they put out of commission all the professional holdup artists and swindlers: bankers, businessmen, judges and corrupt political wheeler-dealers. . . .

We are Quebec workers and we are prepared to go all the way. With the help of the entire population, we want to replace this society of slaves by a free society, operating by itself and for itself, a society open on the world.

Our struggle can only be victorious. A people that has awakened cannot long be kept in misery and contempt.

> Long live Free Quebec!
> Long live our comrades the political prisoners!
> Long live the Quebec Revolution!
> Long live the *Front de Libération du Québec!*

Multiculturalism/1971

Addressing the House of Commons on 8 October 1971, Prime Minister Pierre Elliott Trudeau announced that his government would seek to implement "a policy of multiculturalism within a bilingual framework . . . as the most suitable means of assuring the cultural freedom of Canadians." This was one of the last recommendations of the Royal Commission on Bilingualism and Biculturalism, appointed in July 1963 to inquire into the use of French and the status of French Canadians in Canada. The Commissioners, André Laurendeau and Davidson Dunton, began tabling their reports in 1967. Volume IV, which deals with minorities or ethnic groups, was by far the most forward-looking of the documents tabled . . . so much so that the prime minister caused the Liberal administration's "Federal Response" to be tabled in an appendix to *Hansard*, the record of the Commons' debates, on that date.

Right Hon. P.E. Trudeau (Prime Minister): Mr. Speaker, I am happy this morning to be able to reveal to the House that the government has accepted all those recommendations of the Royal Commission on Bilingualism and Biculturalism which are contained in Volume IV of its reports directed to federal departments and agencies. Hon. members will recall that the subject of this

volume is "the contribution by other ethnic groups to the cultural enrichment of Canada and the measures that should be taken to safeguard that contribution."

Volume IV examined the whole question of cultural and ethnic pluralism in this country and the status of our various cultures and languages, an area of study given all too little attention in the past by scholars.

It was the view of the royal commission, shared by the government and, I am sure, by all Canadians, that there cannot be one cultural policy for Canadians of British and French origin, another for the original peoples and yet a third for all others. For although there are two official languages, there is no official culture, nor does any ethnic group take precedence over any other. No citizen or group of citizens is other than Canadian, and all should be treated fairly.

The royal commission was guided by the belief that adherence to one's ethnic group is influenced not so much by one's origin or mother tongue as by one's sense of belonging to the group, and by what the commission calls the group's "collective will to exist." The government shares this belief.

The individual's freedom would be hampered if he were locked for life within a particular cultural compartment by the accident of birth or language. It is vital, therefore, that every Canadian, whatever his ethnic origin, be given a chance to learn at least one of the two languages in which his country conducts its official business and its politics.

A policy of multiculturalism within a bilingual framework commends itself to the government as the most suitable means of assuring the cultural freedom of Canadians. Such a policy should help break down discriminatory attitudes and cultural jealousies. National unity if it is to mean anything in the deeply personal sense, must be founded on confidence in one's own individual identity; out of this can grow respect for that of others and a willingness to share ideas, attitudes and assumptions. A vigorous policy of multiculturalism will help create this initial confidence. It can form the base of a society which is based on fair play for all.

The government will support and encourage the various cultures and ethnic groups that give structure and vitality to our society. They will be encouraged to share their cultural expression and values with other Canadians and so contribute to a richer life for us all.

In the past, substantial public support has been given largely to the arts and cultural institutions of English-speaking Canada. More recently and largely with the help of the royal commission's earlier recommendations in Volumes I to III, there has been a conscious effort on the government's part to correct any bias against the French language and culture. In the last few months the government has taken steps to provide funds to support cultural educational centres for native people. The policy I am announcing today accepts the contention of the other cultural communities that they, too, are essential elements in Canada and deserve government assistance in order to contribute to regional and national life in ways that derive from their heritage yet are distinctively Canadian.

In implementing a policy of multiculturalism within a bilingual framework, the government will provide support in four ways.

First, resources permitting, the government will seek to assist all Canadian cultural groups that have demonstrated a desire and effort to continue to develop a capacity to grow and contribute to Canada, and a clear need for assistance, the small and weak groups no less than the strong and highly organized.

Second, the government will assist members of all cultural groups to overcome cultural barriers to full participation in Canadian society.

Third, the government will promote creative encounters and interchange among all Canadian cultural groups in the interest of national unity.

Fourth, the government will continue to assist immigrants to acquire at least one of Canada's official languages in order to become full participants in Canadian society.

Mr. Speaker, I stated at the outset that the government has accepted in principle all recommendations addressed to federal departments and agencies. We are also ready and willing to work co-operatively with the provincial governments towards implementing those recommendations that concern matters under provincial or shared responsibility.

Some of the programmes endorsed or recommended by the Commission have been administered for some time by various federal agencies. I might mention the Citizenship Branch, the CRTC and its predecessor the BBG, the National Film Board and the National Museum of Man. These programmes will be revised, broadened and reactivated and they will receive the additional funds that may be required.

Some of the recommendations that concern matters under provincial jurisdiction call for coordinated federal and provincial action. As a first step, I have written to the First Ministers of the provinces informing them of the response of the federal government and seeking their co-operation. Officials will be asked to carry this consultation further.

I wish to table details of the government's response to each of the several recommendations.

It should be noted that some of the programmes require pilot projects or further short-term research before more extensive action can be taken. As soon as these preliminary studies are available, further programmes will be announced and initiated. Additional financial and personnel resources will be provided.

Responsibility for implementing these recommendations has been assigned to the Citizenship Branch of the Department of the Secretary of State, the agency now responsible for matters affecting the social integration of immigrants and the cultural activities of all ethnic groups. An Inter-Agency Committee of all those agencies involved will be established to co-ordinate the federal effort.

In conclusion, I wish to emphasize the view of the government that a policy of multiculturalism within a bilingual framework is basically the conscious support of individual freedom of choice. We are free to be ourselves. But this cannot be left to chance. It must be fostered and pursued actively. If freedom of choice is in danger for some ethnic groups, it is in danger for all. It is the policy of this government to eliminate any such danger and to "safeguard" this freedom.

I am tabling this document, Mr. Speaker, but it might be the desire of the House to have it appended to *Hansard* in view of its importance and long-lasting effect.

Mr. Speaker: Is that agreed?

Some hon. Members: Agreed.

      *

The government accepts and endorses the recommendations and spirit of Book IV of the Royal Commission on Bilingualism and Biculturalism. It believes the time is overdue for the people of Canada to become more aware of the rich tradition of the many cultures we have in Canada. Canada's citizens come from almost every country in the world, and bring with them every major world religion and language. This cultural diversity endows all Canadians with a great variety of human experience. The government regards this as a heritage to treasure and believes that Canada would be the poorer if we adopted assimilation programs forcing our citizens to forsake and forget the cultures they have brought to us.

The federal government hopes that the provinces will also respond positively to those recommendations which the commissioners addressed to them. The Prime Minister has written to each of the provincial premiers outlining the policies and programs which the Federal Government is initiating and asking for their co-operation.Some provinces have already taken the initiative and are responding to the recommendations directed to them.

The government while responding positively to the commission's recommendations, wishes to go beyond them to the spirit of the Book IV to ensure that Canada's cultural diversity continues.

Cultural diversity throughout the world is being eroded by the impact of industrial technology, mass communications and urbanization. Many writers have discussed this as the creation of a mass society — in which mass produced culture and entertainment and large impersonal institutions threaten to denature and depersonalize man. One of man's basic needs is a sense of belonging, and a good deal of contemporary social unrest

— in all age groups — exists because this need has not been met. Ethnic groups are certainly not the only way in which this need for belonging can be met, but they have been an important one in Canadian society. Ethnic pluralism can help us overcome or prevent the homogenization and depersonalization of mass society. Vibrant ethnic groups can give Canadians of the second, third, and subsequent generations a feeling that they are connected with tradition and with human experience in various parts of the world and different periods of time.

Two misconceptions often arise when cultural diversity is discussed.

(a) Cultural Identity and National Allegiance.

The sense of identity developed by each citizen as a unique individual is distinct from his national allegiance. There is no reason to suppose that a citizen who identifies himself with pride as a Chinese-Canadian, who is deeply involved in the cultural activities of the Chinese community in Canada, will be less loyal or concerned with Canadian matters than a citizen of Scottish origin who takes part in a bagpipe band or highland dancing group. Cultural identity is not the same thing as allegiance to a country. Each of us is born into a particular family with a distinct heritage: that is, everyone — French, English, Italian and Slav included — has an "ethnic" background. The more secure we feel in one particular social context, the more we are free to explore our identity beyond it. Ethnic groups often provide people with a sense of belonging which can make them better able to cope with the rest of society than they would as isolated individuals. Ethnic loyalties need not, and usually do not, detract from wider loyalties to community and country.

Canadian identity will not be undermined by multiculturalism. Indeed, we believe that cultural pluralism is the very essence of Canadian identity. Every ethnic group has the right to preserve and develop its own culture and values within the Canadian context. To say we have two official languages is not to say we have two official cultures, and no particular culture is more "official" than another. A policy of multiculturalism must be a policy for all Canadians.

(b) Language and Culture.

The distinction between language and culture has never been clearly defined. The very name of the royal commission whose recommendations we now seek to implement tends to indicate that bilingualism and biculturalism are indivisible. But, biculturalism does not properly describe our society; multiculturalism is more accurate. The Official Languages Act designated two languages, English and French, as the official languages of Canada for the purposes of all the institutions of the Parliament and government of Canada; no reference was made to cultures, and this act does not impinge upon the role of all languages as instruments of the various Canadian cultures. Nor, on the other hand, should the recognition of the cultural value of many languages weaken the position of Canada's two official languages. Their use by all of the citizens of Canada will continue to be promoted and encouraged.

The government is concerned with preserving human rights, developing Canadian identity, strengthening citizenship participation, reinforcing Canadian unity and encouraging cultural diversification within a bilingual framework. These objectives can best be served through a policy of multiculturalism composed of four main elements.

1. The government of Canada will support all of Canada's cultures and will seek to assist, resources permitting, the development of those cultural groups which have demonstrated a desire and effort to continue to develop, a capacity to grow and contribute to Canada, as well as a clear need for assistance.

The special role of the government will be to support and encourage those cultures and cultural groups which Canadians wish to preserve.

The stronger and more populous cultural groups generally have the resources to be self-supporting and general cultural activities tend to be supportive of them. The two largest cultures, in areas where they exist in a minority situation, are already supported under the aegis of the government's official languages programs. New programs are proposed to give support to minority cultural groups in keeping with their needs and particular situations.

However, the government cannot and should not take upon itself the responsibility for the continued viability of all ethnic groups. The objective of our policy is the cultural survival and development of ethnic groups to the degree that a given group exhibits a desire for this. Government aid to cultural groups must proceed on the basis of aid to self-effort. And in our concern for the preservation of ethnic group identity, we should not forget that individuals in a democracy may choose not to be concerned about maintaining a strong sense of their ethnic identity.

2. The Government will assist members of all cultural groups to overcome cultural barriers to full participation in Canadian society.

The law can and will protect individuals from overt discrimination but there are more subtle barriers to entry into our society. A sense of not belonging, or a feeling of inferiority, whatever its cause, cannot be legislated out of existence. Programs outlined in this document have been designed to foster confidence in one's individual cultural identity and in one's rightful place in Canadian life. Histories, films and museum exhibits showing the great contributions of Canada's various cultural groups will help achieve this objective. But, we must emphasize that every Canadian must help eliminate discrimination. Every Canadian must help contribute to the sense of national acceptance and belonging.

3. The Government will promote creative encounters and interchange among all Canadian cultural groups in the interest of national unity.

As Canadians become more sensitive to their own ethnic identity and to the richness of our country, we will become more involved with one another and develop a greater acceptance of differences and a greater pride in our heritage. Cultural and intellectual creativity in almost all societies has been fostered by the interaction and creative relationship of different ethnic groups within that society. Government aid to multicultural centres, to specific projects of ethnic groups, and to displays of the performing and visual arts as well as the programs already mentioned, will promote cultural exchange. The Government has made it very clear that it does not plan on aiding individual groups to cut themselves off from the rest of society. The programs are designed to encourage cultural groups to share their heritage with all other Canadians and with other countries, and to make us all aware of our cultural diversity.

4. The Government will continue to assist immigrants to acquire at least one of Canada's official languages in order to become full participants in Canadian society.

The federal government, through the Manpower and Immigration Department and the Citizenship Branch of the Department of the Secretary of State, already assists the provinces in language training for adults, but new arrivals in Canada require additional help to adjust to Canadian life, and to participate fully in the economic and social life of Canada.

Letter to the Governor General/1974

"Leave them alone and pretty soon the Ukrainians will think they won the battle of Trafalgar," wrote Stephen Leacock in 1937. The author of the eloquent letter that follows may be unknown to the world of authorship, but he has expressed, simply and movingly, the sentiments of millions of Canadians with foreign backgrounds. All I know of Demetrius Paul Demchuk, aside from the fact that he is proudly Ukrainian and resident on the prairies, are the biographical particulars which he has set forth in this letter addressed to Jules Léger on the occasion of his installation as governor general, 14 January 1974. When the governor general spoke to the Annual Dinner of Canadian Press in Toronto on 1 May 1974, he quoted from this letter and concluded: "This has happened in Canada in our generation."

Grandview, Manitoba.
January 15, 1974.

The Right Hon. Jules Leger,
Gov. Gen. of Canada,
Rideau Hall,
Ottawa, Canada.

Your Excellency:

January 14th is the day when Ukrainians Canadians of Orthodox Faith celebrate their New Year according to the Julian Calendar.

And on the same day we were enjoying witnessing your appointment as Governor General of Canada.

THEREFORE, I, being 78 old man of Ukrainian Canadian ethnic group and as an immigrant boy of 16 years landed in the Port of Quebec on June 12th 1911, with $25.00 and with 30 English words.

WITH my wife Maria, born in Canada of the third generation.

WITH our daughter Lida the school teacher.

WITH her husband Henry Podealuk, Postmaster, who was the first Canadian Army officer and set his foot on European continent to fight the Hitler's army.

WITH our second daughter Larissa, the first Ukrainian Canadian girl in Canada, who has been graduated at the Man. U. with the degree of B.Sce in H.E. and Masters degree in Science at the University of Montreal.

WITH her husband Dr. R.F. Hooley, Prof. of Science at the University and a world's Scientist.

WITH our son Modest a graduated druggist and his wife Loraine a teacher.

WITH our daughter Leona graduated in Arts (B.A.) Man. U.

WITH our 13 grandchildren and one great grand child.

WITH ALL DEMCHUKS IN CANADA numbering around one thousand and their name is recorded in Ukraine in the year 1778 A.D.

TO YOU SIR AND YOUR GRACIOUS WIFE
On behalf of all above mentioned I am sending our humble greetings and best wishes with our Prayer to the Almighty God to grant you Health, Happiness and Wisdom in discharging your duties in Canada as representative of Her Majesty the Queen Elizabeth.

GOD SAVE OUR QUEEN!

I remain
Very Respectfully Yours,

Demetrius Paul Demchuk

Dene Declaration/1975

The word *Dene*, pronounced "Dennay," is the Athapaskan term for "the people." It is the name of a proposed separate Indian nation in the Mackenzie district of the

Northwest Territories to be composed of Indians of the Chipewyan, Cree, Dogrib, Loucheux, and Slavey groups. The declaration was passed at the Second Joint General Assembly of the Indian Brotherhood of the Northwest Territories on 19 July 1975, meeting at Fort Simpson. It is reprinted from *Dene Nation: The Colony Within* (1977), edited by Mel Watkins.

Statement of Rights. We the Dene of the Northwest Territories insist on the right to be regarded by ourselves and the world as a nation.

Our struggle is for the recognition of the Dene Nation by the Government and peoples of Canada and the peoples and governments of the world.

As once Europe was the exclusive homeland of the European peoples, Africa the exclusive homeland of the African peoples, the New World, North and South America, was the exclusive homeland of Aboriginal peoples of the New World, the Amerindian and the Inuit.

The New World like other parts of the world has suffered the experience of colonialism and imperialism. Other peoples have occupied the land — often with force — and foreign governments have imposed themselves on our people. Ancient civilizations and ways of life have been destroyed.

Colonialism and imperialism are now dead or dying. Recent years have witnessed the birth of new nations or rebirth of old nations out of the aches of colonialism.

As Europe is the place where you will find European countries with European governments for European peoples, now also you will find in Africa and Asia the existence of African and Asian countries with African and Asian governments for the African and Asian peoples.

The African and Asian peoples — the peoples of the Third World — have fought for and won the right to self-determination, the right to recognition as distinct peoples and the recognition of themselves as nations.

But in the New World the Native peoples have not fared so well. Even in countries in South America where the Native peoples are the vast majority of the population *there is not one country which has an Amerindian government for the Amerindian peoples.*

Nowhere in the New World have the Native peoples won the right to self-determination and the right to recognition by the world as a distinct people and as Nations.

While the Native people of Canada are a minority in their homeland, the Native people of the Northwest Territories, the Dene and the Inuit, are a majority of the population of the Northwest Territories.

The Dene find themselves as part of a country. That country is Canada. But the Government of Canada is not the Government of the Dene. The Government of the Northwest Territories is not the Government of the Dene. These governments were not the choice of the Dene, they were imposed upon the Dene.

What we the Dene are struggling for is the recognition of the Dene nation by the governments and peoples of the world.

And while there are realities we are forced to submit to, such as the existence of a country called Canada, we insist on the right to self-determination as a distinct people and the recognition of the Dene Nation.

We the Dene are part of the Fourth World. And as the peoples and Nations of the world have come to recognize the existence and rights of those peoples who make up the Third World the day must come when the nations of the Fourth World will come to be recognized and respected. The challenge to the Dene and the world is to find the way for the recognition of the Dene Nation.

Our plea to the world is to help us in our struggle to find a place in the world community where we can exercise our right to self-determination as a distinct people and as a nation.

What we seek then is independence and self-determination within the country of Canada. This is what we mean when we call for a just land settlement for the Dene nation.

VI
Some Light Verse

When the Russian poet Yevgeny Yevtushenko crossed our country giving poetry readings in 1973, he was widely quoted as saying, "The best Canadian poet is Phil Esposito." The following poems, verses, and lyrics were not written by our Phil Espositos, but were written (with a few exceptions) by our lesser-known bards. The seventeen works here, beginning with four "boat songs" (perhaps a distinctive Canadian poetic *genre*), take the reader from 1804 to 1974, across one hundred and seventy years of poetic achievement.

A Canadian Boat Song

During the nineteenth century, the best-known and most-loved poem inspired by a Canadian setting was "A Canadian Boat Song: Written on the River St. Lawrence" by Thomas Moore (1779-1852). The Irish poet wrote his lyric at Ste. Anne de Bellevue, south of Montreal, in 1804, while staying with the explorer Simon Fraser. It was first published in *Epistles, Odes and Other Poems* (1806), where Moore added the following explanation: "I wrote these words to an air which our boatmen sung to us frequently. The wind was so unfavourable that they were obliged to row all the way, and we were five days in descending the river from Kingston to Montreal, exposed to an intense sun during the day, and at night forced to take shelter from the dews in any miserable hut upon the banks that would receive us. But the magnificent scenery of the St. Lawrence repays all such difficulties."

A Canadian Boat Song:
Written on the River St. Lawrence/*Thomas Moore*

Faintly as tolls the evening chime
Our voices keep tune and our oars keep time.
Soon as the woods on shore look dim,
We'll sing at St. Ann's our parting hymn.
Row, brothers, row, the stream runs fast,
The Rapids are near and the daylight's past.

Why should we yet our sail unfurl?
Why is not a breath the blue wave to curl?

But when the wind blows off the shore,
Oh! sweetly we'll rest our weary oar.
Blow, breezes, blow, the stream runs fast,
The Rapids are near and the daylight's past.

Utawas' tide! This trembling moon
Shall see us float over thy surges soon.
Saint of this green isle! hear our prayers,
Oh, grant us cool heaven and favouring airs.
Blow, breezes, blow, the stream runs fast,
The Rapids are near and the daylight's past.

Paddling Song

To my knowledge the canoe song which follows, a sweet thing of no great moment, has never been reprinted since its original publication in London in 1823. Now a rare publication, *Canadian Airs: Collected by Lieutenant Back, R.N., During the Late Arctic Expedition under Captain Franklin* was prepared by members of Sir John Franklin's expedition to the Coppermine River "on the shores of the polar sea" made in 1819-22. According to the compiler of *Canadian Airs*, Lieutenant (later Sir) George Back (1796-1879), the air, which is to be played "in moderate time with spirit" to an unnamed tune, was constantly sung on the expedition's trip down the Coppermine River to Coronation Gulf.

Paddling Song/*Unknown Author*

Joy to thee, my brave canoe,
There's no wing so swift as you;
Right and left the bubbles rise,
Right and left the pine wood flies;
Birds, and clouds, and tide, and wind,
We shall leave ye all behind.

Joy to thee, my brave canoe,
There's no wing so swift as you.
Joy to thee, my brave canoe,
There's no wind so swift as you.

Gently now, my brave canoe,
Keep your footing sure and true,
For the Rapid close beneath
Leaps and shouts his song of death,
Now one plunge and all is done;
Now one plunge the goal is won.

Joy to thee, my brave canoe,
There's no foot is half so true.
Joy to thee, my brave canoe,
There's no foot is half so true.

Canadian Boat-Song (from the Gaelic)

"By the bye, I have a letter this morning from a friend of mine now in Upper Canada," wrote an anonymous author in *Blackwood's Edinburgh Magazine*, September 1829. "He was rowed down the St. Lawrence lately, for several days on end, by a set of strapping fellows, all born in that country, and yet hardly one of whom could speak a word of any tongue but the Gaelic. They sang heaps of our old Highland oar-songs, he says, and capitally well, in the true Hebridean fashion; and they had others of their own, Gaelic too, some of which my friend noted down, both words and music. He has sent me a translation of one of their ditties — shall I try how it will croon?" The anonymous author is presumed to be David Macbeth Moir (1798-1851), a Scottish physician and versifier, whose Upper Canadian correspondent was John Galt (1799-1839), colonist and novelist. G.H. Needler discusses the lovely lament in *The Lone Shieling*: "It was not a translation from a Gaelic original. Nor is it in any real sense a boat-song, but the lament of the Highlanders from the Hebrides exiled in Upper Canada." Whatever its provenance, the poem is deeply moving.

Canadian Boat-Song (from the Gaelic)
David Macbeth Moir

Listen to me, as when ye heard our father
  Sing long ago the song of other shores—
Listen to me, and then in chorus gather
  All your deep voices, as ye pull your oars:

  Fair these broad meads—these hoary woods are grand;
  But we are exiles from our fathers' land.

From the lone shieling of the misty island
  Mountains divide us, and the waste of seas—
Yet still the blood is strong, the heart is Highland,
  And we in dreams behold the Hebrides:

  Fair these broad meads—these hoary woods are grand;
  But we are exiles from our fathers' land.

We ne'er shall tread the fancy-haunted valley,
  Where 'tween the dark hills creeps the small clear stream,

In arms around the patriarch banner rally,
  Nor see the moon on royal tombstones gleam:

  Fair these broad meads—these hoary woods are grand;
  But we are exiles from our fathers' land.

When the bold kindred, in the time long-vanish'd,
  Conquer'd the soil and fortified the keep, —
No seer foretold the children would be banish'd,
  That a degenerate Lord might boast his sheep:

  Fair these broad meads—these hoary woods are grand;
  But we are exiles from our fathers' land.

Come foreign rage—let Discord burst in slaughter!
  O then for clansman true, and stern claymore—
The hearts that would have given their blood like water,
  Beat heavily beyond the Atlantic roar:

  Fair these broad meads—these hoary woods are grand;
  But we are exiles from our fathers' land.

The Canadians on the Nile

The first occasion on which a contingent of Canadians took part in an overseas war was the Nile Expedition of 1884. A corps of some four hundred voyageurs sailed up the Nile to the Sudan, part of Lord Wolseley's expedition to rescue General Charles George Gordon. The volunteers reached Khartoum on 28 January 1885, two days following "Chinese" Gordon's death at the hands of the Moslems. This exotic episode in our military history was dramatized in "The Canadians on the Nile" by William Wye Smith (1827-1917), a Scottish-born Ontario clergyman and versifier, who first published his tribute in *Songs of the Great Dominion* (1889), W.D. Lighthall's imperial-spirited anthology.

The Canadians on the Nile/*William Wye Smith*

O, the East is but the West, with the sun a little hotter;
And the pine becomes a palm, by the dark Egyptian
    water:
And the Nile's like many a stream we know, that fills its
    brimming cup, —
We'll think it is the Ottawa, as we track the bateaux up!
  Pull, pull, pull! as we track the bateaux up!
  It's easy shooting homeward, when we're at the top!

O, the cedar and the spruce, line each dark Canadian
    river;
But the thirsty date is here, where the sultry sunbeams
    quiver;
And the mocking mirage spreads its view, afar on either
    hand;
But strong we bend the sturdy oar, towards the Southern
    land!

Pull, pull, pull! as we track the bateaux up!
It's easy shooting homeward, when we're at the top!

O, we've tracked the Rapids up, and o'er many a portage
    crossing;
And it's often such we've seen, though so loud the waves
    are tossing!
Then, it's homeward when the run is o'er! o'er stream,
    and ocean deep—
To bring the memory of the Nile, where the maple
    shadows sleep!
    Pull, pull, pull! as we track the bateaux up!
    It's easy shooting homeward, when we're at the top!

And it yet may come to pass, that the hearts and hands so
    ready
May be sought again to help, when some poise is off the
    steady!
And the Maple and the Pine be matched, with British
    Oak and while,
As once between Egyptian suns, the Canadians on the
    Nile!
    Pull, pull, pull! as we track the bateaux up!
    It's easy shooting homeward, when we're at the top!

Sweet Maiden of Passamaquoddy

"I seized paper and pen and dashed off the following
'Lines to Florance Huntingdon, Passamquoddy, Maine,'"
explained James De Mille (1838-80) in *The New Dominion and True Humourist*, 16 April 1870. "I remember
very little about the composition of that delectable effu-
sion. I found it afterwards in the above state, but could
only recall a few circumstances connected with writing
it." Thus the novelist described the composition of this
amusing (if exasperating) verse in *The Minnehaha Mines*,
a novel published serially in the Saint John publication.
Some day the novel will be given the book publication it
deserves. In the meantime, readers can enjoy De Mille's
tongue-twisters.

Sweet Maiden of Passamaquoddy / *James De Mille*

Sweet maiden of Passamaquoddy.
    Shall we seek for communion of souls
Where the deep Mississippi meanders,
    Or the distant Saskatchewan rolls?

Oh no, — for in Maine will I find thee,
    A sweetly sequestrated nook,
Where the winding Skoodoowabskooksis
    Conjoins with the Skoodoowabskook.

There wander two beautiful rivers
    With many a winding and crook;
The one is the Skoodoowabskooksis:
    The other — the Skoodoowabskook.

Ah, sweetest of haunts! tho' unmentioned
    In Geography, Atlas, or Book,
How fair is the Skoodoowabskooksis
    When joining the Skoodoowabskook!

Our cot shall be close by the waters
    Within that sequestrated nook —
Reflected in Skoodoowabskooksis
    And mirrored in Skoodoowabskook!

You shall sleep to the music of leaflets
    By Zephyrs in wantonness shook,
And dream of the Skoodoowabskooksis,
    And, perhaps, of the Skoodoowabskook!

When awaked by the hens and the roosters,
    Each morn, you shall joyously look
On the junction of Skoodoowabskooksis,
    With soft gliding Skoodoowabskook!

Your food shall be fish from the waters,
    Drawn forth on the point of a hook,
From murmuring Skoodoowabskooksis
    Or wandering Skoodoowabskook!

You shall quaff the most sparkling of water,
    Drawn forth from a silvery brook
Which flows to the Skoodoowabskooksis
    And then to the Skoodoowabskook!

And *you* shall preside at the banquet,
    And *I* shall wait on thee as cook:
And we'll talk of the Skoodoowabskooksis,
    And sing of the Skoodoowabskook!

Let others sing loudly of Saco,
    Of Quoddy, and Tattamagouche,
Of Kennebeccasis, and Quaco,
    Of Merigonishe, and Buctouche.

Of Nashwaak, and Magaguadavique,
    Or Memmerimammericook, —
There's none like the Skoodoowabskooksis
    Excepting the Skoodoowabskook!

The Riders of the Plains

Around the world, the Royal Canadian Mounted Police is
synonymous with Canada and with law and order. The
Force was established to police the prairies in 1873 and
has been celebrated in verse ever since. The best-known
poem about the Force remains "The Riders of the
Plains," which was published anonymously by a Battleford newspaper, the *Saskatchewan Herald*, on 23
September 1878. Its author, said to be a Mountie, has
never been identified. It is reprinted from an amusing
booklet, *Wake the Prairie Echoes: The Mounted Police
Story in Verse* (1973), collected by the Saskatchewan
History and Folklore Society.

The Riders of the Plains/*Author Unknown*

Oh! let the prairies echo with
   The ever-welcome sound —
Ring out the boots and saddles,
   Its stinging notes resound.
Our horses toss their bridled heads,
   And chafe against the reins —
Ring out — ring out the marching call
   For the Riders of the Plains.

O'er many a league of prairie wide
   Our pathless way must be;
And round it roams the fiercest tribes
   Of Blackfoot and of Cree.
But danger from their savage hands
   Our dauntless hearts disdain —
The hearts that bear the helmet up —
   The Riders of the Plains!

The thunderstorm sweeps o'er our way
   But onward still we go;
We scale the weary mountains' range,
   Descend the valleys low;
We face the broad Saskatchewan,
   Made fierce with heavy rains —
With all its might it cannot check
   The Riders of the Plains.

We track the sprouting cactus land,
   When lost to white men's ken,
We startle there the creatures wild
   And fight them in their den;
For where'er our leaders bid,
   The bugle sounds its strains,
In marching sections forward go
   The Riders of the Plains.

The Fire King stalks the broad prairie,
   And fearful 'tis to see
The rushing wall of flame and smoke
   Girdling round rapidly.
'Tis there we shout defiance
   And mock its fiery chains —
For safe the cleared circle guards
   The Riders of the Plains.

For us no cheerful hostelries
   Their welcome gates unfold —
No generous board, or downy bed,
   Await our troopers bold.
Beneath the starry canopy
   At eve, when daylight wanes,
There lie the hardy slumberers —
   The Riders of the Plains.

But that which ties the courage sore
   Of horseman and of steed,
Is want of blessed water —

Blessed water is our need.
We'll face, like men, whate'er befalls,
   Of perils, hardships, pains —
Oh! God, deny not water to
   The Riders of the Plains!

We muster but three hundred
   In all this Great Lone Land,
Which stretches from Superior's waves
   To where the Rockies stand;
But not one heart doth balk,
   No coward voice complains,
That far too few in numbers are
   The Riders of the Plains.

In England's mighty Empire
   Each man must take his stand:
Some guard her honoured flag at sea,
   Some bear it well by land.
It's not our part to face her foes —
   Then what to us remains?
What duty does our country give
   To the Riders of the Plains?

Our mission is to plant the right
   Of British freedom here —
Restrain the lawless savages,
   And protect the pioneer.
And 'tis a proud and daring trust
   To hold these vast domains
With but three hundred mounted men —
   The Riders of the Plains.

W.S., N.W.M.P.
Cobourg, July 1878

A Psalm of Montreal

The most deft satire of our *mores* was composed by Samuel Butler (1835-1902), the English author whose commercial interests took him to Montreal in 1875, where he wrote "A Psalm of Montreal" with its immortal refrain: "O God! O Montreal!" (Before allowing Butler to speak for himself, let me note in passing that the English poet Rupert Brooke, visiting the same city in 1913, noted: "I made my investigations in Montreal. I have to report that the Discobolus is very well, and, nowadays, looks the whole world in the face, almost quite unabashed.") What follows comes from *The Note-Books of Samuel Butler* (1926), edited by Henry Festing Jones.

A Psalm of Montreal/*Samuel Butler*

The City of Montreal is one of the most rising and, in many respects, most agreeable on the American continent, but its inhabitants are as yet too busy with commerce to care greatly about the masterpieces of old Greek art. In the Montreal Museum of Natural History I came upon two plaster casts, one of the Antinous and the other of the Discobolus — not the good one, but in my poem, of course, I intend the good one — banished from public view to a room where were all manner of skins, plants, snakes, insects, etc., and, in the middle of these, an old man stuffing an owl.

"Ah," said I, "so you have some antiques here; why don't you put them where people can see them?"

"Well, sir," answered the custodian, "you see they are rather vulgar."

He then talked a great deal and said his brother did all Mr. Spurgeon's printing.

The dialogue — perhaps true, perhaps imaginary, perhaps a little of the one and a little of the other — between the writer and this old man gave rise to the lines that follow:

Stowed away in a Montreal lumber room
The Discobolus standeth and turneth his face to the wall;
Dusty, cobweb-covered, maimed, and set at naught,
Beauty crieth in an attic and no man regardeth:
O God! O Montreal!

Beautiful by night and day, beautiful in summer and winter,
Whole or maimed, always and alike beautiful —
He preached gospel of grace to the skins of owls
And to one who seasoneth the skins of Canadian owls:
O God! O Montreal!

When I saw him I was wroth and I said, "O Discobolus!
Beautiful Discobolus, a Prince both among gods and men!
What doest thou there, how camest thou hither, Discobolus,
Preaching gospel in vain to the skins of owls?"
O God! O Montreal!

And I turned to the man of skins and said unto him, "O thou man of skins,
Wherefore hast thou done thus to shame the beauty of the Discobolus?"
But the Lord had hardened the heart of the man of skins
And he answered, "My brother-in-law is haberdasher to Mr. Spurgeon."
O God! O Montreal!

"The Discobolus is put here because he is vulgar,
He has neither vest nor pants with which to cover his limbs;
I, Sir, am a person of most respectable connections —
My brother-in-law is haberdasher to Mr. Spurgeon."
O God! O Montreal!

Then I said, "O brother-in-law to Mr. Spurgeon's haberdasher,
Who seasonest also the skins of Canadian owls,
Thou callest trousers 'pants,' whereas I call them 'trousers,'
Therefore thou art in hell-fire and may the Lord pity thee!"
O God! O Montreal!

"Preferrest thou the gospel of Montreal to the gospel of Hellas,
The gospel of thy connection with Mr. Spurgeon's haberdashery to the gospel of the Discobolus?"
Yet none the less blasphemed he beauty saying, "The Discobolus hath no gospel,
But my brother-in-law is haberdasher to Mr. Spurgeon."
O God! O Montreal!

Out West

"The Last Best West Beyond Which One Cannot Dream of Anything Better" is a slogan associated with the vigorous immigration policy of Sir Clifford Sifton, who as minister of the Interior (1896-1905) opened up the prairies to tens of thousands of settlers, who farmed and homesteaded and turned western Canada into "the Breadbasket of the World," another of Sir Clifford's slogans. "Out West" catches some of the wanderlust that inspired the early colonists. It first appeared in the *Saskatchewan Herald*, 18 July 1881, but I found it in "Poems of the Golden West," a selection of anonymous verse made by John Orwell for *White Pelican*, Summer 1972.

Out West/*Author Unknown*

There's a country famed in story,
    As you've often times been told;
'Tis a land of mighty rivers
    Running over sands of gold;
The abode of peace and plenty,
    And with quietness 'tis blest;
But this country that's so famous
    Is away off in the West.

Once a man in Androscoggin,
    Or in some outlandish place,
With a view to find this country
    To the westward set his face.
He was weary at Chicago,
    And he sat him down to rest;
But 'twas only there the centre,
    Not the farther Golden West.

Then he crossed the golden prairies
    Stretching onward like the sea;

"I am bound to find this country,
    If there's such a one," said he;
So he swam the Mississippi,
    Then on Missouri's breast
He explored the wilds of Kansas
    For this country to the West.

Climbing o'er the Rocky Mountains,
    On he kept his weary way,
Till the broad Pacific's waters
    Right before his vision lay;
Here he sat him down and ponder'd,
    But for him there was no rest;
"'Tis an island surely," said he —
    This country in the West.

So a vessel quick he builded,
    And the shore he left behind,
Sailing on with eager longing
    Still this happy isle to find.
After many days, one morning
    He beheld the wish'd-for land;
Steering 'mid the shoals and breakers,
    Quickly reached the golden strand.

From his gallant bark he landed,
    Wading through the curling foam,
With his eyes wide ope'd with wonder,
    For he found himself at home.
Then he learned that one forever
    Might go on and never rest,
Still they would not find this country —
    For 'tis always farther West.

My Address (No. 2)

Of James Gay (1810-91), who styled himself "Poet
Laureate of Canada and Master of All Poets," William
Arthur Deacon wrote, tongue in cheek, "James Gay was a
dear old man. His inspiration is undeniable." The eccen-
tric rhymester, who was by trade an umbrella-maker in
Guelph, Ontario, addressed the following tribute to the
governor general and his wife on the occasion of their
official visit to the Royal City. It appeared in his long-
out-of-print publication, *Canada's Poet: Yours Alway,
James Gay* (1884).

My Address (No. 2)/*James Gay*

To His Excellency the Marquis of Lorne and Her
Royal Highness Princess Louise.

An address for my governor and Her Highness, Princess
    Louise.
Both will leave us soon to cross the salt seas;
Five years have soon passed by, it would not wait for man,

I wish you both safe across the seas to your home and
    native land.
When you arrive in London may they all rejoice and sing,
O'er your safe voyage across the seas, with good health
    and long life to our Queen.
Your lordship puts me in mind of Nelson,
The bravest ever fought on the seas.
His last words were on the "Victory," if I think aright,
Says he, "My boys, you have done your duty!" his spirit
    took flight:
I hope it is in Heaven at rest with angels bright.
I hope my address to you will cause no disgrace,
My wish to both when called away to that most happy
    place;
It's a glorious thing for all mankind,
A happy tale to tell and to leave this world behind
Us, singing, "All is well! All is well!"
I've been in Canada almost fifty years,
To my Queen and my country proved loyal and true,
My colours will never disgrace.
Excuse my inability, my Lord, in my address to you,
Or old England's Red, White, and Blue.
Your Honour, I crossed the seas in '82 to see my gracious
    Queen;
She left for Balmoral on her birthday, so by me she could
    not be seen.
I hope again to cross the seas and to let Old England
    know it,
And to see Her Majesty in her own home, being the
    Master of all Poets.
As the greatest of Poets have passed away,
It appears it's left between Alfred Tennyson and James
    Gay.
Being so long in Canada, according to my belief,
I want to wear on my person the Canadian medal, the
    beaver and the maple leaf;
So when I travel through my native land hundreds can
    have to say,
And also have the pleasure of seeing the world's Poet
    James Gay,
Poet Laureate of Canada up to this present day;
And when I receive my Canadian medal I shall feel happy
    as the flowers in May.
I hope my present Governor will grant me my request,
I shall wear it on my left breast,
Till I am called to rest.
Your Lordship, I take the liberty in sending you my
    likeness and my address. Yours alway, James Gay.

Ode on the Mammoth Cheese

"We have written a number of dairy odes recently; these
and our patriotic songs composed during the past year we
trust will make our work more interesting." These were
the hopes of James McIntyre (1827-1906), the Scottish-

born casket-maker and poetaster and native of Ingersoll, Ontario. McIntyre composed some eighteen poems on the subject of cheese-making, for — as he noted in *Poems* (1889) — "About 800 Cheese factories are in operation in this Province of Ontario." Belated recognition for his compositions came to him from William Arthur Deacon, who in his tongue-in-cheek satire, *The Four Jameses* (1927, 1974), dubbed McIntyre "The Cheese Poet." The title, "casually but affectionately and irrevocably bestowed on him, of the Cheese Poet," has stuck. The text of the "Ode" that follows is taken from McIntyre's second book, *Musings on the Banks of Canadian Thames* (1884).

Ode on the Mammoth Cheese/*James McIntyre*

WEIGHING OVER 7,000 POUNDS.

We have seen the Queen of cheese,
Laying quietly at your ease,
Gently fanned by evening breeze —
Thy fair form no flies dare seize.

All gaily dressed soon you'll go
To the great Provincial Show,
To be admired by many a beau
In the City of Toronto.

Cows, numerous as a swarm of bees —
Or as leaves upon the trees —
It did require to make thee please,
And stand unrivalled Queen of Cheese.

May you not receive a scar as!
We have heard that Mr. Harris
Intends to send you off as far as
The great World's show at Paris.

Of the youth — beware of these —
For some of them might rudely squeeze
And bite your cheek; then songs or glees
We could not sing o' Queen of Cheese.

We'rt thou suspended from baloon
You'd caste a shade, even at noon;
Folks would think it was the moon
About to fall and crush them soon.

My Own Canadian Girl

The following verse may be appreciated today for its innocent charm or for its charming innocence, yet seldom has the Canadian lass been paid a greater compliment! "My Own Canadian Girl" was penned by W.M. MacKeracher (1871-1913), a Presbyterian minister who practised journalism in Montreal and published three volumes of verse, including *Canada, My Land and Other Compositions in Verse* (1908), from which this poem was

taken. It might not be amiss to note that MacKeracher was married, not to a Canadian girl, but to a woman from New York!

My Own Canadian Girl/*W.M. MacKeracher*

The demoiselles of sunny France
    Have gaiety and grace;
Britannia's maids a tender glance,
    A sweet and gentle face;
Columbia's virgins bring to knee
    Full many a duke and earl;
But there is none can equal thee,
    My own Canadian girl.

Thy hair is finer than the floss
    That tufts the ears of corn;
Its tresses have a silken gloss,
    A glory like the morn;
I prize the rich, luxuriant mass,
    And each endearing curl
A special grace and beauty has,
    My own Canadian girl.

Thy brow is like the silver moon
    That sails in summer skies,
The mirror of a mind immune
    From care, serene and wise,
Thy nose is sculptured ivory;
    Thine ears are lobes of pearl;
Thy lips are corals from the sea,
    My own Canadian girl.

Thine eyes are limpid pools of light,
    The windows of thy soul;
The stars are not so clear and bright
    That shine around the pole.
The crimson banners of thy cheeks
    To sun and wind unfurl;
Thy tongue makes music when it speaks,
    My own Canadian girl.

God keep thee fair and bright and good
    As in thy morning hour,
And make thy gracious womanhood
    A still unfolding flow'r.
And stay thy thoughts from trifles vain,
    Thy feet from folly's whirl,
And guard thy life from every stain,
    My own Canadian girl!

The Parson at the Hockey Match

Who was it who once suggested that the Canadian genius is most apparent in two popular institutions, the National Hockey League and the United Church of Canada? The

following verse, written well before the creation of either
body, gives us a churchman's look at the favourite sport
of Canadians. "The Parson at the Hockey Match" was
written by W.M. MacKeracher (1871-1913), the Presbyterian minister turned reporter who also wrote "My Own
Canadian Girl." Both poems come from *Canada, My
Land and Other Compositions in Verse* (1908).

The Parson at the Hockey Match / *W.M. MacKeracher*

It's very disagreeable to sit here in the cold,
And a sinful waste of time — ah, well, it's too late now to
   scold;
I'll think about my sermon and my prayers for Sunday
   next,
And the young folks may be happy — let me see — what
   was my text?
But what a throng of people — an immortal soul in each:
With such an audience this would be a splendid place to
   preach.
I'd have the pulpit half-way down — what ice! without a
   smirch!
Here are the men — I wonder if they ever go to church.
"The teams?" Ah, yes, "the forwards, point, and cover-
   point and goal";
Thank you, my dear, I understand — is that a lump of
   coal?
"Rubber?" Ah, yes, "The puck?" just so! One's holding it, I
   see —
That fellow with his clothes all on — ah, that's the
   referee.
What was he whistling for — his dog? Why, they've
   begun to play;
Well, well, that's rough; I really think we're doing wrong
   to stay.
It's sickening, deafening; dear! I wish this uproar could
   be stilled.
I do sincerely trust there'll not be anybody killed.

It's a wondrous exhibition of alertness, speed, and
   strength.
I suppose there's not much danger — there's a fellow at
   full length.
He's up again; that's plucky. Well, the little lad has pluck —
And now he's master of the ice, possessor of the puck.
He dodges two opponents, but collides with one at last,
A Philistine Goliath — David baffles him and fast
Darts onward o'er the whitening sheet, while from each
   crowded row
The crazed spectators cheer him on — Look! — has he lost
   it? No!
He's clear again. Played, played, my boy. I'd like to see
   him score: —
(I'll have no voice for Sunday if I shout like this much
   more) —
But there his ruthless enemies o'erwhelm him in a shoal —

Well played, you hero, safely passed. Now for a shot on
   goal.
Shoot, shoot, you duffer; shoot, you goose, you ass, you
   great galoot,
You addle-pated idiot, you nincompoop, you — shoot!
You've lost it! Never mind — well tried — that other dash
   was grand.
Why do they stop? "Off side," you say? I don't quite
   understand.
That's puzzling. I suppose it's right. I wish they'd not
   delay.
This is a most provoking interruption to the play.

"Cold?" Nothing of the sort. I was — I'm heated with the
   game.
I'm really enjoying it; indeed, I'm glad I came.
I'd like to see both ends at once; I can't from where we sit.
They've scored one yonder — What's the row? A player
   has been hit?
Such things are bound to happen in a rapid game like
   this;
They'll soon resume the play, my dear; there's nothing
   much amiss, —
Some trifling accident received in a rough body check,
A shoulder dislocated or a fracture of the neck.
Oh, no, it's nothing serious — the game begins again.
They're here, a writhing, struggling mass of half a dozen
   men
Battling and groaning with the strife, and breathing hard
   and fast,
Swayed back and forth and stooping low like elms before
   the blast,
Changing their places like a fleet of vessels tempest-driven
That blindly meet within the waves and part with timbers
   riven,
Waving their sticks with frantic zeal — But isn't this a
   sight?
My goodness! I could sit and watch a game like this all
   night.
There, dirty trousers, there's your chance. Muffed it!
   Why weren't you quick?
This is a sight to make the sad rejoice, to heal the sick,
To rouse the drones and give them life to last them half a
   year —
Hit him again! I wish I had my congregation here.

My stars! and this is hockey. Hockey's the king of sports.
This is the thing to come to when you're feeling out of
   sorts.
This is the greatest holiday I've had for many weeks.
This helps one to appreciate the feeling of the Greeks.
I understand my Homer now — O Hercules, behold
Yon Trojan giant, he that's cast in an Olympian mould,
Ye gods, he more than doubled up that other stalwart
   cove —
Here comes swift-footed Mercury, the messenger of Jove.

Adown the blue, outstripping all, he speeds. Oh, what a
    spurt!
His shoulders have no wings, but see, he has them on his
    shirt.
He's broken through the forward line, baffled the cover-
    point,
Thrown down the other man and knocked their game all
    out of joint.
And now he rushes on the goal—this makes the senses
    reel—
Goal! goal! hurrah! hurrah! well done, men of the winged
    wheel!

At last— how soon!—the game is done; I've scarcely
    drawn a breath.
This getting out is difficult; I'm almost crushed to death.
The cars are packed; how we'll get home I'm sure I do not
    know.
Here's room for you; get up, my dears; I'll walk; away you
    go.

My sermon's gone, but as I walk I cannot help but think
That, after all, perhaps I've found a sermon in the rink.

This world is an arena with a slippery sheet of ice,
And all have skates and hockey sticks and enter without
    price.
And seats are round for those who rest — the idle and the
    old;
But those who are not in the game are apt to find it cold.
Some play defence, some forward, with terrific speed and
    stress.
The puck keeps flying 'twixt the goals of failure and suc-
    cess,
Now up, now down, across and back, here, there, and
    everywhere.

The grit of skates, the crack of sticks, the shouting, fill
    the air.
Some slip and fall a thousand times and spring up in a
    trice;
Some go to pieces on their feet and have to leave the ice;
Some play offside, kick, tackle, trip, try every kind of
    foul;
Some players are forever cheered, some only get a howl.
We seldom hear the whistle of the watchful Referee,
Who mostly lets the game go on as if He didn't see.
No gong rings out half-time to let the players get their
    breath —
To most full time comes only with the solemn stroke of
    death.
The winners are not always those who make the biggest
    score;
The vanquished oft are victors when the stubborn game is
    o'er;
For many things are added to make up the grand
    amount,
And everything is taken at the last into account —

The sort of sticks we played with, and the way our feet
    were shod,
For the trophy is Salvation and the Referee is God.

God prosper our Canadian sports and keep them clean
    and pure,
Whole-hearted, manly, generous, and let them long en-
    dure!
Long live each honest winter sport, each good Canadian
    game,
To train the youth in lusty health and iron strength of
    frame,
To make them noble, vigorous, straightforward, ardent,
    bold,
Nearer a perfect standard than the grandest knights of
    old.

Keep in the path of rectitude the young throughout the
    land,
And guide them ever on their way by thine unerring
    hand,
Along the slippery path of life in safety toward the goal,
And keep their bodies holy as the temples of the soul:
For the river of the future from the present's fountain
    runs,
And a nation's hope is founded on the virtue of her sons.

The glory of a man is strength, Thy wisdom hath
    declared;
Let strength increase, and strength of frame with
    strength of will be paired,
And let these twain go hand in hand with strength of
    heart and mind,
And strength of character present all forms of strength
    combined.
Oh, make our strength the strength of men to perfect
    stature grown,
And use it for thine ends and turn man's glory to thine
    own!

In Flanders Now

Nellie McClung said, "You have the gift, Edna dear, to
ring bells in the hearts of people." W.L. Mackenzie King
said, "I've been your ardent fan for over twenty years."
They were talking about the popular versifier, Edna
Jaques (b. 1891), who has written over a dozen volumes of
light lyrics. In 1918, moved by "In Flanders Fields," she
wrote "an answer" to John McCrae's famous poem, which
was read at the unveiling of the Tomb of the Unknown
Soldier, Arlington National Cemetery, Washington,
D.C., and has been popular ever since. The text is taken
from Jaques's *Beside Still Waters* (1939). "One sees why
Edna Jaques is popular: she is probably our most
genuinely popular writer of verse," explained the critic
E.K. Brown. "She enables us to see what Canadian taste
really is."

In Flanders Now/*Edna Jaques*

We have kept faith, ye Flanders' dead,
  Sleep well beneath those poppies red
That mark your place.
The torch your dying hands did throw,
  We've held it high before the foe,
And answered bitter blow for blow,
  In Flanders' fields.

And where your heroes' blood was spilled,
  The guns are now forever stilled
And silent grown.
There is no moaning of the slain,
  There is no cry of tortured pain,
And blood will never flow again,
  In Flanders' fields.

Forever holy in our sight
  Shall be those crosses gleaming white,
That guard your sleep.
Rest you in peace, the task is done,
  The fight you left us we have won,
And Peace on Earth has just begun,
  In Flanders now.

The Athabasca Trail

It was the British imperialists like Sir Arthur Conan Doyle (1859-1930) who saw the romance of Canada in all its colour and configuration. They knew the Dominion of Canada to be "a vaster Britain" and a cornerstone of the British Empire, but they also sensed the epic sweep of the ancient land which was now a new nation. These are some of the sentiments expressed by Sir Arthur when he addressed the Canadian Club of Ottawa on 2 July 1914. It was a festive occasion and his speech was followed by prolonged cheers. It ended like this: "Before I sit down I will read a verse or two in which I was able, perhaps, to compress a little more of that feeling which Canada has awakened, than can be done in prose. Poetry is like the pemmican of literature: it is compressed thought, and one can mingle emotion with it, which one cannot always do in prosaic speech. I will read you, if I may, these few lines before I take my seat. I call it 'The Athabasca Trail,' since Athabasca is the place where we have for some time been living an open-air life."

The Athabasca Trail/*Sir Arthur Conan Doyle*

My life is gliding downwards; it speeds swifter to the day
When it shoots the last dark canon to the Plains of Far-
  away,
But while its stream is running through the years that are
  to be,
The mighty voice of Canada will ever call to me.

I shall hear the roar of rivers where the rapids foam and
  tear,
I shall smell the virgin upland with its balsam-laden air,
And shall dream that I am riding down the winding
  woody vale,
With the packer and the packhorse on the Athabasca
  Trail.

I have passed the warden cities at the eastern water-
  gate,
Where the hero and the martyr laid the corner stone of
  State,
The *habitant, coureur-des-bois*, and hardy *voyageur,*
Where lives a breed more strong at need to venture or
  endure?
I have seen the gorge of Erie where the roaring waters
  run,
I have crossed the Inland Ocean, lying golden in the sun,
But the last and best and sweetest is the ride by hill and
  dale,
With the packer and the packhorse on the Athabasca
  Trail.

I'll dream again of fields of grain that stretch from sky to
  sky,
And the little prairie hamlets, where the cars go roaring
  by,
Wooden hamlets as I saw them — noble cities still to be
To girdle stately Canada with gems from sea to sea;
Mother of a mighty manhood, land of glamour and of
  hope,
From the eastward sea-swept Islands to the sunny western
  slope,
Ever more my heart is with you, ever more till life shall
  fail,
I'll be out with pack and packer on the Athabasca Trail.

Away With Tunics

The following ditty deserves a far happier fate than languishing unread in the back issues of the *International Journal*, published by the Canadian Institute of International Affairs. It seems that a memo was circulated requiring consular officers to decline politely those foreign honours that might be offered them. This occurred while Lester B. Pearson was minister of external affairs (1946-48), and Pearson himself offered a bottle of spirits to the author of the best verse describing the memo. Lord Garner, British high commissioner in Ottawa (1956-61), writing in "Mike: an Englishman's View," *International Journal*, Winter 1973-74, identifies the author of the verse published here as Raymond Bell, a member of his staff, now Sir Raymond Bell. Sadly, Lord Garner does not tell us who won the bottle of spirits.

Away With Tunics/*Sir Raymond Bell*

Away with tunics, cocked hats, swords
In proof of stern endeavour
We'll wear (where Adam wore the fig)
The Maple Leaf for Ever.

Dief Will Be the Chief

Those who have yet to hear The Stringband perform "Dief Will Be the Chief" will be at a loss to know what to make of the lyrics that follow. What is lost on the printed page is the catchy tune and the manic innocence of the Toronto folk group's performance style. The words and music were written by Bob Bossin (b. 1946), the founder of The Stringband, and the song was first heard nationally on CBC Radio's "As It Happens," 10 April 1975. One listener was John G. Diefenbaker, the former Conservative prime minister, whose eightieth birthday in 1975 was celebrated with much merriment and well-wishing. What did Diefenbaker think of the musical tribute? "As a connoisseur of good music," he told the programme's hosts, Barbara Frum and Al Maitland, "I am simply delighted." The song was number one on the Prince Albert hit parade. The lyrics are reprinted from the *Globe and Mail*, 4 February 1978. The Stringband is now known as the "Whilom Stringband (formerly The Stringband)."

Dief Will Be the Chief/*Bob Bossin*

In 1957, when you were just a kid in school
And Cassius Clay was just an amateur
Hustlin' down in Louisville,
Dief came out of Prince Albert
And he said he was a man with a dream,
Now in '74 Clay's the champ once more and I know
Dief will be the chief again.

Dief is the chief, Dief is the chief,
Dief will be the chief again.
Everybody's happy back in '57
And nobody's happy since then.
There was law in the land, order in the home,
Swimmin' in the river back then,
And I know in my heart
That Dief will be the chief
And a dollar worth a dollar again.

Well, he lost in '25 and he lost in '26 and '29
But he never lost heart.
He lost in '33 and he lost in '38
And the forties were mostly dark.
But in '53 he married Olive,
And together they ruled the land,
And with Olive as his guide

The Queen of his heart,
Dief will be the chief again.

Now we've got a man up in Ottawa,
He's got cold water in his veins.
You know that he
Don't give a shit about you.
And he don't hear when you complain.
But Dief came out of Prince Albert,
He was raised in the prairie grain,
And he always had a hand
For the working man,
Dief will be the chief again.

Dief is the chief, Dief is the chief,
Dief will be the chief again.
Everybody's happy back in '57
And nobody's been happy since then.
There's a famine in the land,
A mortgage on the home,
And strikes without any end,
But I know in my heart that Dief will be the chief
And a dollar worth a dollar again.

He's Chief Walking Buffalo
To the people of the Sioux,
Honorary Chief Eagle to the Cree;
He's a customary colonel up in Saskatoon
And a personal acquaintance of the Queen;
He's a Baptist and a Kinsman and Kiwanis man too
And he's eighty on September 18,
And he's always had a hand
For the working man.
Dief will be the chief again.

1838

"Ultimately, the reason why William Lyon Mackenzie King has been our highly respected prime minister for twenty years is that the anything-but-respectable William Lyon Mackenzie was beaten in 1837," remarked W.H. Underhill. Students of Canadian history are quick to realize that far from flourishing here, the revolutionary tradition has withered on the vine, at least to the extent that the hopes of rebels and reformers and revolutionaries were dashed by the failure of the Rebels of '37 and the two Riel rebellions. Dennis Lee (b. 1939), the poet and editor, had this in mind when he wrote "1838," which he published in *Nicholas Knock and Other People* (1974).

1838/*Dennis Lee*

The Compact sat in parliament
To legalize their fun.
And now they're hanging Sammy Lount
And Captain Anderson.

And if they catch Mackenzie
They will string him in the rain.
And England will erase us if
Mackenzie comes again.

The Bishop has a paper
That says he owns our land.
The Bishop has a Bible too
That says our souls are damned.
Mackenzie had a printing press.
It's soaking in the Bay.
And who will spike the Bishop till
Mackenzie comes again?

The British want the country
For the Empire and the view.

The Yankees want the country for
A yankee barbecue.
The Compact want the country
For their merrie green domain.
They'll all play finders-keepers till
Mackenzie comes again.

Mackenzie was a crazy man,
He wore his wig askew.
He donned three bulky overcoats
In case the bullets flew.
Mackenzie talked of fighting
While the fight went down the drain.
But who will speak for Canada?
Mackenzie, come again!

VII
National Songs

"Let me make the songs of a nation," wrote Andrew Fletcher in 1703, "and I care not who makes its laws." In selecting the lyrics to appear in this section, I have not limited myself to the National Anthem ("O Canada") and the Royal Anthem ("God Save the Queen") but have gone beyond them to include some of the "national" songs of Quebec as well as quasi-official songs popular in the other provinces. Here are eleven songs, sanctioned by the people or by their governments and known by heart, in whole or part, by the Canadian people. I would dearly have loved to have extended the coverage to include such lovely folk songs with provincial identifications as "Farewell to Nova Scotia" or "The Poor Little Girls of Ontario" or "Saskatchewan" or "Alberta Land," but I had to draw a line somewhere. The words and music of these and other delightful songs may be found in such excellent collections as *Canada's Story in Song* (1965), compiled by Edith Fowke and Alan Mills. What follows are those songs that are frequently sung at official gatherings across the country and around the world wherever Canadians are gathered.

Alouette!

"This is by far the best known of all Canadian songs," explains the folksong collector Edith Fowke. "It has long been used by both French and English Canadians for community singing." An *alouette* is a skylark, and the lark, in this traditional French-Canadian song is warned: "Alouette, gentle alouette, alouette, I will pluck your feathers yet." Verse by verse, different parts of the bird's body are mentioned: *la têt'* (head), *le bec* (beak), *le nez* (nose), *les yeux* (eyes), *le cou* (neck), *les ail's* (wings), *le dos* (back), *les patt's* (feet), *la queue* (tail).... This is a nonsense song with an uncanny hold on Canadians of both language groups.

Alouette!

Alouette, gentille alouette, alouette, je t'y plumerai.
Alouette, gentille alouette, alouette, je t'y plumerai.

Je t'y plumerai la têt', je t'y plumerai la têt',
Je t'y plumerai la têt', je t'y plumerai la têt',
Et la têt',
Et la têt',
Et la têt',
Et la têt',
Alouett',
Alouett', O....

Je t'y plumerai le bec, je t'y plumerai le bec,
Je t'y plumerai le bec, je t'y plumerai le bec,
Et le bec,
Et le bec,
Et le bec,
Et le bec,
Et la têt',
Et la têt',
Et la têt',
Et la têt',
Alouett',
Alouett', O....

À la Claire Fontaine

"One is not *Canadien* without it," wrote the folksong collector Ernest Gagnon of "À la Claire Fontaine." It was sung by Champlain's men at Port Royal in 1608 when they formed the Order of Good Cheer to banish the miseries of winter, and it was lustily sung by both the *coureurs de bois* and the *habitants* in New France. According to Edith Fowke in *The Penguin Book of Canadian Folk Songs* (1973), this mediaeval jongleur song became an unofficial anthem of French Canada. The English version is by Edith Fowke.

À la Claire Fontaine

By the clear running fountain
I strayed one summer day.
The water looked so cooling
I bathed without delay.

Beneath an oak tree shady
I dried myself that day
When from the topmost branches
A bird's song came my way.

Sing, nightingale, keep singing,
Your heart is always gay.
You have no cares to grieve you,
While I could weep today.

You have no cares to grieve you,
While I could weep today,
For I have lost my loved one
In such a senseless way.

She wanted some red roses
But I did rudely say
She could not have the roses
That I had picked that day.

Now I wish those red roses
Were on their bush today,
While I and my beloved
Still went our old sweet way.

CHORUS
Many long years have I loved you,
Ever in my heart you'll stay.

Vive la Canadienne!

"A lively toast to the Canadian girl" is how Edith Fowke
describes this popular song. Sometime during the seventeenth century a Quebecker, perhaps a *voyageur*, composed a new set of words for the old French melody. The
English words here are by Edith Fowke and come from
The Penguin Book of Canadian Folk Songs (1973). When
the song is sung, the last two lines of each verse are
repeated.

Vive la Canadienne!

Of my Canadian girl I sing,
  Gaily our voices ring!
Of my Canadian girl I sing
And her sweet eyes so blue,
  And her sweet eyes so blue, blue, blue,
  And her sweet eyes so blue.

Here's to a lovers' meeting!
  Gaily our voices ring!
Here's to a lovers' meeting!

I know that she is true,
  I know that she is true, true, true,
  I know that she is true.

Quickly our hearts are beating!
  Gaily our voices ring!
Quickly our hearts are beating,
As we go on our way,
  As we go on our way, way, way,
  As we go on our way.

So go the hours a-flying,
  Gaily our voices ring!
So go the hours a-flying
Until our wedding day,
  Until our wedding day, day, day,
  Until our wedding day.

O Canada, Mon Pays, Mes Amours

"He spoke to us of his poems, he even sang to us one of his
songs, the one which all the world knows," wrote Sir
Wilfrid Laurier in 1871 of Sir George-Étienne Cartier
(1814-73), the French-Canadian statesman and Father of
Confederation, and of the song he composed, "O
Canada, Mon Pays, Mes Amours," which was for half a
century one of the most popular of patriotic songs in
French Canada. Cartier wrote it when he was twenty and
first sang it to an old French air in Montreal on St-Jean
Baptiste Day, 24 June 1834. It is now sung, when sung at
all, to the melody of J.B. Labelle. The original version of
"O Canada, Mon Pays, Mes Amours," which is published
here, comes from *Sir George-Étienne Cartier, Bart.: His
Life and Times* (1914), written by John Boyd, who is
responsible for the metrical version of Cartier's stirring
lyric.

O Canada, Mon Pays, Mes Amours

Comme le dit un vieil adage:
Rien n'est si beau que son pays;
Et de la chanter, c'est l'usage;
Le mien je chante à mes amis
L'étranger voit avec un oeil d'envie
Du Saint-Laurent le majestueux cours;
À son aspect le Canadien s'écrie:
O Canada! mon pays! mes amours!

Maints ruisseaux et maintes rivières
Arrosent nos fertiles champs;
Et de nos montagnes altières,
On voit de loin les longs penchants.
Vallons, côteaux, forêts, chutes, rapides,
De tant d'objets est-il plus beau concours?
Qui n'aimerait tes lacs aux eaux limpides?
O Canada! mon pays! mes amours!

Les quatre saisons de l'année
Offrent tour à tour leurs attraits.
Au printemps, l'amante enjouée
Revoit ses fleurs, ses verts bosquets.
Le moissonneur, l'été, joyeux s'apprête
À recueillier le fruit de ses labours.
Et tout l'automne et tout l'hiver, on fête.
O Canada! mon pays! mes amours!

Le Canadien, comme ses pères,
Aime à chanter, à s'égayer.
Doux, aisé, vif en ses manières,
Poli, galant, hospitalier,
À son pays il ne fut jamais traitre,
À l'esclavage il résistait toujours;
Et sa maxime est la paix, le bien-être
Du Canada, son pays, ses amours.

Chaque pays vante ses belles;
Je crois bien que l'on ne ment pas;
Mais nos Canadiennes comme elles
Ont des grâces et des appas.
Chez nous la belle est aimable, sincère;
D'une Françoise elle a tous les atours,
L'air moins coquet, pourtant assez pour plaire
O Canada, mon pays! mes amours!

O mon pays! de la nature
Vraiment tu fus l'enfant chéri;
Mais l'Albion la main parjure,
En ton sein le trouble a nourri.
Puissent tous tes enfants enfin se joindre,
Et valeureux voler à ton secours!
Car le beau jour déjà commence à poindre.
O Canada! mon pays! mes amours!

O Canada, Mon Pays, Mes Amours

"One's own land is best of all,"
So an ancient adage says;
To sing it is the poet's call,
Mine be to sing my fair land's praise.
Strangers behold with envious eyes
St. Lawrence's tide so swift and grand,
But the Canadian proudly cries,
O Canada, my own beloved land!

Rivers and streams in myriad maze
Meander through our fertile plains,
Midst many a lofty mountain's haze,
What vast expanse and vision chains!
Vales, hills and rapids, forest brakes —
What panoroma near so grand!
Who doth not love thy limpid lakes,
O Canada, my own beloved land!

Each season of the passing year,
In turn, attractions hath to bless,
Spring like an ardent wooer, dear,
Besports fair flowers and verdant dress;
Summer anon prepares to wrest
The harvest rare with joyful hand;
In Fall and Winter, feast and jest.
O Canada, my own beloved land!

Canadians, like their sires of old,
Revel in song and gaily live,
Mild, gentle, free, not overbold,
Polite and gallant, welcome give.
Patriots, to country ever leal,
They, foes of slavery, staunchly stand;
Their watchword is the peace and weal
Of Canada, their beloved land.

Each country vaunts its damsels fair,
(I quite agree with truth they boast)
But our Canadian girls must share
The witching charm of beauty's host,
So lovely they and so sincere,
With that French charm of magic wand,
Coquettish just to make them dear.
O Canada, my own beloved land!

O my country, thou art blest,
Favoured of all the nations now!
But the stranger's vile behest
Would the seeds of discord sow.
May thy brave sons for thy sake
Join to help thee, hand in hand,
For thy great day doth e'en now break,
O Canada, my own beloved land!

Mon Pays

"A country, like a conscience, is something that all of us have deep within ourselves," Gilles Vigneault (b. 1928) once explained. On another occasion the Quebec *chansonnier* said: "I'm trying to make a people — whom I watch disappear with great anger — believe that its fate can be reversed." Certainly the single song most expressive of the need the *Québécois* have to assert their identity and individuality is "Mon Pays," which first appeared in a collection of Vigneault's poems called *Avec les vieux mots* (1965). The version published here is the authorized English adaptation by the Quebec writer Jo Ouellet. Both the original French lyrics and a different poetic translation may be found in my edition of *The Poets of Canada* (1978).

This My Land

This my land I call home is a blanket of snow;
This my road that I travel has no place to go;
This my garden is barren where nothing will grow:
It's a homeland called Winter — a country of snow.

In this white and frozen track,
Where some would choose to turn their back,
A Winterland they'd call a tomb,
My father chose to build a home;
And I intend to prove him right,
I'll build another just in sight,
With rooms so gay — with rooms so bright
That guests who come to pay a call
Will then stay on to their delight.

This my land I call home is a blanket of snow,
This my voice is the echo where winds fiercely blow,
This my house is of ice for those who don't know
It's a homeland called Winter — a country of snow.

And from my lonely land so vast,
I've got to shout while still I last,
To all the corners of the earth:
My home is yours, it was from birth;
Within its walls of frigid cold,
I toil and sweat, you must be told,
To stoke the fire, I must enfold
All humans come from everywhere
'Cause they're my kin, both young and old.

This my land I call home is a blanket of snow;
This my road that I travel has no place to go
This my garden is barren where nothing will grow:
It's a homeland called Winter — a country of snow.

This my land's just the opposite of what it could be,
Not a country at all yet 'twas time it should be;
This my song is my life and it's simple you see:
Let's make Winter a country for you and for me.

The Maple Leaf for Ever

"I think I will write about the maple leaf," Alexander Muir (1830-1906) told his wife one evening in 1867. Muir recalled the experience of walking under a silver maple tree on Laing Street (and more than a century later it is still standing, at 62 Laing Street in the east end of Toronto, shedding its leaves in the fall) when a leaf fell onto his sleeve and resisted his efforts to brush it off. That evening Muir composed the patriotic words and stirring tune of "The Maple Leaf for Ever." Muir had to publish the sheet music at his own expense and he never did benefit financially from his composition, but the Toronto highschool teacher had the satisfaction of knowing he had written a song that had become a patriotic favourite in English Canada. The version of the lyrics reproduced here is familiar to generations of primary and secondary school students who sang it, as the sheet music advises, "*con spirito*." The popular version differs from the earlier version in two ways. Muir originally wrote: "In days of yore the hero Wolfe,/Britain's glory did maintain. . . ." The first verse used to end with a reference to French

Canada's *fleur-de-lys*: "With Lily, Thistle, Shamrock, Rose,/The Maple Leaf for ever."

The Maple Leaf for Ever

In days of yore, from Britain's shore,
Wolfe the dauntless hero came,
And planted firm Britannia's flag,
On Canada's fair domain.
Here may it wave, our boast, our pride,
And joined in love together,
The Thistle, Shamrock, Rose entwine
The Maple Leaf for ever!

The Maple Leaf, our emblem dear,
The Maple Leaf for ever!
God save our Queen, and Heaven bless
The Maple Leaf for ever!

At Queenston Heights and Lundy's Lane,
Our brave fathers, side by side,
For freedom, homes, and loved ones dear,
Firmly stood and nobly died;
And those dear rights which they maintained,
We swear to yield them never!
Our watchword ever more shall be,
The Maple Leaf for ever!

The Maple Leaf, our emblem dear,
The Maple Leaf for ever!
God save our Queen, and Heaven bless
The Maple Leaf for ever!

Our fair Dominion now extends
From Cape Race to Nootka Sound;
May peace for ever be our lot,
And plenteous store abound:
And may those ties of love be ours
Which discord cannot sever,
And flourish green o'er Freedom's home,
The Maple Leaf for ever!

The Maple Leaf, our emblem dear,
The Maple Leaf for ever!
And flourish green o'er Freedom's home,
The Maple Leaf for ever!

On merry England's far-famed land
May kind Heaven sweetly smile;
God bless Old Scotland evermore,
And Ireland's Emerald Isle!
Then swell the song, both loud and long,
Till rocks and forest quiver,
God save our Queen, and Heaven bless
The Maple Leaf for ever!

The Maple Leaf, our emblem dear,
The Maple Leaf for ever!
God save our Queen, and Heaven bless
The Maple Leaf for ever!

The Ode to Newfoundland

"Pine-clad hills" are words Newfoundlanders traditionally associate with their Great Island, although pines taking root today in Newfoundland are few and far between. The phrase comes from "The Ode to Newfoundland," verses written by Sir Cavendish Boyle (1849-1916) upon assuming governorship of Newfoundland (1901-04). It was set to music by C.H. Parry, the noted British composer who also arranged Blake's "Jerusalem," and first performed in public in St. John's on 21 January 1902. Unlike the pine, the "Ode" has stood the test of time and was adopted by unanimous consent as "the National Ode of our Island Home." As J.R. (Joey) Smallwood wrote in the first volume of *The Book of Newfoundland* (1937): "This is the national ode of Newfoundland and is sung by the school children and also at public gatherings. Many teachers have adopted it as a closing exercise for the daily school session to promote love of our own country in the youthful mind." Newfoundland, Britain's oldest overseas colony, is Canada's youngest province, having joined Confederation on 31 March 1949.

The Ode to Newfoundland

When sunrays crown thy pine-clad hills
  And summer spreads her hand,
When silvern voices tune thy rills,
  We love thee, smiling land.

We love thee, we love thee, we love thee,
  Newfoundland,
We love thee, we love thee, we love thee,
  Newfoundland.

When spreads thy cloak of shimmering white
  At winter's stern command,
Through shortened day and starlit night
  We love thee, frozen land.

We love thee, we love thee, we love thee,
  Newfoundland,
We love thee, we love thee, we love thee,
  Newfoundland.

When blinding storm-gusts fret thy shore,
  And wild waves lash thy strand:
Through spindrift swirl and tempest roar
  We love thee, windswept land.

We love thee, we love thee, we love thee,
  Newfoundland,
We love thee, we love thee, we love thee,
  Newfoundland.

As loved our fathers, so we love,
  Where once they stood we stand:
Their prayer we raise to Heaven above:
  God guard thee, Newfoundland.

God guard thee, God guard thee, God guard thee,
  Newfoundland,
God guard thee, God guard thee, God guard thee,
  Newfoundland.

This Land is Your Land

"This Land Is Your Land" is the signature song of The Travellers, the first folk-song group to perform topical and patriotic songs in English Canada. The group was formed by five singers and musicians from Toronto in 1954, and it was their manager, Martin Bochner, who in the late fifties adapted the words of "This Land Is Your Land," composed in 1956 by Woody Guthrie (1912-67), to Canadian needs. The song has been widely sung ever since. In addition to the American original, popularized by Pete Seeger, there are Canadian, British, Australian, and Spanish versions. The adaptation has one shortcoming, as Norman DePoe, the broadcaster, noted in 1972: "One phrase rankled: 'From the Arctic Circle to the Great Lakes waters.' Is there nothing north of 60? Where are Dangerous Dan McGrew and Sam McGee? What were Franklin, Davis and McClure doing trying to open the Northwest Passage?...A phrase which would scan equally well would be 'From the northern ocean....' Since we claim sovereignty right up to the Pole, I'm inclined to suggest it should be 'From the Polar ice cap to the Great Lakes waters,' except that I feel a good many soft southerners might not feel that land was 'made for you and me.'"

This Land is Your Land

This land is your land,
This land is my land,
From Bonavista
To the Vancouver Island,
From the Arctic Circle,
To the Great Lakes waters,
This land was made for you and me.

Le plus cher pays
De toute la terre,
C'est notre pays,
Nous sommes tous frères
De l'île Vancouver
Jusqu'à Terre-Neuve,
C'est le Canada, c'est notre pays.

When the sun came shining
And I was strolling
And the wheatfields waving
And the dust clouds rolling,
As the thought was living
A voice was chanting, saying,
This land was made for you and me.

This land is your land,
This land is my land,
From Bonavista
To the Vancouver Island,
From the Arctic Circle
To the Great Lakes waters,
This land was made for you and me.

A Place to Stand

One of the films specially commissioned for Expo 67 was *A Place to Stand*, which was produced by David Mackay and directed by Christopher Chapman for the Ontario Pavilion. The seventeen-minute film was a great success and went on to win an Academy Award for short subjects. One reason for its great success was the theme song, popularly known as "Ontar-i-ar-i-ar-i-o," written by Richard Morris (words) and Dolores Claman (music). Next to "Mon Pays," Gilles Vigneault's evocation of Quebec, "A Place to Stand" is the most widely recognized of provincial anthems, official and unofficial. It is to be sung with "a swinging march tempo."

A Place to Stand

Give us a place to stand
and a place to grow
and call this land
On-ta-ri-o,
On-ta-ri-ta-ri-o.

A place to live
for you and me
with hopes as high
as the tallest tree.

Give us a land of lakes
and a land of snow
and we will build
On-ta-ri-o.

From western hills
to northern shore
to Niag'ra Falls
where the waters roar.

Give us a land of peace
where the free winds blow
and we will build
On-ta-ri-o.

A place to stand,
a place to grow,
On-ta-ri-a-ri-a-ri-o.

A place to stand,
a place to grow,
On-ta-ri-a-ri-a-ri—
O-N-T-A-R-I-O.

God Save the Queen

"This must be the best-known tune in the world," suggested Percy A. Scholes in *The Oxford Companion to Music* (9th edition, 1956). "If any attribution is necessary in song-books, the word 'traditional' seems to be the only one possible, or, perhaps, '*Traditional; earliest known version by John Bull, 1563-1628.*'" In their present form, the words and music of Great Britain's national anthem go back to 1744. Although sung in Canada since the earliest of times, it was not until 16 February 1968 that Parliament proclaimed "God Save the Queen (King)" to be the Royal Anthem in Canada. There are at least three French versions of the lyrics; the version here is the official one.

God Save the Queen (King)

God save our gracious Queen (King),
Long live our noble Queen (King),
God save the Queen (King);
Send her (him) victorious,
Happy and glorious,
Long to reign over us;
God save the Queen (King).

Dieu Protège Notre Reine (Roi)

Dieu protège la reine (le roi)
De sa main souveraine!
Vive la reine (le roi)!
Qu'un règne glorieux,
Long et victorieux
Rende son peuple heureux.
Vive la reine (le roi)!

O Canada

Let us begin by making a distinction. "O Canada," in either English or French, is the National Anthem of Canada. "God Save the Queen (King)," in either English or in French, is the Royal Anthem of Canada. This distinction dates from 1964, when a resolution to this effect was introduced in the House of Commons but not immediately adopted. The distinction became official on 16 February 1968, and the "recommended texts" of the National Anthem follow.

O Canada

O Canada! Our home and native land!
True patriot love in all thy sons command.
With glowing hearts we see thee rise,
The true North, strong and free.

From far and wide, O Canada,
We stand on guard for thee.
God keep our land glorious and free!
O Canada, we stand on guard for thee.
O Canada, we stand on guard for thee!

Ô Canada

Ô Canada! Terre de nos aïeux,
Ton front est ceint de fleurons glorieux!
Car ton bras sait porter l'épée,
Il sait porter la croix!
Ton histoire est une épopée
Des plus brillants exploits.
Et ta valeur, de foi trempée,
Protégera nos foyers et nos droits.
Protégera nos foyers et nos droits.

On public occasions only the first verse of the National Anthem is usually sung. Perhaps the quintessential Canadian experience is attending a game of the Montreal Canadiens at the Forum and rising to attention, English and French alike, shoulder to shoulder, to hear the strains of "O Canada" sung in a bilingual version by the throaty tenor voice of Roger Doucet. (The experience is in striking contrast to Kate Smith's rendition of "God Bless America" or, earlier, Gracie Field's singing "There'll Always Be an England.")

As an anthem, "O Canada" is a perfect amalgam of the two races. The original French lyrics were written by Sir Adolphe-Basile Routhier (1839-1920), a Quebec judge and writer, as a thirty-two line poem, "Chant National," which appeared in his collection of poems, *Les Échos* (1882).

Chant National

O Canada! terre de nos aïeux,
Ton front est ceint de fleurons glorieux.
    Car ton bras sait porter l'épée,
        Il sait porter la croix;
    Ton histoire est une épopée
        Des plus brillants exploits;
    Et ta valeur de foi trempée,
Protégera nos foyers et nos droits.

Sous l'oeil de Dieu, près du fleuve géant,
Le Canadien grandit en espérant.
    Il est né d'une race fière;
        Béni fut son berceau.
    Le ciel a marqué sa carrière
        Dans ce monde nouveau:
    Toujours guidé par sa lumière,
Il gardera l'honneur de son drapeau.

De son patron, précurseur de vrai Dieu,
Il porte au front l'auréole de feu.

Ennemi de la tyrannie,
    Mais plein de loyauté,
Il sait garder dans l'harmonie
    Sa fière liberté,
Et par l'effort de son génie
Sur notre sol asseoir la vérité.

Amour sacré de trône et de l'autel,
Remplis nos coeurs de ton souffle immortel.
    Parmi les races étrangères
        Notre guide est la loi;
    Sachons être un peuple de frères
        Sous le joug de la Foi;
    Et répétons comme nos pères
Le cri vanqueur: Pour le Christ et le Roi!

The French words were set to music by the Quebec composer Calixa Lavallée (1842-91) and the stately patriotic composition was first performed in Quebec City on St. Jean Baptiste Day, 24 June 1880. One of the best early translations was by William McLennan (1856-1904), a Montreal writer and translator, published in *Songs of French Canada: Translated into English* (1909), edited by Lawrence J. Burpee.

O Canada!

O Canada! land of our sires,
    Whose brow is bound with glorious bays,
The sword thy valorous hand can wield
    And bear the Cross that faith inspires,
What mighty deeds hast thou beheld,
    An epogee of glorious sights!
The faith, thy shield through all thy days,
    Shall still protect our homes and rights,
    Shall still protect our homes and rights.

By the broad river's giant stream,
    Beneath God's ever-watchful sights,
Canadians thrive in Hope's bright gleam,
    Sprung from a great and noble race,
Cradled by self-denial's hand,
    In the new world high Heaven did trace
The pathway of their progress grand,
    And ever guided by its light
They'll guard the banner of their land,
They'll guard the banner of their land.

Christ's forerunner, their patron saint,
    From him they bear a crown of fire,
Enemies of the tyrant's base restraint
    The depths of loyalty their deeds inspire.
And their proud liberty they would keep
    With never-ending concord blest,
While by their genius sown deep
    Upon our soil the truth shall rest,
    Upon our soil the truth shall rest.

O sacred love of altar and of throne,
    May thy immortal breath our spirits fire!
'Midst other races as we hold
    Thy law whose sway we ever own,
May we as brethren all aspire,
    With faith's control, while clear shall ring,
As from our sires in days of old,
    The conquering cry, "For Christ and King,"
    The conquering cry, "For Christ and King."

But it is not McLennan's version that is known across
English Canada; it is the version written by R. Stanley
Weir (1856-1926), Montreal judge and author, prepared
for the Tercentenary of Quebec in 1908. Weir published
the lyrics in *After Ypres and Other Verse* (1917).

O Canada!

"THAT TRUE NORTH." — *Tennyson*

O Canada! Our Home and Native Land!
True patriot-love in all thy sons command;
With glowing hearts we see thee rise,
The True North, strong and free,
And stand on guard, O Canada,
    We stand on guard for thee.
    O Canada, glorious and free!
    We stand on guard for thee!

O Canada! Where pines and maples grow,
Great prairies spread and lordly rivers flow,
How dear to us thy broad domain,
From East to Western Sea;

Thou land of hope for all who toil!
    Thou True North, strong and free!
    O Canada, glorious and free!
    We stand on guard for thee!

O Canada! Beneath thy shining skies
May stalwart sons and gentle maidens rise,
To keep thee steadfast through the years,
From East to Western Sea.
Our Fatherland, our Motherland!
    Our True North, strong and free!
    O Canada, glorious and free!
    We stand on guard for thee!

Ruler Supreme, Who hearest humble prayer,
Hold our dominion in Thy loving care.
Help us to find, O God, in Thee,
A lasting, rich reward,
As waiting for the Better Day
    We ever stand on guard.
    O Canada, glorious and free!
    We stand on guard for thee!

Weir is remembered today as the author of the English
words of "O Canada." He was not a great poet, but then
how many great poets have been the authors of national
anthems? Instead, Weir was a patriot and a skilled versifier, as witness "My Song," the last poem from *Poems
Early and Late* (1922):

My song is but a sigh,
A fragmentary thing;
The perfect music, I
Shall never, never sing;
And yet forever try.

VIII
Some Facts, Some Figures

Perhaps the phrase most descriptive of Canada, even to this day, is the one pressed into service by Bruce Hutchison in 1942 for the title of his popular and influential book about Canada: *The Unknown Country*. To the world at large, Canada remains unknown, a veritable *terra incognita*, a land area once pink and now snowy white on many maps of the world. And it continues largely as an unknown quantity on the home front too. There are any number of reasons for the relative ignorance of Canadians about themselves and their country. These are too well known to bear enumeration or discussion here, except for one. One reason for our lack of self-knowledge as a country and a people is that we do not really know where to look for information about ourselves. The only general encyclopedia of Canadian life, published by a branch-plant operation, is badly in need of revision. Instead of a general index, it acquired coloured photographs. While sets of this Canadian encyclopedia may be found in all the public libraries in the country, there are fewer than four thousand of these libraries. One seldom sees the ten-volume set in private libraries in homes. For this reason I have decided to include here some facts and figures that all Canadians should know about their country. Perhaps the information here will settle not a few arguments or spark greater interest in the geography and demography of the country. I want to thank B.G. Fingerote, M.L.S., for amassing much of the information that follows, which has, in the main, been taken from the following reference sources: *Canada Year Book: 1975* (1975); *Canada Year Book: 1976-77* (1977); *Gazetteer of Canada* (1961-74); *Census of Canada* (Reports of 1973 and 1977); *Rand McNally Cosmopolitan World Atlas* (1975); *The World Almanac and Book of Facts: 1977* (1976); *The 1977 Corpus Almanac of Canada* (1977); *Canadian Almanac and Directory* (1977); *Canada Goes Metric* (1974) by Gerald J. Black; and *Conversion Factors and Tables* (third edition, 1961) by O.T. Zimmerman and Irvin Lavine.

DOMINION OF CANADA

Characteristics

NAME: Dominion of Canada

CAPITAL: Ottawa
Created by the Act of Confederation, effective 1 July 1867.

AREA:	LAND	FRESHWATER	TOTAL
	3,560,238 mi.^{2}	291,571 mi.^{2}	3,851,809 mi.^{2}
	9,220,975 km^2	755,165 km^2	9,976,140 km^2

SOUTHERNMOST POINT:
Middle Island, Lake Erie 41°41′N
NORTHERNMOST POINT:
Cape Columbia, Ellesmere Island 83°07′N
DISTANCE BETWEEN: 2,875 mi.   4,627 km

EASTERNMOST POINT:
Cape Spear, Newfoundland 52°37′W
WESTERNMOST POINT:
Mount St. Elias, Yukon Territory 141° W
DISTANCE BETWEEN: 3,223 mi.   5,187 km

HIGHEST POINT:
Mount Logan, Yukon Territory   19,524 ft.   5,951 m

BORDER WITH THE UNITED STATES:
3,986.8 mi.   6,416 km
BORDER WITH ALASKA:
1,539.8 mi.   2,478 km

MOTTO: *A mari usque ad mare* (From sea to sea; *D'un océan à l'autre*)

Rivers, Lakes, Islands

MAJOR DRAINAGE BASIN	MAJOR RIVERS
Atlantic	St. Lawrence, St. John
Hudson Bay	Churchill, Nelson, Saskatchewan
Arctic	Mackenzie, Peace
Pacific	Fraser, Columbia, Yukon

GEOLOGICAL CATEGORIES: SEVENTEEN REGIONS

CONTINENTAL SHELF	OROGEN	PLATFORM	PRECAMBRIAN SHIELD
Atlantic	Cordilleran	Interior	Grenville
Pacific	Appalachian	Arctic	Churchill
Arctic	Innuitian	Hudson	Southern
		St. Lawrence	Bear
			Superior
			Slave
			Nutak

LENGTH OF MAJOR RIVERS	MILES	KILOMETRES
St. Lawrence	1,900	3,058
St. John	418	673
Churchill	1,000	1,609
Nelson	1,600	2,575
Saskatchewan	1,205	1,939
Mackenzie	2,635	4,241
Peace	1,195	1,923
Fraser	850	1,368
Columbia	498	801
Yukon	714	1,149

AREA OF MAJOR LAKES	SQUARE MILES	SQUARE KILOMETRES
Superior*	31,700	82,103
Huron*	23,000	59,570
Erie*	9,910	25,667
Ontario*	7,340	19,011
Great Bear	12,096	31,328
Great Slave	11,031	28,570
Winnipeg	9,417	24,390
Athabasca	3,064	7,936
Reindeer	2,568	6,651
Winnipegosis	2,075	5,374
Manitoba	1,799	4,659
Dubawnt	1,480	3,833

Partly in the United States

AREA OF MAJOR ISLANDS	SQUARE MILES	SQUARE KILOMETRES
Baffin	195,928	507,451
Victoria	83,896	217,290
Newfoundland	42,031	108,860
Ellesmere	75,767	196,236
Banks	27,038	70,028
Devon	21,331	55,247
Axel Heiberg	16,671	43,178
Melville	16,274	42,149
Southampton	15,913	41,214
Prince of Wales	12,872	33,338
Vancouver	12,079	31,284

Populations, Groups

POPULATIONS OF CANADA SINCE 1851

1851	2,436,297
1861	3,229,633
1871	3,689,257
1881	4,324,810
1891	4,833,239
1901	5,371,315
1911	7,206,643

1921	8,787,949
1931	10,376,786
1941	11,506,655
1951*	14,009,429
1961	18,238,247
1971	21,568,310
1976	22,992,604
1981†	24,041,400
1991†	26,591,400
2001†	28,369,700

*Includes Newfoundland
†Estimated

POPULATION BY ETHNIC GROUP, 1971

Canada	21,568,310
British Isles	9,624,115
English	6,245,970
Irish	1,581,730
Scottish	1,720,390
Welsh	74,415
Other	1,610
Other European	11,139,805
French	6,180,120
Austrian	42,120
Belgian	51,135
Czech & Slovak	81,870
Finnish	59,215
German	1,317,200
Greek	124,475
Hungarian	131,890
Italian	730,820
Jewish	296,945
Lithuanian	24,535
Netherlands	425,945
Polish	316,430
Romanian	27,375
Russian	64,475
Scandinavian	384,790
Danish	75,725
Icelandic	27,905
Norwegian	179,290
Swedish	101,870
Ukrainian	580,660
Yugoslav	104,955
Other	194,850
Asian	285,540
Chinese	118,815
Japanese	37,260
Other	129,455
Other	518,850
Indian and Eskimo	312,760
Negro	34,445
Other & Unknown	171,645

POPULATION BY MOTHER TONGUE, 1971

Canada	21,568,310
English	12,973,810
French	5,793,650
German	561,085
Italian	538,360
Ukrainian	309,855

Indian and Eskimo	179,820
Netherlands	144,925
Polish	134,780
Greek	104,455
Chinese	94,855
Portuguese	86,925
Magyar	86,835
Croatian/Serbian	74,190
Yiddish	49,890
Czech/Slovak	45,150
Finnish	36,725
Indo-Pakistan	32,555
Russian	31,745
Arabic	28,550
Norwegian	27,405
Danish	27,395
Spanish	23,815
Swedish	21,680
Japanese	16,890
Lithuanian	14,725
Estonian	14,520
Flemish	14,240
Lettish	14,140
Romanian	11,300
Icelandic	7,860
Welsh	3,160
Other	63,025

POPULATION BY RELIGIOUS DENOMINATION, 1971

Canada	21,568,310
Adventist	28,590
Anglican	2,543,180
Baptist	667,245
Buddhist	16,175
Chinese & Missionary Alliance	23,630
Christian Reformed	83,390
Churches of Christ, Disciples	16,405
Confucian	2,165
Doukhobor	9,170
Free Methodist	19,125
Greek Orthodox	316,605
Hutterite	13,650
Jehovah's Witnesses	174,810
Jewish	276,025
Lutheran	715,740
Mennonite	168,150
Mormon	66,635
Pentecostal	220,390
Presbyterian	872,335
Roman Catholic	9,974,895
Salvation Army	119,665
Ukrainian Catholic	227,730
Unitarian	20,995
United Church	3,768,800
Other	293,240
No religion	929,570

POPULATIONS OF CAPITALS AND MAJOR CITIES

	1971 Census	1976 Census
Calgary, Alta.	403,343	469,917
Charlottetown, P.E.I.	25,253	24,837
Chicoutimi, Que.	126,401	128,643
Edmonton, Alta.	496,014	554,228
Halifax, N.S.	250,581	267,991
Hamilton, Ont.	503,122	529,371
Kitchener, Ont.	238,574	272,158
London, Ont.	252,981	270,383
Montreal, Que.	2,729,211	2,802,485
Oshawa, Ont.	120,318	135,196
Ottawa-Hull	619,861	693,288
Quebec City, Que.	501,365	542,158
Regina, Sask.	140,734	151,191
Saint John, N.B.	106,744	112,974
Saskatoon, Sask.	126,449	133,750
St. Catharines, Ont.	285,802	301,921
St. John's, Nfld.	131,814	143,390
Sudbury, Ont.	157,721	157,030
Thunder Bay, Ont.	114,708	119,253
Toronto, Ont.	2,602,098	2,803,101
Vancouver, B.C.	1,082,352	1,166,348
Victoria, B.C.	195,800	218,250
Whitehorse, Y.T.	11,217	13,311
Windsor, Ont.	248,718	247,582
Winnipeg, Man.	549,808	578,217
Yellowknife, N.W.T.	6,122	8,256

Principal Industries

AGRICULTURE:

Principal field crops

wheat	rapeseed
oats	potatoes
barley	mustard seed
rye	sunflower seed
flaxseed	tame hay
corn	fodder corn
soybeans	sugar beets

Livestock and products

cattle	poultry
hogs	eggs
sheep	forest and maple products
dairy products	

MINING AND MINERAL PRODUCTION:

Principal areas
metallics
non-metallics
fuels
structural materials

FORESTRY:

Principal areas
lumber production
sawmills and planing mills
pulp and paper production

MANUFACTURING:

Principal areas
durable goods

nondurable goods
foods and beverages
tobacco processing and products
rubber products
leather products
textile products
knitting mills
clothing
machinery
furniture and fixtures
transportation equipment
electrical products

CONSTRUCTION:
Principal areas
building
engineering

TRANSPORTATION, COMMUNICATION, AND
OTHER UTILITIES:
Principal areas
transportation
storage
communications

ELECTRIC POWER, GAS, AND WATER

TRADE:
Principal areas
wholesale
retail

FINANCE, INSURANCE, AND REAL ESTATE:
Principal areas
financial institutions
insurance and real estate

SERVICE:
Principal areas
recreational
business
personal
industrial composite
tourism

FISHERIES AND FUR:
Principal areas
freshwater
sea water
wildlife

Provinces and Territories

NEWFOUNDLAND

CAPITAL: St. John's
Entered Confederation: 31 March 1949

AREA:	LAND	FRESHWATER	TOTAL
	143,045 mi.²	13,140 mi.²	156,185 mi.²
	370,485 km²	34,032 km²	404,517 km²
Newfoundland:	41,164 mi.²	2,195 mi.²	43,359 mi.²
	106,614 km²	5,685 km²	112,299 km²
Labrador:	101,881 mi.²	10,945 mi.²	112,826 mi.²
	263,871 km²	28,347 km²	292,218 km²

HIGHEST POINT:
Unnamed peak in the Torgnat Mountains 5,232 ft. 1,595 m

MOTTO: *Quaerite prime regnum Dei*
(Seek ye first the Kingdom of God)

FLORAL EMBLEM: The pitcher plant

PRINCIPAL RIVER: Churchill

PRINCIPAL LAKE: Melville

POPULATION	1971	1976
	522,104	557,725

PRINCIPAL INDUSTRIES:

Fisheries	Mining	Electrical power
Forestry	Agriculture	Manufacturing

PRINCE EDWARD ISLAND

CAPITAL: Charlottetown
Entered Confederation: 1 July 1873

AREA:	LAND	FRESHWATER	TOTAL
	2,184 mi.²	—	2,184 mi.²
	5,657 km²	—	5,657 km²

HIGHEST POINT:
Caledonia Triangulation Station 450 ft. 137m

MOTTO: *Parva sub ingenti*
(The small under the protection of the great)

FLORAL EMBLEM: Lady's slipper

POPULATION	1971	1976
	111,641	118,229

PRINCIPAL INDUSTRIES:
Agriculture   Fishing   Tourism

NOVA SCOTIA

CAPITAL: Halifax
Entered Confederation: 1 July 1867

AREA:	LAND	FRESHWATER	TOTAL
	20,402 mi.²	1,023 mi.²	21,425 mi.²
	52,841 km²	2,650 km²	55,491 km²

HIGHEST POINT: Cape Breton 1,747 ft. 532m

MOTTO: *Munit haec et altera vincit*
(One defends and the other conquers)

FLORAL EMBLEM: The trailing arbutus

PRINCIPAL RIVER: St. Mary's

PRINCIPAL LAKE: Bras d'Or

POPULATION	1971	1976
	788,960	828,571

PRINCIPAL INDUSTRIES:

Fisheries	Agriculture	Mining
Manufacturing	Forestry	Tourism

NEW BRUNSWICK

CAPITAL: Fredericton
Entered Confederation: 1 July 1867

AREA: LAND   FRESHWATER   TOTAL
     27,835 mi.²   519 mi.²   28,354 mi.²
     72,092 km²   1,344 km²   73,436 km²

HIGHEST POINT: Mount Carleton 2,690 ft. 820m

MOTTO: *Spem reduxit*
(She [England] restored hope)

FLORAL EMBLEM: The purple violet

PRINCIPAL RIVER: Saint John

PRINCIPAL LAKE: ---

POPULATION **1971**   **1976**
     634,557   677,250

PRINCIPAL INDUSTRIES:

Mining   Agriculture   Fisheries
Manufacturing   Forestry   Tourism

QUEBEC

CAPITAL: Quebec City
Entered Confederation: 1 July 1867

AREA: LAND   FRESHWATER   TOTAL
     523,860 mi.²   71,000 mi.²   594,860 mi.²
     1,356,791 km²   183,889 km²   1,540,680 km²

HIGHEST POINT: Mont D'Iberville 5,210 ft. 1,588 m

MOTTO: *Je me souviens*
(I remember)

FLORAL EMBLEM: The white garden lily

PRINCIPAL RIVER: St. Lawrence

PRINCIPAL LAKE: Mistassini

POPULATION **1971**   **1976**
     6,027,764   6,234,445

PRINCIPAL INDUSTRIES:

Agriculture   Electrical power   Forestry
Manufacturing   Hunting   Mining
Fisheries   Tourism

ONTARIO

CAPITAL: Toronto
Entered Confederation: 1 July 1867

AREA: LAND   FRESHWATER   TOTAL
     344,092 mi.²   68,490 mi.²   412,582 mi.²
     891,194 km²   177,388 km²   1,068,582 km²

HIGHEST POINT: Timiskaming District 2,275 ft. 693 m

MOTTO: *Ut incepit fidelis sic permanet*
(Loyal she began, loyal she remains)

FLORAL EMBLEM: The white trillium

PRINCIPAL RIVER: Ottawa

PRINCIPAL LAKE (completely in province): Nipigon

POPULATION **1971**   **1976**
     7,703,106   8,264,465

PRINCIPAL INDUSTRIES:

Agriculture   Electrical power   Mining
Manufacturing   Forestry   Tourism
Fisheries   Fur production

MANITOBA

CAPITAL: Winnipeg
Entered Confederation: 15 July 1870

AREA: LAND   FRESHWATER   TOTAL
     211,775 mi.²   39,225 mi.²   251,000 mi.²
     548,495 km²   101,592 km²   650,087 km²

HIGHEST POINT: Baldy Mountain 2,729 ft. 832 m

MOTTO: No official motto.
Unofficially, Home of the Bay; The Prairie Province

FLORAL EMBLEM: The prairie crocus

PRINCIPAL RIVER: Nelson

PRINCIPAL LAKE: Winnipeg

POPULATION **1971**   **1976**
     988,247   1,021,506

PRINCIPAL INDUSTRIES:

Agriculture   Manufacturing   Mining   Electrical power

SASKATCHEWAN

CAPITAL: Regina
Entered Confederation: 1 September 1905

AREA: LAND   FRESHWATER   TOTAL
     220,182 mi.²   31,518 mi.²   251,700 mi.²
     570,269 km²   81,631 km²   651,900 km²

HIGHEST POINT: Cypress Hills 4,567 ft. 1,392 m

MOTTO: No official motto.
Unofficially, Home of the RCMP; Wheat Province

FLORAL EMBLEM: The prairie lily

PRINCIPAL RIVER: Saskatchewan

PRINCIPAL LAKE: Athabasca

POPULATION **1971**   **1976**
     926,242   921,323

PRINCIPAL INDUSTRIES:

Agriculture   Mining   Manufacturing

ALBERTA

CAPITAL: Edmonton
Entered Confederation: 1 September 1905

AREA: LAND   FRESHWATER   TOTAL
     248,800 mi.²   6,485 mi.²   255,285 mi.²
     644,389 km²   16,796 km²   661,185 km²

HIGHEST POINT: Mount Columbia 12,294 ft. 3,747 m

MOTTO: No official motto.
Unofficially, Next Year Country

FLORAL EMBLEM: The wild rose

PRINCIPAL RIVER: Peace

PRINCIPAL LAKE: Lesser Slave

POPULATION	1971	1976
	1,627,874	1,838,037

PRINCIPAL INDUSTRIES:
Agriculture   Forestry   Mining (includes oil)
Electrical power   Manufacturing

BRITISH COLUMBIA

CAPITAL: Victoria
Entered Confederation: 20 July 1871

AREA:	LAND	FRESHWATER	TOTAL
	359,279 mi.²	6,976 mi.²	366,255 mi.²
	930,528 km²	18,068 km²	948,596 km²

HIGHEST POINT: Fairweather Mountain 15,300 ft. 4,663 m

MOTTO: *Splendor sine occasu*
              (Splendour without diminishment)

FLORAL EMBLEM: The dogwood

PRINCIPAL RIVER: Columbia

PRINCIPAL LAKE: Williston

POPULATION	1971	1976
	2,184,621	2,466,608

PRINCIPAL INDUSTRIES:
Fisheries   Electrical power   Forestry
Manufacturing   Agriculture

YUKON TERRITORY

CAPITAL: Whitehorse
Created a territory: 13 June 1898

AREA:	LAND	FRESHWATER	TOTAL
	205,346 mi.²	1,730 mi.²	207,076 mi.²
	531,844 km²	4,481 km²	536,325 km²

HIGHEST POINT: Mount Logan 19,524 ft. 5,951 m

MOTTO: No official motto.
Unofficially, Home of the Klondike

FLORAL EMBLEM: The fireweed

PRINCIPAL RIVER: Yukon

PRINCIPAL LAKE: Kluane

POPULATION	1971	1976
	18,388	21,836

PRINCIPAL INDUSTRIES:
Mining   Forestry   Electrical power
Tourism   Furs and game

NORTHWEST TERRITORIES

CAPITAL: Yellowknife

Created a territory with present boundaries: 1 September 1905

AREA:	LAND	FRESHWATER	TOTAL
Total:	1,253,438 mi.²	51,465 mi.²	1,304,903 mi.²
	3,246,390 km²	133,294 km²	3,379,684 km²
Franklin:	541,753 mi.²	7,500 mi.²	549,253 mi.²
	1,403,134 km²	19,425 km²	1,422,559 km²
Keewatin:	218,460 mi.²	9,700 mi.²	228,160 mi.²
	565,809 km²	25,123 km²	590,932 km²
Mackenzie:	493,225 mi.²	34,265 mi.²	527,490 mi.²
	1,277,447 km²	88,746 km²	1,366,193 km²

HIGHEST POINT: Mount Sir James MacBrien 9,062 ft. 2,762 m

MOTTO: No official motto.
Unofficially, The New North

FLORAL EMBLEM: Mountain avens

PRINCIPAL RIVER: Mackenzie

PRINCIPAL LAKE: Great Bear

POPULATION	1971	1976
	34,807	42,609

PRINCIPAL INDUSTRIES:
Mining   Commercial development   Fisheries   Forestry

Monarchs of French and English Canada

(With dates of birth, death, and accession)

FRENCH MONARCHS

François I (1494-1547), 1515
Henri II (1519-59), 1547
François II (1544-60), 1559
Charles IX (1550-74), 1560
Henri III (1551-89), 1574
Henri IV (1553-1610), 1589
Marie de Médicis (1573-1642)
    Regent, 1610
Louis XIII (1601-43), 1610
Anne d'Autriche (1601-66)
    Regent, 1643-51
Louis XIV (1638-1715), 1643
Louis XV (1710-74), 1715

ENGLISH MONARCHS

(House of Tudor)
Henry VII (1457-1509), 1485
Henry VIII (1491-1547), 1509
Edward VI (1537-53), 1547
Mary I (1516-58), 1553
Elizabeth I (1533-1603), 1558

(House of Stuart)
James I (1566-1625), 1603
Charles I (1600-1649), 1625

(The Commonwealth)
Oliver Cromwell (1599-1658)
    Lord Protector, 1653
Richard Cromwell (1626-1712)
    Lord Protector, (1658-59)

(House of Stuart [Restored])
Charles II (1630-85), 1660
James II (1633-1701), 1685
William III (1650-1702), 1689
 and
Mary II (1662-94), 1689
Anne (1665-1714), 1702

(House of Hanover)
George I (1660-1727), 1714
George II (1683-1760), 1727
George III (1738-1820), 1760
George IV (1762-1830), 1820
William IV (1765-1837), 1830
Victoria (1819-1901), 1837

(House of Saxe-Coburg and Gotha)
Edward VII (1841-1910), 1901

(House of Windsor)
George V (1865-1936), 1910
Edward VIII (1894-1972), 1936
 20 Jan. to 11 Dec. (abdication)
George VI (1895-1952), 1936
Elizabeth II (b. 1926), 1952
 Coronation, 2 June 1953

The present Queen, as Princess Elizabeth, celebrated her marriage to Philip Mountbatten, Duke of Edinburgh, on 20 November 1947. She acceded to the throne as Elizabeth II on the death of her father in 1952, and was crowned at Westminster Abbey on 2 June 1953. The Queen and her consort have four children: Prince Charles, Prince of Wales, born in 1948; Princess Anne, born in 1950; Prince Andrew, born in 1960; and Prince Edward, born in 1964.

Governors General Since Confederation

	TERM
The Viscount Monck of Ballytrammon	1867-68
The Baron Lisgar of Lisgar and Bailieborough	1869-72
The Earl of Dufferin	1872-78
The Marquis of Lorne	1878-83
The Marquis of Lansdowne	1883-88
The Baron Stanley of Preston	1888-93
The Earl of Aberdeen	1893-98
The Earl of Minto	1898-1904
The Earl Grey	1904-11
Field Marshal H.R.H. the Duke of Connaught	1911-16
The Duke of Devonshire	1916-21
General the Baron Byng of Vimy	1921-26
The Viscount Willingdon of Ratton	1926-31
The Earl of Bessborough	1931-35
The Baron Tweedsmuir of Elsfield	1935-40
Major General the Earl of Athlone	1940-46
Field Marshal the Viscount Alexander of Tunis	1946-52
The Right Honourable Vincent Massey	1952-59
General the Right Honourable Georges P. Vanier	1959-67
The Right Honourable Roland Michener	1967-74
The Right Honourable Jules Léger	1974-

Prime Ministers Since Confederation

PRIME MINISTERS	PARTY	TERM
Sir John Alexander Macdonald	Conservative	1867-73
Alexander Mackenzie	Liberal	1873-78
Sir John Alexander Macdonald	Conservative	1878-91
Sir John Joseph Caldwell Abbott	Conservative	1891-92
Sir John Sparrow David Thompson	Conservative	1892-94
Sir Mackenzie Bowell	Conservative	1894-96
Sir Charles Tupper	Conservative	1896
Sir Wilfrid Laurier	Liberal	1896-1911
Sir Robert Laird Borden	Conservative/ Unionist	1911-20
Arthur Meighen	Conservative/ Unionist	1920-21
William Lyon Mackenzie King	Liberal	1921-26
Arthur Meighen	Conservative/ Unionist	1926
William Lyon Mackenzie King	Liberal	1926-30
Richard Bedford Bennett	Conservative	1930-35
William Lyon Mackenzie King	Liberal	1935-48
Louis Stephen St. Laurent	Liberal	1948-57
John George Diefenbaker	Progressive Conservative	1957-63
Lester Bowles Pearson	Liberal	1963-68
Pierre Elliott Trudeau	Liberal	1968-

Premiers Since the Centennial

NEWFOUNDLAND:
Joseph Roberts Smallwood, 1949-72
Frank Duff Moores, 1972-

PRINCE EDWARD ISLAND:
Alexander Bradshaw Campbell, 1966-

NEW BRUNSWICK:
Louis Joseph Robichaud, 1960-70
Richard B. Hatfield, 1970-

NOVA SCOTIA:
George Isaac Smith, 1967-70
Gerald A. Regan, 1970-

QUEBEC:
Daniel Johnson, 1966-68
Jean Jacques Bertrand, 1968-70
Robert Bourassa, 1970-76
René Lévesque, 1976-

ONTARIO:
John Parmenter Robarts, 1961-71
William Grenville Davis, 1971-

MANITOBA:
Walter C. Weir, 1967-69
Edward Richard Schreyer, 1969-77
Sterling M. Lyon, 1977-

SASKATCHEWAN:
William Ross Thatcher, 1964-71
Allan Emrys Blakeney, 1971-

ALBERTA:
Ernest Charles Manning, 1943-68
Harry Edwin Strom, 1968-71
Edgar Peter Lougheed, 1971-

BRITISH COLUMBIA:
William Andrew Cecil Bennett, 1952-72
David Barrett, 1972-75
William Richards Bennett, 1975-

Lieutenant-Governors Since the Centennial

NEWFOUNDLAND:
Fabian O'Dea, 1963-69
Ewart John Arlington Harnum, 1969-74
Gordon Arnaud Winter, 1974-

PRINCE EDWARD ISLAND:
Willibald Joseph MacDonald, 1963-69
J. George MacKay, 1969-74
Gordon L. Bennett, 1974-

NEW BRUNSWICK:
John Babbitt McNair, 1965-68
Wallace S. Bird, 1968-71
Hedard J. Robichaud, 1971-

NOVA SCOTIA:
Henry Poole MacKeen, 1963-68
Victor de Bedia Oland, 1968-73
Clarence L. Gosse, 1973-

QUEBEC:
Hughes Lapointe, 1966-78
Jean-Pierre Côté, 1978-

ONTARIO:
William Earl Rowe, 1963-68
William Ross Macdonald, 1968-74
Pauline M. McGibbon, 1974-

MANITOBA:
Richard S. Bowles, 1965-70
W. John McKeag, 1970-76
F.L. Jobin, 1976-

SASKATCHEWAN:
Robert L. Hanbridge, 1963-70
Stephen Worobetz, 1970-76
George Porteous, 1976-78
Cameron Irwin McIntosh, 1978-

ALBERTA:
J.W. Grant MacEwan, 1965-74
Ralph Garven Steinhauer, 1974-

BRITISH COLUMBIA:
Major-General George R. Pearkes, 1960-68
John Robert Nicholson, 1968-73
Walter Stewart Owen, 1973-78
Henry Pybus Bell-Irving, 1978-

YUKON TERRITORY:
Commissioner James Smith, 1966-76
Commissioner A.M. Pearson, 1976-

NORTHWEST TERRITORIES:
Commissioner S.M. Hodgson, 1967-

The Fathers of Confederation

Here are the thirty-six delegates from the British North American colonies who attended one or more of the three conferences, held in Charlottetown, Quebec, and London between 1864 and 1866, which resulted in the drawing up of the articles of Confederation, given Royal Assent on 29 March 1867, to take effect 1 July 1867.

CANADA
Étienne-Paschal Taché
John A. Macdonald
George-Étienne Cartier
William McDougall
William P. Howland
George Brown
Alexander Tilloch Galt
Alexander Campbell
Oliver Mowat
Hector-L. Langevin
James Cockburn
Thomas D'Arcy McGee
Jean-Charles Chapais

NOVA SCOTIA
Charles Tupper
William A. Henry
Robert B. Dickey
Jonathan McCully
Adams G. Archibald
John W. Ritchie

NEW BRUNSWICK
Samuel Leonard Tilley
John M. Johnson
D.R. Wilmot
Peter Mitchell
Charles Fisher
Edward B. Chandler
William H. Steeves
Col. John Hamilton Gray

NEWFOUNDLAND
Frederick B.T. Carter
Ambrose Shea

PRINCE EDWARD ISLAND
John Hamilton Gray
Edward Palmer
William H. Pope
George H. Coles
T. Heath Haviland
Edward Whelan
A.A. Macdonald

Capital Cities

Quebec was the capital of:
    New France from 1608 to 1763
    The Province of Quebec from 1763 to 1791
    Lower Canada from 1791 to 1841
    The Province of Canada from 1851 to 1855;
        from 1859 to 1865
    The Province of Quebec since 1867

Newark (now Niagara-on-the-Lake) was the capital of:
    Upper Canada from 1791 to 1794

Toronto (formerly York) was the capital of:

Upper Canada from 1794 to 1841
The Province of Canada from 1849 to 1851;
    from 1855 to 1859
The Province of Ontario since 1867

Kingston was the capital of:
The Province of Canada from 1841 to 1844

Montreal was the capital of:
The Province of Canada from 1844 to 1849

Ottawa (formerly Bytown) has been the capital of:
The Dominion of Canada since 1867; chosen by Queen
Victoria in 1857; proclaimed capital of the Province of
Canada in 1865; first functioned as capital of the Province
of Canada in 1866

Halifax has been the capital of:
Nova Scotia since 1749

Saint John (formerly Parrtown) was the capital of:
New Brunswick from 1784 to 1786

Fredericton has been the capital of:
New Brunswick since 1786

Charlottetown has been the capital of:
Prince Edward Island since 1769

Fort Garry was the capital of:
The District of Assiniboia from 1812 to 1870

Winnipeg has been the capital of:
Manitoba since 1870
The Northwest Territories from 1870 to 1876

Victoria has been the capital of:
British Columbia since 1858
Vancouver Island from 1843 to 1858

Fort Livingstone, Swan River, was the capital of:
The Northwest Territories in 1876

Battleford, Saskatchewan, was the capital of:
The Northwest Territories from 1877 to 1882

Regina has been the capital of:
Saskatchewan since 1905
The Northwest Territories from 1882 to 1905

Edmonton has been the capital of:
Alberta since 1905

Dawson was the capital of:
The Yukon Territory from 1898 to 1952

Whitehorse has been the capital of:
The Yukon Territory since 1952

Yellowknife has been the capital of:
The Northwest Territories since 1967

St. John's has been the capital of:
Newfoundland since 1583

Wars and Rebellions

Iroquois and the French colonists	1609-24
Between England and France	1626-30
Iroquois and the French colonists	1633-45
	1652-54
	1661-66
Between England and France	1666-67
Iroquois and the French colonists	1687-1700
King William's War (War of the Grand Alliance)	1689-97
Queen Anne's War (War of the Spanish Succession)	1702-13
King George's War (War of the Austrian Succession)	1744-48
Seven Years' War	1756-63
Pontiac's Conspiracy	1763-64
American Revolutionary War	1775-83
War of 1812 with the United States	1812-14
Lower Canada Rebellion	1837-38
Upper Canada Rebellion	1837
"Aroostook War" between New Brunswick and Maine	1839
Fenian Raids	1866-71
Red River Rebellion	1869-70
North-West Rebellion	1885
South African (Boer) War	1899-1902
First World War	1914-18
Spanish Civil War	1936-39
Second World War	1939-45
Korean War	1950-53

Time Zones

TIME ZONES	HOURS BEHIND GREENWICH MEAN TIME
Newfoundland Standard Time	3 hours 30 minutes
Atlantic Standard Time	4 hours
Eastern Standard Time	5 hours
Central Standard Time	6 hours
Mountain Standard Time	7 hours
Pacific Standard Time	8 hours

Statutory Holidays

New Year's Day	1 January
Good Friday	Friday preceding Easter Sunday (March or April)
Easter Monday	Monday following Easter Sunday (March or April)
Victoria Day	24 May (observed on a Monday)
Dominion Day	1 July
Labour Day	1 September (observed on the first Monday in September)
Thanksgiving Day	Second Monday in October
Remembrance Day	11 November
Christmas Day	25 December

The federal government also recognizes the fifty-two Sundays of
the year to be statutory holidays. Most of the provinces and

territories extend statutory status to Boxing Day (26 December) and to other individual holidays (*e.g.*, Quebec has designated 24 June to be the Fête de Saint-Jean-Baptiste).

Metric Conversion Factors

Imperial measures to metric measures
Metric measures to imperial measures

To convert	Multiply by
LENGTH	
Inches to centimetres	2.54
Centimetres to inches	0.3937
Feet to metres	0.3048
Metres to feet	3.2808
Miles to kilometres	1.6093
Kilometres to miles	0.6214
AREA	
Square inches to square centimetres	6.4516
Square centimetres to square inches	0.155
Square feet to square metres	0.0929
Square metres to square feet	10.7639
Acres to hectares	0.4047
Hectares to acres	2.471
Square miles to square kilometres	2.5899
Square kilometres to square miles	0.386
VOLUME (CUBIC)	
Cubic inches to cubic centimetres	16.387
Cubic centimetres to cubic inches	0.061
Cubic yards to cubic metres	0.7646
Cubic metres to cubic yards	1.308
VOLUME (LIQUID OR DRY)	
Pints to litres	0.5683
Litres to pints	1.7598
Quarts to litres	1.1364
Litres to quarts	0.8799
Gallons to litres	4.5459
Litres to gallons	0.2199
MASS (WEIGHT)	
Ounces (avdp) to grams	28.349
Grams to ounces (avdp)	0.03527
Pounds (avdp) to kilograms	0.4536
Kilograms to pounds (avdp)	2.2046

COMPARATIVE TEMPERATURES

Degrees Fahrenheit	Temperature	Degrees Celsius
350	oven heat	177
212	water boils	100
100	heat wave	38
98.6	body	37
78.8	ideal swimming	26
68	ideal room	20
32	water freezes	0
14	ideal skating	-11
-40	systems equal	-40
-459.67	absolute zero	-273.15

RULE-OF-THUMB TEMPERATURE CONVERSIONS

Celsius (°C) to Fahrenheit (°F.), multiply by 2, then add 32.
Fahrenheit (°F.) to Celsius (°C), subtract 32, then divide by 2.

MILEAGE EQUIVALENCES

Miles per hour (mph)	Kilometres per hours (km/h)
20	32.19
30	48.28
40	64.37
50	80.47
60	96.56
70	112.65
80	128.75
90	144.84

IX
A Chronology

Dates of Interest to Canadians

Long before there was a Canadian nation, long before there was a Canadian people, long before there was a *Canadien* people, there were people in this part of the world. The aboriginal Canadian people did not leave written records, but they did leave other evidence of their presence and state of civilization. I think Edward Mc-Court, the novelist, expressed this superbly in *Saskat-chewan* (1968): "Troy town rose and fell ten times on the hill Hissarlik above the Hellespont; the Indian village sited a few miles west of Moose Jaw went Troy three better — thirteen distinct cultural levels have been uncovered in the Mortlach 'midden,' first stumbled upon by a local farmer who observed an unusual number of arrowheads in a pasture cowpath." Archaeologists working in 1975-76 found preserved in the permafrost of Old Crow, within the Arctic Circle, man-made implements which carbon dating demonstrates to be 25,000 years old, the oldest evidence of man in North America. And even before the creation of artifacts, there are the remains of immense dinosaurs and miniscule trilobites that bear silent witness to life forms that predate our own. And before *that*, there is evidence of geological upheavals in the Canadian Shield, among the oldest rock formations on the planet. The chronology here, beginning some 2,400 years ago, cannot convey the sense of our prehistory, but it does give us some indication of the variety of events that have affected us during our historical past. This compilation of 365 (or so) dates of historical, cultural, and social importance and interest is based on much original research. It is also based on information found in such standard sources as *Webster's New Twentieth Century Dictionary* (1958), *Canadian Chronology, 1497-1960* (1961), and *Canadian Chronology* (1970) compiled by Glen W. Taplin.

430 B.C.	Herodotus, Greek historian called "the father of history," describes travellers' reports of conditions in the Arctic where "the ground is frozen iron-hard."
499 A.D.	Hoei Shin, Chinese Buddhist missionary, describes his visit to Fusang, a new land which resembles British Columbia in some aspects.
875	Celt-Irish monks from Iceland may have landed on Brion Island, Gulf of St. Lawrence, and established a settlement on Cape Breton Island which Scandinavians refer to as Huitramannaland (Country of the White Men).
982	Eric the Red, from Iceland, may have landed at Cumberland Peninsula, Baffin Island.
986	Bjarni Herjulfsson, from Iceland, may have sailed along the east coast from Vineland (Wineland, now Newfoundland) to Markland (Forest Land, now Labrador) and on to Helluland (Stony Land, now Baffin Island).
1004-5	Leif Ericsson, son of Eric the Red, from Greenland, may have wintered at Vineland (L'Anse aux Meadows, Newfoundland).
1005-8	Thorwald Ericsson, brother of Leif Ericsson, from Greenland, may have spent two winters at Vineland and died there, killed by the natives.
1012-16	Thorfinnr Karlsefni Thordarson, from Greenland, married to Guidridr, Thorwald's widow, may have spent three winters at Vineland.
1013	Snorri, son of Thorfinnr and Guidridr, may have been born at Vineland, the first white child born in North America.
1298	Marco Polo, Venetian traveller, in dictating his memoirs, makes mention of an Arctic isle, possibly Ellesmere Island, as the source of the gerfalcon.
1390	Traditional date of the founding of the Iroquois Confederacy by Dekanawidah and his assistant Hiawatha, thus uniting the Five (later Six) Nations Indians.
1497	John Cabot, from Bristol, sights Cape Bonaventure, Newfoundland, 24 June.

1501	Gaspar Corte-Real, from Portugal, visits Newfoundland and Labrador.
1524	Giovanni de Verrazano, Italian pilot in the service of France, explores the Newfoundland coast.
1534	Jacques Cartier, from Saint-Malo, erects his cross at Gaspé, 24 July.
1535	Cartier, on his second voyage, reaches the Iroquois village of Stadacona (Quebec City), 14 September; and the Huron village of Hochelaga (Montreal), 2 October.
1541	Sieur de Roberval named lieutenant-governor of Acadia by Francis I, 15 January.
1576	Sir Martin Frobisher, from England, enters Frobisher Bay, Baffin Island, 21 July.
1583	Sir Humphrey Gilbert, returning from Newfoundland which he claimed for England, is lost off Sable Island, 9 September.
1605	Port Royal, French colony, founded at Annapolis Basin, Nova Scotia, August.
1607	Marc Lescarbot, French poetaster, stages *The Masque of Neptune* at Port Royal, 14 November.
1608	Samuel de Champlain establishes France's premier colony in New France at Quebec, 3 July.
1611	Henry Hudson, English navigator, is set adrift in Hudson Bay, 23 June.
1617	Louis Hébert, first French colonist, sets sail with his family for Quebec, 11 March.
1627	The Company of New France is formed by Cardinal Richelieu, 29 April.
1629	Quebec is surrendered by Champlain to the British brothers, David and Lewis Kirke, 20 July.
1632	Quebec is restored to the French by the Treaty of St. Germain-en-Laye, signed 29 March.
1633	Champlain is named first governor of New France, 23 May.
	Étienne Brûlé, French explorer, is believed eaten by Hurons in southern Ontario, June.
1635	Champlain dies in Quebec, 25 December.
1642	Ville-Marie (Montreal) is founded by Sieur de Maisonneuve, 17 May.
1643	Hôtel-Dieu, the first hospital in New France, is opened in Montreal, 8 October.
1649	Jean de Brébeuf, French Jesuit, is martyred by the Iroquois, near Midland, 16 March.
1655	First medical insurance plan is offered by a physician in Montreal, 3 March.
1660	Dollard des Ormeaux and sixteen companions withstand an Indian attack at Long Sault, 1 May.
1661	Pierre-Esprit Radisson and Sieur de Groseilliers may have visited Hudson Bay.
1663	Earthquake rocks Quebec the evening of 5 February.
	New France is proclaimed a royal colony by Louis XIV, 24 February.
	First immigration act is proclaimed in New France, 10 October.
1670	"The Governor and Company of Adventurers of England Trading in Hudson's Bay" is chartered, 2 May.
1672	Comte de Frontenac is appointed governor of New France, 6 April.
1674	François de Laval, Jesuit, is appointed bishop of Quebec, 1 October.
1681	First hospital insurance plan is offered by the Hôtel-Dieu in Montreal, 20 August.
1682	Sieur de La Salle, French explorer, claims the delta of the Mississippi River for France, 9 April.
1687	New France's first recorded suicide — that of Pierre Lefebvre, September.
1688	First stone of the church of Notre-Dame-des-Victoires, Quebec, is laid, 1 May.
1691	Henry Kelsey, HBC explorer, takes part in a buffalo hunt on the prairies, 23 August.
1692	Madeleine de Verchères, at fourteen, defends "Fort Dangerous" against an Indian siege, 22 October.
1693	First mental patient admitted to the Hôtel-Général, Montreal.
1713	Treaty of Utrecht is signed, ceding Acadia and Newfoundland to the English, 11 April.
1732	Sieur de La Vérendrye, first native-born explorer, erects Fort St. Charles on the west side of the Lake of the Woods, July.
1750	Fort Rouillé (later York, then Toronto) is constructed by Joseph Dufeaux, French contractor, beginning 15 April.
1752	*Halifax Gazette*, first newspaper in Canada, is published, 25 March.
1754	Anthony Henday, HBC agent, is the first known white man to see the Rocky Mountains, near Innisfail, Alberta, 17 October.
1755	Expulsion of the Acadians at Grand Pré, Nova Scotia, 5 September.
1758	Louisbourg, on Cape Breton Island, falls to the British, 26 June.
1759	The conquest of Quebec by the British, 13 September; the death of James Wolfe; the death of the Marquis de Montcalm, 14 September.
1763	France renounces all claims in North America except for St. Pierre and Miquelon, by the Treaty of Paris, 10 February.
	La Corriveau, celebrated murderess, is hanged near the Plains of Abraham, 18 April.
	Royal Proclamation establishes the British government of Quebec, 7 October.
1765	*Catéchisme du Diocèse de Sens*, first book printed in Canada, is published.
1769	Frances Brooke publishes *The History of Emily Montague*, the first Canadian novel.
1774	The Quebec Act, extending the boundaries of Quebec, is passed 22 June.
	Juan Pérez, Spanish explorer, visits Nootka Sound, Vancouver Island, 17 August.
1775	Bruno Hecata, Spanish explorer, lands at Point Grenville, Vancouver Island, and claims it for Spain, 14 July.
	James Montgomery, American general, is killed attacking Quebec, 31 December.

1778	James Cook, British captain, lands at Nootka Sound, 28 May.
1782	Guy Carleton named commander-in-chief of British North America, 23 February.
1783	United Empire Loyalists settle at what is now Saint John, New Brunswick, about 11 May.
1790	Spain surrenders exclusive rights on the Pacific Coast by the treaty of Nootka Sound, 28 October.
1791	The Constitutional Act, dividing Quebec into the provinces of Upper and Lower Canada, is passed, 26 December.
1793	Sir Alexander Mackenzie crosses the continent by land, the first explorer to do so north of Mexico, and inscribes the rock at Dean Channel, British Columbia, 22 July.
	George Vancouver, British captain, explores the Pacific Coast, 26 May to 20 September.
1806	*Le Canadien*, first newspaper wholly in French, issued, 22 November.
1807	Joseph Brant, Mohawk chief, dies at Burlington, Ontario, 24 November.
1809	The first steamboat, the *Accommodation*, makes its maiden voyage, 31 October.
1811	David Thompson, distinguished surveyor, reaches the mouth of the Columbia River, 15 July.
1812	General Isaac Brock dies in the Battle of Queenston Heights, Ontario, but the American invaders are repulsed, 13 October.
1813	Victory of the H.M.S. *Shannon* over the U.S.S. *Chesapeake*, 1 June.
	Laura Secord, Loyalist housewife, commences her celebrated trek of nineteen miles to Beaver Dam, 21-22 June.
1816	The Massacre of Seven Oaks, at present-day Winnipeg, takes place, 19 June.
1817	First bank office is opened in Montreal of the Bank of Montreal, 3 November.
1821	A royal charter is granted to McGill University in Montreal, 31 March.
1826	Ottawa is founded — called Bytown from 1827 to 1854 — by Colonel John By, a British engineer, 26 September.
1827	A royal charter is granted to King's College (now the University of Toronto), 15 March.
1829	First issue of the *Christian Guardian*, forerunner of the *United Church Observer*, published, 21 November.
1830	Josiah Henson, the original Uncle Tom, crosses over to Upper Canada, 28 October.
1831	The *Royal William* makes the first Atlantic crossing under steam, arriving in England on 11 September.
1834	The City of Toronto is incorporated, 6 March.
1835	Joseph Howe, journalist and future statesman, defends himself against libel charges, May 1835.
	Asylum for the insane opened in Saint John, New Brunswick, 14 November.
1836	Thomas Chandler Haliburton publishes *The Clockmaker*.
1837	The Rebellion of 1837 breaks out in Lower Canada, 6 November; in Upper Canada, 5 December.
	The *Caroline*, an American supply ship used by the Rebels, plunges in flames over Niagara Falls, 29 December.
1839	Lord Durham submits his famous *Report* to the British Parliament, 11 February.
1840	James Evans, missionary at Norway House, now Manitoba, devises and prints hymns in the basic syllabic alphabet still in use among the Cree and the Inuit, 17 November.
1841	The Act of Union, uniting Upper and Lower Canada into the Province of Canada, is effective, 10 February.
1844	*The Globe* (now *The Globe and Mail*) is published by George Brown, 5 March.
1845	François-Xavier Garneau, French-Canadian historian, publishes his influential *Histoire du Canada*.
1846	Kerosene or coal oil is invented by Dr. Abraham Gesner in Nova Scotia.
1847	Disappearance of Sir John Franklin, English explorer, in the eastern Arctic, last seen 26 July.
1848	Responsible government comes in the Reform ministry of Robert Baldwin and Louis-H. La Fontaine, 11 March.
	Paul Kane, artist, returns to Toronto from his two-year wanderings in the West, 1 October.
1849	Lord Elgin signs the Rebellion Losses Bill, 25 April.
	The "Montreal Annexation Manifesto" appears in the *Montreal Gazette*, 11 October.
1851	The Three-Pence Beaver, Canada's first postage stamp, designed by Sandford Fleming, is issued, 23 April.
1852	Université Laval is founded in Quebec City, 8 December.
1855	Ice hockey is played for the first time anywhere in the world on Kingston ice, Christmas Day.
1857	First oil well in the world is drilled rather than dug by Charles N. Tripp at Enniskillen, near Sarnia, Ontario.
	Ottawa is chosen by Queen Victoria to be the capital of Canada, 31 December.
1858	First Canadian coins — 1¢, 5¢, 10¢, and 20¢ pieces, depicting Queen Victoria — are minted, 1 July; bills are not regularly issued until 1870.
	The Atlantic cable carries the first message from North America to Great Britain, 5 August.
1860	The Queen's Plate is run for the first time, Toronto, 27 June.
	Cornerstone of the old Parliament Building is laid by Edward, Prince of Wales, 1 September.
1863	Aubert de Gaspé's famous novel of habitant life, *Les Anciens Canadiens*, is published.

1864   *Selections from the Canadian Poets*, the first poetic anthology, edited by E.H. Dewart, is published.

Charlottetown Conference is held to discuss the union of the British provinces, 1 September; Quebec Conference follows, 10-29 October.

1866   Defeat of the Fenian invaders from the United States at Ridgeway, near Fort Erie, Ontario, 2 June.

London Conference begins on 4 December.

1867   Astrolabe, lost by Champlain near Pembroke, Ontario, on 7 June 1613, is found by a youngster, E.G. Lee.

The British North America Act, 1867, effects a legislative union of New Brunswick, Nova Scotia, and Canada (East and West), 1 July.

1868   Thomas D'Arcy McGee is assassinated in downtown Ottawa, 7 April.

First Dominion Militia Act is given assent, 22 May; first active Canadian militia units are formed three years later.

The new Dominion acquires Rupert's Land, 31 July.

1869   Red River Rebellion breaks out at St. Vital, Manitoba, 11 October.

Timothy Eaton establishes the T. Eaton Co. Ltd. in Toronto in December.

1870   Louis Riel, Métis leader, orders the execution of Thomas Scott at Fort Garry, Manitoba, 4 March.

The Northwest Territories are transferred to the Dominion of Canada, 15 July; on the same day, Manitoba enters Confederation as the fifth province.

1871   The First Dominion census: Population 3,689,257.

British Columbia enters Confederation as the sixth province, 20 July.

1873   George Munro Grant publishes *Ocean to Ocean*, his nationalistic narrative.

The North-West Mounted Police is created as a civil force, 23 May.

Prince Edward Island enters Confederation as the seventh province, 1 July.

Canadian Labour Union, an effective early association of unions, is founded in Toronto on 23 September.

1874   Edward Blake, statesman, delivers his famous Aurora Address, urging the cultivation of a national spirit, Aurora, Ontario, 3 October.

1876   The University of Montreal is established as a branch of Laval, 15 May.

First sitting of the Supreme Court of Canada, 5 June.

Alexander Graham Bell makes the world's first long-distance call between Paris and Brantford, Ontario, 10 August.

1878   Sir Samuel Cunard founds the Cunard Steam-Ship Co. Ltd., to consolidate operations begun in 1838.

Secret ballot is introduced into the federal election of 17 September.

1880   Sir Charles G.D. Roberts publishes *Orion and Other Poems* which inspires Archibald Lampman and others.

Night riders murder the Donnelly family, near Lucan, Ontario, 4 February.

Royal Canadian Academy of Arts meets for the first time, 6 May.

"O Canada" with words by Sir Adolphe-Basile Routhier and music by Calixa Lavallée is premiered in Quebec City, 24 June.

Blondin, famous funambulist, crosses Niagara Gorge on a rope, his manager on his back, 19 August.

1882   Royal Society of Canada meets for the first time, 25 May.

1883   Standard Time, promoted by Sandford Fleming, is adopted 18 November.

1884   The Nile Voyageurs set sail for Egypt, 15 September.

1885   North-West Rebellion breaks out at Batoche, 18 March; Louis Riel surrenders 15 May; Riel is hanged, 16 November.

The "Last Spike" ceremony is held at Craigellachie, British Columbia, 7 November.

1887   *Saturday Night* magazine is founded in Toronto, 3 December.

1889   W.D. Lighthall edits *Songs of the Great Dominion*, a nationalistic anthology of poetry and song.

1890   The "Chateau Style" is created by architect Bruce Price for the Château Frontenac in Quebec City, completed in 1893.

1891   Sir John A. Macdonald declares in Ottawa, 7 February: "A British subject I was born, a British subject I will die."

1893   Stanley Cup is first awarded for amateur (later professional) hockey to the Montreal Amateur Athletic Association, 23 February.

1896   Seventy-three volumes of *The Jesuit Relations and Allied Documents*, edited by R.G. Thwaites, begin to appear.

Gold is discovered on Bonanza Creek, Klondike River, Yukon, 16 August.

1897   Almighty Voice, maverick Indian, is surrounded and shot to death after a two-year search, 30 May.

1898   Yukon Territory is constituted as a separate territory of the Dominion, 13 June.

1899   First Canadian Contingent leaves Quebec for the Boer War, 29 October.

1900   Alphonse Desjardins establishes the first credit union in North America at Lévis, Quebec, 6 December.

1901   Richard Maurice Bucke, psychiatrist and author, publishes *Cosmic Consciousness*.

Death of Queen Victoria and accession of Edward VII, 22 January.

Guglielmo Marconi, Italian inventor, sends the world's first wireless messages across the Atlantic from Signal Hill, St. John's, Newfoundland, 11-12 December.

1903   Marquis wheat, ideally suited to prairie conditions, is developed by Sir Charles E. Saunders, Dominion Cerealist.

Frank Slide kills eighty people at Frank, near Crow's Nest Pass, British Columbia, 29 April.

1904   Sir Wilfrid Laurier, prime minister, in an address in Ottawa, 18 January, proclaims: "The twentieth century belongs to Canada."

Designation "Royal" is extended to the North-West Mounted Police, 24 June.

1905   Alaska Boundary Award, giving the United States much of the panhandle, is concluded, 25 March.

Alberta and Saskatchewan enter Confederation as the eighth and ninth provinces, 1 September.

1906   Ontario Hydro-Electric Power Commission, the first such nationalized service, is created, 7 June.

1907   Robert Service, a Yukon bank teller, offers to pay a Toronto publisher to issue *Songs of a Sourdough*.

1908   L.M. Montgomery publishes *Anne of Green Gables*, to be followed by seven sequels.

Dr. Frederick Cook, American explorer, attains the North Pole, 21 April.

Celebration of the Tercentenary of Quebec, 19-31 July.

1909   J.A.D. McCurdy becomes the first British subject to fly in a heavier-than-air ship, the *Silver Dart*, Baddeck, Nova Scotia, 23 February.

Department of External Affairs is created by statute to handle Canada's foreign relations, proclaimed in force, 1 June.

Captain J.E. Bernier, Arctic explorer, claims the Arctic Archipelago for Canada, 1 July.

1910   Royal Canadian Navy is formed, 4 May.

1911   Members of the RNWMP's "Lost Patrol" perish near Fort McPherson, Northwest Territories, 5 February.

Busy Man's Magazine, founded in 1905, is renamed *Maclean's Magazine*, March.

1912   Stephen Leacock published his third book, *Sunshine Sketches of a Little Town*.

1914   Louis Hémon, French journalist, dies the year before the publication of his classic novel *Maria Chapdelaine*.

Nellie McClung and other feminists stage the well-known Women's Parliament in Winnipeg, 28 January.

Canada declares war on Germany, 4 August.

1915   "In Flanders Fields," the most famous of World War I poems, is written by Lieutenant-Colonel Dr. John McCrae in twenty minutes, Ypres, Belgium, 3 May.

1916   The Great Fire guts the Parliament Building, Ottawa, 3 February.

National Research Council of Canada is established in Ottawa to further scientific planning and development; advisory committee appointed, 29 November; act assented to, 29 August 1917.

1917   Income tax legislation is introduced in the House of Commons as "a temporary war measure," 18 January.

Canadian Corps takes Vimy Ridge in the most celebrated of all Canadian engagements, 9 April.

Tom Thomson, woodsman and painter, drowns under mysterious circumstances, Canoe Lake, Algonquin Park, on or about 8 July.

The Halifax Explosion shatters much of the city, 5 December.

1918   The Red Baron, nickname of Germany's leading air ace, is shot down by the Canadian airman A. Roy Brown, 21 April.

Armistice ending the First World War is signed at 11:00 A.M., 11 November.

1919   Death of Sir Wilfrid Laurier, 17 February.

The Winnipeg general strike is called and lasts over a month, 15 May.

Sir John Alcock and Sir Arthur Brown make the first non-stop transatlantic flight from Newfoundland, 14 June.

Cornerstone of the new Parliament Building is laid by Edward, Prince of Wales, 1 September.

Canadian National Railways is organized, 20 December.

1920   RNWMP becomes the Royal Canadian Mounted Police, 1 February.

The Group of Seven exhibits for the first time in Toronto, 7 May.

The Canadian Forum, an independent monthly of opinion and the arts, is incorporated in Toronto, 14 May.

1921   The Canadian Authors Association is formed in Montreal, with Stephen Leacock as president, weekend of 12 March.

The Fifth Thule Expedition to the Canadian Arctic, under Knud Rasmussen, begins its three-year explorations.

St. Francis Xavier University at Antigonish, Nova Scotia, begins extension work that develops into the Antigonish Movement.

The famous clipper *Bluenose* is launched at Lunenburg, Nova Scotia, 26 March.

Agnes Macphail, elected to the British Columbia legislature, is the first female parliamentarian in the British Empire, 6 December.

1922   *Nanook of the North*, the world's first feature-length documentary film, photographed by Robert Flaherty in the eastern Arctic, is premiered in New York.

1923   Foster Hewitt, sports reporter, coins the phrase "He shoots! He scores!" in a broadcast on 23 March.

Failure of the Home Bank in Montreal, the last of the bank failures, 17 August.

F.G. Banting and J.J.R. Macleod are named Nobel Prize laureates for their discovery of insulin; citation dated 25 October.

1924	Royal Canadian Air Force is formed, 1 April.
1925	The Power Corporation of Canada, Ltd., one of the major holding companies, is incorporated under federal law, 18 April.
	The United Church of Canada holds its first service, Toronto, 10 June.
1926	Arvida, a company town on the Saguenay River, is founded by the Aluminium Company of Canada Ltd.
	The Balfour Report, which defines the dominions as "autonomous," is adopted at the Imperial Conference, 18 November.
1927	Mazo de la Roche publishes *Jalna* and begins work on its fourteen sequels.
	Labrador is granted to Newfoundland and not to Quebec by a decision of the British Privy Council, 1 March.
	The Diamond Jubilee of Confederation, marking sixty years of nationhood, is celebrated with live radio broadcasts from Parliament Hill, 1-3 July.
	The Toronto Symphony Orchestra plays its first concert under this name, 11 October.
1928	The Canadian rumrunner, *I'm Alone,* is sunk by the U.S. Coast Guard in the Gulf of Mexico, creating an international incident, 22 March.
1929	The British Privy Council renders its decision that women are "persons" within the meaning of the law and hence may be summoned to the Senate, 18 October.
1930	Gilbert LaBine, prospecting at Echo Bay, Great Bear Lake, Northwest Territories, discovers pitchblende, 16 May.
1931	"The Romance of Canada" series of live weekly radio dramas is produced by Tyrone Guthrie from Montreal, 22 January.
	The Statute of Westminster, which formally recognizes the autonomy of the British dominions, is enacted, 12 December.
1932	The Dominion Drama Festival's first annual competitive festival is held, 24 April.
1934	The Dionne Quintuplets are born at Callandar, Ontario, 28 May.
1935	The Bank of Canada, a central bank, commences operation, 11 March.
	The On to Ottawa Trek of the unemployed begins in Vancouver, 3 June.
	William Aberhart leads the Social Credit Party to victory in Alberta, 22 August.
1936	Red Ryan, notorious bank robber, is killed in a gun fight, Sarnia, Ontario, 24 May.
	The Vimy Memorial in France is unveiled by King Edward VIII, 26 July.
	The Canadian Broadcasting Corporation, the largest system in the world, is created, 2 November.
	The Globe and Mail is born of a merger of *The Globe* and *The Mail and Empire* in Toronto, 23 November.

1937	"The Happy Gang" is first heard on CBC Radio, 14 June.
	Trans-Canada Air Lines (now Air Canada) makes its inaugural flight, 1 September.
	The Governor General's Literary Awards are given for the first time; awarded 24 November for books published in 1936.
1938	The Winnipeg Ballet is founded in Winnipeg; it is granted the "Royal" prefix in 1953.
1939	The National Film Board is formed to interpret Canada to itself and the world, 2 May; begins making wartime propaganda films.
	Royal visit of King George VI and Queen Elizabeth, 17 May to 15 June.
	Canada declares war on Germany, 10 September.
	Norman Bethune, medical doctor, dies of infection after operating in northern China, 12 November.
1940	Report of the Rowell-Sirois Commission on dominion-provincial relations is tabled in the House of Commons.
	E.J. Pratt's narrative poem *Brébeuf and His Brethren* is published.
	Quebec women are granted the franchise in Quebec elections, 25 April.
1941	Hugh MacLennan's novel *Barometer Rising* is published.
	CBC Radio establishes its national news service, 1 January.
	The Atlantic Charter is signed by Winston Churchill and Franklin Delano Roosevelt in Placentia Bay, Newfoundland, 14 August.
	Winston Churchill, prime minister of Great Britain, delivers his celebrated "some chicken, some neck" speech in the House of Commons, Ottawa, 30 December; later that day, in a Commons office, he is memorably photographed by Yousuf Karsh.
1942	Publication of Earle Birney's *David and Other Poems* and Bruce Hutchison's *The Unknown Country.*
	C.W. Jefferys issues the first of three volumes in his famous series "The Picture Gallery of Canadian History."
	Evacuation of the Japanese from coastal British Columbia, 26 February.
	The *St. Roch,* under Sergeant Henry A. Larsen, leaving Vancouver 23 June 1940, completes the Northwest Passage, arriving at Halifax two years later, 11 October.
	Dieppe raid by Canadian troops with Allied support is a disaster, 19 August.
	Alaska Highway is formally opened from Dawson Creek to Fairbanks, at Soldiers Summit, Kluane Lake, 20 November.
1943	A.J.M. Smith's edition of *The Book of Canadian Poetry* is published.
	First Quebec Conference of Allied leaders is held at the Château Frontenac, 10-24 August.

1944   First CBC Stage series of dramas is directed by Andrew Allan, 23 January.

Normandy invasion with Canadian troops is a success, 6 June.

The Family Allowance Act, giving monthly "baby bonuses" to parents of children under eighteen, is approved in the House of Commons, 1 August.

Second Quebec Conference of Allied leaders is held at the Château Frontenac, 11-16 September.

Prime Minister Mackenzie King announces the resignation of his minister of national defence, 2 November.

1945   Hugh MacLennan publishes his novel *Two Solitudes.*

Germany surrenders at Reims, France, ending the Second World War in Europe, 5 May.

Igor Gouzenko, Russian cipher clerk, defects from the Russian Embassy in Ottawa with a sheaf of intelligence reports, 5 September.

The Argus Corporation, now Canada's largest holding company, founded by E.P. Taylor and others in Toronto, is incorporated under Ontario law, 24 September.

1946   Canadian Citizenship Act is passed on 14 May, proclaimed on 1 July, providing for the creation of a Canadian citizen, to take effect on 1 January 1947.

1947   Northrop Frye's *Fearful Symmetry* and W.O. Mitchell's *Who Has Seen the Wind* are published.

Oil strike at Leduc No. 1, south of Edmonton, ushers in the oil boom, 13 February.

1948   Prime Minister Louis St. Laurent recommends the creation of "a collective-security league" — the future NATO — in the House of Commons, 29 April.

Tit-Coq, Gratien Gélinas's popular play, is premiered in Montreal, 22 May.

Refus global [Global refusal], a manifesto written by Paul-Emile Borduas, is issued in Montreal, 9 August.

W.L. Mackenzie King, prime minister longer than anyone else in the Commonwealth, resigns, 15 November.

1949   The asbestos strike breaks out at Asbestosville, near Sherbrooke, Quebec, 14 February.

Newfoundland enters Confederation as the tenth province, with J.R. (Joey) Smallwood as first premier, 31 March.

Dr. William F. Giauque, Canadian-born American scientist, awarded the Nobel Prize in chemistry for "work in the field of chemical thermodynamics," delivers his Nobel lecture, 12 December.

1950   Red River floods 600 square miles in and around Winnipeg, 5 May.

The *St. Roch,* the first vessel to circumnavigate the North American continent, reaches Halifax through Panama Canal, 29 May.

Cité Libre, influential quarterly published until 1966, is founded by P.E. Trudeau and others, June.

1951   Morley Callaghan's novel *The Loved and the Lost* is published.

James Houston, arts administrator, encourages Eskimo carvers on Baffin Island to market their carvings through co-operatives, then experiment with print-making.

The Massey Report on national development in the arts, letters, and sciences is tabled in the House of Commons, 1 June.

Le Théâtre du Nouveau Monde is founded in Montreal, August.

The National Ballet of Canada is formed in Toronto, its first official performance being 12 November.

1952   Norman McLaren's famous short film *Neighbours* is released.

The Young Politician, the first part of Donald G. Creighton's two-volume life of Sir John A. Macdonald, and E.J. Pratt's "verse panorama" *Towards the Last Spike* are published.

Vincent Massey is sworn in as the first native-born governor general, 28 February.

James Nicholson, Toronto philanthropist, dies, 29 June; a bequest permits work to begin on the multi-volume *Dictionary of Canadian Biography,* the first volume of which appeared in 1966.

First telecasts in Canada, with CBFT in Montreal transmitting on 6 September, and CBLT in Toronto on 8 September.

Harold Adams Innis, distinguished scholar and teacher, dies, 8 November.

1953   National Library of Canada is formally established, 1 January.

Coronation of Princess Elizabeth as Elizabeth II in Westminster Abbey, 2 June.

The Stratford Shakespearian Festival opens in Stratford, Ontario, the first season being from 13 July to 22 August.

Announcement that Canada is co-operating with the United States in erecting an early-warning system for protection against air attack, 30 September.

1954   Painters Eleven, including such abstract painters as Harold Town, Jock Macdonald, and William Ronald, holds its first exhibition at the Roberts Gallery, Toronto, 12-28 February.

"The Investigator," a satire on Senator Joseph McCarthy, is broadcast on "Stage 54," CBC Radio, 30 May.

Marilyn Bell becomes the first person to swim across Lake Ontario, 9 September.

1956   Wilbert Coffin, a Gaspé prospector, is hanged for the murder of three Pennsylvania hunters, 10 February.

The Canadian Labour Congress, an association of labour unions, is formed, effective 1 May.

Pipeline debate dominates the House of Commons, 13 May to 1 June.

1957   *The Encyclopedia Canadiana,* in ten volumes, is launched.

Les Grands Ballets Canadiens is given its present name in Montreal.

My Fur Lady, a lively musical from McGill, premieres in Montreal, 7 February, and subsequently tours the country.

The Canada Council is established to encourage the arts, humanities, and social sciences; royal assent, 28 March.

Herbert Norman, Canadian ambassador to Egypt, leaps to his death from a Cairo apartment building, 4 April.

John G. Diefenbaker becomes the first Conservative prime minister in twenty-seven years, 21 June.

The first in a series of international conferences on science and world affairs (known as the Pugwash Conferences) is held at Pugwash, Nova Scotia, 7-10 July.

NORAD, a Canadian-American air-defence alliance, is formed, 12 September.

Lester B. Pearson receives the Nobel Peace Prize for defusing the Suez Crisis at the United Nations, 12 October.

1958   The Manitoba Theatre Centre, the first of the regional theatres, mounts its first production in Winnipeg, 16 July.

1959   The famous Ski-Doo is manufactured by J.-A. Bombardier at Valcourt, Quebec.

Cancellation of the ill-fated Avro *Arrow,* 20 February.

The St. Lawrence Seaway is opened by Queen Elizabeth and American President Dwight D. Eisenhower, 26 June.

Canadian Literature, a quarterly edited by George Woodcock, is launched in Vancouver, summer.

Maurice Duplessis, long-time Quebec premier, dies, 7 September.

1960   "The Enchanted Owl," the most famous of all Eskimo prints, is drawn by Kenojuak at Cape Dorset.

Liberals under Jean Lesage assume power in Quebec and begin the Quiet Revolution, 22 June.

Canada's Indians are finally granted complete franchise, 1 July.

The Canadian Bill of Rights is given royal assent, 10 August.

Canadian Opera Company is formed as an association, 20 September.

The National Theatre School of Canada, a co-lingual institution, is opened in Montreal.

1961   Dr. Marcel Chaput, separatist spokesman, resigns from the Defence Research Board, 4 December.

1962   Marshall McLuhan publishes *The Gutenberg Galaxy.*

The Trans-Canada Highway is officially opened at Rogers Pass, Alberta, 3 September.

Alouette, the world's first domestic communications satellite, is launched, 29 September.

1963   Lester B. Pearson leads the Liberal Party to victory in the general election, 8 April.

First bombings of federal buildings and mailboxes in Montreal by the FLQ, spring.

1964   L'Arche, a movement to care for the mentally handicapped, is launched near Paris by Jean Vanier.

Northern Dancer, owned by E.P. Taylor, is the first Canadian horse to win the Kentucky Derby, 2 May.

1965   John Porter publishes *The Vertical Mosaic* and George P. Grant publishes *Lament for a Nation.*

TCA changes its name to Air Canada, 1 January.

The Auto Pact, a Canadian-American trade agreement for automobile parts, is signed, 16 January.

The Maple Leaf flag is flown officially for the first time, 15 February.

The Great Hydro Blackout hits eastern Canada and the United States at 5:25 P.M., 9 November.

1966   Dr. Charles B. Huggins, Halifax-born medical scientist, shares the Nobel Prize for Chemistry.

The Munsinger Case is drawn to the attention of Parliament and the country, 4 March.

Paul-Joseph Chartier, the "mad bomber," dies attempting to blow up the Parliament Building, 18 May.

Rose Latulippe, Canada's first full-length ballet, choreographed by Brian Macdonald to music by Harry Freedman, is premiered at Stratford, 16 August.

1967   Death of Governor General Georges Vanier in Ottawa, 5 March.

Expo 67, the world fair, opens in Montreal, 28 April.

Climax of centennial celebrations of one hundred years of nationhood, Parliament Hill, 1 July.

Louis Riel, the opera written by Harry Somers to Mavor Moore's libretto, premieres in Toronto, 23 September.

The Ecstasy of Rita Joe, a play by George Ryga, is premiered in Vancouver, 23 November.

1968   Unification of the services (Royal Canadian Navy, Canadian Army, Royal Canadian Air Force) into the Canadian Armed Forces, 1 February.

Pierre Elliott Trudeau becomes prime minister, 6 April.

Premiere of *Les Belles-Soeurs,* a play in joual by Michel Tremblay, at the Théâtre du Rideau Vert, 28 August.

"As It Happens," CBC Radio's phone-out show, is launched, 18 November.

1969   National Arts Centre for the performing arts is for-
        mally opened in Confederation Square, Ottawa,
        31 May.

        The American supertanker *Manhattan* requires
        assistance of the Canadian icebreaker *John A.
        Macdonald* to navigate the Northwest Passage,
        September-October.

        Supreme Court overturns the conviction of Joseph
        Drybones on the basis of denied equality before
        the law, 20 November.

1970   *Goin' Down the Road,* Don Shebib's feature film,
        is released.

        Fifth Business, the first novel in Robertson Davies's
        Deptford trilogy, is published.

        The first legal lotteries are introduced by Montreal
        Mayor Jean Drapeau, 1 January.

        White Paper on metric conversion is tabled in the
        House of Commons, 16 January.

        First Arctic Winter Games are held at Yellowknife,
        Northwest Territories, 9-14 March.

        October Crisis begins with the FLQ kidnapping of
        James Cross, 5 October.

1971   *Mon Oncle Antoine,* Claude Jutra's feature film, is
        released.

        Constitutional Conference is held in Victoria,
        14-16 June.

        Canada Development Corporation is established to
        encourage national investment; royal assent
        given 30 June.

        House of Commons declares in favour of a policy
        of multilingualism within the framework of bi-
        lingualism, 8 October.

        Gerhard Herzberg of the National Research Coun-
        cil is awarded the Nobel Prize for Chemistry, 2
        November.

1972   Margaret Atwood's influential study *Survival* is
        published.

        Anik, the world's first geostationary commercial
        satellite, is launched, 9 November.

1973   Karen Kain and Frank Augustyn of the National
        Ballet of Canada place first in duet ensemble
        work, Moscow's International Ballet Competi-
        tion, 19 June.

1974   Appointment of Jules Léger as governor general,
        14 January.

1975   More than a million workers observe a general
        strike—called "Day of Protest"—against wage
        and price controls, 14 October.

        The Anti-Inflation Board is established to intro-
        duce wage and price controls, 16 October.

1976   Joe Clark is elected leader of the Conservative
        Party, 22 February.

        Final issue of the Canadian edition of *Time* maga-
        zine appears with Joe Clark on the cover, 2
        March.

        The Games of the XXI Olympiad are held in Mon-
        treal from 17 July to 1 August.

        The Parti Québécois under René Lévesque is
        elected, the first separatist government in North
        America, 15 November.

1977   Canada unilaterally declares the 200-mile limit on
        sovereignty of the seas, 1 January.

        The Berger Inquiry issues its report which recom-
        mends a ten-year moratorium on any Arctic
        pipelines, 11 April.

        Quebec's controversial language law, Bill 101, is
        passed by the National Assembly, 26 August.

        Television cameras are allowed inside the House of
        Commons, 18 October.

1978   Sun Life Assurance Company of Canada an-
        nounces it will move its head office from Mon-
        treal to Toronto, 6 January.

        Débris from a nuclear-powered Soviet satellite falls
        near Fort Reliance, Northwest Territories, 24
        January.

        "See Canada First," government-encouraged pack-
        aged tours, are publicized, 10 February.

        Anti-Inflation Board begins to phase out its wage
        and price controls, 14 April.

        Prime Minister Trudeau tables in the House of
        Commons a document titled "A Time for Ac-
        tion," which calls for a renewal of the Canadian
        federation and a new constitution, 12 June.

Credits

author. ROBERT W. SERVICE: "The Spell of the Yukon," from *The Complete Poems of Robert Service* (New York: Dodd, Mead, 1944). Reprinted from *Collected Poems of Robert Service*. Reprinted by permission of McGraw-Hill Ryerson Limited. PIERRE-ELLIOTT TRUDEAU: "The Ascetic in a Canoe," from "Exhaustion and Fulfilment: The Ascetic in a Canoe," from *Wilderness Canada* (Toronto: Clarke Irwin, 1970), edited by Borden Spears. Copyright © 1970 by Clarke, Irwin & Company Limited. Used by permission. GILLES VIGNEAULT: "Mon Pays," translated by Jo Ouellet. From *Avec les Vieux Mots*. Copyright © Nouvelle Éditions de l'ARC, Montreal, traduction de Jo Ouellet. Used by permission. "Gens du Pays," translated by Alexandre L. Amprimoz. "Gens du Pays" de Gilles Vigneault. Copyright © Nouvelle Éditions de l'ARC, Montreal. Used by permission. MIRIAM WADDINGTON: "Canadians," from *Driving Home: Poems New and Selected* (Toronto: Oxford University Press, 1972). Reprinted by permission of the publisher.

Picture Credits

Securing photographs and illustrations for specific purposes is painstaking and time-consuming work, as I discovered when I set myself the task of selecting the visual materials that appear between pages 128 and 129 of this book. My workload was lightened considerably by three people, in particular, and made possible by some two dozen government departments and other institutions. Bill Brooks, the Toronto photographer (and author in his own right), gave me professional advice from the first and supplied some of the photos. Assistance on heraldic matters was graciously rendered by Conrad Swan, York Herald of Arms, College of Arms, London, England; Dr. Swan and Harald Bohne, Director of the University of Toronto Press, permitted materials that first appeared in *Canada: Symbols of Sovereignty* (1977) to be reproduced here. Dave McIntosh of the National Capital Commission in Ottawa supplied photos (and enthusiasm) when most needed. The government departments and other institutions are acknowledged in the credits that follow, identified by page number, left to right, top to bottom. These are, in particular: The National Film Board's Photothèque; Public Archives of Canada (abbreviated to the customary PAC); The National Gallery of Canada; and the tourism departments of the provincial and territorial governments. Curiously, the Canadian Government Office of Tourism found my request for photos to be "outside" of their mandate.

i, ii, iii, iv: Courtesy Conrad Swan and the University of Toronto Press from *Canada: Symbols of Sovereignty* (1977).

v: PAC (C 1015); PAC (C 63529); PAC (C 23958); Government House/Bedford Ottawa.

vi, vii: First fourteen: PAC (C 11415); fifteenth: Prime Minister's Office (PC-33).

viii: Ontario Ministry of Industry & Tourism; NFB Photothèque/Hans Blohm; NFB Photothèque/Hans Blohm; NFB Photothèque/Hans Blohm.

ix: Ontario Ministry of Industry & Tourism; PAC (PA 9123); PAC (PA 43785); Ontario Ministry of Industry & Tourism; PAC (C 3353).

x: Government of Newfoundland & Labrador, Dept. of Tourism/John Byrne; Nova Scotia Communications, Information Centre; New Brunswick Dept. of Tourism; NFB Photothèque/Shin Sugino.

xi: Gouvernement du Québec/Tourisme; Ontario Ministry of Industry & Tourism; Manitoba Government Travel, Dept. of Tourism & Recreation; Saskatchewan Dept. of Tourism; Alberta Government Photographic Services; British Columbia Government Photograph, Dept. of Travel Industry.

xii: PAC (PA 24270); Ontario Ministry of Industry & Tourism; National Capital Commission; Gouvernement du Québec/Tourisme; Nova Scotia Communications, Information Centre; Ontario Ministry of Industry & Tourism.

xiii: National Capital Commission for all photographs except Riel, courtesy Saskatchewan Dept. of Tourism.

xiv: Ontario Ministry of Industry & Tourism; PAC (C 7472); National Capital Commission; Manitoba Government Travel, Dept. of Tourism & Recreation.

xv: TravelArctic, Government of the Northwest Territories; Ontario Ministry of Industry & Tourism; British Columbia Government Photograph, Dept. of Travel Industry; Ontario Ministry of Industry & Tourism.

xvi: Ontario Ministry of Industry & Tourism; NFB Photothèque/Cedric Pearson; National Capital Commission.

xvii: All photographs: Ontario Ministry of Industry & Tourism.

xviii: Canadian Football Association; Canadian Hockey League/Arnott & Rogers Ltd.; Association of Canadian Television and Radio Artists; Bill Brooks; Canadian Film Awards; The Order of Canada.

xix: Stamps: National Postal Museum, Ottawa, Canada. Coins: National Currency Collection, Bank of Canada.

xx: Musées des Beaux-Arts de Besançon, France; The National Gallery of Canada, Ottawa (Gift of the Duke of Westminster, 1918); PAC (C 2149); Hudson's Bay Company; PAC (C 33866); PAC (C 70251); PAC (C 3693); RCMP, Ottawa.

xxi: Copyright © Karsh, Ottawa; Gallery Moos Ltd., Toronto; CN Photo; CP Photo; Air Canada Photo; Department of Indian Affairs and Northern Development, Ottawa; Department of Indian Affairs and Northern Development, Ottawa/National Indian Arts and Crafts Corporation; CBC Photo; CTV Photo.

xxii, xxiii: Colour photos, Bill Brooks.

xxiv: Colour photos: Inukshuk and Alert, courtesy Information Department, Government of the NWT; other colour photos: Bill Brooks.

Index of Contributors

DESIGN
David Shaw & Associates Ltd.

ILLUSTRATION
Graham Pilsworth

COMPOSITION
ATTIC typesetting

MANUFACTURING
T.H. Best Printing Company Ltd.